NATURAL LAW MODERNIZED

Hobbes, Locke, Hume, and Rousseau are classic modern philosophers, widely consulted in matters of ethics and political theory. In this provocative study David Braybrooke challenges received scholarly opinion by arguing that these canonical theorists took St Thomas Aquinas as their point of reference, reinforcing rather than departing from his natural law theory.

The natural law theory of St Thomas Aquinas is essentially a secular theory, says Braybrooke. He argues that Hobbes, Locke, Hume, and Rousseau share a core of thought that not only has roots in St Thomas but offers an alternative to other ethical theories now current. According to Braybrooke, this surviving and reinforced core qualifies as an ethical theory viable by the most sophisticated standards, meeting the main challenges of analytical metaethics, and thus standing up to the scrutiny that any ethical theory must undergo in contemporary philosophical discussions.

Braybrooke's study takes the reader into a rich and compelling intellectual universe, one in which medieval natural law theory, widely ignored as obsolete, survives robustly through the modern canon and into the third millennium.

(Toronto Studies in Philosophy)

DAVID BRAYBROOKE, a Canadian philosopher working in the United States, holds the Centennial Commission Chair in the Liberal Arts at The University of Texas at Austin, and is Professor of Government at Texas as well as Professor of Philosophy.

DAVID BRAYBROOKE

Natural Law Modernized

UNIVERSITY OF TORONTO PRESS
Toronto Buffalo London

© University of Toronto Press Incorporated 2001
Toronto Buffalo London
Printed in Canada

Reprinted in paperback 2003

ISBN 0-8020-3543-4 (cloth)
ISBN 0-8020-8644-6 (paper)

∞

Printed on acid-free paper

Toronto Studies in Philosophy
Editors: James R. Brown and Amy Mullin

National Library of Canada Cataloguing in Publication

Braybrooke, David
 Natural law modernized/David Braybrooke.

 (Toronto studies in philosophy)
 Includes bibliographical references and index.
 ISBN 0-8020-3543-4 (bound).   ISBN 0-8020-8644-6 (pbk.)

 1. Natural law.   2. Ethics.   I. Title.   II. Series.

 K455.B72 2001   340'.112   C2001-930448-X

University of Toronto Press acknowledges the financial assistance to its publishing program of the Canada Council for the Arts and the Ontario Arts Council.

University of Toronto Press acknowledges the financial support for its publishing activities of the Government of Canada through the Book Publishing Industry Development Program (BPIDP).

To the cohorts of students, undergraduates and teaching assistants at Dalhousie, and graduates at Texas, who have worked with me on the topic of this book.

Contents

Preface

Like the book of mine published just preceding this one, which was *Moral Objectives, Rules, and the Forms of Social Change* (University of Toronto Press, 1998), the present book originates in a number of papers, presented and published on various occasions, serving different purposes, and here brought together for the first time. The origin shows in the degree of independence that the several chapters have from one another; in the variation in rigour of treatment (especially in respect to the use of formal logic and some instances of minute scholarship); and in a degree of repetitiveness, remaining even after a strong effort to minimize it.

However, in the present book, unlike the one preceding, there is an overall argument running from end to end, bringing a number of great modern authors into line with St Thomas in a modernized natural law theory. All the parts function much more firmly as contributions to (shall I say?) an organic whole. There is a much larger proportion of new material written especially for this occasion and with an integrating purpose. The variation in rigour and the use of logic affect mainly the treatment of Hobbes, where these things are prominent, if not obtrusive; and this is a consequence simply of my finding my way through logic and minute scholarship to saying some new things about Hobbes's system of natural laws for which (who knows?) scholars may be grateful, quite independently of the significant contribution that the discovery makes to my overall argument here. The unreduced repetitiveness lies mainly in the natural laws brought forward to illustrate, turn by turn, what the several authors that I mainly discuss have in mind. Individual laws are repeated, though something like a full list of natural laws is given only once, when I put Hobbes's catalogue of them together with some of the chief instances of laws to be found in St Thomas. The list is drawn upon selectively in the chapter in which I show that Hume and Locke jointly establish a point of departure for, not just reporting claims about the universality of laws, but also for defending those claims.

Like all my work in philosophy – like, I would wish to say, all or almost all work in philosophy whoever carries it on – the present book results from a series of collaborative enterprises, during the course of which I have heard and taken into account the comments of my students and my colleagues. I shall not be able to name all of them; I would not have the space to name all of them even if I could recall them all person by person. I nevertheless acknowledge with thanks their multiple stimulations and provocations. I wish to mention specifically that in making as much as I do of the term 'thriving,' I am following my cherished colleague Sue Sherwin, who made impressive and stimulating use of it in her doctoral dissertation. I wish to acknowledge the help of undergraduate students at Dalhousie University, who in one cohort after another took my year-long course 'Justice, Law, and Morality,' not my name to begin with, and renamed in its last years at the behest of the university computer 'Ethics and Politics'; and of a number of cohorts of graduate students in government and philosophy at The University of Texas at Austin who took my seminar 'Natural Law Modernized,' not coincidentally the same title as the title of this book. All of them will find the argument outlined in the courses referred to repeated again, but with a number of refinements many of them developed during our joint efforts. Ha Kim Dao, a first-rate Texas student in my undergraduate honours seminar on another topic, enlarged my views on the history of natural law in modern times by writing an honours thesis under my direction on natural law in American political history.

Two of the graduate students at Texas must be given special mention: Xiusheng Liu and Michael McLendon. Liu's work with me on Hume and Mencius shows up not only in his essay on natural law theory in classical Chinese philosophy in the appendix to this book, but it also shows up in the use that I make of Chinese philosophy in the chapter on moral education. McLendon, like Liu, served for a time as a research assistant while he was writing an essay on natural law theory, in this case an essay on Ibn Khaldun (after initially exploring Maimonides as well). This essay, too, appears in the appendix.

For a term I had point-by-point assistance from Brenna Troncoso, a student in my natural law seminar and a research assistant of matchless energy and perspicuity; to my great benefit, Brenna returned to help me in the very final stage of the project. I had effective research assistance also, more briefly, from Mikel Richardson-Bryan in Halifax, Steve Bilakovics, Sunila Kale, and Bobby Parks in Austin, and in Halifax again, Nanette Morin. In Halifax Susan MacLeod carried out the final stage of word-processing, with ready helpfulness, and efficiently and conscientiously as well. The chore of correcting page proofs was more efficient and much more fun, done as it was with the help and company turn by turn of my daughter Linda McAdams and her husband David Dixon, than it would have been had I done it by myself.

During an early stage of my work on the present book, I had, as I wish to acknowledge with thanks, the support of a sabbatical leave fellowship from the Social Sciences and Humanities Research Council of Canada, as well as sabbatical pay from Dalhousie University. Very congenial provisions for residence and daily life during the sabbatical leave were given me as a visiting fellow at Wolfson College, Cambridge, and for this I am grateful, too. The funds for paying the research assistants came from the research funds associated with my chair at The University of Texas, as will, if all goes well, a final subsidy (in lieu of a subsidy from Ottawa) for the publication of the book. I am grateful for this ready support. In the near-to-final stages of word-processing, I have had to appeal again and again to Bill Bova, the computer expert at The University of Texas Department of Government and sometimes to his newly joined colleague Mindy Bonine; I am glad and grateful to have had them on hand; and to have had in this as in many other ventures, the kind assistance in word-processing and other matters of my Dalhousie colleague Robert Martin.

For encouragement in the project of the book from his first hearing of it, and a lot of encouragement along the way, I wish to thank Ron Schoeffel, editor-in-chief of University of Toronto Press. During the final stages of going into production, I have again had the help of Barb Porter at the Press and of Kate Baltais as copy-editor. I thank both. Kate Baltais caught a number of slips, some minor, some not so minor, and I have adopted many of her suggestions. Other people at the Press, whom I cannot so readily name, helped, too, and I thank them as well.

Some of the material in chapter 3 originally appeared in an article on Rousseau and the General Will that I contributed to a festschrift for Frederick Barnard (J.M. Porter and R. Vernon, eds., *Unity, Plurality and Politics* [London: Croom Helm, 1986]); I hold the copyright to the material. I wish to thank, respectively, *The Vital Nexus* and *The Cana-dian Journal of Philosophy* for some material in chapter 8, on moral edu-cation, originally published in 1991, and for pretty much the whole of chapter 9, on natural law and jurisprudence, originally published in 1990 (in a supplementary volume of the *CJP*).

Colleagues at Dalhousie and Texas have heard a number of the chap-ters of the book presented in departmental colloquia, and their com-ments have made a great difference, I am sure for the good, in what I have ended up saying. So have the comments of three philosophers who gave their critical assessment of the book to the University of Tor-onto Press, encouragingly favourable in every case, but also fertile in arresting suggestions for improvements; one in particular had the effect of multiplying the number of current authors that I have con-sulted and now refer to.

I name some of my colleagues at Dalhousie and Texas, along with colleagues at more remote locations, in the acknowledgments given in the individual chapters. Here I shall name, with my thanks, my col-league Arthur P. Monahan of St Mary's University, to whom I have turned for counsel a number of times and got both counsel and encour-agement. I wish also to name and thank Quentin Skinner, John Dunn, Noel Malcolm, and Richard Tuck, with whom I talked about the project of the book during my year in Cambridge. I must express, too, my gratitude to James Fishkin for rescuing me from mandatory retirement in Canada and literally giving my career a new lease on life. He did so by ushering me into a job at The University of Texas at Austin wonder-fully rewarding in every respect. I must thank him for never-failing encouragement while I have held the job. Were it not for the fact that some of the cohorts of students to whom I have dedicated the book take temporal precedence over him, I would have dedicated it to him. Wait till next year.

Note on Translations from St Thomas: I have used the Blackfriars edition of the *Summa Theologiae* in Latin and English (London: Eyre and Spot-tiswoode, 1964 and following years) as my source for his teachings and as the standard for checking my references. However, chiefly because my research assistants sometimes used the older translation by the Fathers of the English Dominican Province (New York: Benziger Broth-ers, 1947), some quotations have found their way into my text from there. I have let them stand, finding that they check out as equally accurate, and considering that they are sometimes more idiomatic.

Note on Capitalization: I capitalize a number of nouns when they are functioning as proper names, as when I refer to Hobbes's First Law. Similarly, using for my own purposes the distinction that John Rawls makes between 'concept' and 'conception' in *A Theory of Justice* (Cambridge, Mass.: Harvard University Press, 1971, 5), I capitalize nouns that stand for conceptions, for example, the conception, the Common Good, that I find in Rousseau (and the conception, the General Will, that corresponds to it there). Under the relatively vague concept of what people might have in common as a good or goods fall various conceptions, some almost equally vague, though Rousseau's is not.

NATURAL LAW MODERNIZED

Chapter One

Did Medieval Natural Law Die Out?

Natural Law Modernized is a deliberately ambiguous title. Ambiguous, too, is the project of the book, which may be described as 'modernizing medieval natural law theory.' This fuller description does distinguish what is at issue in the book from the 'natural law' position in late-twentieth-century jurisprudence. There the reference to natural law may mean simply that there are moral rules, more basic than ordinary (positive) laws, which these must express or satisfy. Various views of moral rules might serve in this connection, most of them different in perspective, and perhaps different, too, in the rules that they champion from the perspective and rules of medieval natural law theory. I mean to present and stand by the basic view of moral rules found in St Thomas Aquinas's medieval natural law theory, a theory that makes three chief claims: first, there is a set of universally applicable moral rules, with principled allowances for variations in circumstances; second (another empirical thesis), people will thrive and their societies will thrive only if these rules prevail; and third (a further empirical thesis), human beings by and large are inclined to heed the rules.

The second and third claims are the criteria by which the rules falling under the first are identified. Though they can hardly be thought trivial, all of these features may appear banal; or, on the point of inclination to obey the rules, both banal and wishful thinking. They are not banal. Sorting out moral rules that can be effectively defended as universal is not something that can be done without critical thinking; and some of the rules most famously put forward as universal ones turn out not to be so on close examination. 'Universally applicable' is itself a notion that demands close analysis. The defensibly universal rules may in some cases turn out to be unfamiliar ones, and when they are familiar they may well have a different footing after they have survived critical examination. Likewise, there is more work to do in establishing what thriving amounts to than simply recount familiar opinions. What are all the various things that count in a person's thriving, and which count for more than others? How is the thriving of persons to be related to the thriving of a society?

The natural law theory that I shall set forth has distinctive broad answers to these questions, answers in which the ways in which a person's thriving is fully integrated, along with the thriving of others, in the thriving of a society are specially insisted upon. They are not in alternative ethical theories like utilitarianism (which seeks the greatest happiness of everyone affected, whether on a social basis or not) or contractarianism (which would accept a social contract among egoistic rational agents as the foundation of ethics). The natural law theory presented here does not make as much of people's preferences as these other theories; it is more concerned with people's needs. This point, however, does not present an obstacle to acknowledging that people are inclined – so far as they are, as the result of favourable education in favourable circumstances – to heed the laws or rules that the theory upholds.

I shall demonstrate that the core of the theory that St Thomas sets forth survives in modern thinkers, specifically, Thomas Hobbes, John Locke, David Hume, and Jean-Jacques Rousseau. Thus the theory is modern, since it is upheld by modern thinkers. I shall also demonstrate that the same core, embellished by the contributions of these modern thinkers, can stand – at the beginning of the third millennium – as an ethical theory viable by the most sophisticated current tests. Thus, the theory is modern, because it is current, or deserves to be. The theory can meet all the subtle challenges of analytical metaethics. It will not succumb to sceptical claims that there are devastating counterexamples to every comprehensive position in ethics. It will not collapse in the face of postmodernist objections.

The Core Medieval Theory Freed from Notoriously Controversial Features

This modern natural law theory is very different from what most people, especially most people in the general public, think of as the natural law position. Natural law theory has not in name aroused much enthusiasm in recent generations outside the Catholic church. One reason for this is precisely that subscription to it has been thought to entail subscription to Catholic beliefs about the existence of God for one thing, and about a variety of other things, including divorce, the status of women, and sexual activity, embracing, in regard to the latter – most notoriously – opposition to contraception and abortion, as well as to fornication and masturbation.

Some passages in St Thomas's writings, for instance, 2a2ae, Q.153, 4 of the *Summa Theologiae*, can be read as prohibiting any orgasmic sexual activity that is not aimed by both partners in a heterosexual union at the conception of a child. There, after pointing out that 'the exercise of sex is of capital importance for the Common Good, namely, the preservation of the human race,' St Thomas flatly says that 'the discharge of semen,' unlike other 'superfluities of the body,' 'ought to be in such manner as to fit the end for which it is needed.' That, of course, and not coincidentally, rules out masturbation, with by itself enormous consequences in human misery through the centuries, as well as any intercourse with women past the age of bearing children, and a lot of intercourse commonly carried on (with contraceptive precautions) before women get past that age. No concession on these points is made, in the passage cited, to the biological facts that in a great number of people the sexual drive is very urgent and that the orgasms in which sexual tension is discharged are enormously enjoyable whether or not they occur as incidents of efforts at procreation.[1]

John Finnis[2] argues convincingly, however, on the basis of passages elsewhere in St Thomas's writings that even St Thomas (not to speak of Catholic teachings at the present day) takes a somewhat more liberal view of these matters. Sexual union in marriage has two purposes: procreation, and besides procreation, the expression of a loving commitment to the marriage bond. When procreation is not intended, or even possible, sexual union can be wholly justified by the second purpose. This is certainly a significant allowance. However, the principle leaves under prohibition every other form of sexual activity, in or out of marriage, solitary or in partnership (indeed, heterosexual intercourse in marriage not carried on expressly to manifest commitment – if not to procreate – is prohibited, too). The procreative purpose, moreover, retains a certain priority: When procreation is possible, the partners must not forestall procreation by contraception.

Where do prohibitions like these come from? Finnis holds that the violations of these prohibitions all deviate from the 'intelligible good' of 'truly marital intercourse' and offer no intelligible good of their own, at most, evidently, only 'bodily and emotional satisfaction, pleasurable experience, unhinged from basic human reasons for action and posing as its own rationale' (153, 151). Among those basic reasons, the only 'hinge' available for sexual activity is a matrimonial ideal, vigorously and repeatedly maintained by Robert George and other allies of Finnis: 'Only in marriage can sexual acts constitute a real union of persons,'[3] and 'only in marriage can sexual acts realize a Common Good rather than induce self-alienation or produce a merely illusory experience of personal unity.'[4] All 'non-marital sexual acts' in marriage or out of it are wrong, because in all of them orgasm is unfulfilling, that is to say, inconsistent with heeding 'the first principle of morality,' 'the principle of integral human fulfillment,' in which true human goods have their place.

Where does this matrimonial ideal come from, and why is it prescribed for people who are not married or who though married have some other conception of marriage? One may well suspect that it arose originally, with its limited licence for sexual activity, from making procreation basic by applying to it an arbitrary use of the idea of the biological functions of specific bodily organs, that is, of the necessary parts that they play in the life of the organism. The clitoris has no necessary part in procreation, but does it not have a function, namely, to give sexual pleasure? Moreover, organs need not have only one function; the penis already has, besides the function connected with procreation, another one in urination. Might it not be recognized as having a third, namely, to be the source of a distinctive (and for many people an extraordinarily urgent) pleasure? Moreover, why is the pleasure not an intelligible good, especially if it is intelligibly sought under recognized conditions answering, short maybe of answering to the proffered matrimonial ideal, to mutual consent and other things? That it is not on Finnis's or George's list of human goods brings their list into question. In any case, the prohibitions that arbitrarily and unconditionally would obstruct this pleasure do not figure in the core of natural law theory that I am concerned with; nor do they figure in the definitive passages of St Thomas's writings that I shall draw upon.

George claims that arguments from biological function are passé for the sort of natural law theorists among whom he counts himself.[5] George prefers what he considers a much more powerful argument. However, this turns out, I am afraid, to be more question-begging than anything else, relying on notions about the unified activity of each person and about union in activity between persons that, respectively, assume that activity is worthless if it is not unified in the sense prescribed (which calls for mind and body to be together wholly committed) or assume the matrimonial ideal in question. Under the principle of integral human fulfilment, other forms of sexual activity are not just less fulfilling, they are not fulfilling in any degree acceptable even as an approximation, because in them people treat their own bodies as mere external instruments to cheap and transitory pleasures. What George says about masturbation typifies the line of thought. In masturbation, 'the physical activities (stroking, rubbing) are chosen as merely extrinsic means of producing an effect (gratification) in consciousness.'[6] To engage in such physical activities is to alienate oneself from one's body, or, worse, from one's self as a person in whom soul and body should act in unison. George and his co-author Lee seem to have overlooked the fact that masturbation is very commonly not just physical activity leading to a physical climax with an accompanying sensation of gratification; it involves by way of fantasies (often essential to success) the mind as much or more than the body. George and Lee are equally imperceptive and arbitrary in ruling out other sexual activities, including even the activities of lovers who cannot, they hold, have a real experience of unity with each other if they are not married.

I am not sure that I can believe that this approach has really left reasoning from biological functions behind. 'Integral human fulfillment,' even if it is an ideal that cannot be fully realized, is something evidently distinctively and uniquely appropriate for human beings. I have no objection to that. But, again, how did the matrimonial ideal, with its exceedingly controversial features (controversial in themselves, doubly controversial as candidates for universalization), get into the picture of integral human fulfilment, if not by way of the thought that sexual activity has an important function in human lives, namely, procreation, which cannot be accomplished unless a man and a woman unite to play their different parts in carrying it out, as a prelude to raising the children that may issue from it? But, again, affirmation of this fact about human biology need not exclude other functions, or any of a variety of more liberal ways of treating sexual activity.

The core medieval natural law theory that I shall be occupied with does not include the specific prohibitions regarding sexual activity that I have just been discussing. I do not argue that the core theory is incompatible with them. I would, however, give a sceptical reception in most cases to arguments for adding them, as I would for arguments against divorce.[7] (I do not need to oppose George and Finnis on the subordination of women; except perhaps for accepting women as priests, I would grant that they are no more inclined than I to retain this feature of the medieval theory, and they like me have also discarded any licence given to human slavery.)[8] In respect to abortion, which troubles me as the subjects of the other prohibitions do not, I must acknowledge a shortfall in the core theory. The core natural law theory is concerned with the relations of people who are already members of communities. In principle it can be expanded relatively easily to embrace people who happen to be outside a given community; but what it is to do with questions about beings who are arguably not yet people is not something it is prepared to say. St Thomas himself thought that human souls were imparted to embryos only a number of weeks after conception.[9]

What the core natural law theory carries forward from St Thomas is rooted in the nature of man and worldly circumstances to a degree that, given the controversies they invite, the special features regarding sex and other matters that I discard cannot plausibly be conceded. The features retained – answering to the three chief claims already cited at the beginning of this chapter – rules universally applicable, the thriving of persons under the rules in thriving societies, and the inclination to heed the rules, can all be derived from the view of human beings in nature outlined by St Thomas in the paramount passage, *ST*, 1a2ae, Q.94, 2, which treats them as in the first place material substances, as a species of animal in the second place, and in the third place as a species having properties unique among animals such as language and reason. The rules have to take into account the fact that as substances human beings cannot be in several places at once (which constrains the number of duties that can be placed upon them) and that everything they do must be done from persistent material platforms with limited capacities, namely, their bodies (so that they cannot act except on information that reaches them there, in ways accessible to them there). The rules have to take into account the needs of human beings, just from being the sort of substances that they are, for such things as food, shelter, and clothing; and hence the possibility of conflicts among persons over the same, possibly very limited, provisions for these needs. The rules have to take into account procreation and the prolonged, vulnerable infancy of human offspring. (Contrary, however, to the theorists that we just visited, the core theory leaves open a number of possibilities for successful provisions on these matters: along with monogamous families, for example, polygamous ones, or villages attentive to all the miscellaneous children on hand.) The rules having to do with language and reason must include rules providing for children to learn the language of their communities, extending to literacy and numeracy when these are required for full social participation. Beyond that, the rules will provide for deliberation about laws and the deliberated use of laws to bring about and maintain social cooperation. These remarks about the subject-matter of the rules – the natural laws – already give some notion of the character and range of the core theory; details about content will follow in later chapters.[10]

The core theory does not invoke the will of God to establish the content of the moral rules that it upholds or to confer upon them their standing as natural laws. One cannot lightly disregard the theistic perspective that St Thomas brings to natural law theory; and all the modern thinkers that I shall be concerned with, except for Hume, give God an important place in their views, lending support to the opinion (expressed, for example, by Alan Ryan, cited by Anthony J. Lisska[11]) that natural law without God is 'dead,' and 'a secular natural law theory is simply incoherent.' Nevertheless, I shall argue that even theorists as theistic in outlook as St Thomas and John Locke recognize in principle that the content of natural law can be arrived at without invoking the existence of God. Hobbes and Rousseau would join them, it is true, in holding that God is the authority who gives natural law its ultimate imperative force. However, Hobbes and Rousseau themselves show how we can dispense with God in this connection, too, if we are not satisfied to follow Hume in ignoring Him – Hobbes by resting the laws (both civil and natural) in practice upon the authority of the Sovereign, whose necessity he reaches by empirical argument, Rousseau by ascribing the authority behind the laws to the General Will, which aims to do what is empirically necessary to achieve the Common Good. Far from being a contradiction in terms because God has been set aside, the core of natural law theory is essentially naturalistic and secular in all these thinkers, including St Thomas and Locke, though both of the latter two have to be treated on this point with some delicacy.

Believers, of course, will put the core natural law theory in a theistic perspective, and there is nothing incongruous in doing so. The theistic perspective will do nothing to win non-believers as adherents to the core theory; it may repel them. However, all my great authors, except Hume, do present the core theory in a theistic perspective; and it is clear that St Thomas and Locke cherish that perspective. (Hobbes's commitment to theism is a notoriously controversial issue.) Insofar as

St Thomas adheres to a secular natural law theory, it is under the auspices of a belief that God has arranged the world to make it possible for people to participate in His eternal law through reasoning that does not invoke His existence or will, but relies instead on human nature and circumstances. In the face of a secular presentation of the core natural law theory, believers might adopt St Thomas's view, or even, without striking out anything in the theory, hold that it becomes richer and more persuasive (as it does for them) if it is associated with God's purposes.

The Core Natural Law Theory Ascribed to Canonical Authors in Modern Political Thought

My project derives some interest from the selection of authors in my modern set: Hobbes, Locke, Hume, and Rousseau. If one were going to collect from seventeenth- and eighteenth-century writers a robust doctrine of natural law, correcting the errors and filling the gaps left by some by drawing on others, this is not the most likely set to turn to, because they are not the most straightforward champions: Knud Haakonssen and J.B. Schneewind have persuaded me[12] one would do better, or at least one would do more easily, by turning to the other seventeenth-century writers like Hugo Grotius, Richard Cumberland, and (above all) to Samuel Pufendorf; or, in the eighteenth century, to Francis Hutcheson. Some commentators, like Norberto Bobbio, treat Hobbes as belonging without question to the natural law tradition.[13] Others, like H.A. Rommen, treat him as falling wholly outside it.[14] Hobbes certainly says things that put him dramatically at odds with St Thomas; Locke's ethical theory has seemed to some (Schneewind)[15] to give too much weight of an egoistic cast to pleasure and pain; Hume's use of natural law terminology has seemed to some (Annette Baier)[16] ironical; and Rousseau can be found explicitly repudiating any attachment to natural law theory (Lloyd Weinreb).[17] I aim to show that notwithstanding these points, all the authors in the set are basically in agreement with St Thomas in supporting a natural law theory with the same character and core content, and also (though this is more controversial) on there being a source, apart from the God of the Bible or of natural theology, for its imperative force.

Perhaps this would be interesting even if the set of authors in question had been chosen at random. They have not been chosen at random. The three of my seventeenth- and eighteenth-century authors who wrote in English have (to a degree exceeding the others I mentioned) canonical status in the teaching of modern ethics and political philosophy in English-speaking countries; and Rousseau surpasses all Continental authors of the seventeenth and eighteenth centuries, even Pufendorf, in influence in political philosophy, and hence in canonical status. I do not regard canonical status as sacrosanct in respect to being definitive; but it does go along with the authors concerned being prominent and familiar. If natural law theory survives robustly with them, it cannot be written off as a concern of minor authors.

I shall be making corrections, as needed, to the contributions of these canonical authors to the core theory in the course of arguing for the recognition of their contributions as reinforcements rather than departures. Doing so is indispensable if natural law theory is to be attractive at the end of the twentieth century. However, more must be done if the theory is to be shown to have answers to the challenges presented to any ethical theory in twentieth-century philosophical discussions. I have in mind challenges to cognitivism – the position that moral judgments have truth value – and realism – the position that some moral judgments truly correspond to features of the world. I have in mind also the challenge to sort out the aspects of ethics that are important to the distinction between internalism and externalism in moral motivation: Does believing in the truth of moral judgments commit one to heeding them, or does the commitment spring from a source external to the judgments themselves?

David Copp's 1995 book *Morality, Normativity, and Society*[18] seems to me to have the state-of-the-art answers that natural law theory needs to meet these challenges. Copp's book, in fact, is a good approximation to a contemporary statement of natural law theory, though it does not sail under its colours, and is almost entirely unmindful of the texts and history with which the present book is preoccupied. I shall ransack Copp's book for my own purposes. In what a disinterested judge might consider fair compensation (drawing on traditional natural law notions among other things), I shall try to improve on Copp in several respects, for example, in bringing back a fuller conception of moral sentiment, in supplying a definition of rules, and in sorting out his curiously unconsolidated account of how a social choice of a moral code justifies it. Copp is still in the grip of the notion that justified rules presuppose some unique legislating authority, with social choice serving as a vestige of the Divine choice found in Locke's account and others. Copp, moreover, puts no restrictions on the motivations of the agents taking part in the social choice of a moral code (except that they know that what they are doing will have this effect); and this may be looked upon as combining with a vestige of divine legislative authority a vestige of theological voluntarism (the idea that things are good because God chooses them, not that He chooses them because He recognizes that they are good).

Is this going to be a scholarly book? I do not take all of the teachings in ethics of any of these authors into the core theory, any more than I take all of the teachings of St Thomas. In every case I am very selective; I do not aim to give a full or balanced account of the whole teaching of the author concerned, just extract components of the core theory that can be found there and accurately ascribed to the author concerned or that he could be brought by argument to endorse given what I have extracted from the rest of his teaching. I shall certainly be leaving a lot of scholarship to others. There is an abundance of points to make about the relations of St Thomas's thinking about ethics to other aspects of his thinking, let alone to the thinking of other medieval philosophers; an abundance of points to make, too, about the relations of Hobbes's, Locke's, Hume's, and Rousseau's thinking to the teachings of other authors with claims to attention comparable to theirs, even if they do not figure in everybody's conception of the canon. There are relations to authors more obscure than these, who like Richard Cumberland may have more subtle and convincing things to say about natural law than many who are more famous. Then there are the aspects of Hobbes's and Locke's thinking – maybe also of the thinking of Hume and Rousseau – that can be fully understood only by considering the full political context in which they wrote – the debates in and out of Parliament, the pamphlets, the plots, the apprehensions of their times. I shall not be attempting a synoptic, much less an exhaustive account of the intellectual development of any of the individual thinkers that I do treat.

Nevertheless, if I am right that the core of ethical theory to be found in all these thinkers is the same, that each makes contributions that strengthen the theory, and that the theory, taken together with their contributions and with what I have taken from Copp, can meet contemporary philosophical challenges, this is a big – complex – fact about the history of ethics and political philosophy. If I shall be very far from noticing everything to be said about the thinkers that I treat, I may hope to be accurate in respect to the views that I do pick out and ascribe to them. Thus, I hope to demonstrate a big scholarly fact with accurate supporting historical evidence.

Big it may be. Is it interesting? Why should one bother to carry out this demonstration? I can invoke a number of reasons: First, the demonstration throws light on the continuity from St Thomas through modern thinkers to the present day. Many, perhaps most, scholarly studies emphasize the differences between the authors treated; it is important now and then to redress the balance in favour of continuity. Second, the demonstration extends the range of present options in ethical theory. People who think about these things may reject emotivism, the view that moral judgments do no more than express emotions; they may escape emotivism/imperativism, the view that moral judgments both express emotions and some sort of commands, nothing more; they may not be tempted by the error theory variant of cognitivism, according to which moral judgments are in principle true or false, but all happen to be strictly speaking false. These people will be left, in many cases, under the impression that the remaining options in ethical theory are confined to utilitarianism, contractarianism, and some version of Kant's rationalism. In fact, natural law theory is a further option. But third, simple and familiar as some of the content of natural law theory is (and should be if it is right) in the course of carrying out the demonstration a number of interesting issues (for example, about the place of needs in ethics, universality of moral rules, and moral education) come up in forms that may not be encountered on other approaches to ethical theory. An up-to-date, modernized natural law theory that deals with these issues in a convincing way, the sort of theory I hope to present, will not only light up again points received from the tradition, but will set a number of new lights shining.

My Project Contrasted with the Projects of Other Current Writers

John Finnis, in his book *Natural Law and Natural Rights*,[19] and in other works, some of them written in collaboration with Germain Grisez (an author of independent importance in this field), has undertaken, in the words of one of their admirers and critics, to retrieve 'the systematic core of natural law theory [in St Thomas][20] in a way that is congruent with the older tradition and in a way that is persuasive to contemporary ethicians.'[21] How, one might well ask, is my project different from theirs?

It is different in a number of ways – to speak in particular of Finnis, he is a fervent Catholic believer, who gives to God and church doctrine as much place in his conception of natural law as to St Thomas and who would keep in his theory a lot about procreative activity that I would discard. Finnis presents an argument, more intricate and detailed than anything that I shall attempt, in which an elaborate concept of 'practicable reasonableness' governs the identification and pursuit of a set of supposedly incommensurable human goods. I want to operate with lighter baggage, in part because the lighter baggage will make it easier to assimilate standard modern authors, and have them contribute some of the details of the theory. Finnis is not interested in spelling out any convergence of views between St Thomas and the modern authors whom I treat; indeed, he is ready, which I am not, to disparage them by comparison with St Thomas.[22] I read *Natural Law and Natural Rights* with interest and admiration when it was new; and it has no doubt affected my thinking in more ways than I cite in the present book. However, I had come in my teaching to the main lines of the argument of the present book maybe a dozen years before I encountered Finnis; and in the main I mean to be steering my own independent course.

I mean to be doing that, too, in respect to Finnis's more recent book on Aquinas, to which I have referred several times already, and shall refer again. Again, in spite of great respect for Finnis's learning and scholarship, I take a different view on a number of points. The disagreement may for the most part have to do with my tendency to parse the core theory differently from anything that would fully reflect Finnis's outlook: I mean to be more straightforward in emphasizing the connection with the thriving of society; simpler in the conception of what this thriving, considered as the Common Good, entails; simpler again in the treatment of motivation. In all these connections I am preoccupied with social ethics, while Finnis and his allies (for example, Grisez, Boyle, George) are preoccupied with personal ethics. The ranges of our preoccupations, of course, intersect: Telling the truth, for example, is an important consideration in the private relations of persons; but what preoccupies me is the contribution that a rule – a natural law – prescribing the telling of truth makes to the thriving of a society. Even in the perspective of personal ethics, the various forms of sexual intercourse seem to me to be insignificant matters for moral concern, if they are matters of concern at all, compared to truth-telling, kindness, reliability, even *joie de vivre* (cheerfulness). In the perspective of social ethics, they are hardly visible compared to high rates of imprisonment, the proliferation of firearms in civilian populations, persistent unemployment, and poverty. Yet I have learned from Finnis's more recent book to make more of the natural inclination of human beings to heed the natural laws; and perhaps if we look upon these laws and natural inclinations in the perspective of social ethics, I come out in the neighbourhood of Finnis's position. I do not suppose that we disagree about the importance to social peace of truth-telling, promise-keeping, and mutual accommodation.

Finnis and Grisez, and their collaborator Joseph M. Boyle, Jr, I should note, are not the only figures in the field who are trying like me to make use in ethical theory today of 'the systematic core of natural law theory' in St Thomas. Robert George, a very productive author, has already been noted as an ally of Finnis on the restriction of sexual activity; and though like Finnis, he is preoccupied with personal ethics, George's interest in upholding natural law theory extends in harmony with Finnis's beyond an intense concern with that subject. However, George is no more concerned than Finnis or Grisez, as I am, with bringing the core of St Thomas's natural law theory up to date by demonstrating its presence in the canonical authors of modern political thought.

Alasdair MacIntyre has presented himself in several works, most recently in *Three Rival Versions of Moral Inquiry* (Notre Dame, Indiana: Notre Dame University Press, 1990) and in *Dependent Rational Animals* (LaSalle, Ill.: Open Court, 1999), as a Thomist or 'Thomistic Aristotelian' and his interest in the history of thought is omnivorous. However, MacIntyre does not make anything special of my canonical authors; though on other points there are major affinities between his thinking and mine, including taking inspiration from Vicki Hearne's work on training animals and making a good deal of human needs (see the chapter 'Moral Education,' below). Nor does MacIntyre pursue anything like my project with the core of natural law theory, embellished by points collected from the canonical modern authors who subscribed to it and illustrated in the secular ethical theory of the present day. In *Dependent Rational Animals*, MacIntyre makes what I accept as an important and poignant addition to other treatments of human needs, including mine – see *Meeting Needs* (Princeton: Princeton University Press, 1987) – by stressing our vulnerability to disabilities and the importance because of this of provisions for mutual aid. I entirely reject, however, MacIntyre's contention in *Three Rival Versions of Moral Enquiry* that to make any headway in moral inquiry one must accept principles (like God and God's creation) that do not admit of dissent; in the West, at least, this means for MacIntyre accepting Thomistic doctrine as a whole. At one point in *Three Rival Versions of Moral Inquiry*, MacIntyre says that 'to read [the *Summa Theologiae*] in its own terms from within the tradition which Aquinas reconstituted [by combining Augustine's doctrines with Aristotle's] in the course of writing it is the only way to reckon with it in other than mock and distorting encounter' (135). He goes on immediately, and it seems to me with much less than perfect consistency, to admit that by the 'knowledge of the natural law which human beings have by nature ... we can surely all judge equally of what he says, plain persons and philosophers or theologians alike' (135–6). This is the position that I take and that I ascribe to St Thomas himself in the texts that I draw upon; and if this means that I shall not be going so deeply into his doctrines as MacIntyre, Finnis, Grisez, Boyle, and George – another great difference, I am ready to concede, from their approach – it also means that I shall not fail, as I think they do, to give full credit to the connections that St Thomas makes in the perspective of social ethics between the natural laws and their adaptation, for the sake of utility, to empirical consequences.[23]

Arguments by Strauss, Sabine, and Schneewind for Thinking Medieval Natural Law Died Out

My contention that the core of St Thomas's natural law theory survives in a successful natural law theory upheld by the modern authors that I treat is something that will have to be made good by producing it from the texts. That is the business of the chapters to come. Before launching upon those chapters, however, I shall clear the way for the theory to be produced by disposing of some current scholarly opinions that stand in the way of believing such a theory can be produced.

Leo Strauss has asserted that modern natural law theory, that is to say, the theory running under the name of natural law theory in the seventeenth and eighteenth centuries, is radically different from medieval natural law theory. I have particularly in mind Strauss's article in the *International Encyclopedia of Social Sciences* (1968), a reference work not yet superseded by anything else of the kind.[24] George Sabine, another writer still current on this subject because nothing later has surpassed in breadth of scholarship his history of political theory, comes close to this position in arguing that in the seventeenth and eighteenth centuries natural law theory became secularized as a rationalistic theory before being displaced by an empirical approach to ethics.[25] J.B. Schneewind, in a work published just a few years ago,[26] joins Sabine in thinking that the natural law theory prevailing in the seventeenth century and up to the middle of the eighteenth century was discredited by the empirical approach. None of these scholars think, as I do, that there is a successful natural law theory kept up in the seventeenth and eigtheenth centuries. For Strauss, modern political philosophy, modern natural law theory included, is a grievous departure from the insights of ancient philosophy. Schneewind entitles a section of one of his chapters 'The Collapse of Modern Natural Law Theory.' Sabine is clearer than Schneewind about what he views as the reason for the collapse, namely, that putting ethics on an empirical foundation, as was done pre-eminently by Hume, undermined natural law theory – in the end completely.

I argue the contrary: A successful natural law theory was present in the seventeenth and eighteenth centuries, in the authors that I treat among others; it was superseded and lost from sight; but it did not collapse.[27] The empirical foundation proclaimed for it was not a complete innovation, since it was foreshadowed in earlier authors – in St Thomas, to go no further back – and clearly revived by Hobbes and Locke. It is true that this successful theory was distinct from any version of natural law theory that looked to God (the God of the Bible and revelation) to promulgate the laws that the theory justifies.[28] The theory is distinct also from any version of natural law theory that so much emphasized the role of reason in working it out as to obscure the empirical issues at stake, giving the impression that the whole theory could be worked out a priori and demonstratively. (Allusions to the possibility of demonstration do not by themselves commit an author to this excessively rationalist view; the demonstration may begin with empirically founded axioms and lead to a model that stands or falls with its empirical fit.)

Strauss's views, at least as expressed in his confused article in the *International Encyclopedia of Social Sciences*, do not offer much of an obstacle to my project. Having in mind, as he specifically says, Hobbes, Locke, and Rousseau (to whom I add Hume), Strauss asserts that modern natural law, in distinction from natural law as understood in medieval times and earlier, was originated by Hobbes, who relied on self-preservation rather than on 'the hierarchical order of man's natural ends.' But self-preservation is very prominent, indeed basic, for St Thomas, too, since it is an end that he takes human beings to share, not just with all other animals, but with all substances; and the hierarchy of ends[29] given by St Thomas can be regarded up to a point as amplifying in accordance with human nature, more advanced than other substances and other animals, what self-preservation means in the case of human beings, including participation in social life. The love and service of God, admittedly, transcend these things, even to the degree that the love and service are directed by an illusion; and mating, which St Thomas mentions as an end that human beings have in common with other animals, fits only awkwardly under self-preservation. But Hobbes, too, would have a problem with mating; and Hobbes, distinguishing as he does between mere survival and commodious living, has something that takes self-preservation a fair distance up St Thomas's hierarchy of ends.[30]

Two paragraphs earlier, in the course of enumerating other supposed differences between modern natural law and traditional natural law, Strauss asserts that according to modern natural law, 'Natural law by itself is supposed to be at home in the state of nature,' that is to say, that people there know and heed natural law. This is true in so many words of Locke; and perhaps may be made out by argument to be true of Hume, if the situation after the adoption of the conventions regarding property and justice (but before the institution of government) is counted as the state of nature, not the situation before the conventions have been adopted. However, it is something specifically denied by Rousseau, as regards the content of natural law on the received view; and nothing could be further from Hobbes's teaching: People in the state of nature may know what the natural law is and may wish to live by it, but they do not dare try, because they do not dare expose themselves to pre-emptive attacks by others.

Strauss says that traditional natural law was 'essentially conservative,' while 'modern natural law' is 'essentially revolutionary.' Hobbes would be very surprised to hear this; likewise Hume, though Hume does preserve the principle of appeal against unjust laws that can be found in St Thomas and Locke, who are both very cautious (to say the least) about inciting revolution, but who do not rule it out. St Thomas, in his brief work *On Kingship*, refuses to authorize in so many words the assassination of a tyrant, but he allows that people in power may be justly killed as enemies of God or the people; and he also asserts that rulers who abuse their power may legitimately be removed from office, without explaining how this is to be done without violence in some cases.[31] Spectacular use for revolutionary purposes was made of Rousseau's writings as well as of Locke's. Locke does outline circumstances in which revolution would be justified. Rousseau does not, and in his writings, for all his strictures on French society, he does not come forward as someone with an ardent revolutionary program.

Earlier in his article Strauss described, in what I accept as useful and accurate accounts, the doctrines of Plato and Aristotle, who along with the Stoics that came after them in antiquity laid the groundwork for natural law thinking in medieval and modern times. Perhaps having in mind Plato's ideal Republic more than Aristotle's best polity, Strauss goes on to assert that the laws of modern natural law 'do not declare what the best political order is, which by its nature is not realizable except under very favorable conditions, but they state the conditions of legitimacy which obtain regardless of place and time.' This is not a point of distinction between medieval natural law and modern, since exactly the same thing can be said of St Thomas's views, at least of the general principles with which all legitimate applications must accord.

Are rights – 'the rights of man' – rather than duties more prominent in modern natural law, as Strauss holds? It is true that St Thomas does not make anything explicit of rights – he was writing, on the present generally accepted scholarly account, at a time when the modern notion of rights was just being innovated by other thinkers, whose lead he did not follow.[32] Hobbes makes a good deal of the 'right of nature,' a very odd right since it does not come with any limit or any protection from interference, but Hobbes hardly treats this as a foundation for rights in organized society; it is something that must be renounced, so far as it is rationally possible to do so, to have an organized society. Hume has little to say about rights, even in his account of justice and property. Locke and Rousseau may be looked to as champions of rights, but even they say less about rights than one would expect from the general reputation that they and rights have acquired from association with the Declaration of Independence and the Declaration of the Rights of Man. Moreover, an entirely convincing case can be made, and has been made by John Finnis, that the addition of rights to natural law theory does no more at bottom than add a useful device for giving natural law effect.[33]

Strauss also asserts that modern natural law reflects 'the belief that natural law can be treated "geometrically," that is, that the conclusions possess the same certainty as the principles.' Both Hobbes and Locke did have this belief, which St Thomas explicitly disavows; there is no sign of it in Hume or in Rousseau. St Thomas, unlike Hume and Rousseau, does hold that natural laws are related by deduction, where they do not come down to equally eligible options given particular circumstances. Just how this is to be reconciled with the uncertainty, which according to St Thomas increases more and more as the deductions descend toward particularization, is left unexamined, as is the possibility (which St Thomas overlooks) that if one presses for the best solution in particular circumstances the options may not any longer seem equally eligible.[34]

Strauss says of Hobbes's teaching that in it 'man is not by nature ordered toward society, but he orders himself toward it prompted by mere calculation.' But Hobbes does treat human beings as naturally inclined to obey natural laws – the conditions of having an ordered society – if they can find a safe way of doing so. Furthermore, 'the mere calculation' in question is not one that leaves disregard of the laws as anything more than a desperate alternative. It is not a matter of balancing pleasures and pains, but a matter of recognizing and seizing if one can the only chance of peace and personal security.

'Mere calculation' figures in Strauss's dual formulation of what he regards as the basic issue about natural law. Is the right solution to the issue about having a society 'merely the condition of the living together of a particular society ... or is there a justice among men as men which does not derive from any human arrangement? In other words, is justice based only on calculation of the advantage of living together, or is it choiceworthy for its own sake and therefore "by nature"?' Both formulas present false antitheses. If human beings recognize that, given their nature and their circumstances, they cannot thrive unless they heed the natural laws as conditions of living together, they are recognizing a fact about themselves and the world that transcends any arbitrary choice. Justice – an arrangement that fulfils the natural laws – is thus not merely conventional. Perhaps it is choiceworthy only as a condition of realizing 'the advantage of living together,' but that advantage is not to be belittled as a subject of mere calculation. It at least is choiceworthy for its own sake; people either care about it – care about human beings thriving in societies that themselves flourish – or they do not.

To sum up this critique of Strauss: He does not have good grounds for holding that Hobbes, Locke, and Rousseau (all of whom he identifies among the 'great modern natural law teachers' as distinct from 'university professors' appointed to teach natural law theory), much less Hume, all have in common the positions that Strauss asserts make the difference between modern natural law and traditional natural law, of which he takes St Thomas to offer 'the classic form of teaching.' Nor does Strauss have any good ground for holding that what these modern thinkers do have in common is not substantially, give or take minor adjustments, identical with the core of St Thomas's theory, except for some improvements added in the spirit of that core.

In *The Invention of Autonomy*, Schneewind gives a picture of what, according to him, is the demise of natural law theory in the eighteenth century and the rise to replace it of another sort of ethical theory, one that culminates in the work of Immanuel Kant. This, according to Schneewind, was a shift between thinking of ethics as a matter of obedience to given laws to thinking of it as a sphere in which the laws are adopted by autonomous choices of the persons subject to them.

This may well be an important distinction, but it rests on thinking of natural laws as laid down for our obedience by God. It does not, logically, make a secular natural law theory, of the sort that one can find in Hume, obsolete. Schneewind gives no attention and no weight to Hume's contention, put forward in an argument that does not contain even a token invocation of God's legislative authority and rests solely on empirical grounds (including the observation that human beings are naturally inclined to approve the thriving of others along with themselves), that the rules of justice are natural laws. Schneewind gives no attention or weight either to the aspects of natural law to be found in the teaching of Rousseau, which may be regarded as founded on empirical discovery, with the God of civil religion added on for political purposes later.[35]

Moreover, any shift from obedience to personal autonomy requires special care in handling if it is to be related to natural law theory. Traditional natural law theory no doubt made less allowance for a variety of life-plans than modern moralists would want to; what allowance it did make did not extend to letting everybody in principle construct his or her own life-plan within the limits of mutual non-interference. But the notion of the Common Good is elastic enough to accommodate a great variety of choices. The choices, indeed, have to be both in the natural law view and in Kant's view consistent with the rules or laws of morality. The choice of the laws themselves is certainly not for Kant an exercise of personal autonomy in any idiosyncratic dimension: Each of Kant's rational agents arrives by the test of universalization at the same moral laws. In principle, Rousseau's citizens also converge on the same laws when they seek to identify which laws promote the Common Good. The laws are laws of the citizens' own choosing, but they choose under certain conditions. The laws, moreover, are to be obeyed just as stringently as under the former theistic regime in ethics. So one might equally well portray the shift from natural law to the ethics of personal autonomy as a shift from obedience to God to obedience to laws chosen by human beings for themselves under suitable provisions for legislation. Then the displacement of natural law theory looks like a displacement of divine authority, with the possibilities of secular development of natural law theory (already realized in St Thomas, according to Finnis and Lisska) accidentally discarded in the process.

Schneewind says (82), 'Hobbes and Cumberland originated views whose descendants are still live options for us. Pufendorf's theory is dead.' 'Dead' because currently passed over as an effect of prevailing (though not utterly prevailing) disregard for natural law theory? Or 'dead' because of intrinsic defects? Schneewind does not make any intrinsic defects prominent in his chapter on Pufendorf. Schneewind charges Pufendorf with failing to show how free will can be efficacious in a causal world, and there is a hint of a general charge of not resolving the problem of God's untrammeled will. But on this Pufendorf has a neat formula, as Schneewind himself reports: God need not have created man as he is; but once God had done so, what is good for man is determined by man's nature (140), and man has certain duties that he must perform on pain of punishment. True, this formula (not unique to Pufendorf, though clearly stated by him in Schneewind's citation) leaves some difficulty about how to handle the enforcement of rules about imperfect duties, which leave us some discretion as to where and when we are to fulfil them (for example, give to the poor); the threat of punishment seems out of place with them. Schneewind ascribes (164) to Pufendorf a 'fatal incoherence' respecting the relation of obligation to imperfect duties. Schneewind goes on to consider Thomasius, but in the account that he gives of this philosopher he omits to consider how Thomasius's notion of God the Father counselling the performance of these duties might be used to repair Pufendorf; Schneewind treats Thomasius's changes as, in effect, repudiations of Pufendorf, which does not seem plausible, on the face of the account given of both.

As the three distinctive marks of 'modern natural law theory' Schneewind gives (144): [1] our unsocially sociable psychology causes basic problems that [2] empirically discoverable law shows us how to resolve [3] without any substantive conception of the highest good' (I have put in the numbers). [1] makes no difference from St Thomas, who could hardly forget the fractiousness exhibited by human beings in original sin and in the consequences of original sin. [2] is not a point of difference with St Thomas either, since for St Thomas natural law is discovered by reflecting on human nature and circumstances. What is the basis for [3]? Hobbes offers peace and commodious living as goods that depend on having an effective system of natural laws. Locke offers self-preservation and the preservation of others – but commodious living, too, as can be gathered from his defence of private property as an incentive to increasing the social product. Rousseau offers a Common Good with specifiable concrete features; Hume offers whatever is useful to happiness and social life. It is true, that none of these would be pursued as goods for people whose preferences did not align with them; but why should it not be appropriate to take people's preferences and dispositions into account?

The difficulties ascribed by Schneewind to 'modern natural law theory' seem to arise mainly from the theorists' (not just Pufendorf's) insisting on voluntarism, an insistence to which the theorists were led by a dilemma: either voluntarism, open to anything turning out to be good if God wills it so, or intellectualism, identifying what is good before considering whether God wills it. Haakonssen similarly portrays the natural law theorists of the late seventeenth century as struggling continually to reconcile theistic voluntarism with moral realism.[36] Some authors may have been unable to arrive at a consistent system of natural law just because of this problem.[37] However, if we set God aside in favour of a secular system, we escape the problem, which is just as well, because it is, strictly posed and followed up, quite insoluble. Take God out of the picture: Infer what is basically – indispensably – good for a person from empirical findings about human nature and circumstances. The inferences extend without trouble to what is good for groups of persons taken together. Individual persons may not be committed even to their own individual goods. If they commit themselves to goods for the group, it may only be on a self-interested basis. But suppose we find statistically significant numbers of people committed to further levels of good for groups (or for persons in groups). The commitments can as a matter of observed fact be induced with no resort to fear or only a minimal amount. The obligations come along with commitments to the rules that promote the various levels of good. As a matter of historical inheritance, an ethics reasonably impressive and far-reaching in content and structure obtains. It is perverse to attempt to stand outside this inheritance entirely and ask for a justification that is not arbitrary or question-begging. (Kant, preoccupied with this dilemma, attempted to stand outside, but no sense can be made of his results unless we bring into moral legislation references to the consequences of the legislation for human good.)

Sabine anticipated Schneewind in holding that natural law theory collapsed in the eighteenth century, but for Sabine the collapse comes not from inability to cope with God's will and theodicy. According to Sabine, natural law theory became secularized in the seventeenth century, beginning with Grotius,[38] and the collapse came about because the a priori rationalism that Sabine ascribes to natural law theory gave way to a thoroughly empirical outlook, as in Hume, who Sabine believes wholly undermined natural law and natural rights. Sabine disregards the long tradition of appeal to empirical evidence in natural law theory, and disregards, too, Hume's specifically speaking of the rules of justice as natural laws. Sabine treats Rousseau as too muddled to be taken seriously, however influential he may have been, and argues that the Common Good in Rousseau is too individualistic in conception to be classed with the Common Good as traditionally conceived. Sabine does not take into account Rousseau's many natural law arguments, sometimes announced as such, sometimes not. Furthermore, Sabine had the misfortune of writing about Rousseau's Common Good without having the theory of public goods in hand, and so he does not appreciate the force of what I shall show to be, on the basis of its public goods ingredients, the transindividualistic nature of the Common Good in Rousseau.

It is nothing to wonder at that the empirical basis of natural law theory as presented by St Thomas, and even more so as presented by his more rationalistic successors, should have been less than clear even to so percipient a historian of ideas as Sabine. St Thomas and the others meant to stand by a strong claim for there being universal moral principles. One apparently inviting way of making sure of universal moral principles is to concentrate on the traditional attribution of rationality to human beings, and to try to extract the principles a priori from what it means to be rational. Then the principles may appear to have a status something like the principles of logic. Even going this way, however, does not shake the theory loose from an empirical grounding. For if human beings were not, as a matter of empirical fact, rational (or consistently rational to the degree required to appreciate the bearing on them of the principles), the relevance to them of the principles would be questionable. (I shall elaborate in the chapter to follow on this and other aspects of the empirical perspective to be attributed to St Thomas.)

For St Thomas, even universal moral principles are principles only imperfectly known to us, since for one thing we do not know all the exceptions that circumstances will call for. With this uncertainty there comes provision for flexible adaptation to changing circumstances, which may distinguish St Thomas's teaching from what present-day followers like Finnis and Grisez have made of that teaching by, as it were, filling in some of the gaps that St Thomas left.[39] We come closer to identifying the universal moral principles step by step, as our knowledge (and perhaps our subtlety in formulation) increases.

It may seem anomalous that significant discoveries about natural law may come up very late in the history of people's acquaintance with it – doubly anomalous, if we consider that the most important rules should lie well within the grasp of non-specialists, and non-specialists have had centuries, indeed millennia, to think about the rules and lead lives in accordance with them. Yet the claims of women to equal status with men as citizens and workers and otherwise, which now would be granted by almost anyone adhering to a modern natural law theory, offer an example of how a matter of the highest importance might be a late discovery. How could this have happened? In other cases, the discovery might have to do with whether a given rule should be dropped from the corpus or added or reformulated. In this case, the discovery concerns rather which people shall benefit from the application of the rules. But how could it have been so long ignored that women should benefit as much (and in the same ways) as men? The explanation may lie mainly in the persistence of certain conventions, which in turn were founded on a misapprehension of fact. People used to believe that women could not do as well as men as citizens or workers (that is, as workers in occupations reserved for men). How did things change? Some women refused to believe the supposed facts, and agitated for change. They were taking an initiative on premises that most of their contemporaries, including most of the contemporaries adhering to natural law, would have rejected. They won some victories. Then women demonstrated by actual performance that they could do as well as men. Finally (but within the time of only a few generations), this impressive new evidence was generally accepted, so that hardly anyone can now be found who would argue, in the face of it, that women cannot make proficient lawyers and physicians, not to speak of airline pilots.

Natural law theory is in this perspective open to new discoveries, whether they are inspired by new circumstances or not, a perspective that is perfectly consistent with some rules remaining established all along as a matter of historical fact ('Do not do wanton injury to other people'; 'Offer peace to people who offer peace to you') and calling for inclusion in any axiomatic system offered for natural law theory, such as Hobbes's. The representation of natural law theory must always be tentative, though some points will be much less tentative than others; it is a representation of what we have so far come to know as approximations to the universal principles. Nor does the tentativeness stand in the way of systematic deduction, since deductions will go through from one proposition or rule qualified with a 'ceteris paribus' clause (covering allowable exceptions to the rule, both exceptions already known and exceptions yet to be discovered) to another proposition or rule qualified in the same way. All the propositions or rules in the system may be formulated with the qualification: Instead of saying, 'Do not do wanton injury to other people,' we say, 'Do not do injury to other people ceteris paribus.'

Is there a difficulty about the step-by-step process taking the wrong path, leading us ever farther away from the correct principles? This seems gratuitous scepticism. The process of beginning with what will be admitted to be imperatively efficient rules can cite the fact that they hold for most circumstances, and then be careful to add only convincing exceptions that preserve the aim of the underlying rule. The watchman at the city gate preserves the aim of increasing the security of the city's defences when he makes an exception to the rule that the gate must be closed at sunset and admits a late-returning party of soldiers, rather than leaving them to be cut to pieces by the pursuing enemy.[40]

The way is open to claim, with my project in this book, that the changes brought in by modernization have left the core of natural law unchanged. But, as my project means to bring out, they have done more: They have strengthened the arguments for the position and where (as in the case of Hobbes's unrelenting reliance on egoistic agents) they have not exactly done this, they have at least clarified the meaning of the position. Hobbes shows that the core or at least some of its basic components, though not the spirit in which people have traditionally been expected to adhere to it or the full sense of the Common Good even at the minimum that adherence to it implies, can be arrived at by fully developing the traditional theme of self-preservation. Moreover, Hobbes supplies, what St Thomas only hinted at, a fully explicit axiomatic system for the core. Locke transposes social contract to a non-egoistic perspective (resuming the tradition) and relaxes the presuppositions about conflict that Hobbes insists on. Hume develops the secularized, a posteriori argument for natural laws, though he takes a narrow view of the core, and Hume (like Locke) makes private property in land basic in a way that jeopardizes the universality of the core taken so narrowly. Rousseau, even if on occasion he disavows support for natural law theory, makes a contribution as important as any of the others, perhaps more so, by approaching the Common Good as an object to be defined by what in the twentieth century has become known as the theory of public goods, and by insisting on the generality of the legislation undertaken by the General Will in pursuit of the Common Good.

Following this chapter, in which the way has been opened to arguing that a core of medieval natural law theory persists in modern political thought, the succeeding chapters lay out the argument. I begin, as this chapter already intimates, with St Thomas because the primary issue that I treat is whether medieval natural law theory, as expounded classically by St Thomas, survives in modern political thought, specifically, in the canonical authors that I take up. First, I show that Locke is allied with St Thomas in treating natural law as having secular content and an empirical foundation. Then, I show that Rousseau is allied with St Thomas in having an empirical and (in Rousseau's case, at least) a precise conception of the Common Good. In the chapter following, Hobbes's systematized catalogue of the natural laws takes on consistent additions from the more expansive doctrine of St Thomas. Thus, Hobbes, too, figures as an ally of St Thomas. So does Hume, in a chapter devoted to showing that he is (contrary to prevailing impressions) a moral realist and (what prevailing opinion hardly thinks of) a natural law theorist as well, and allied with St Thomas. In the chapter following, I show that Hume's doctrine of private property and Locke's are complementary; and that though they do not establish the rules of private property as universal ones, universal rules can be found on the same path that they take, at greater depth. I then turn, in a chapter on David Copp's society-centred theory of ethics, from the primary issue of whether medieval natural law theory survives in the canonical authors of modern political thought to the secondary issue of whether it has a footing among present-day ethical theories. By showing that Copp's theory is an unwitting instance of the core medieval natural law theory set forth earlier in the book, I show that it does have such a footing even where it is not anticipated to have one. In the two final chapters, I consider how the natural laws are to be inculcated by moral education, and how enduring the demands are that they make on positive law. Two appendices by other hands – the hands of two of my students, now junior colleagues – show how natural law theory figures respectively in the thought of the great Arab political theorist Ibn Khaldun and in classical Chinese philosophy.

Chapter Two

Locke's Natural Law and St Thomas's: Secular in Content, Empirical in Foundation

It is easier to establish the presence of a natural law theory like St Thomas's in Locke's case than in the case of the other canonical authors who figure in the present work. The present chapter will take advantage of this fact, first, to establish a firm footing for medieval natural law theory in the seventeenth century – modern times – as exemplified by my canonical authors. But, second, in the course of expounding Locke's position and demonstrating a basic convergence with St Thomas's, I shall be showing how a secular natural law theory can be detached from the theistic auspices under which both set forth their teachings. Third, I shall be showing, with more extensive treatment of St Thomas on this point, because he has a richer variety of things to say, how he as well as Locke may be taken to give natural law theory an empirical foundation.

I shall make the point about detaching a secular natural law theory in Locke's case by focusing on what Locke gives, in passing, toward the end of his *Essays/Questions on the Law of Nature*, as 'an a posteriori argument' for natural law;[1] and though my exposition of Locke will be otherwise very brief and broad, this focus will distinguish my exposition from other commentators'. A. John Simmons, for example, in *The Lockean Theory of Rights*,[2] gives, besides his detailed critical account of Locke's treatment of rights, a critical account of Locke's basic position in moral theory, more detailed than anything I attempt, or for my purposes need to do. Simmons does not, however, give any attention to the a posteriori argument, or to how this argument can be used, as I shall use it, to decompose Locke's theistic argument for natural law, and identify a detachable secular component that the argument contains. Simmons recognizes (citing, as I have done, Alan Ryan in opposition)[3] that 'secular natural law theory is a perfectly intelligible enterprise'(103), but he does not consider whether it is an enterprise that is a detachable part of Locke's moral theory.[4] I shall detach it; and I shall do the same thing for St Thomas's teaching, too. I shall, also, as a feature of my exposition, defend the claim that Locke remains committed to natural law theory, in spite of late developments in his thought that have seemed to some scholars inconsistent with that commitment.

In the *Essays/Questions*, Locke not only frankly presents natural law in a theistic perspective like St Thomas's; whether through direct reading or through his reading of the works of 'the judicious Hooker,'[5] Locke seems in many places to be echoing St Thomas's thoughts. For example, in a passage at the very end of the affirmative answer that Locke gives to the Fifth of his Questions, 'Can Reason arrive at a knowledge of the law of nature through sense experience?' Locke says that man is 'impelled to form and preserve a union of his life with other men, not only by the needs and necessities of life,' but also because 'he is driven by a certain natural propensity to enter society and is fitted to preserve it by the gift of speech and the commerce of language.'[6] The transition from needs to sociality and language (the basis for reasoning) harmonizes perfectly with the movement of St Thomas's thought in the paramount passage, *ST*, 1a2ae, Q.94, 2, in which St Thomas lays out the three-part division of natural law as applying, first, in respect to what human beings have in common with all other substances, second, in respect to what they have in common with all other animals, and third, in respect to the rationality that makes them unique among animals. I shall begin with what Locke says and show that in substance it is the same thing as St Thomas's theory, at least with respect to the core of the latter.

Locke and St Thomas: A Core of Natural Law Theory Detachable for Secular Rendition

Toward the end of his *Essays/Questions on the Law of Nature*, Locke offers in passing an approach to identifying the content of natural law, what he calls an a posteriori argument, as an alternative to his official, full-dress argument presented earlier. That earlier argument explicitly begins by arguing to the proposition that God exists, goes on to the proposition that He regulates us according to His purposes and our nature, and hence that He commands us to obey certain laws in order to realize the good appropriate to our species. The a posteriori argu-

ment runs 'from the disadvantages which would follow were it supposed that this obligation would not be in force at some place or other.
For [then] there would exist no religion, no society among men, no
faith, and countless disadvantages of this kind that it is enough to have
touched on them only lightly.'[7]

The a posteriori argument need not mention God or religion; and
'faith' may be taken to refer to trust among men (see below). The heart
of the argument lies in the reference to 'countless disadvantages' and
'no society among men.' Moreover, religion and faith come into the
argument as stated, not accompanied by any invocation of God as
the author of natural law, but simply as among the things that would
be absent were the natural law not to be observed.

The omission to argue here from God's authority and purpose no
doubt does not imply any slackening in Locke's attachment to these
things, but it does show how what the natural laws amount to in content can be identified without (expressly) considering that God created
human beings and may be supposed to have certain purposes with
them. In the a posteriori argument, we are to consider only what consequences in social disruption would follow if certain laws were not by
and large conformed to. Precisely because the alternative to heeding
them would be everywhere disruption, these are the natural laws, corresponding to respect for the constitution of a constitutional government and the keeping of covenants[8] and to the virtues besides 'faith in
keeping promises' of 'obedience towards ... superiors ... truthfulness,
clemency, liberality, purity of morals, and the other virtues.'[9] (Locke
mentions also 'reverence and love for the divinity,' but he is not here
arguing to the other virtues from God's existence and will.) Put
another way, as Hume will put it, thinking of the basic rules regarding
private property as the rules of justice, the natural laws are the laws
indispensable to having a thriving society. (We might think, a richer set
of laws if we set a higher standard for thriving; in principle, we must
allow for the possibility of there being multiple sets at every level of
richness.)

If we go back to the earlier, official argument, we find that the presence of God in the argument will only take us so far, that is to say, only
to the point at which it is held that God wants our good and commands us to act only in ways consistent with attaining it. Locke's presentation somewhat obscures this limit. What I have been calling the
earlier official argument is laid out under the Fifth Question. Having
experienced the variety of things in the world, and the order that they

display, the mind moves to asking what could be the origin of these things, and thereby comes upon a proof of God's existence. It then recognizes that in mind and body human beings are creatures of God, and that God must have had some purpose in giving them their remarkable powers along with a natural propensity to belong to and preserve society. Accordingly, man 'perceives that he is impelled to form and preserve a union of his life with other men.'[10] The natural laws will follow as rules that people must be ready to observe on entering society and taking part in it once having entered.

The official argument can also be abstracted from the answer to the First Question, though Locke is not committed to all that he says there. Offering it as an answer to a question in a scholastic disputation, he is at liberty to set forth some propositions that will later succumb to dialectical objections, and this is specially true of the arguments from universal consent and tradition, both of which, at least as naively understood, are refuted under later Questions. However, for what it is worth, one may note that after postulating the existence of God, Locke expounds five subarguments each giving an affirmative answer to the question whether God has given laws for human beings to obey. They are: First, reason leads us to recognize laws holding for all peoples (an argument taken from Aristotle); second, disputes over the content of these laws presuppose their existence; third, human beings cannot be supposed to be an exception to the regulation by God of everything else in the world; fourth, there could be no expectation that constitutional government would be respected or covenants kept without a foundation in natural laws; fifth, virtue and vice would lose their meaning if there were not natural laws transcending the interests, pleasures, or whims of human beings. I have the third and fourth of these arguments especially in mind in what I would abstract as 'the official argument.' Given that God commands us to act in accordance with natural laws and that it is by doing so that we attain our good, we must identify our good, and in particular the good that we are to pursue together. Will this not be our thriving together in society and our happiness so far as it is compatible with thriving together?[11] Simmons cites from the Eleventh and final *Essay/Question* the passage in which Locke says, 'By the foundation of natural law we understand that which supports and upon which are erected, as upon a foundation, all the other precepts of this law, even the less obvious, and that from which [these precepts] can be deduced in some manner. As a consequence, these derive their entire force and their binding power from this foundation because they are in agreement with this primary and, as it were, fundamental law, which is the rule and measure of all the other laws which depend on it.'[12]

Simmons identifies this foundation with the principle that 'mankind as a whole is to be preserved,' and this identification is borne out by some of the citations that he makes of the *Second Treatise*.[13] Perhaps, not quite borne out, since Locke does not use the phrase 'mankind as a whole,' instead referring to 'all mankind' (par. 7), 'Man' (par. 16), 'the rest of mankind' (par. 171), or 'all mankind in general,' identified with 'Society' in the state of nature (also par. 171). It is at least not entirely clear that the prevailing idea is collective (take human beings the world over en masse), rather than distributive (take the rest of mankind one by one, as they come within the scope of any contemplated action). Locke's generation was not in the position that present generations have put themselves into of being able to literally jeopardize the preservation of 'mankind as a whole.'

In any case, not all of Simmons's citations bear out his preferred language. Simmons cites par. 134, but there Locke gives 'the first and fundamental natural law' as 'the preservation of the Society, and (as far as will consist with the public good) of every person in it.'[14] We evidently have a choice here. Simmons himself notes,[15] citing the *Essay on Human Understanding*, that Locke holds that 'morality' necessarily promotes 'public happiness' and 'the preservation of society.' This, moreover, not the reference to 'the preservation of mankind' is the language that prevails in the *Essays/Questions*. So I shall use this language, that is to say, the language of par. 134 of the *Second Treatise*, as just cited, for the fundamental natural law, ready to argue that the preservation of the rest of mankind is reached by promoting the joint thriving of neighbours, together with that of further members of a given society (the civil society at issue), together again of people outside it who have not adopted a hostile posture.

Locke does not seriously try to make good the gesture at having a deductive system of natural laws, in which the other precepts are derived from the fundamental natural law, any more than he seriously follows up the similar stand, which he takes in the *Essay on Human Understanding*, about ethics being a deductive science. But Locke does tell us something about how to expand the account beyond the first and fundamental law. The natural laws are the laws that human beings must obey in order to thrive together in society. Locke draws no help from the reference to God at this point.[16] We have to consider the nature of human beings and the circumstances in which they (typically, at least) find themselves. Just as much as with the a posteriori argument, the issue is an empirical one. Given that nature and given those circumstances, as we observe them, what laws must human beings obey in order to thrive together? Among our authors, strangely, this question becomes fully explicit only with Hume,[17] but it is clearly identifiable in them all. Moreover, deduction alone will not take us all the way to spelling out the corpus of natural laws, once we have discovered what in an elementary way the nature and circumstances amount to. We cannot know without experience (or experiment), for example, just what people will come into conflict about, or what rules will be most effective in forestalling such conflicts. Just what exceptions (if any are to be allowed) would come along with an effective and indispensable law against homicide?

So far as discovering the content of the natural laws goes, God turns out, then, to be a spare wheel in Locke's account, except for the specific prescription of 'reverence and love for the divinity,' and even this, as an ingredient of content, one law among others, may be thought to demand justification on the basis of its contribution to thriving personal and social. It is true that this justification may proceed (as it certainly would in Locke's case and in St Thomas's, too) by way of referring to the difference heeding this prescription makes to the attitude with which members of the community regard the natural laws; the members will obey them all in the spirit of showing reverence and love for their author. This, however, is not a point about content; nor is the reference to God as the authority that gives the laws their force.

The reference to God supplies a clear-cut answer to the question of authority, and simultaneously an ultimate answer to the question of enforcement. At least the reference to God may do this for those who believe in Him, unhelpful as it may be to those who do not. One alternative approach to authority might be to think of the laws as not having and not needing any more authority (or more enforcement) than custom does. But this really is the same thing as to think of the laws as something that people impose upon themselves, with some sort, maybe a very informal, even implicit sort, of coordination without any necessary resort to deliberation, much less to the operation of a social decision procedure. If this does not seem enough authority, the operative alternative seems to be that the authority comes from a society imposing the laws upon itself with a decision procedure. That is not the same thing as having individual people impose the laws upon themselves, even with some sort of coordination; but it may not seem different enough to give the laws solid authority. Societies, like persons and collections of persons, can arrange to do quite bizarre things, and their decisions may be quite arbitrary.

The lesson to draw from this, however, is that the question of authority should not be separated from the question of content (which we shall find David Copp doing, very incongruously, and I expect quite inadvertently, at the last stage of an appeal to social choice in what is in effect a current version of natural law theory).[18] Arrived at by considering the empirical conditions of thriving, the content of the natural laws is not arbitrary. We need to have an authority that heeds this content in prescribing the laws. Some people – the voluntarists – have argued that in principle God might not do so; to think that He could not prescribe otherwise would be inconsistent with ascribing Him unlimited power. So the reference to God does not necessarily give a more satisfactory answer to the question of authority, even for believers. If it gave a satisfactory answer for Locke, it is because he is ready to make something of the – intellectualist – assumption that God is mindful of what is good for human beings, given their nature and circumstances, and prescribes laws accordingly.[19] But if a society or its members were similarly heedful, the possibility that its choices might be bizarre or arbitrary would not be troublesome. So Locke's theory, though it is offered in a theistic perspective, could possibly be divested of theism without disintegrating.

This can be said even of St Thomas's theory, and some commentators in effect do say it.[20] True, this may seem at best to be a point about content, and even as a point about content it must be qualified in St Thomas's case, as in Locke's, by recognizing that St Thomas treats 'Thou shalt love the Lord thy God' as one of the natural laws; indeed St Thomas makes it a first general, self-evident principle of natural law (*ST*, 1a2ae, Q.100, 3). However, as an ingredient of content, this can be treated as instrumental to thriving, or simply set aside for secular purposes, that is, for purposes of convincing non-theists. Again, it is true, the principle would make for St Thomas and other believers a difference important to them in the spirit in which they obey the natural laws. Furthermore, the natural laws have their place for St Thomas in the eternal God-given scheme of things (the eternal law), consisting as they do of matters that human beings come to know by participating through their own reason in that scheme: It is ordained by God that there be laws suited to human beings and that human beings, reasoning about their nature and circumstances, come to recognize the content of these laws, through recognizing their advantages (emphasized in the a posteriori argument). On the other hand, neither the Bible nor post-Biblical revelation is required in St Thomas's view for that much recognition. Not even natural theology is required. People can reason their way to the content (with the exception noted) and to the advantages of the natural laws without reference to there being a god, even the god of natural theology.[21] Recognizing the advantages of obeying those laws, will people not find, if they must, some way of imposing the laws upon themselves?

The detachable part of Locke's official argument that leaves the theological preface behind can be found in St Thomas, too, though in the texts from which I am working it is not laid out in a straightforward way. Given human nature and circumstances, people will thrive together only if they heed the natural laws. This is an empirical argument because what human nature and circumstances amount to has to be discovered by observation (even if, as it may be in some cases, the observation is very direct and familiar), and so does what laws promote thriving. Philosophy and science (both natural and social) cooperate in establishing that human beings cannot thrive without having full provisions for their need for food, including, for example, vitamins.

The a posteriori argument is essentially the same as the official argument, run backwards. Given human nature and circumstances, if people are not heeding the natural laws, they are not thriving. The form of the official argument is H&C $\rightarrow$ (T $\rightarrow$ L); of the a posteriori argument, H&C $\rightarrow$ (~L $\rightarrow$ ~T). T $\rightarrow$ L and ~L $\rightarrow$ ~T may be substituted for each other as logically equivalent formulas.

Considered informally, at least, the a posteriori formulation gives a more incisive impression, because it does not (as the official argument does) seem to demand a full account of thriving; it suffices to bring the argument home to be able to specify some aspects of thriving that will fail if people do not heed the laws. Locke holds that they will fall into disorder; and disorder frequently comes up for attention in St Thomas's thinking. St Thomas advises people to defy unjust laws that do not directly repress the practice of true religion only if they can do so without worse consequences in disorder and scandal than the laws create themselves. He declares also that if they are not trained to heed the laws people will, in spite of their 'natural aptitude for virtue,' be too much given to 'undue pleasures,' and a number of them will resist training in virtue so much as to require being brought to order through 'force and fear.'[22]

A Core Theory Empirical in Foundation

On the whole, what can be cited in the texts of St Thomas as empirical grounds for the natural laws falls more easily into the official argument than into the a posteriori one. There are three main lines of thought on which the empirical grounds can be seen to be operating: (1) observations about one or another aspect of human nature, which can be pieced together to establish an empirical perspective; (2) the attention given to the need to adapt the laws to different circumstances, which implies that circumstances must be taken into account both before and after any specific adaptation; and (3) reasoning from the essence of the human species. The third line of thought brings to bear St Thomas's fundamental views in epistemology, but it is by itself perhaps less persuasive to modern readers than the other two are, just because it brings in technical notions that are not now current. I shall invoke it in last place to corroborate the imputation of the other two lines of thought, and show that they fall in with his official epistemology.

According to *ST*, 1a2ae, Q.90, 2, 'Nothing stands firm with regard to the practical reason unless it be directed to the last end which is the Common Good,' and the laws that are established when so directed 'are adapted to produce happiness and its parts for the body politic.' But observation and experiment are required to discover the adaptation. 'Man is helped by industry in his necessities, for instance, in food and clothing. Certain beginnings of [providing for] these he has from nature, viz., his reason and his hands, but he has not the full complement, as other animals have, to whom nature has given sufficiency of clothing and food' (*ST*, 1a2ae, Q.95, 1). Thus, in *ST*, 1a2ae, Q.91, 3, St Thomas quotes Cicero, in agreement with him: 'Justice has its source in nature; thence certain things come into custom by reason of their utility.' Furthermore, 'Many things are done virtuously to which nature does not incline at first, but which, through the inquiry of reason, have been found by men to be conducive to well-living' and therefore are prescribed by natural law (*ST*, 1a2ae, Q.94, 3). Among these social inventions we may rank private property, the rules governing which constitute 'an addition to natural law contrived by reason,' on the observable grounds that these rules supply incentive for self-support, promote an orderly use of resources by determining just what everyone is to take care of, and reduce the number of quarrels, for 'it is to be observed that quarrels arise more frequently where there is no division of the things possessed' (*ST*, 2a2ae, Q.66, 2). This point may be contested; but whether it is true or false will turn on further observation; and all these passages, which are just a sampling, show St Thomas working, and meaning to work, with empirical evidence.

In a number of other remarkable passages, St Thomas gives sensitive attention to the need to adapt laws to changing circumstances. Though the basic principles of natural law are unchangeable, he says, 'Many things, for the benefit of human life, have been added [to the natural laws] over and above the [received] natural law both by the divine law and by human laws' (*ST*, 1a2ae, Q.94, 5). Where does the need to make these additions come from? Evidently from the fact that, though the initial lawgivers endeavoured 'to discover something useful for the human community,' they could not take everything into account, in particular changes in the 'conditions of life,' with differences resulting in what is beneficial (*ST*, 1a2ae, Q.97, 1). So the laws that they made call for alteration to adapt to the new conditions. St Thomas cautions that they 'should never be changed unless, in some way or other, the common weal be compensated according to the extent of the harm done' by the unsettling effect of making the change (*ST*, 1a2ae, Q.97, 2). Clearly, he is moving back and forth here between the laws and the circumstances, including (if we give 'the condition of man' a reading that it easily invites) changes in people's outlook and character; the adaptation of the laws is being thought of as an empirical process of adjustment.

It is true that in many of these passages, St Thomas is concerned with changes in human laws rather than with the natural laws themselves, considered apart from human laws. That is not the case in all the passages, however – see, again, Q.94, 3 and 5, where changes (by addition) to the natural laws are explicitly at issue. There changes in the natural laws are said to be brought in by changes in the human laws. Furthermore, human laws, if they are genuine laws, must accord with the natural laws. They must be deducible from the natural laws (and hence themselves belong to the corpus), or they must be constructions that harmonize with the natural laws and decide certain questions on which the natural laws do not of themselves prescribe one way or another. (The distinction, as I noted in the Introduction, will disappear in circumstances where it makes sense to press for optimal solutions of these questions.) Accept it that human laws must be adjusted to accord with observations of 'the condition of man'; so will some natural laws, as a consequence. Some natural laws will not change; but is this not because they accord with the unchanging features of human nature and with all circumstances in which human beings ever find themselves? And is it not the most plausible assumption about what could establish this accordance that it is by observation, or better, by confirming to a reasonable degree a hypothesis suggested by observation and standing or falling with observation that the accordance is established?

There is another sort of adaptation to observed circumstances that St Thomas repeatedly considers, which does not involve changes in the laws, rather, at most changes in the formulations of them. It is continually discovered, one may presume by observation, since the challenges come up to begin with as unanticipated experiences, that laws properly framed 'to suit the majority of instances ... were not framed according to what might possibly happen in an individual case' (*ST*, 1a2ae Q. 96, 1, quoting 'the Jurist'). 'It often happens' that a measure which is conducive to the common welfare in the majority of cases 'in some cases is highly harmful' (*ST*, 1a2ae Q.96, 6). So rulers should make exceptions in these cases; or people, if they have no chance to refer back to the rulers for permission, must make exceptions on their own, as a sensible watchman will do at the time for closing the city gate.

Given some assumptions (often ignored) about the circumstances that human beings will find themselves in, the natural laws can be presented as arrived at by reasoning about the nature or essence of human beings. This, too, is an empirical approach.[23] It is empirical even if we ascribe to St Thomas (and to Aristotle) the all-at-once-view that when in one moment of sudden illumination the knowing agent seizes the essence from sense-experiences,[24] all the features that belong to the essence, in this case of human beings, crystallize in the agent's mind and are available for reflection ever afterwards. For even in this case, it is only by observation that one can establish that human beings have an essence of just this sort (with the feature of needing food, for example). Another, more plausible view, would hold that, even when one recognizes that one is in the presence of a natural kind, and has hit upon a defining feature that will not be relinquished, other features will be discovered feature by feature, though from time to time some features may be ascribed mistakenly, and set aside later. That is a view even more empirical in spirit, and it does no damage to St Thomas's general position about the dependence of the natural laws on empirical evidence.

There are other reasons, besides the attractions of the high a priori route to moral principles, why the universal principles that St Thomas and the others meant to stand by might not seem to have an empirical grounding. First, it is hard to imagine a human being thriving who did not live in a society in which the rules are heeded; and though the rules suited to different societies vary, at a suitable level of generality they will turn out, as I shall show, to be everywhere the same. A society of saints is imaginable in principle, and may even be regarded as practical, if it were composed of the well-disposed people that can be observed even outside of it. But this would be, not a society that lived at odds with the rules, but one in which the rules were heeded without any need of sanctions or perhaps even any need of corrections. Second, St Thomas does follow Aristotle in holding that the essence of human beings, that is to say, the nature of human nature, is seized by an intuition (though it is an intuition extracting the universal from sense-experience). This is not enough to ground the rules, unless we suppose that in the essence is seized also an idea of what circumstances human beings are designed for (or have evolved to cope with), namely, not only social life, but social cooperation as an indispensable means of self-protection and of coping with scarcity. But it does invite the a priori route through rationality, if this feature of the essence is stressed. Third, if natural law theory is right, the rules that it upholds should be in some cases, if not in all, familiar. They may seem (and have seemed to some philosophers) self-evident; and a systematic representation of them by someone committed to them may be constructed by a priori reasoning from one or more of the self-evident principles taken as axiomatic.

None of these points really derogate from the empirical grounding of the universal principles, or, put another way, from their being universal only in depending on facts themselves observed to be universal. The essence of human beings might have been quite different: For example, they might not by nature have been able to remain in the company of any other human being more than five minutes without putting themselves into mortal danger from some violent allergic (anaphylactic) reaction. Or, for psychological reasons, human beings could not help but be at cross-purposes when they tried to cooperate with one another. In either case the rules calling for social cooperation would have at the very least to be drastically modified. Perhaps social life could not even get started. So it is possible to imagine a society, not one of human beings as we know them, but of beings in physical and mental powers very much like human beings, in which the moral rules, if any, would be very different from those familiar to us and upheld by natural law theory.

It is true that St Thomas does not contemplate the possibility that the case for the universal principles will be refuted by empirical evidence. Moreover, he does not supply an explicit empirical argument connecting the natural laws with the achievement of thriving societies. This omission goes hand in hand with his omission to define the Common Good. St Thomas was thinking that knowledge of the natural laws, like knowledge of the Common Good, is something that every human being can easily come by, or at least could come by if the basic disposition to attain knowledge had not been twisted; because of original sin, people turn away from the knowledge in practice. However, St Thomas might have considered, it comes back in obvious truths once people consider ethics theoretically. This way of thinking no doubt encourages people to regard recourse to an empirical argument – to what Locke, not quite ready to recognize it as indispensable, calls the a posteriori argument for natural law – as hardly worth bothering to set forth even if it is assumed. Believers may think, why go all the way round about through an empirical argument to discover natural laws, when the clouds can be dispersed by active faith, and by consulting the Bible and other believers?

I have been treating the natural laws in St Thomas's conception as rules, and I think of rules as systems of imperatives, with some imperatives manifest from time to time and some of them continually latent.[25] Finnis says that, as practical principles, the rules of natural law are not imperative, but directive, though he does not do much to explain the general difference that he has in mind.[26] Grisez is more helpful: He says, 'For Aquinas ... natural law includes counsels as well as precepts.' The latter refer 'to the good which must be done'; the former, 'to the nonobligatory good it would be well to do.'[27] I do not think my view differs substantially from these, if we take into account that rules for me are not by definition accompanied by sanctions and that their imperative force can be softened to almost any degree by specifying broad ranges of exceptions. Thus, the rule to give alms to the poor would allow (a conditional component) for not doing this when one does not have the means or when the case presented is not so needy as others or it is going to be dealt with by a public agency; and it would not be backed by sanctions, anyway, but simply by corrections, reminders by other people that a given occasion is an appropriate one not excluded by any reasonable exception. This seems enough allowance for counsels.

Locke no doubt differs from St Thomas about how empirical knowledge is to be gathered; and he differs from him, in particular, in not regarding empirical science as a matter of deduction from real essences seized in sense-experience. If the ingredients of the essences are seized step by step, even if this is a matter of filling in the details of the essence that a certain kind of being (for example, human beings) exhibits, then the gathering of knowledge from observation will be broadly what common sense would expect it to be without postulating essences. Various things will turn out to fall into certain natural kinds of things, but in each case the natural kind with the persistent differences that it implies will be something that is discovered by repeated observations. Even if all the details of an essence are seized in one moment of sudden illumination, the core of natural law theory – with its reliance on the principle of empirically founded indispensability to thriving – will be the same for both Locke and St Thomas, in spite of their difference over the details of epistemology.

Neither Locke nor St Thomas believes that the descriptions 'inscribed in the heart' or 'discovered by the natural light of reason' imply that knowledge of natural law is innate, in the sense that it is not derived from sense-experience. Some commentators have thought that Locke's famous stand against innate knowledge in his *Essay the Human Understanding* was something that he simply ignored in his references to the knowledge of natural law in the *Treatises on Government*.[28] On the face of it, given that all these works went to the press at about the same time, that seems implausible. It is even more implausible if one takes into account the fact that the source of the critique of innate knowledge lies in the *Essays/Questions on the Law of Nature*, and that Locke had not forgotten or repudiated that work. Locke refused to publish it, in spite of being urged to do so by at least one friend acquainted with it,[29] at the same time as *Human Understanding* and the *Treatises on Government*. However, he had taken the trouble, a few years earlier, when those works were under way or almost under way, to have a fair copy made of the *Essays/Questions*, and he took pains to preserve the copy among his manuscripts.[30]

St Thomas distinguishes between general and indemonstrable principles of natural law and 'certain particular determinations of the laws' that are deduced from them (*ST*, 1a2ae, Q.91, 3), presumably by combining the general principles with other premisses derived from the observation of variable features of human character and circumstances. He also distinguishes 'primary principles,' which he says are 'altogether unchangeable' (*ST*, 1a2ae, Q.94, 5, 6), and which can be identified with the 'general principles or precepts' just cited, by contrast with 'secondary principles' (*ST*, 1a2ae, Q.94, 6). Furthermore, the general principles are said to be 'self-evident' (*ST*, 1a2ae, Q.94, 2). Many readers have made a good deal of these things, but I think they do no more than sketch the beginnings of a program of reducing natural laws to a deductive system, a program that St Thomas did not carry out, and might not have found congenial to pursue anyway.

St Thomas offers no definitive list of primary principles, self-evident or otherwise, though he says there are several of them (*ST*, 1a2ae, Q.94, 2). They include 'Thou shalt love thy neighbour' (*ST*, 1a2ae, Q.100, 3), and somewhat less straightforwardly, 'No man should work for the destruction of the commonwealth or betray the political community to its enemies' (*ST*, 1a2ae, Q.100, 8).[31]

Suppose that 'self-evident' is taken, broadly, to mean that the proposition at issue, if it is contingent and empirical, requires of an ordinarily competent adult observer no further observational research for it to be known to be true; and, whether or not it is contingent and empirical, no complex chain of reasoning to establish. (Thus, 'self-evident' covers some empirical propositions and some a priori ones as well; but there are other propositions, empirical on the one hand and maybe a priori on the other, that are not self-evident.) The second of the primary principles just cited, the one about not working for the destruction of the commonwealth, is closer to being self-evident in the sense supposed than the first; and to make it out to be self-evident one does not need to resort to the additional dimension of St Thomas's conception of self-evident, which would make deductions from the essences of natural things self-evident for anyone who grasped the essences.[32] The clause in the second primary principle, about not working for the destruction of the community, can be regarded as following immediately from accepting the basic argument connecting rules with thriving personal and social. The other clause follows immediately thereafter as a special case of the first, taken as a more general rule. Both clauses have a contingent and empirical foundation; but neither requires further observational research and both are arrived at by the simplest reasoning.

'Love thy neighbour' is another matter. Attractive as it is as a moral precept, it does not come in so many words clearly enough defined to be established without further specification; and the parable about the Good Samaritan does not give specification enough to make it self-

evident. Even if the rule is taken minimally to mean simply that everyone should keep the peace with everyone else and offer help on occasion, reasoning may be required to connect it with empirical evidence
about the importance to thriving of keeping the peace and being ready
to help. Moreover, the occasions on which help should be offered
under an 'imperfect' obligation to do so still need specification, calling
upon further empirical evidence. One may also wonder, if I may be
permitted an exegetical comment, whether to take it as self-evident
misses the point of the injunction to love thy neighbour, by failing to
see that Jesus originally meant it to be extraordinary and challenging.

One first principle that St Thomas emphasizes, 'Good is to be done
and pursued, and evil avoided' (*ST*, 1a2ae, Q.94, 2), may be self-
evident given the meaning of 'good' and 'evil,' but it is of little use
as a source of other principles, though St Thomas seems ready to treat
it as useful. In the main, one cannot know (as I am sure St Thomas
would have been the first to agree) what rules fall under it and
what do not until one has defined the good and evil at issue. That is to
be done by considering 'all those things to which man has a natural
inclination' and are 'naturally apprehended by reason as being good
and objects of pursuit' (Q.94, 2 again). One example would be the natural inclination to consume food when hungry. We might take it to be
self-evident, given our familiarity with human nature, that human
beings need food and have a natural inclination to provide themselves
with it.

From this and other inclinations we can construct a fertile set of
unchangeable general first principles; indeed, from the need for food
and the corresponding inclination alone we can go a long way toward
deducing a robust set of secondary rules or principles. This would be
from beginning to end thoroughly empirical, and in the spirit of
St Thomas's thinking, but it is notable that St Thomas does not try to
do anything of the sort, perhaps because he felt that to do so would be
to go too far in labouring the obvious.

Nevertheless, he does assert that some rules can be deduced from
others, and this needs to be cleared up. It can be cleared up simultaneously with clarifying the relation between the formulas of the laws
and the laws underlying the formulas, as this relation operates in
empirical adaptations of the second kind, in which exceptions are
brought into the laws as framed or formulated.

In the case of universal rules of natural law, C in the formula H & C
$\rightarrow$ (T $\rightarrow$ L) might mean any possible circumstances in which human

beings find themselves, or any circumstances in which we might reasonably expect to find human beings (for example, Hume's circumstances of justice, on the circumstances side). Likewise, H might mean human nature as manifested in any possible circumstances or in any circumstances reasonably expectable (turning to Hume, again, the circumstances of justice on the human nature side). If in following St Thomas we think of the essence of the species as fixed, once and for all, we would have in H the first alternative. If we think (taking up some things that St Thomas says about changes in 'the condition of man,' for example, after the original sin) that human nature might be modified for the better or worse, the second alternative would obtain.

If we think of universal rules as rules that apply in every society, we may be inclined to distinguish two classes of them:

First, those that in no society have any exceptions;
Second, those that in any society come with exceptions.

With changes in circumstances, rules may move from one class to another. The rule, 'Do not slay the innocent,' might be undermined by such changes. After the germ theory of disease becomes known in a poor community, there might be cases in which there is no means of keeping someone alive in quarantine. Imagine someone who is carrying the Ebola virus.[33] However innocent, might he not have to be killed, to save everybody else? If technology advances to provide sure means of forestalling the infection without the expense of a quarantine, the rule would move back to the first class. But contrary to the opinion that some students of St Thomas[34] hold and ascribe to him, the rule in question may always have been liable to have exceptions, given sufficiently stringent circumstances. Consider the Inuit expecting Grandpapa, once he has become more a consumer of food than a producer, to go to sea on an icefloe, or old-time Japanese in Tohoku sending Granny into the mountains. The exceptions, moreover, are arguably not just permissible exceptions (excusable departures), but required ones. The community may not be able to survive, much less thrive, without making the exceptions.

We have to distinguish between rules as formulated (which according to St Thomas's sensible teaching will do little if anything to mention the exceptions) but just speak to what works for the majority of cases, and the relevant underlying rules,[35] in which the exceptions (so far known) would be mentioned. Both the rule as formulated and the underlying rule may be thought of as having three components: **volk** (pronounced 'folk') for the demographic scope of the rule, that is to say, the population to which it applies; **wenn** (pronounced 'when') for the conditions under which the rule is to be heeded; **nono** for the actions or sequences of actions prohibited. Defining an imperative noncircularly as 'a blocking operation' (physical or verbal) 'targeting some specifiable action type,' a rule may be defined as 'a system of imperatives, that is to say, of action types that are blocking operations targeting (**nono**ing, more or less precisely) specified other action types (by given agents falling under **volk** in circumstances specified by **wenn**). The **nono** in the underlying rule does not make stealing a **nono**, but stealing-with-exceptions, or stealing qualified, or to follow St Thomas more exactly, taking another's property qualified. The exceptions could be mentioned (so far as known) in the underlying rule either as additions qualifying the object of the **nono**, or under the **wenn** clause, narrowing the conditions under which the prohibition applies.

What is the basis for deduction? In some cases we may be simply inferring from a general rule to a less general one that falls under it: 'Do not do evil (or injury) to any man,' thus, falls under 'Seek the good, shun the evil,' though already we must understand 'the good' to embrace more than the person's own advantage; and we need to understand – on empirical grounds – something at least of what is to a person's advantage. Like 'Do not do anything destructive of the community,' mentioned above, the rule about not doing evil to any man might equally well be taken to be an immediate implication of the basic argument about thriving in persons and in the community. In other cases, further empirical evidence has to be brought in. In each case, the core rule derives from this evidence taken together with the basic argument for the pursuit of the Common Good (thriving personal and social), and the exceptions are added on the same basis, as with the rule about taking another person's property.[36] Sometimes the empirical evidence is familiar and obvious; sometimes, it is not. 'Some matters are approved or disapproved with minimal attention to invoking general principles, while some matters cannot be the subject of judgment without much consideration of the various circumstances' (*ST*, 1a2ae, Q.100, 1). The rules or laws dealing with matters of the first sort may be regarded as self-evident, under a sufficiently relaxed conception of self-evidence.

Locke is committed (in *The Reasonableness of Christianity*, for example)[37] to allowing that the heathen may have discovered enough of natural law 'by the light of nature' for some of them to live good lives and escape eternal punishment.[38] For most people in Christian countries, the Christian revelation has been an essential means of discovery, just as it has been an essential means both of enforcement and encouragement. The two positions are compatible: The heathen could have discovered without revelation the content of natural law far enough to discern that wilful homicide is forbidden and that theft and false witness are forbidden, too. Perhaps neither the heathen nor the generality of Christians could discover without revelation just what in hard cases is to count as homicide or theft or false witness. In each case, any of a number of rules might make a substantial contribution to a thriving community. So revelation would contribute details that people would not be able to arrive at by empirical investigation and deductive argument on their own. This formula of reconciliation establishes the compatibility at issue. Unfortunately, it does not seem that in fact revelation does contribute details of content: 'Love thy neighbor,' for example, gives strong guidance, but it is somewhat vague as to what 'love' will amount to or one's 'neighbour.' What revelation does do is give some specific assurance that virtue will be rewarded and vice punished, if not in this world, then in the next.

The Content of the Common Core

My claim that Locke's and St Thomas's theories are the same is not a claim that they offer the same systems of laws (which can be axiomatized with the same axioms and theorems) or basic systems (which are already perfectly receptive to additional axioms and theorems, perhaps receptive respectively to different additional axioms and theorems, but giving in the end systems that are the same in the sense just invoked). I do not claim that they enumerate the same laws or would accept the same laws as additions to the ones that they do enumerate. Both Locke and St Thomas give, they are bound to give, incomplete enumerations, and there is no reason to expect that the enumerations that they do give correspond entirely law for law. They might well disagree about whether an item on either of their lists or an item that either may add is genuinely a natural law. But this need not be a disagreement about the core of natural law theory. It could be a disagreement about an empirical issue, which they both would understand must be settled by reference to the principle that any genuine natural law must be indispensable to a society's fully thriving. (I use 'indispensable' here and elsewhere as shorthand for a more adequate notion, which I shall outline in a moment.) One could imagine both Locke and St Thomas considering only what laws are indispensable to a society to barely carry on and perpetuate itself. Then, not even the natural law against homicide would have to give comprehensive personal security: Societies have continued in spite of having frequent feuds and duels. However, I shall assume that Locke and St Thomas, and my other authors, too, are agreed that the natural laws should aim at a high level of thriving, a level to be explained in a succeeding chapter by teasing out all the various aspects of a rich notion of the Common Good.[39]

It follows that natural law theory, just as much as utilitarianism, offers a criterion for distinguishing good laws from bad. The criterion, pressed home, may raise empirical questions as complex as those raised by Jeremy Bentham. Meanwhile, we have to rely on common-sense approximations, on what has seemed to work reliably, time and again, in specific connections in the past, but we would also have to do this if we tried to apply the principle of utility. No one has ever carried the felicific calculus out; no one ever will. We may assume, however, that certain actions and policies, by meeting related, surrogate criteria, like the meeting of basic needs, would make advances towards the maximization of utility, or towards a more fully thriving society.

The principle of indispensability, treated as generating empirical issues, is at the core of natural law theory. One might as well say, Locke's a posteriori argument is at the core. In the core, one would expect to find, also, a set of laws (or a disjunction of sets) sufficient, taken together with the more particularized laws that could be deduced from them, for a society's thriving. One does find, in all the canonical authors whom I treat, much the same collection of examples that can be taken as approximations to the natural laws in the core. They are examples that answer roughly to commonsense notions of morality; hence, the impression that Peter Levi got during his Jesuitical studies that natural law theory was 'warmed over common sense.'[40]

The core of natural law theory may not be far from being itself common sense; nor should it be. It nevertheless raises subtle and far-reaching issues that go far beyond the present resolving powers of social science. Every law, if it is to be regarded as indispensable, must be indispensable as a member of an indispensable set. But might there not be many alternative sets, which might turn out to be equally effective in promoting thriving personal and social? This seems to be in principle quite possible, especially if we do not think of thriving as something subject to an exact calculation, like utility. If so, the idea of a given rule being indispensable will not work so well, generally, as the idea of a rule being at least an INUS condition for thriving, to borrow from Mackie's analysis of causation.[41] INUS is an acronym: An INUS condition is an Insufficient but Necessary ingredient in an Unnecessary but Sufficient combination of conditions that will have a certain effect – here, having in force the rule in question is a causal condition of thriving. Thus, it is at least an INUS condition of having a thriving society that there be, in Locke's view, an effective rule demanding respect for private property. It may well be (it would be surprising if this were not the case) that several rules will figure in every sufficient combination; those rules alone (for example, a rule against continually discarding provisions for needs) would qualify for being called 'indispensable' *tout court*.

Establishing whether one plausible combination of rules will be as effective as conditions for thriving as another is a matter for deep and prolonged empirical research,[42] which (so far as I know) no theorist of natural law has ever engaged in. To do so would take us far from this discussion of the basic orientation of natural law theory. Here we follow other natural law theorists, who have implicitly relied on the evidence that at some times and places there have been thriving societies, and in those societies (they have assumed) much the same set of laws has been observed. But any one of these laws might turn out on investigation to have been not strictly indispensable in every feature. To be sure, natural law theory would be implausible if certain familiar laws, broadly conceived, and identified as core rules possibly coming with exceptions, did not seem convincing without further investigation. There must be some law having the effect of restraining homicide in every indispensable set. Yet the details remain open to investigation.

Is Locke unlike St Thomas in any important way in postulating, as he does, that the natural laws obtain in the state of nature? For some people, like Leo Strauss,[43] this has indeed been an important point, but I think it amounts to little more, apart from picturesque expression, than a contention that it would be possible for thoroughly well-disposed people to live together without government. Perhaps it amounts, in addition, to the contention that it is possible for people to be thoroughly well-disposed, since examples of such people can be found even now. On neither of these points would St Thomas disagree, as is shown by his contemplating just such possibilities in the case of a community of saints. Locke is not even entirely at odds with Hobbes on these points. Locke may be more sanguine than Hobbes about finding a substantial proportion of well-disposed people in any actual circumstances, but he treats people as by and large so quarrelsome as to have 'every the least difference ... apt to end' in war,[44] which brings Locke for practical purposes, in particular as regards the need for organized government originating in an explicit social contract, close to Hobbes.[45] The most significant difference between them does not have to do with the in principle possibility of living peaceably in the state of nature, though Locke begins by giving the possibility much more weight than Hobbes does. It has to do, for one thing, with the fact that people do not, in Hobbes's view, violate any standing obligations when they quarrel and indeed wage war without restraint. Locke's people quarrel (among other things) about how what they know to be the standing obligations of natural law are to be applied. Moreover, an associated fact, Locke's state of nature is a society of sorts, unlike Hobbes's, and unlike the situation in Hume's account of the origin of justice that precedes the arrival of the rules about property.[46]

Schneewind asserts, in a passage that I have already brought up (in the Introduction, for its general bearing on modern natural law theory), 'Locke's thought on natural law is ... built around the three points that mark what I have called a distinctively modern form of the view: [1] our unsocially sociable psychology causes basic problems that [2] empirically discoverable law shows us how to resolve [3] without appeal to any substantive conception of the highest good.'[47] Locke, in his description of the state of nature, does not treat human beings as unsociable; and even the liability of that state to degenerate into a state of war does not, strictly speaking, imply that people were unsociable to begin with or persistently unsociable even now. They might be eager for the mutual assurance that would save them from conflict. Schneewind himself says, perhaps with less than perfect truth, of Locke's state of nature that 'although war may occur [in it], it is neither inevitable nor frequent' (142–3). However this may be, recognition of the unsociable tendencies of human beings cannot serve as a point of distinction between 'modern natural law' and St Thomas's theory. Thomas is well aware of the fractiousness of human beings, and of all the recalcitrance deriving from original sin to conducting themselves virtuously. As a matter of observation, people who are not saints have difficulties in living together; and for St Thomas as for Locke, 'empirically discoverable laws' show them how to resolve the problems. So neither point (1) nor point (2) is a point of distinction between Locke's 'modern natural law' and St Thomas's theory. Point (3) might be a point of distinction if Locke had left 'the highest good' without any fixed or fixable content. Or it might be such if the content was determined entirely by human preferences, varying every which way regarding pleasure and pain, which is the ground on which Schneewind cites Locke as repudiating any hope of finding agreement on the highest good.[48] I think this makes too little of Locke's commitment to charity[49] and (as an Anglican mindful of the Book of Common Prayer) to the forgiveness of trespasses, ingredients of morality neither of which reduces in any simple way to pleasures or pains, though they may certainly contribute to happiness.

Locke's insistence in his *Essay on Human Understanding*[50] that every human good can be reduced to pleasure (or relief from pain), taken together with the strong stand (much stronger and more explicit than anything in St Thomas) that ethics is in principle a demonstrative science proceeding from 'real essences' or 'archetypes,' not ideas nominally defined that represent the world and may represent it imperfectly,[51] make Locke seem a proponent of a narrow abstract utilitarianism. But I think we need to be cautious about looking back at Locke through two centuries or more of attacks on the Benthamite conception of pleasure and pain as too narrow to accommodate all the dimensions of human good. If we take Locke talking about 'pleasure' and 'pain' to be talking about what is in the whole range of experiences agreeable or disagreeable to human beings, he will not seem to be so narrow. He will be approaching use of the concept of happiness in the broad sense; and we must bear charity and forgiveness in mind, even if Locke does not succeed in integrating those notions into his very sketchy ideas of the deductive structure for ethics. Certainly he wishes to allow for the agreeable experiences of study, and even more emphatically, for the bliss or terror that may wait beyond the grave.

Moreover, by Schneewind's own account, the arrangements, including property and justice, under which human beings prosper, can be included in 'the General Good of those under [the] Law.' Schneewind denies that in this reference to 'the General Good' Locke is adverting to 'a substantive Common Good.' Schneewind says, 'He is saying that law gives each of us what we want, namely security in disposing as we please of our person, actions, and possessions' (143). Where is the argument for this dismissal of substantial content for 'the General Good'? The arrangements mentioned and other conditions for our happiness figure in 'the General Good,' and the principle stated in the *Second Treatise* that we should preserve ourselves and others, too, when their preservation does not conflict with ours implies that the happiness of others as well as our own figures in 'the General Good,' not just for them, but for us their neighbours, and their brothers and sisters, too. This is true even if we take the narrowest view of the principle, and read it as implying only that we should not stand in the way of other people's endeavours at happiness so long as what they need in these endeavours takes away nothing or only a negligible amount from what we need for our own happiness. But there is no reason to read the principle this narrowly in the *Second Treatise* and what Locke says in the *First Treatise* about our charitable duties stands against the narrow reading. So does Locke's belief in an 'obligation to mutual love amongst Men' (Schneewind, 157, citing *Second Treatise*, par. 5), even if Schneewind is perfectly right in holding that the chief embarrassment that prevented Locke from writing out a systematic account of his ethical views was that he could not find 'a solid grounding' for this 'great maxim of charity' (157).

This is not to say that Locke explicitly endorsed a notion of the Common Good as rich as the one that in the chapter following I shall draw (with some embellishments) out of Rousseau. I can assert no more than that Locke does not reject such a notion, or imply rejection; and that in some passages he moves toward endorsing it. In other passages (much emphasized by Schneewind) in which he uses the language of egoistic hedonism even if he is not himself committed to that doctrine, Locke moves away. These passages include, in particular, the account of ethics as a deductive science, in the *Essay Concerning Human Understanding*. Had Locke given a systematic account of his ethics and in doing so put all his weight behind egoistic hedonism, the passages favourable to received natural law theory, in the conception of the Common Good and otherwise, would either have been rejected or drastically modified. But why should it be supposed that the adjustments would all have been on this side? The *Essay Concerning Human Understanding* and the *Treatises on Government* were produced contemporaneously. It is at least as plausible to suppose that, in the hypothesized synthesis, Locke would have put most weight on the *Treatises* and the passages there that can be readily assimilated to the view of natural law theory which he adopted in his *Essays/Questions*. Then egoistic hedonism would have been disavowed (as it is, explicitly, in the *Essays/Questions*), and the appearance of his commitment to it removed.

The insistence in the *Essay Concerning Human Understanding* on viewing ethics as a deductive science does not threaten the position that for Locke, as for St Thomas, ethics has an empirical basis. (Endorsements of deduction in ethics by St Thomas and by Hobbes do not threaten their empiricism either.) A brief account of how natural law theory can be empirically based and represented in a deductive system notwithstanding would make the following points: First, any and all of the rules in the system could as a matter of separate observation be found to be indispensable to a thriving society; second, it would be a matter of empirical proof whether any of the rules were being currently upheld in a society under observation; third, whether or not they were being currently upheld, one or more of these rules could be taken as axioms and the rest of the rules deduced from them.

The system might seem to be a priori in some sense. There are a great number of senses of 'a priori' on offer, with none of them so outclassed by any other that it has been retired from the field. [52] Some of them are in spirit or by definition further removed from empirical considerations than others. One might, I think, be mistakenly inclined to go some distance with a tendency to think the system of natural laws a priori rather than empirical for at least two reasons: The rules, taken as axioms, might not seem to require any observation because they are taken to be self-evident, given their familiarity and their immediate connection with human nature, as with, for example the rule that property is to be respected; second, the system might be put forward as a consolidated view of the ethics to which the proponent of the system was already attached. A system of received and familiar themes in the ethics actually operating in the case of the proponent and other members of her society might easily induce a tendency on the proponent's part to think of it as a priori. But it would not be a priori, if ultimately it stood or fell by the a posteriori argument and the principle of indispensability, with empirical evidence about what it takes for a society to thrive.

Chapter Three

Rousseau and St Thomas on the Common Good

The Common Good is a key notion in natural law theory. According to the theory, genuine moral rules, the natural laws, are the rules that people in a society must obey in order to achieve the Common Good. St Thomas builds this point into his principal definition of a law – a genuine law: 'An ordinance of reason for the Common Good made by the authority who has care of the community and promulgated' (*ST*, 1a 2ae, Q.90, 4). The Common Good may be taken here to embrace both the good of the political community as such ('the specifically political common good' distinguished by Finnis) and what Finnis calls the 'all-inclusive Common Good' of the people involved, which would also take into account the common goods of families and various other groupings internal to the community, for example, associations (religious and otherwise) of its members.[1] The specifically political common good takes precedence over these goods in cases of conflict; and the specifically political common good, so far as it is achieved, creates a favourable environment for the activities of the groupings. On the other hand, the groupings make their own decisions about how their common goods are to be pursued, in harmony with the decisions about the specifically political common good, without (in many matters) having these decisions pre-empt theirs. All the other authors of main concern in this book would go along with these points, though I am not sure that they would all be willing to speak of a common good for all human beings, much less the common good of the universe.[2]

But just what does the Common Good amount to? For all that St Thomas continually invokes the notion, in many different connections, he does not anywhere (to my knowledge) elaborate a definition for it, perhaps because he thought that the notion was familiar and obvious, a view that, as we shall see, is easily understood, even though it by no means embraces the whole of what is at issue.

St Thomas does give us something to go on besides familiarity. Consolidating remarks about the Common Good in *Summa Theologiae* 1a2ae, QQ.90, 91, 92, 94, 95, 96, 97, and 2a2ae, QQ.58, 61 (and filling out what we can gather from these texts with points cited by Finnis, as we have done above), we find that for St Thomas the Common Good comprises, in the first place, the minimum conditions for realizing peaceful intercourse among human beings and a shared conception of cooperation (Finnis); and, in the second place, whatever arrangements contribute to the community thriving as a whole (which for St Thomas means leaving some things unregulated that it would be infeasible to regulate, or, were they regulated, too intrusive into the affairs of families, other substate groupings, and individual persons). The thriving of the community includes the thriving of members of the community; their thriving includes their earthly happiness (and, for St Thomas, some assurance of good prospects in the life beyond); and their earthly happiness very prominently includes the happiness that comes from friendship.[3] The precept 'Love thy neighbour' may be thought of as reaching for the Common Good through friendship and beyond.[4]

The Common Good is the final cause of right actions in particular matters – that is, such actions (including actions in pursuit of private goods or for the good of a household) must be consistent with the minimum conditions of cooperation and make whatever net contribution is relevant and feasible to maintaining and strengthening the conditions for the community's thriving. Those actions must accordingly conform to genuine (natural) law. The specific structure of income distribution (and along with it the specific rule for distributing common stocks of goods) must assure the poor of minimum provisions for their needs (natural concupiscences) and forestall social unrest, since both justice and peace are aspects of the Common Good. Any differential rewards for merit (specified following Aristotle as geometrical equality, proportioning the rewards to the merit) must be consistent with this.

This is just enough about St Thomas's conception of the Common Good to justify assimilating it to Rousseau's, and it is to Rousseau that I shall turn now for a scheme of elaboration. By virtue of his public goods conception of the Common Good Rousseau is to be counted as a major contributor to strengthening the theory of natural law and keeping it up. Yet Rousseau (alone among the authors that I chiefly treat) explicitly repudiates natural law theory; so it may seem a specially perverse project to try to assimilate him. I could limit myself to holding that the concept of the Common Good that is associated with Rousseau's concept of the General Will can be taken over, leaving the rest of his ideas behind. Or I could point out in addition that Rousseau does, inconsistency notwithstanding, often use the language of natural law theory, or equivalent language.[5] But I think I can do something much more ambitious than that. I can confront Rousseau's repudiation and show that it does not stand in the way of treating him as a natural law theorist.

The repudiation that Rousseau expresses in the preface to the Second Discourse (on inequality) could hardly be more explicit. There he chides received natural law theory for not offering a good definition of law and for not reducing to one consistent set the various and contradictory laws that it identifies. He stresses, more than these points, that the received theory misuses the term 'natural,' for the laws that it variously purports to identify have no bearing upon people in the state of nature; they are all laws that presuppose a settled civil society. Instead of considering what people could think and know in the state of nature,

> On commence par rechercher les règles dont, pour l'utilité commune, il serait à propos que les hommes convinssent entre eux; et puis on donne le nom de loi naturelle à la collection de ces règles, sans autre preuve que le bien qu'on trouve que résulterait de leur pratique universelle. Michel Launay, ed., Rousseau, *Oeuvres Complètes* (Paris: Editions du Seuil, 1971, vol. 2, 210)

> (One begins by looking for the rules that, for their common utility, it would be suitable for men to agree upon; and then one gives the name of natural law to the collection of these rules, without any other ground than the good that one finds would result from their universal practice.)

'What's wrong with that?' a natural law theorist might ask. Indeed, this minimal proof is precisely the basic argument for natural law that is found in St Thomas, Locke, and the others; and precisely the argument that I shall return to again and again in this book. Rousseau scornfully dismisses it with the words: 'Voilà assurement une manière très commode de composer des définitions, et d'expliquer la nature des choses par des convenances presque arbitraires' (Launay, vol. 2, ibid.). (That's a convenient way for sure of making up definitions and explaining by quite arbitrary conventions the nature of things.) The phrasing does not even accurately express the basis of the dismissal, which is that this way of proceeding to identify the natural laws will not turn up any laws properly so named, because it will not turn up laws that apply in the state of nature.

If Rousseau is conceded this point, it becomes clear that his dispute with natural law theory in respect to the way of proceeding is mainly a terminological one. He is reserving the term 'natural' for use outside a settled society; other theorists are using 'natural' to apply only when a settled society is in view (at least settled far enough to have agreed-upon conventions, for example, regarding property). They are arguing that the natural laws are indispensable for every settled society, at any rate for any settled society that means to thrive. Given the very exten-sive allowances in their theory for variations in circumstances and cul-ture, there is no reason why Rousseau would not be ready to entertain this thesis. Indeed, he implicitly subscribes to it, for example, in the dedicatory passage that precedes the preface to the Second Discourse. In that passage, Rousseau praises the city of Geneva as realizing in respect to its laws and other features a government that invites univer-sal admiration.

Rousseau not only invites treatment as one natural law theorist among others; he makes an outstanding contribution to natural law theory in respect to defining one of its central notions: the Common Good. Appreciating the power of his definition goes hand in hand with clarifying his doctrine of the General Will, which, like any legisla-tion that accords with natural law, aims at the Common Good.

In the experience of Rousseau's readers and commentators, the Gen-eral Will easily turns into a metaphysical mystery. Is it the will of soci-ety or the body politic, hypostatized as a Person superior to any of its members, none of whom might have a will coinciding with it? If this is not a mystery, it may be said that it is at least 'a fiction. What is the State? Always a set of people, maybe only one, who command; the many must obey willy-nilly. It is not possible for everybody to be at once the subject of his own law and the sole author. Rousseau's deter-mination to moralize politics can only overload it with an excessive finality foreign to it, offering to regenerate humanity but never suc-ceeding. The pursuit of Virtue or Fraternity ends in Terror.'[6]

Sabine, citing Rousseau's language in the Encyclopedia article on Political Economy, is justified in asserting that the idea of the General

Will presupposes 'the theory that a community has a corporate personality or *moi commun*, the organic analogy for a social group.'[7] Rousseau himself, in that article, maintains, 'The body politic ... is ... a moral being possessed of a will.'[8] Indeed, it 'can be considered as an organized body, living and like that of a man.'[9] This language, with the organic analogy fully exploited, leads not only to mystery, but also to bypassing Kenneth Arrow's problem about getting logically satisfactory social choices by combining personal ones. If, notwithstanding, we did bring the language within the ambit of social choice theory, violation of the anti-imposition axiom easily follows, with violation of the anti-dictatorship axiom an additional possibility.

Rousseau's language in the final version of *The Social Contract*, however, is much soberer, and need not be taken to have sinister consequences. The General Will there becomes the will of 'a being of Reason because it is not a man,'[10] phrasing that already betokens a shift away from the organic analogy. More important, Rousseau explicitly characterizes the General Will as formed from the wills of individual citizens, when these aim at their own interests in a certain way. With this characterization, the theory of the General Will, or at any rate the ingredient of that theory most basic in *The Social Contract*, invites treatment as an intuitive exercise in what we know as the theory of public goods. It is not a mystery at all. It is intelligible and prescient. Moreover, it establishes a perspective for understanding the rationale of voting that reduces the impact of Arrow's problem, even if it does not escape the impact entirely. Arrow himself, in a sympathetic though inconclusive discussion already present in the first edition of *Social Choice and Individual Values* allows for such a use of Rousseau's theory: 'Voting, from this point of view, is not a device whereby each individual expresses his personal interests, but rather where each individual gives his opinion of the general will,' and this is to be found in 'consensus' on a 'moral imperative.'[11]

Rousseau's Distinction between the General Will and the Will of All

The General Will, Rousseau tells us, aims at what is in everyone's common interest.[12] Yet it is not, he insists, to be confused with the will of everyone, in which everyone may aim just at his own interest.[13] Is there anything that can figure as the object of the one without being the object of the other? We have to find something that is in everyone's own interest, yet susceptible of being disregarded when everyone's own interest is, nevertheless, being pursued. This may sound impossible. But there is such an object, and it vindicates Rousseau in giving us a trenchant distinction between the General Will and the will of everyone.

What is in everyone's own interest, as the object of the General Will, is to be found, according to Rousseau, by taking away from the particular wills directed at the private interests of individual citizens 'the pluses and the minuses that are mutually destructive to themselves.'[14] I take it that what Rousseau means are the interests that people may have in gains associated with losses for other people of equal amounts, reckoned in physical terms or money income, not utility. Such gains all involve limitative benefits, that is to say, benefits which some can enjoy only if others are forestalled from enjoying them. They fall into two categories: first, gains by expropriative transfer that imply other people must give up goods in their possession; second, what I shall call 'other limitative benefits,' breaking these down into two subcategories: benefits from goods that would be present in any case though not yet firmly appropriated and benefits that would not be present, for example, because they would not have been produced, had there not been some prior agreement to respect allocating them to those who hold them.

I shall for the time being take the condition about pluses and minuses in a strong sense, embracing all these categories and subcategories. Hence, I shall be supposing that in aiming the General Will at its proper objects, not only are transfers or possible transfers of goods by force, fraud, and the abuse of political power ruled out, but also all goods that have limitative benefits. Limitative benefits are characteristic of private goods, the consumption of which in any instance is to the benefit of one person and to the detriment of anyone else. What Eve ate of the apple, it was impossible for Adam to eat. By contrast, the benefits characteristic of public goods (like a lighthouse, a broadcast of classical music, monetary stability, a safe environment) are such that consumption by one person does not impair or limit consumption by others.[15]

Now we can say, the will of everyone may aim wholly at private goods. The General Will, by contrast, aims at public goods. The latter are certainly in everyone's own interest, and may be willed accordingly, by persons who give them due attention. However, people may disregard them in favour of pursuing private goods, which also are in their own interest. They may be preoccupied with private goods because of a certain lack of vision. Or they may be, as Rousseau explicitly notes, tempted to get what they can of public goods as free riders.[16]

The General Will must not only be distinguishable from the will of everyone. It must be coherent and immutable.[17] Will aiming at public goods guarantee these properties? It is true that one person may benefit more from consumption of a public good than another person. Indeed, for every person who rejoices in hearing a Bach concerto over the air, there may be a dozen people who obtain at most only a mild pleasure. But this is not in itself an obstacle to everyone's benefiting from willing to have the public good, in his own interest. A more telling objection lies in the possibility that people vary in their preferences for mixes of public goods. Some, for example, may favour pure air and water more than a public radio broadcasting string quartets, while others want relatively more resources to go into broadcasting; and these people in turn may differ as to what programs they want.

This difficulty can be turned by granting Rousseau the assumption that the General Will aims not at all public goods, but at a subset of public goods from which everyone benefits, and which therefore every prudent and well-informed person will want. To get full value from this assumption, we need to rule out variations between people respecting their preferences for public goods as against private ones or respecting public goods compared with each other, whether or not they are public goods that belong to the subset. On Rousseau's conception of the problem, this is to be done by appealing to the full development, sooner or later, of a feeling for the Common Good,[18] a matter that I shall take up in a moment. For now, I shall just assume that once the subset has been identified, everyone (or at least a majority) will demand that each good in the subset be produced in some substantial quantity. This further assumption can be reinforced by taking the subset in question not to include all public goods that benefit everyone (which might possibly make it a very large set, unmanageable to contemplate), but to include only those public goods indispensable to the thriving of the people and the community in question. Shrinking the subset in this way also helps make sure (without making it strictly speaking implied) that providing an adequate quantity of each good in the set will not outrun the resources at the disposal of the community.[19]

The voters in their votes express their opinions that the public goods in question will indeed benefit everyone. (They express, simultaneously, a commitment to assist in bringing them into being, or whatever other goods into being that are correctly determined to belong to the set, taking the opinion of a majority of voters as the best available indication of correctness). The benefits are objective provisions for needs, for example, making a vaccine against smallpox available to every member of the population; or at any rate well-suited provisions for heeding preferences that do not conflict with needs (for example, look-out points at places where especially spectacular views are present).

Proceeding with the objective-benefits view of the Common Good, but wanting, nevertheless, to simplify the discussion by assuming that there is unanimous agreement in the expression of the General Will calling for these benefits, I need to rule out conflicts of preferences among the public goods in the subset, ranking them in comparison with each other. We could do this by assuming that though the benefits received from any good in the subset vary from person to person, the order of benefits from the subset is the same for all, in their own eyes. Without denying that an intelligible conception of the General Will could be worked out on this assumption, I shall work with the stronger and simpler assumption that the order of benefits from the subset is the same for all and that everyone (in a sense that I am about to specify) gets an equal benefit from each good. There are public goods that fit into the set so circumscribed. They include public goods that are of chief importance in the work of governments: having a legal system; having police and fire departments; having means of national defence; having a safe environment in other respects; having monetary stability. Government, in a sufficiently simple society, might be entirely occupied in providing such goods. We need not invoke the concept of utility, with its difficulties, refined or unrefined, to explain how the benefits from these goods are equal. We need not, and the citizens engaged in aiming the general will at its proper objects need not, depend on any subjective estimates of benefits to oneself. They may consider, respecting the goods mentioned, that it is reasonable to ascribe to everyone an equal benefit. Everyone, they may hold, benefits equally in having her life and limbs protected. They may hold, furthermore, that everyone benefits equally from having his property protected. If the property varies in amount, it may be considered that the loss of any item of property from larger possessions would do less to jeopardize life-plans than the loss of any equivalent item from smaller possessions. With this inverse variation in jeopardy, the benefit from having the property protected may be held, by a reasonably pragmatic stipulation, to remain always the same.

Since the Common Good consists of public goods, all its benefits will be available to everyone without any extra marginal cost; in the case of some public goods, those specially relevant here, no one could even be excluded from enjoying the benefits. Consequently, the 'free-rider' problem arises in respect to contributions from individual citizens to the production of any of the public goods in question. Knowing that she will enjoy the benefit of the good, if it is produced, anyway, each citizen may be tempted to shirk paying the taxes or shirk putting forward the effort (turning out to vote; working alongside others to pile sandbags against the levee) that all are expected to contribute. Rousseau clearly states the free-rider problem (thus giving convincing evidence that he is thinking of public goods) and solves it by holding that any citizen tempted to shirk shall be 'forced to be free.' He shall be compelled, in other words, to heed the legislation that he has had a part in enacting; and to make whatever contributions are demanded of every citizen for the legislation to succeed. The passage has notoriously struck many readers as sinister; but they read the passage without public goods and the free-rider problem in mind.

For the moment, I leave the General Will at the point of having identified some of the goods in the subset of public goods that on the most narrow view form its proper objects. Noting only that the citizens may mistake the answer, I leave open the question whether other public goods should be recognized as belonging to the subset: for example, provisions for civic education. I postpone the question of what level of production of the goods shall be decided upon. Even on the most narrow view, the General Will should resolve this question; but how it is to go about doing so is best discussed on a broader view, because there the thinking that goes into the decision is most convincing.

Public and Private Goods

Can more than the subset of public goods just mentioned be embraced among the objects of the General Will? I think we can find more to be embraced, if we return to the condition about taking away the pluses and the minuses, and if we are willing to brave certain complications that we need not face with a General Will aimed solely at a restricted subset of public goods. It is unrealistic to leave private goods (and other public goods) entirely out of account among the concerns of politics. On the other hand, they can become objects of the General Will only insofar as that will contemplates them within a framework of distributive justice and as matters of common interest. Complications arise in both of these connections; and the framework of distributive justice becomes determinate for the General Will, if it does become determinate, only by grace of argumentation something less than apodictic.[20]

We made some sense of the condition about pluses and minuses by taking the condition in a strong sense of setting aside both gains by transfer and other limitative benefits. We can make further sense of the condition by taking it more weakly, as setting aside expropriative transfers only. That is to say, we may take it as setting aside just those objects of one's own interest in which one aggrandizes one's own benefits by taking private goods away from other people. The General Will certainly could not aim at these benefits. Could it aim at any limitative benefits?

With (non-excludable) public goods, by contrast with goods obtainable only by expropriative transfers, one could not deny anyone else the goods and still consume them oneself. The second subcategory of other limitative benefits, which are present only as a result of an agreement to respect the allocation of private goods from which they arise, meets something like the same condition. For to deny these goods to anyone by refusing to agree to an allocation and thus forestalling their presence implies denying the goods to oneself; indeed, it implies denying any goods to oneself that one might gain depending on an agreement about allocation. Everyone would have an interest in any scheme for producing private goods under which everyone substantially shared in the output.

Any such scheme would have a dual aspect: It would be a scheme for producing and distributing private goods (including, it might well be, an appropriate system of taxes) some or all of them answering to self-interest of the narrowest sort; but having a scheme of some sort, in which everyone had a substantial share of private goods, would be a matter of common interest. Would having a scheme be a public good? The shares that people have are shares that they could be denied; and one person's consumption of his share stands in the way of another person's consuming it. On the other hand, the benefit of having some share or other does not impair anyone else's having the benefit of having some share or other. Everyone can enjoy the scheme in that respect simultaneously, and like everyone else, benefit from it fully. Nor could anyone be excluded from having a share unless the scheme were transformed into another scheme that did not fit the definition of giving everyone a substantial share. Either having a scheme is a public good, of a somewhat attenuated sort, or having one is an analogue of a public good.

Unfortunately, it is not, if it is a public good, necessarily one that belongs to the restricted subset considered earlier. It is not necessarily a public good from which it could be held that everyone got equal benefits in every respect that it was reasonable to take into account. The General Will would be intelligible – free of mystery – if it stopped with the conclusion that it was in the common interest to have some such scheme, and did not try to choose which one. Yet to stop there would be a disappointment. The General Will would not be doing all the work that Rousseau, or we, might ask of it; and it would leave no ready alternative way to a justifiable choice. Can we get it to make a choice among schemes? I shall go about answering this question indirectly, by way of a closer analysis of the Common Good and a discussion of the role that a cognitive standard for the Common Good designates for voting.

The Common Good

Nannerl Keohane, in a model discussion of Rousseau's conception of the common interest (the Common Good), distinguishes three types: one embracing the parallel interests that are served by a common scheme of cooperation, as in the example of the deer hunt; a second embracing interests that people have in the shared pleasures of social intercourse; the third embracing the interests that citizens have in the general 'abstract and lofty' benefits of having a political community that upholds liberty, equality, and the rule of law.[21] I shall elaborate on this scheme, consistently I think with its basic insights, and distinguish four types of common interest: parallel but solitary interests served by a common scheme of cooperation; interests in joint consumption, with pleasure taken in the presence and concurrent consumption of other people; interests in joint consumption and in the joint effort of cooperation, with pleasure taken not merely in having other people present, consuming too and contributing to the noise and jollification, but also, vicariously, in having the others enjoy themselves; finally, shared interests resting on loyalty to the other members of the community and the community itself.

In effect, what I have done is mainly to subdivide Keohane's second category. It may be thought that the division is artificial: how plausible is it that people could enjoy having other people present during joint consumption without sympathizing with their enjoyments? But, in fact, people can use others as instruments of pleasure without caring whether the others are pleased; this is notoriously a possibility in sexual intercourse. So the division marks off real possibilities. However, I agree that people's feelings naturally move across the distinction. More often than not, they come to care for the enjoyments of their sexual partners. It is just my point in elaborating Keohane's distinctions to bring out the natural tendency, which she herself has in mind, for people to develop common interests of all four types. Were people to begin with parallel interests only, they would tend to develop the others in the order given. In reality, the priorities are no doubt not so simple. At the very least, one could not expect people to be fully cognizant of the earlier types until after they had begun to be attached to some of the later ones. Nevertheless, on the essential point reality will vindicate Rousseau: In what he would reasonably consider a healthy community, the common interest will be generally felt to comprise all four types; and everyone's own interest will be shaped accordingly.

Social intercourse, properly managed, will, according to views in which *The Social Contract* corroborates *Emile*, induce in any individual person a sympathetic concern with the happiness of others.[22] Even without the development of a sense of joint efforts, this concern for other people enlarges one's conception of one's own interest to coincide at least in part with other people's. Hence the interest that each person has in having a scheme for producing private goods that answers to the general interest becomes an interest attached not just to parallel objects but to shared ones. But the same enlargement of concern may occur with the subset of public goods that were discussed earlier. There, too, the goods become objects of shared (overlapping) interests rather than of interests merely parallel.

The development of a sense of joint efforts goes hand in hand with this shift from parallel interests to shared ones. If, by living with other people, one acquires a sympathetic concern with their interests, one will be helping them out from time to time, and receiving help from them in turn. Thus starts up a foundation for regarding the association with other people as a community of mutual aid. On the other hand, when specific new projects for cooperation are broached, one of the attractions for any individual person of participating in them will be the opportunity that they offer of benefiting others, along often with the camaraderie with which the benefits are produced.

Sooner rather than later, it will be recognized that foremost among such projects are the undertakings of government to supply the public goods mentioned earlier: a legal system, internal protective services, national defence, and monetary stability. Like Keohane, we can conceive of recognizing them as something that is superimposed upon the recognition of the shared interests in private goods just mentioned. Recognizing them may be looked upon simultaneously as an outgrowth of the loyalty of each member of the community to the others with whom she shares the efforts of mutual aid as well as in joint consumption of the results of those efforts. Upon mutual loyalty is built loyalty to the community as a whole.

Thus, a rich notion of the Common Good, each element of which is a clear and simple idea, answers to the General Will. Moreover, the Common Good, as Rousseau conceived it, offers a foundation for choosing, among the schemes that give everyone a substantial share of private goods, a just scheme. 'Justice' (like kindness), Rousseau says, is 'a true affection of the soul enlightened by reason, and nothing but an orderly development of our primitive affections,' which 'of all the virtues [is] the one that conduces most to the Common Good of men.'[23] One may well think that it has the primacy among virtues that St Thomas attributes to justice; and this passage is one more bit of evidence about Rousseau's attachment along with St Thomas to natural law.

Contemplating schemes for producing and distributing private goods everyone might find an interest in a scheme of subsistence farming or of fending for oneself in the market, in either case with provisions for security brought in with a government. We have a more robust sense of the Common Good, and hence of something answering closely to Rousseau's conception of the General Will, however, with schemes that prescribe a just distribution of the proceeds of joint efforts. What joint efforts are in this connection is not, however, something entirely given by nature. What joint efforts are depends on what the participants are willing to recognize as joint efforts. Do they think of each other as contributing something to producing the private goods produced under the scheme, if the contribution is only (through taxes or otherwise) to maintaining the scheme, and that perhaps only by refraining from sabotaging it? An economy of subsistence farming or a *laissez-faire* market economy might be looked upon in this way. No doubt, however, it is easier to cultivate a sense of joint effort in a society with substantial public undertakings that enlist widespread participation. There all concerned might be satisfied that the scheme is in their own interest if it prescribed equal incomes, or Rawls's Difference Principle, or equality in meeting needs plus the Difference Principle applied to distributing a surplus answering to matters of preference only, in all cases taking taxation into account as appropriate. In suitable circumstances, it seems to me, the General Will would gravitate toward adopting some such scheme as its object. But that is to say, simultaneously, every person whose individual will is combined in the General Will would find it to her own interest to have such a scheme. The citizens would thus tend to converge on a unanimous endorsement, founded on a cognitive standard, of the idea of having some such scheme or other. I shall consider in a moment how the endorsement can be narrowed to fix, among approximately just schemes, upon a single one of them.

Voting and Choice of a Scheme

What role, however, is left for voting in the expression of the General Will? Some readers take the fact that the General Will works to a cognitive standard to imply that voting is superfluous. Yet Rousseau insists upon it. Every citizen must vote; every vote must be counted;[24] no representatives must intervene between the voting and the choice of general social policy.[25] Rousseau might join William Riker in finding some use for voting as a means of throwing representatives out of office, if there were representatives;[26] or of replacing magistrates in the executive that Rousseau does assume will administer the day-to-day business of government.[27] For Rousseau, however, though not for Riker, recourse to voting would be a means not just of unsettling things. It would be a means of making sure that the magistrates do not deviate too far from the cognitive standard of pursuing the objects aimed at by the General Will.

Yet this is not, in Rousseau's eyes, the primary task of voting. In his eyes, the primary task set the whole body of citizens is to establish what the proper objects aimed at by the General Will are and to prescribe their production. Were citizens to let representatives do these things on their behalf, they would be forfeiting their freedom, consisting as it does after the social contract in having to obey only laws that are fully of their own making.[28] They would, moreover, be shirking responsibility, a somewhat different point, since it has to do with a failing in character, from the even more serious point that they are also falling short in performing their twofold civic duty, which is to offer along with their opinions of how well the proposals for legislation fit the Common Good their commitment to obey laws that accord with those opinions or with the opinions of the majority as to the Common Good (which will be a more reliable indicator of the Common Good than the opinions of a minority).[29]

Bringing in commitment alongside opinion may seem to move away from a full cognitive basis for assessing the Common Good toward the position (of which Trachtenberg's is one variant) that the Common Good is whatever, given their preferences, the citizens choose to make of it. One way of understanding how the pairing of opinion and commitment would work would have the extent of the Common Good tailored to suit the commitments that the citizens are willing to make to it.[30] But even on this way of understanding the pairing there is irreducibly some cognitive content about the objective benefits in the Common Good. Moreover, it seems much more in accordance with Rousseau's standpoint to suppose that the opinion of the Common Good to be expressed by every citizen is to be expressed disinterestedly, that is to say, without even so much infection from any voter's separable private interest as variable commitment would allow. The commitment follows the opinion without qualifying it.

If representatives were sincerely concerned to choose for the citizens what citizens would choose for themselves, were this convenient, the representatives could aim their choices at the Common Good of the whole body of citizens;[31] and their opinions of whether a given proposal for legislation suited the Common Good of the whole body of citizens might be as accurate, or more accurate, than the opinions of the majority of citizens. However, as an empirical matter, any set of representatives are sooner or later likely to go by their own interests – the common good of their subgroup. Moreover, voting (on a Burkean basis) for uninstructed representatives does not give them any guidance as to what the whole body of citizens believes to be for the Common Good; the voting would be on an entirely different issue. On the other hand, voting for instructed representatives may lead to a majority opinion among the representatives different from the majority opinion in the electorate as a whole. Overwhelming majorities in some constituencies might succumb in the net result to very narrow ones in others. Proportional representation would have its own difficulties. Most important of all remains the consideration that the people represented would not be giving in their own persons the commitments to heed the legislation along with their opinions as to what legislation should pass, that is to say, what legislation promotes the Common Good.[32]

This may not be a very hard problem, especially if we suppose the General Will aims only at a restricted subset of public goods. It does require some calculation, that is to say, some consideration as to what must be set aside as matters of conflicting particular interests. Thus, in my account so far, limitative benefits must be set aside unless they figure in schemes of production that redound to the substantial interest of everyone; and set aside also must be interests in those public goods in respect to which people's preferences conflict. The goods that remain will be the objects aimed at by the General Will, though it has not yet been settled whether the General Will will choose any particular scheme for producing limitative benefits. But these goods may be wrongly or incompletely identified if the calculation of what is to be set aside goes astray. Rousseau's view is that the best chance of getting the calculation right lies in having everyone attempt the calculation and vote accordingly. Assembled to deliberate on the calculations, the citizens are to be asked, 'What is to the advantage of the State?'[33] I would rather ask, 'What is to the advantage of the political community?' One could also ask, 'What promotes the common interest or is for the Common Good?' However expressed, it is not a question to which the voters, either by majority or in unanimity, can return an infallible answer.[34] It is a question requiring an analysis at least as complicated as the one that I have been giving, and on all the points coming up in the analysis, any citizen, or all of them together, may be mistaken.

Yet Rousseau was not being blindly enthusiastic in holding, empirically, that the closer the voting results approach unanimity, the closer is the approach to expressing the General Will. By ruling out private 'communication' among the assembled voters, Rousseau does something to rule out coalitions, and with them a good deal of the instability to which the results of voting are ordinarily subject.[35] Furthermore, Condorcet's theorem about juries gives some formal support to the notion that on a cognitive issue a majority is more likely to be correct than a minority; and a larger majority, more than a smaller one.[36]

The argument for the theorem assumes that each participant has a probability of being correct greater than one-half. Can we count upon rank-and-file citizens to be experts to this modest degree on what issues properly come before the General Will and how they are to be decided? In respect to recognizing conflicts of interests and preferences, I think they are experts enough. At least in a society simple enough to open up no opportunities for elaborate swindles, they can recognize, with tolerable accuracy each speaking for herself, when they are liable to be victimized by the aggrandizement of another. Each can recognize with tolerable accuracy when a scheme for producing private goods does not promise substantial benefits for himself. Each can recognize with tolerable accuracy when a conflict with others in preferences among public goods has cropped up. (One way of bringing such conflicts to light would be to have a straw or trial vote before proceeding to a would-be definitive expression of the General Will.) On all these matters the people may be mistaken, even when they are sincerely trying to make the proper calculations and vote accordingly. By and large most of them may be expected to reach the right answers, setting aside the objects that the General Will cannot properly aim at, and identifying its proper objects as including at least the provision of a restricted subset of public goods and, as well, the conclusion that some scheme or other affording everyone substantial shares shall be adopted for producing private goods.

Moreover, most people may be expected to reach the right answers on the other issues that I have tentatively allowed may call for an expression of the General Will. There is a class of questions, generally lost sight of in epistemology, for which the fact that a majority opts for one answer rather than another forms part of the evidence that it is the correct one. 'Is our climate a comfortable one?' is one question in the class. It must be quite a heterogeneous class if it includes also the present questions. Yet arguably it does. I have already provided a model of how it does in the question about what respects it was reasonable for the citizens to take into account when they judged whether or not equal benefits from a given public good were to be ascribed to everyone. The view of a majority, if a majority took this view, that everyone was to be ascribed equal benefits from protecting property, because everyone had a life to protect and plans equally dependent on whatever amount of property they have, deserves some respect. For those are respectable reasons, which the majority may well regard as decisive.

If we draw upon Rousseau's conception of how people acquire, progressively, richer and richer notions of the Common Good, we can see how the reasons to which the majority give decisive weight might expand to resolve further questions. Even in a healthy community, we may suppose that it will take time for people to acquire such notions. It might take time for a majority of people with such notions to develop even after they had reached adulthood and begun playing their full part as citizens. But suppose that a majority of the citizens are brought up well enough to have a substantial attachment to every level of the Common Good. Then one might expect this majority to increase, though perhaps only gradually, as everyone felt more strongly the effects of correct decisions by the General Will in fostering more intense attachments on everyone's part to the Common Good in every aspect. Rousseau himself is thinking on these lines when he thinks of a people being prepared to exercise the General Will by sustained experience living under the laws laid down for them by a Lawgiver.[37]

One of the remaining issues tentatively allowed for was the issue about what level of production shall be fixed upon for any of the restricted set of public goods in respect to which it is held that people benefit equally. A criterion that the majority might regard as reasonable for fixing the level, given the nature of these goods, would be that the level should suffice to make the citizens feel comfortably secure. Are the police and fire departments large enough to meet this criterion? Are there enough administrators and judges and courts to uphold an effective system of legal protection? Every citizen is in a position to answer these questions in his own case. Those with a fully developed sense of common interest will take into account the feelings of others. Some others they will judge too anxious; some, too sanguine. Every citizen, moreover, is in a position to consider whether the provisions are ample enough to keep on creating feelings of security in the long run. The issue, insofar as it regards provisions for national defence, has since Rousseau's time become enormously complicated by technology.[38] But at least in a simpler world, with information of ordinary kinds about external threats, the estimates of a majority of citizens as to the adequacy of their armed forces would deserve some respect. They would not, as reasonable people attached to their common interests at every level, feel secure with a corporal's guard of untrained soldiers, if neighbouring states bristled with arms. On the other hand, if they themselves have pacific intentions, they would justifiably not consider it necessary to have every able-bodied man and woman continuously mobilized, while the neighbouring states ran down their forces.

The other issue tentatively allowed for was the issue about which scheme to choose in the range of schemes for producing private goods all of which, besides offering substantial benefits to everyone, meet some standard or other of distributive justice. Here, in the absence of arguments convincing everyone, or everyone imbued with a lively sense of the common interest, that one such standard is uniquely justified, the General Will may have to make an arbitrary choice within the range specified. Such a choice, however, even if arbitrary, resolves the difficulty that if a unique scheme is not fixed upon, no benefits from any scheme will be realized. Moreover, offsetting the arbitrary features of the choice will be the fact that arguments reasonable if not conclusive exist for being content with any scheme within the range. For example, a scheme calling for equality in meeting needs plus the Difference Principle for matters of preference only can be backed by such arguments from the writings of Rawls and others.[39] The General Will, adhering to such arguments, would have an appropriate foundation.

The private goods at issue in such schemes are other limitative benefits of the second kind, benefits that arise from goods that would not be present without agreement on some such scheme. But other limitative benefits of the first kind, where the goods are present regardless of such agreement, can be brought within the compass of the General Will on the same approach. A majority, seeking to have them distributed in the way that most fully accorded with the common interest, would distribute them under the same ultimate scheme, for example, making sure of equality in meeting needs first and then considering whether any incentive effects (in the production of other goods) called, under the Difference Principle, for an unequal distribution in dealing with matters of preference only.

Have I, in opening up some room for shifts of judgment respecting ultimate schemes of distributive justice, fallen into inconsistency with Rousseau's stipulation that the General Will is 'immutable'? We need not foist upon Rousseau the notion that the General Will gives the same answers regardless of circumstances. It would be immutable enough – no more immutable than is reasonable – if it gave the same answers in the same circumstances. It would also be immutable enough to make sense of Rousseau's stipulation if it was immutable in the end, though reached by successive approximations.

Generality of Laws

The General Will aims to achieve the Common Good by enacting general laws. This idea, so expressed, falls in more easily with some of the public goods ingredients of the Common Good than others, for example, a law prohibiting sexual intercourse even between people who have reached the age of consent, let it be fourteen, unless both parties give their unconstrained consent. What about a decision to build fire stations? But this too can be expressed as a general law: Fire stations shall be established in every built-up area, one for every three square miles. In the first case, there is a law that is itself a public good; in the second, the law calls for the production of a public good. This does not seem to matter.

What matters very much more, and something stressed by Rousseau, is that the laws shall be perfectly general: They shall not mention any citizen by name. Nor, by a ready elaboration of the idea, should they deal with any citizen by a definite description; similarly, for groups of citizens, set apart by their names or by their localities. We can also rule out subterfuges, like the one under which the New York State Legislature might pass a law applying to every city in the state with a population greater than five million, which is true only of New York City. I say we can rule out such subterfuges, but it is difficult and perhaps impossible, to find a formula that will operate to do so in all cases. Difficult, because inevitably, some laws will require some members of the population (all able-bodied men and women between the ages of eighteen and forty, say) to do things (serve in the armed forces) that it does not require of other members. Setting aside the use of proper names, perhaps every case will call for inspection to decide whether a discriminatory subterfuge is being used or a legitimate purpose is being served in which every member of the community has an interest (for example, defence from invasion).

However this may be, and however difficult to find the optimal formula, it is clear that what Rousseau means to do by his insistence on generality is protect individual members of the community against the tyranny of the majority, in particular, protect them against being compelled to make personal sacrifices not legitimated by general purposes. The idea is one that not only makes natural law theory more attractive, especially in the feature that expressly subordinates the good of the individual person to the good of the whole community. It is something that might be drawn upon in defence of utilitarianism. Bentham, after all, was as much concerned – literally, expressly, as much; perhaps, in fact, more concerned – with 'measures of government,' especially laws, as well as with the actions of persons; and it is by insisting on the generality of those measures that many invidious or gratuitous personal sacrifices are prevented.

The Laws in Rousseau's Scheme as Natural Laws

Generality assists us in seeing the laws legislated by the General Will as natural laws. It would be very anomalous to have natural laws, even the adaptations of natural laws most particularized regarding circumstances, aim at individual people by name or definite description. But is generality enough? Are there really natural laws prescribing a certain density of fire stations? If we invoke St Thomas's distinction between deduction and construction, I think we can see that there are. In all circumstances, human beings will find it a public good to have adequate security for their persons and their belongings against the danger of fire. It will be, moreover, a natural law that they should do their part in keeping up this security. But in some circumstances, when, for example, we have a dispersed population living in a climate with abundant rainfall, no more may be required of them than to control the fires on their hearths and to refrain from throwing firebrands about. In a dry climate, or during a drought, they may be required to turn out to fight brushfires around their villages. In other circumstances, with people living in towns, security against fire will demand further arrangements for cooperation, and these may include provisions for demolishing some houses in case of fire to create firebreaks protecting other buildings not yet ablaze. They may demand (as legislation since the Second World War has demanded in Japan) that the houses be built of relatively fireproof materials to begin with.

Sooner or later during the course of these developments, the advantages of establishing a public firefighting service will emerge. The people will not be comfortable with a level of security that dispenses with such a service; they will, accordingly, judge that the level is inadequate unless the service is established. Finally, we come to a law about the density of fire stations; and reasonable decisions about the minimum time for response, perhaps ten minutes, to bring firefighting equipment to any location in town. If no good argument can be produced for thinking this exceeds an optimum or falls short of it, the law about the density of fire stations is a construction on the basis of the basic natural law about having precautions against the danger of fire suited to the circumstances. (Again, if there is an argument specifying ten minutes as optimal, the law becomes a deduction from the basic law about precautions against fire.)

This is not to say (and here St Thomas's distinction, reported by Finnis, between the political common good and the common good realized elsewhere, for example, in families, might be cited) that all aspects of the Common Good are going to be legislated by the General Will of the body politic. There can no doubt be legislation protecting children against abuse; but it will not be useful to require parents to be actively kind. Hobbes, we shall be reminded in the next chapter, thought that there was a basic natural law requiring gratitude; but, again, that is a subject that legislation has too heavy a hand to address usefully. The natural laws on such matters will have to be represented by customs, under which people remind family members or neighbours, when reminders are called for, that certain conduct is abnormally cruel or ungrateful. Both St Thomas and Rousseau make an allowance for the role that custom can play in this connection (see, for example, *ST*, 1a2ae, Q.97, 3; and *Contrat*, Book II, Chapter 12).

Conflicts of Preference

The General Will, on the foregoing account, has already been given room to speak on the objects that it can speak to intelligibly – (perhaps, given the problematic features of some of the objects mentioned, more room than it can properly use). The space accorded it embraces most, perhaps, of the issues that come up in politics. Yet there is something left over: issues about public goods about which people's preferences conflict, because they prefer different mixes of the goods. What shall be done about these issues? There are several possibilities. They could be ignored; or, what comes to much the same thing except for constitutional protection, assigned to private spheres set aside from social choice. People could form 'clubs' to produce them. Another possibility, realized under most governments nowadays, is to make use of the taxing, subsidizing, and organizing powers of the state to produce a variety of public goods answering to the demands of different groups. Is there any way of rationalizing such a practice as falling among the objects properly aimed at by the General Will?

I think there is, though to avoid complications that would jeopardize the rationale, one may have to assume that this extension is limited to a small set of issues, with simple alternatives. For example, public subsidies for making music, including broadcasting music, might be allocated among a number of kinds of music, categorized according to some simple scheme, relative to the proportions of the population most attached to each category. The scheme might lump together aficionados of baroque trio sonatas with those who delight most in Rachmaninoff and leave it to one broadcasting service for classical music to range over this variety. According to a prior scheme of allocation, the subsidies going to all categories of music might be related to those going to sports, according to the relative proportions of music lovers and sports fans.

Leaving the various goods in question to be supplied to individual consumers in the market or as club goods may leave everyone with less of the goods that they most relish than would action through the state. If this is so (on the evidence), then the General Will, calling upon the state to produce them according to some fair scheme of allocation, like the one just described, advances everyone's interest in a non-limitative way.[40]

On the other hand, without flying in the face of this caution, it may be possible to form a firm majority for an allocation that skews the proportions in favour of goods of higher cultural aspiration. A majority might concur in doing this in order to discourage its professional elite from emigrating to other countries. Moreover, regardless of emigration, a majority, most of whom have other tastes, may be persuaded that the vitality of their society in the long run depends on having more robust provisions for high art and the higher learning than an allocation according to present tastes would warrant. The consideration is one, I fear, that is often abused by arguments that are specious even if successful. In principle, however, is not the long-run interest of the community one to which everyone; at least at the end of full moral development, can attach his own? The attachment is certainly something to be expected from the full development of the loyalties extolled by Rousseau. As such, the long-run interest of the community is a proper object of the General Will. If, for the time being, only a majority of the people are ready to endorse it, that may be because they have a fuller view of the Common Good. Their endorsement in this connection will be all the more impressive if it runs for most of them against their personal present tastes.

Reservations about My Interpretation

Whatever sense I have made of the General Will has been made without trying to show just how it is to operate in a complex modern society or even, in a simpler society, in conjunction with specific forms of government as Rousseau conceived of them.[41] Moreover, if I have succeeded in showing that the General Will need not be taken to be 'an ideal entity as indeterminate as it is absolute,'[42] and, so taken, to licence the sinister consequences that in some quarters it has been charged with, I by no means have offered to justify all the inferences to which Rousseau's doctrine has given some colour.

Most sinister of these have been the ventures of self-appointed prophets and tyrants to speak for the General Will before even a majority have come to agree on the policies at issue. There is too much of an opening for repression and terror in the idea of forcing people to be free. Misguided by the prophets or tyrants, or acting upon prejudices that prevent even an overwhelming majority from seeing what is truly for the Common Good, citizens sincerely seeking to express the General Will may go astray. They may break through the safeguard that requires laws to be truly general in spirit, not just in letter; and instead of distributing justly indispensable burdens, be creating various classes of victims. But even a benign, spontaneous development of consensus about the common interest, of the kind that I have sketched, might lead to heavy pressures upon dissenters in opinions and ways of life. Rousseau stands for *Gemeinschaft*, not for the cosmopolitan liberties of *Gesellschaft*. A healthy democracy must have some combination of the two.

Complexity at the Lofty Level of the Common Good

More needs to be said about the complexity of the Common Good when the commitments that correspond to it reach the 'lofty' level far transcending self-interest. Fully developed, at this level the features will include recognition on the part of members of the community that the community is a natural and necessary vehicle for producing public goods and meeting needs (including the needs for private goods produced and distributed under a settled framework itself a public good), and a concomitant understanding by everyone that everyone is committed to stick with the community even in times of trouble and exigency. Self-interest reflects forward in this recognition and understanding; but these things are social, not personal, in orientation. This orientation extends to everyone's understanding that life in a community with such mutual commitments is a necessary condition for personal happiness. The program given with human nature and the derived program for carrying on social life in a community imply that people will thrive in a way attractive to all of them only by drawing upon mutual commitments and expectations. (Already it becomes anomalous that through slavery or some other form of oppression there should be mixed with members of the community people on the scene who do not have a part in the mutual commitments and in the life-chances for personal thriving that they make available.)

Fully developed, the Common Good at the 'lofty' level will embrace a mutual concern by all members of the community that they all have enough in public goods and in private goods as well to meet their needs, and, indeed, not merely to do that, but thrive. There will also be mutual concern that the work done to supply these goods, both private and public, will be steady work under decent conditions. This concern, joined with the one mentioned just before, will lead to every member of the community recognizing that the community is a public good with the special character of serving as an instrument for fulfilling humane purposes (the humane purposes of the members) regarding the needs, work, and entitlements of all the members of the community as required. Both those helped at any given time and those who want the help given benefit from the existence of a public good with this charac-ter. In the full achievement of these features of the Common Good, the members of the community will have occasion to rejoice that they have laws and institutions that meet the needs and serve the purposes of their fellow-citizens along with their own. They will rejoice in the attachment that they and all the others feel for the Common Good; and they will rejoice in the virtue and happiness attained on the basis of that attachment. They will rejoice in living in a community that thrives by the members sharing commitment, attachment, and rejoicing.[43]

These are all, no doubt, very agreeable things. Though there may well be cautions to observe about not heightening the mutual commit-ments to the point of jeopardizing the personal liberties of the mem-bers of the community or to the point of overriding the needs of people for the moment outside the community first given, it is not to be expected that anyone will rise in disapproval. But how realistic is it to expect people to have the corresponding motivations?

The motivations certainly are not to be counted upon. However, Rousseau, to follow Keohane's interpretation of him, does show how the corresponding motivations — we may suppose, all the correspond-ing motivations — might develop from self-interest (or at least egocen-tricism) as a point of departure. Social practice, if carried on at all the levels described, would induce the motivations. This pattern of devel-opment, though very uncertain of success, will seem to many as realis-tic as the subject admits of, just by beginning in self-interest and egocentricism. But I think it is the reference to social practices that makes the pattern realistic. It is no doubt an exaggeration to say that rational self-interest comes about simply as a limitation of an orientation originally social and cooperative; but the social orientation is there, at the beginning of the development of persons, side by side with the egocentricism. As I shall try to show in the chapter to come on moral education, the problem is not transformation and redirection of an originally unqualified self-interest; the problem is to maintain and increase the weight on socially oriented (other-regarding) motivations.

Effectiveness of the Notion

Is the Common Good so conceived an effective notion, that is to say, does it enable us to determine at least some issues of social (and personal) policy? Many instances of its effectiveness have already been given. However, its full power to determine issues can be assessed only when the specificity of the rules that it may generate is assessed. Yet even without specifying any significant number of these, which will be done beginning with the next chapter, taking Hobbes's axiomatic system of the laws of nature as a point of departure, the conception in hand of the Common Good can be further vindicated. The interchangeability of this conception of the Common Good with the conception of the common interest forestalls attempts to identify it with the good of a state or a regime or a social class. Of course, in practice, it is liable to be more or less deliberately confused with one or another of these matters; but that is an abuse of the concept, and it is questionable whether it is any more liable to abuse than other general notions about the objectives of ethics and social policy. In accordance with the dimensions of attachment to it that I have elaborated, again following Rousseau, it answers, moreover, not just to the recognition of a common interest and cooperation in achieving it, but to a common interest and cooperation coloured by the mutual affection of the citizens.

States or regimes, even in a sense societies, can thrive without caring about the thriving of every member of the society. (Consider Japan in the Tokugawa years and the licence given samurai, including the practice of testing a new sword by beheading a chance passerby: *tameshi kiri.*) But this is not the sort of thriving implied by the Common Good as natural law theory understands it. Natural law theory is compatible with a class structure; but it endorses one only if it is a structure in which the lives and welfare of members of the lower classes are safeguarded with attentive humanity (as much as they can be). Shall we add, to a degree that other regimes or societies could not match, at least for the members of their lower classes? Is this to bring in Rawls's Difference Principle anachronistically? But the Difference Principle may just spell out a precise version of what was already, vaguely, always implicit in the natural law conception of the Common Good as the thriving of a society. Consider how naturally that vague principle may have led that traditional Christian thinker, R.H. Tawney, to the Difference Principle.[44]

This conception of the Common Good is effective enough, before specific rules are set forth, to denounce shortfalls in respect to the public goods that it embraces, for example, neglect of precautions against floods, the pollution of all the convenient sources of pure water, systematic attempts by the operators of pinball arcades to encourage children to absent themselves from schools. These are all actions against the Common Good, while the contrary actions are for it. Likewise, to have part of the population homeless and otherwise miserable while other parts have resources enough to indulge themselves in luxurious living is an offence against the Common Good.[45]

Appendix 3.1: The Common Good Underappreciated in Current Political Science

Contrary to the opinion of some leading political scientists, the concept of the Common Good can play an incisive part in the basic assessment of important recent political developments.

Samuel Huntington on the Supposed Conceptual Inadequacy of the Concept

In a recent book,[46] Samuel Huntington describes a turn toward democracy – a 'third wave' of democratization – in many countries in Latin America and elsewhere that laboured under authoritarian regimes, and in many cases suffered, worse, the violence of civil war. He deliberately takes, however, as many have done in premature despair, a procedural view of democracy, expressly setting aside the Common Good along with other values that democratic procedure has been supposed to promote, as a fuzzy notion, therefore best ignored when one adopts a working definition of democracy.

The Common Good is not to be dismissed as a fuzzy notion, either with respect to the structure into which multiple ingredients of the notion must be fitted or with respect to the determinacy of the individual ingredients. It may be a fuzzy notion at the margins – where we are not dealing – as I mean to be dealing here with central or paradigmatic aspects of the Common Good, like arrangements for meeting basic needs. It is not centrally fuzzy. Moreover, it would not make the definition of democracy fuzzy or uselessly idealistic to incorporate into it reference to the Common Good. It would make the definition more complex and more stringent. As a consequence, we might have far fewer cases of democracy or of democratization to rejoice in than Huntington presents, perhaps a third wave in which none appear. But that would be an observational fact established like any other, though more distressing than most.

In many or most of the cases that Huntington presents, the change to democratic procedure has led to advances in realizing the Common Good, for example, in reducing the number of people dealt with violently or held in prison, and so far in the perspective of the Common Good the changes are to be approved. Moreover, it is just because of the service that democratic procedure does for the Common Good, so far as that service goes, which includes offering peaceful solutions to problems that otherwise would be dealt with violently, that the procedure invites attachment.

Huntington makes a convincing argument that the change could not have been carried through in most of these cases or consolidated without compromises between the upholders of the supplanted regimes and their opponents. Extremists on either side who were not ready to compromise, for example, in accepting the received distribution of property, were shut out and had to be shut out. I do not think this was entirely a good thing, however, and Huntington himself gives us some licence to think it was not entirely a good thing when he declares, 'Democracy is a solution to the problem of tyranny, but not necessarily to anything else' (263). In some cases, perhaps in all, the compromises may have had the consequence that the democratic procedure brought in by the change is the procedure of a stalled, or de-moralized democracy – a democracy without morals, or at least without further moral objectives, in which important aspects of the Common Good will be forfeited indefinitely, perhaps forever. One factor that Huntington notes as favouring democratization is the proportionate increase within a country of the urban middle class as compared to 'the industrial working class. The potential threats democracy posed to middle-class groups thus decline ... and those groups [become] increasingly confident of their ability to advance their interests through electoral politics' (66–7). Electoral politics would not only not endanger their interests, say in property and profits; it would presumably also offer these people the advantage of greater safety from terrorist attacks upon themselves or from being caught in crossfires during counterinsurgency operations.

Consider a regime democratic in procedure in which 50 per cent of the electorate do very well for themselves in material goods. If only 70 per cent of the electorate vote, the 50 per cent can keep a succession of governments in power, which may peacefully turn over again and again, but which nevertheless one with another ignore the plight of the worst-off 30 per cent of the population: black or Hispanic perhaps, crowded into the central cities or in squatter areas surrounding the cities, demoralized in the usual sense of absent morale. They are citizens, too, but the privileged 50 per cent (convinced perhaps that the Common Good is too fuzzy a notion to bother with) feel no concern for them and no readiness to undertake a redistribution of resources (in education and employment projects, say) on the scale that would rescue them from their misery.

This is not necessarily a revolutionary situation. It may be a stagnant one: demoralization in both senses continuing indefinitely. Either way, Huntington would perhaps incline to treat it as a *systemic* problem, about the performance of democratic procedure once established, and put it outside the scope of his chosen subject, *transition* to democratic procedure. Huntington means the scope of this to go no further than to see whether the attachment to the procedure is consolidated, say, by continuing through two successive peaceful changes in elected governments. Huntington is not unreasonably rigid about this distinction, however, and he does put forward a hypothesis about the performance of democratic procedure that should increase our uneasiness about its stalling, perhaps because of the very terms on which the procedure is introduced, in a demoralized democracy. After distinguishing between 'performance legitimacy' and 'procedural legitimacy,' Huntington asserts that 'performance legitimacy plays a role in democratic regimes, but it is nowhere near as important as the role it plays in authoritarian regimes and it is secondary to procedural legitimacy' (258–9). This division of honours seems questionable on both sides. Furthermore, if performance legitimacy is secondary in democratic regimes (not only by definition – Huntington's definition – but by reference to the sentiments of the people affected), maybe that is so because people in the middle class have no special reason to be unhappy about the performance as it affects them.

We can hardly understand the significance of the current transitions if we do not take into account demoralized democracy and its failure to achieve the Common Good as a possible systemic fate. Some of the extremists caught up or set aside by the compromises that make the transition to democratic procedure feasible may, however crazy they were in other respects, have been reluctant to compromise because of attachment to a principle that may be taken to be an ingredient of the Common Good. I give it in a modified non-sexist form, 'From all according to their abilities, to all according to their needs.' This principle, in which Marx joins the *Acts of the Apostles*, captures the aspect of the Common Good, made explicit in the conception elaborated in the present chapter, in which mutual concern among the members of a community calls for mutual aid. It is determinate enough to reject some outcomes and some distributions of property and income. Will the reformers or revolutionaries who compromise it away in the course of democratization ever get a chance to put it into effect? The compromise instituting democratic procedure may in some cases have the consequence of putting such a principle forever out of reach, which associates with the transition to democracy a bitter dilemma. Either continue, hopelessly, with unconscionable violence or settle for a demoralized democracy *in perpetuo*.

The democracy that supervenes on the transition to democratic procedure will be a demoralized democracy unless there is (or unless there comes to be) an effective widespread attachment to principles ingredient to the Common Good; and the presence or absence of such attachment before, during, and after the transition to democratic procedure is as important for empirical political science to observe as it is for normative political theory to demand.

Robert A. Dahl on the Common Good as a Procedural Notion

The Common Good may be an effective notion. Is it too effective? If it has all this effective content – which will increase when specific rules are derived from it, does it leave any room for deliberation? Does it constrain deliberation on the Common Good in ways that threaten democracy? It is common among current writers (for example, John Dryzek and Robert Dahl)[47] on democratic politics to call for opening up everything for deliberation, short (for some theorists only) of having deliberation take place under certain constraints about procedure. Dahl apprehends that if there were a standard for the Common Good identifiable independently of democratic procedures, it might serve the claims of a political elite to make better choices of policy than the general public. It could furnish knowledge – an ingredient of the science of politics – that an elite, as Plato and the Bolsheviks have both held, would be in a better position to apply than the masses. If there is not such a standard, then it would be mere pretence for an elite to claim to know it better, or know better how to apply it, than the people left to themselves. Dahl might wish to say that this premiss alone will not enable anyone to conclude to democracy (see, for example his *Democracy and Its Critics*, hereafter *DIC*, 180). Nevertheless, it clears guardianship out of the way on a ground that in his overall argument Dahl himself makes much of (*DIC*, 31, 98). (It does so, of course, at the expense of begging the question as to whether there is an independent standard.) If we exclude the possibilities of anarchism and random choice, we have a dilemma to deal with: either someone else chooses for the people or the people choose for themselves. Scepticism about the Common Good undermines the case for an elite's choosing. It is not the only way of doing this, but it is neater and more trenchant than the alternatives.

Can we defend the Common Good, without falling into the hands of Plato or the Bolsheviks, as something identifiable as a matter of knowledge? Something that the people can be counted on to know and aim at in the Common Good, at least as well as the experts? Or something that whatever features of it need to be worked out in precise forms by experts, can sensibly be put to the people for discussion and ratification in every dimension? Then we shall not have to consider trading off, at the risk of oppression, some or all of the people's authority in order to have well-founded choices by the experts.

We have, following Rousseau, identified something of this sort, at least in simple cases, where citizens consider basic public goods and decide what are adequate levels of production of them. But if we are to stick with the Common Good so conceived, we must put aside one assumption that Dahl works with, namely, that the interests that it covers can be defined without further constraints as sets of preferences consistent person by person. With his criterion of enlightened understanding (*DIC*, 180), Dahl would demand that the preferences reflect the 'fullest attainable understanding' of 'the choices that people make in expressing the preferences'given their 'most relevant alternatives.' But logically (unless we follow Socrates and hold that people could not knowingly prefer anything to virtue) this leaves the range of preferences untouched. People with the fullest attainable understanding of what they want may stand by preferences destructive in implications to other people, even to themselves; and in some cases they do. Natural inclinations to do otherwise may have been weaker in them to begin with than in most people, or, weak or not, displaced by unfortunate experiences.

The Common Good that I have elaborated following Rousseau covers a great deal, having been built up in the course of elaboration to include elementary public provisions for peace, order, health, and safety, going on to having the other features of institutional infrastructure that make a productive use of the division of labour possible, ending up with some provisions for humane assistance and distributive justice. It is not, however, determinate about everything that figures in personal and social life. Beyond the provisions for the Common Good, a great variety of personal preferences may come into play, and insofar as they relate to issues about public policy the problems of social choice theory return, though they are not now so basic or so important. Let us continue to steer away from those problems.

Public provisions for health and safety are elements of the Common Good.

Can people oppose such provisions? Certainly: They may put their preferences, their profits, even their own health and safety, ahead of the Common Good, trying to ensure comfortable positions for themselves regardless of the danger to arrangements that would keep everybody at least afloat. But it is no injury to the conception of the Common Good that people may act against it; like its cousin, the public interest, by design the Common Good draws a contrast between what falls under it and what is opposed to it as alternative goals. Suppose public provisions for health and safety are elements of the Common Good. Can the people be counted on to make the best, or even just sensible choices respecting them? Here we must confront, with Dahl, the complexities of modern society, including the complexities of technology at issue in the production of public goods. It may seem that the people cannot be counted on to come even close, even if they strive with the best of good will to make enlightened choices. Will not the dangers to health and safety, as well as the remedies for them, be in some respects matters, inherently complex, and complicated further by considerations of risk and uncertainty, that only experts have the knowledge to assess? Furthermore, will there not be trade-offs between having remedies for one danger and having remedies for others, and will not people differ in the trade-offs that they call for, thus, bringing the problems of social choice theory back into the tent – not just the camel's nose, but the whole camel?

The trade-off problem can be wholly or at least in large part deferred by assuming that, in pursuing the Common Good, the people are working within a region in which minimum provisions will be made for all the dangers that they face; trade-offs will come up lexicographically only in dealing with whatever surplus of resources is left after the minimum provisions have been made. At least that is where trade-offs must finally be reckoned with; there may be trade-offs in design before the outlays in a final budget have to be considered.

However, does not setting aside and deferring the trade-off problem still leave the problem about discovering effective provisions? Are the people or the experts to say whether fluoridating the public water supply does more good than harm? Moreover, questions about dangers and remedies may well be more complicated, in matters of health and safety, than this example suggests; they may in some cases approach being as complicated as the question of how to keep everybody employed and productivity rising. Without conceding that we can rely on the advice of economists in this connection, I should concede, and do concede, that this is a question on which the people cannot be counted on to make sensible choices ahead of time; what they make of extended experience with any specific recommendations from economists is another matter. In parallel, I should concede, and do concede, that there are some questions about the Common Good in respect to public provisions for health and safety that the people cannot be counted on to decide sensibly. They may decide against fluoridation; or perhaps, if the mistake has now shifted sides, for it. That does not mean that the people have no sensible part to play on such issues, but it is a part that requires further argument, which I shall touch on at the end of this comment.

At this point, I am concerned to show simply that there are aspects of the Common Good that the people are perfectly competent to deal with even in large, complex, modern societies. To take two topics of concern in the news in recent years, the people can tell that to allow the percentage of the population not vaccinated against measles to rise substantially poses a danger to public health; the people can tell that reducing the number of emergency rooms when even the present number is overcrowded jeopardizes public health and safety. If there are observations to make to establish the facts in such cases, the observations are well within the competence of members of the public to make, whether they make them personally or not. To take another example: The people are perfectly competent to tell that to supply every man, woman, and child in the United States with a hand grenade or a flame-thrower would pose an intolerable danger to the Common Good.[48]

What lies behind Dahl's criterion of enlightened understanding is the quite reasonable expectation that when people see how, for example, their preferences for a free choice of hunting equipment or for personal safety relate to preferences for the casual distribution of live hand-grenades, if not of semi-automatic weapons, they will put personal safety first. But why, I might ask, should Dahl or we care, in theorizing about the justification of democracy, that things would probably turn out this way? Is it not because we hold that keeping people alive, whether or not this is a matter of consistent preferences, is a good thing? But this is the Common Good point of view: People have a common interest in health and safety that they might, insofar as it is just a matter of having consistent preferences, repudiate. We hope they will not; we do not expect they will. Public provisions for health and safety answer to these interests, whether or not this person or that chooses in accordance with them. Moreover, people can see that they answer to the same interests in the case of other people, and value having the interests of those others served along with their own. This does not commit them to paternalism; they may scruple not to interfere with other people's choices when those choices damage only the persons concerned, but still deplore the damage.

Sceptical as he is of there being any objective criterion for results answering to the Common Good (beyond some reference to enlightened self-interest, considered as enlightened personal preferences), Dahl is inclined to find the Common Good more in 'process' than in 'substance.' Going to an extreme with this inclination at one point (*DIC*, 182), Dahl says, 'It seems to me highly reasonable to argue that *no* [his emphasis] interests should be inviolable beyond those integral or essential to the democratic process.' In another passage (*DIC*, 167), Dahl relaxes this position to allow for two further categories of substantial good: 'Rights or goods ... external to the democratic process but necessary to it' (like some limit on inequalities in personal resources), and rights or goods 'external to the democratic process and not necessary to it,' yet implied, like the right to a fair trial, by the idea that people should in some respects be treated equally — the Idea of Intrinsic Equality, which Dahl looks upon (for instance, at *DIC* 85) as a crucial argument for having a democratic process. Neither of these categories fully allows for public provisions for health and safety: We could have people treated equally by simply omitting to provide vaccinations, emergency rooms, and regulations for the possession of weapons. I think that — again — Dahl has in the back of his mind a robust enough notion of at least some elements of the Common Good to find omissions like these painful, dare I say, objectively objectionable from a moral point of view. He makes some room for them in his last word on the Common Good (*DIC*, 307): 'Our Common Good, then — the good and interests we share with others — rarely consists of specific objects, activities, and relations; ordinarily it consists of the practices, arrangements, institutions, and processes that ... promote well-being of ourselves and others.'

We could consider public provisions for health and safety 'practices, arrangements, [or] institutions,' even as 'processes' that 'promote well-being,' though why they should not also rank as 'specific objects, activities, [or] relations' I do not know. They certainly are not rare; and along with other compelling aspects of the Common Good, they certainly form an important and urgent part of current public business or of what it would generally be agreed should be current public business. The Common Good on such questions is 'specific enough to provide guidance,' and its relevance is fully vindicated by such questions, even if 'some kinds of goods' and some 'specific cases' of policy choices escape it in accordance with the skeptical next-to-last word (*DIC*, 305)[49] that Dahl offers about the Common Good.

Whether or not the doubts about fixing the definition of the Common Good are linked to a need to accommodate a diversity of preferences in procedures of political choice, it may still seem that to fix the definition (beyond stipulating some points about procedures) does too much to constrain deliberation. Does it not remove from the discretion of citizens their right to determine the Common Good for themselves? But there is an ambiguity and confusion here. The Common Good is not something that I or any other theorist should impose on citizens who are democratically deliberating about the Common Good. But we can predict that if an ingredient in their deliberations consists in reasoning about human nature and circumstances, as natural law theorists do, they will draw similar conclusions about the general features of the Common Good. Thus, they determine what the Common Good is as they might agree in determining any other matter of knowledge, and they can no doubt be thought of as ratifying the Common Good so determined as a touchstone for choosing social policies. They can deliberate further, and at length, about what rules the Common Good entails and how the rules are to be applied to current affairs. In the course of deliberation, they will thus determine aspects of the structure of the Common Good sketched during its elaboration above following Rousseau, and this will make the concept effective on more issues. But it is already effective, determining at least some choices of social policy.

The question about the competence of the people in democratic deliberation to pass upon the recommendations of experts can also be firmly resolved in favour of the people. For the recommendations, however esoteric their generation, can be required to translate scientific knowledge into accounts of the impacts of alternative policies on matters that the public is competent to judge: for example, the issue about the warming of the atmosphere. It is true that the public cannot assess how likely the impacts are without putting some trust in the experts – without, in most cases, choosing which experts to put their trust in. But their position in this respect is no different from the position of anyone, however highly educated, not a doctor or lawyer herself, choosing between different sources and different statements of medical or legal advice.

Variation in Content of the Common Good between Societies

I have been deploying in my critique of Huntington and Dahl some features of a conception, elaborated earlier in the chapter, of the Common Good defined independently of procedures and transcending them. In effect I have been treating these features as fixed, not only in respect to procedures, but across societies. I should not leave the subject without conceding that the Common Good, even if it is defined independently of procedures, in practice varies in content (or at any rate in the attention given to different aspects of content) in a number of dimensions.

First, it varies in attachment and concurrently in the features to which attachment is directed. Some people may be interested only in the personal benefits that they derive from the public goods features of the Common Good. Even among these people, moreover, different people may be interested in different features – some may not care at all about having sports facilities; some may not care about having classical music broadcasts.

Second, there is to be expected a good deal of variation in which of the features (with corresponding attachments) that do transcend personal interests are pursued or recognized in different societies. Some may not get beyond recognizing the community as a vehicle for supplying public goods and calling for cooperative commitment on this basis. Many may not get to the point of rejoicing in mutual attachment and commitment, much less to the point of rejoicing in one another's rejoicing.

Third, even in those societies where all the features surveyed in this chapter (in particular, during the examination of the lofty level) have been substantially realized, there may be a good deal of variation in the technology supporting the achievement. Some societies may be very simple in respect to the supporting provisions and none the worse for that (they may be better adapted to the environment than societies with complex fossil-fuel cultures).

Fourth, given realization of all the features and the same technology (or ready technological possibilities), there may be variation among societies, as among persons, in tastes for forms of provision and for the values to be pursued once needs have been met. These dimensions and subdimensions open up room for a great deal of variation in the operative content of the Common Good in different societies. Incautiously treated, they foster the impression that the Common Good is infinitely variable and amounts to nothing more than a possible, but far from foreordained, convergence of preferences, something that could be brought about by deliberation under favourable procedures, nothing more. But variation in these dimensions does not imply infinite variability. The variation allowed for is quite consistent with the Common Good in every society having, among others, the features that I have invoked in this chapter. In every society, people need arrangements that enable them to consume provisions for their needs; in every society, they must have arrangements that restrict the use of deadly weapons. It is consistent, too, with the structure of the Common Good having many or most of the same features at the lofty level, whether or not people act upon them. They may not be ready to act upon them, even if they recognize the attractions of acting upon them.

Chapter Four

Hobbes Allied with St Thomas:
An Axiomatic System of Laws

Thomas Hobbes, with his unrelenting reliance on self-interest in the exposition of his ethical and political theory, and the licence that he gives for mayhem, murder, and cannibalism under the Right of Nature, may seem to be operating worlds apart from the perspective of natural law theory. Certainly, Hobbes is on these points very different in spirit from St Thomas. Leo Strauss, as we have seen,[1] holds that with other exponents of natural law in the seventeenth and eighteenth centuries Hobbes is radically different with respect to the content and application of natural law. Modern natural law in general, Strauss holds, is worlds apart from medieval natural law theory. J.B. Schneewind, a much more careful and lucid commentator, aligns himself with Strauss on this point, as we have also seen, though for different reasons, which are almost equally inadequate.[2] (I am delighted, however, to have Schneewind on the scene, contributing by his opposition to the dialectical interest of my project.)

In his careful discussion of Hobbes, Schneewind does not, however, pronounce one way or the other on whether Hobbes falls outside medieval law theory and into a modern school. Hobbes's picture of the state of nature, summed up in what must be the single most famous and striking statement in the history of English-speaking philosophy, about the life of man there being 'solitary, nasty, brutish, and short,' and worst of all, afflicted with 'continual fear,' has no precedent, so far as I know, in St Thomas's writings. However, Hobbes most certainly does not recommend the state of nature or the formally untrammeled liberty enjoyed there with the so-called Right of Nature. He recommends organized society; only there can life under the natural laws be carried on. This, as I shall argue, brings Hobbes back, respecting content and application, to the perspective of St Thomas. On the other hand, Norberto Bobbio's confident assimilation of Hobbes to the natural law tradition, though in the end correct, does not take sufficiently into account the difficulties of aligning Hobbes with previous natural law theorists.[3] Hobbes's reliance on self-interest and the licence given under the Right of Nature do set him apart; and the fact, which I shall explain in detail, that half of his system of natural laws has to be suppressed in order to assimilate him to other natural law theorists suggests that the project of assimilation is unpromising, perhaps even crazy.

Yet Hobbes does offer, in a truncated, but cogent and systematic form, what Locke calls 'the a posteriori argument' as proof of natural law. A community cannot thrive – it cannot even be a community – unless the people belonging to it have peace and order, public goods that are ingredients of the Common Good as elaborated above, and necessary conditions for the further public goods and the private goods that sustain 'commodious living.' To have those things the people must have a community organized, so far as organization is necessary, to maintain a set of moral rules: the natural laws – as Hobbes, in perfectly traditional terms, speaks of them. Setting aside questions of motivation to obey them, Hobbes's laws thus fall in with the conception of the Common Good that can be extracted from Rousseau and elaborated congenially to his views, a conception attributable also to Locke (who holds that we must preserve others as well as ourselves), and to Hume (for whom the chief of the natural virtues, and the origin of the moral dimension of the artificial virtues, is humanity), as well as to St Thomas.

Hobbes's Argument Setting Up His System of Natural Laws

The laws of nature that figure in *Leviathan* all fall into an axiomatic system that is deducible from the prohibition of behaving in ways destructive to one's life. The system set forth and the systematic argument that it embodies are important contributions to natural law theory, though Hobbes is rarely given credit for them. Moreover, Hobbes's system can serve here as a stage in collecting the natural laws that are accumulating, often in single examples (as one chapter of this book succeeds another), to fill in the corpus of laws that we can identify at least tentatively as the persisting core of natural law theory. Indeed, taking the laws reproduced from Hobbes's list together with the laws that I shall add working from St Thomas's enumeration of virtues, this chapter will serve as the main collecting point for laws of nature presented in the book.

Some of the laws in Hobbes's *Leviathan* list are laws that apply to people living together after peace has been established; only then is it possible for people to fully heed the laws without danger to themselves. Others – the Ninth and Tenth Laws, for example, 'Against Pride' and 'Against Arrogance' respectively – also apply (even in Hobbes's account of them) as conditions for establishing a society that is organized (under a Sovereign) to keep the peace under laws of the kind just described. This is true even more conspicuously of the First Law, calling for everyone to seek peace. Hence, not all the laws entirely fit Hobbes's thesis that the laws of nature that he enumerates cannot be obeyed in *foro externo*[4] outside of a society at peace under a Sovereign. At the very least, the thesis needs to be modified to allow for some public obedience during the transition to a properly organized society. 'Seeking peace' can cover both sorts of laws, though more felicitously perhaps only the latter, since we may think first when we hear of 'seeking peace' of people who do not have it. However, people who do have it, but who fear that it will break down can approach others 'seeking peace.'

'Seeking peace' is not the ultimate source of the deductions in Hobbes's system. At the end of his *Leviathan* list, as set forth in Chapters 14 and 15, Hobbes mentions as laws of nature laws that forbid 'things tending to the destruction of particular men (as drunkenness and all other parts of intemperance).' These can be deduced along with the others, which are concerned with 'dictating peace for a means of conservation of men in multitudes' and 'only concern the doctrine of civil society.' They are evidently not deduced from the prescription to seek peace, but rather from something like the statement at the beginning of Chapter 14 of *Leviathan* that 'a law of nature (*lex naturalis*) is a precept or general rule, found out by reason, by which a man is forbidden to do that which is destructive of his life or taketh away the means of preserving the same, and to omit that by which he thinketh it may be best preserved.'

Is this basic statement a definition or an axiom? Hobbes does not say. It can be read as either; and it is noteworthy that it takes rules to be prohibitions or reducible to such; being forbidden to omit an action reduces a prescription to do it to a prohibition.[5] Hobbes goes on to supply an argument leading from the statement in question to what he calls in *Leviathan* 'the First Law': 'To seek peace.' This justifies treating the basic statement as the fundamental axiom of a larger system, one department or division of which has to do with forbidding intemperance and other things 'tending to the destruction of particular men,' while the other division (Hobbes's concern here) has to do with 'the doctrine of civil society.' A crucial step in the argument is the deduction of 'a precept, or general rule of reason *that every man ought to endeavour peace, as far as he has hope of obtaining it, and when he cannot obtain it, that he may seek and use all helps and advantages of war'* (Hobbes's italics). The italicized statement, taken as a whole, can be regarded as an alternative formulation of the First Law, more compelling because with its two-branch structure it better fits the definition of a law of nature in the basic statement. In *Leviathan* it just precedes Hobbes's saying that the first branch is by itself the First Law, and treating the second branch as a licence to exercise the Right of Nature. Reading the alternative formulation as having two branches corresponding to the two branches of the basic statement, the second branch invites being read as a prescription (a prohibition of doing otherwise than exercise the Right of Nature, so far as the exercise is called for); and in this respect the alternative formulation corresponds to what Hobbes calls the First Law of Nature in *De Cive*.[6]

Then the division, our primary concern, like Hobbes's, that has to do with civil society, consists of a system of laws affirmed (under a certain condition) in one subdivision and in the other, parallel subdivision withdrawn (under the opposite condition). The affirmations are deduced from the First Law identified as the principle of seeking peace; or, in the alternative formulation, from the rule in the first clause of the conjunction. The withdrawals are deduced from the second clause of that conjunction, taking the clause as prescribing that the Right of Nature be resumed by anyone whose attempts at peace have been rebuffed. The rule combining the prescription to seek peace with the prescription (failing peace) to resume the Right of Nature is the ultimate principle in the division, though not, as I observed above, in the larger system. It is itself deduced from the basic statement, combined with an assumption, based for Hobbes on empirical grounds, that people are either in a condition where seeking (or keeping) peace is in order, or in a condition that demands a warlike posture. A diagram will help (see Figure 4.1).

How exactly does the argument in Division II go? It runs in Subdivision 1 from the basic statement about what laws of nature are to the

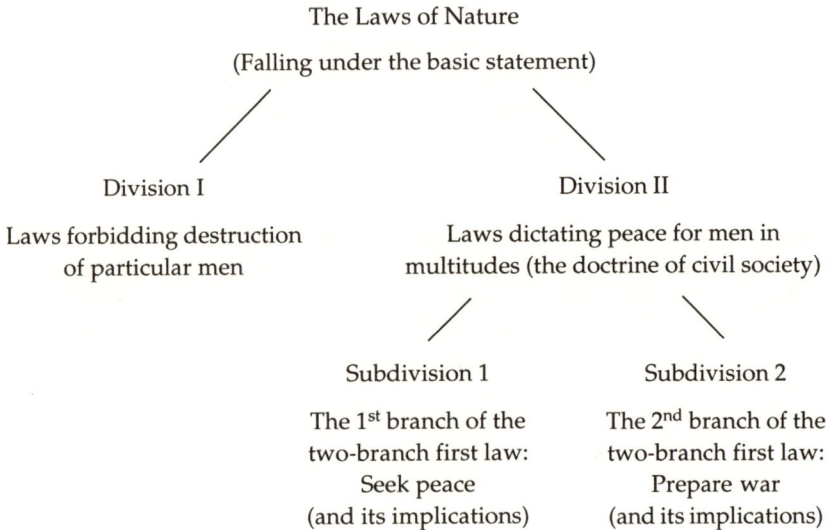

The Laws of Nature

(Falling under the basic statement)

Division I

Laws forbidding destruction
of particular men

Division II

Laws dictating peace for men in
multitudes (the doctrine of civil society)

Subdivision 1

The 1st branch of the
two-branch first law:
Seek peace
(and its implications)

Subdivision 2

The 2nd branch of the
two-branch first law:
Prepare war
(and its implications)

Figure 4.1.

first branch of the First Law of Nature in the alternative formulation, thus to what Hobbes in *Leviathan* calls the First Law, To seek peace. The later numbered laws derive turn by turn from this branch. The argument runs in Subdivision 2 from the basic statement to the second branch of the First Law of Nature in the alternative formulation, that is to say, 'Prepare war,' with further laws, the negative counterparts of the derived laws in Subdivision 1, to follow. The argument to both branches and beyond in their respective subdivisions is very simple, at least once it gets going, as a brief resort to symbolic logic emphatically brings out. Brief as it may be, however, the resort is not universally digestible; and to get going it does requires for felicitous expression very limited use on one point of the second-order and even of the third-order predicate calculus (or something equally récherché). So I relegate the symbolic logic to an appendix to this chapter; and here give in a natural language the argument the precise features of which in all its simplicity the logic helped me establish.

As set forth at the beginning of Hobbes's chapter 14, the argument goes by way of a reference to the Right of Nature. This is in the main superfluous for the deduction, though it is a reference formally required for the deduction of the Second Law, which is expressly about giving up the Right of Nature. Setting aside the Right of Nature, the argument to the First Law may be put as follows. (I am not suggesting that it, or even the revised form that will succeed it, is the only way of putting it.)

The basic statement, again, defines a Law of Nature as a general rule 'by which a man is forbidden to do that which is destructive of his life or taketh away the means of preserving the same, and to omit that by which he thinketh it may be preserved.' Hobbes holds that as a matter of fact every man finds himself in one or the other of two mutually exclusive personal situations or states. In one he has some hope of obtaining peace; in the other, this hope is not present. Suppose he does not know which. Then at least in the sense that he has not yet been disappointed in his endeavour to have peace he may be held to have hope of obtaining it; and he should seek to obtain it by overtures of his own to other people or by responding favourably to overtures by others. Moreover, he is forbidden to do anything else, since to do anything else, considering the dangers that other people pose for him, is destructive of his life. But if he is rebuffed in his overtures – if ignoring them or rejecting them, the people that he meets attack him or at any rate assume a warlike posture, then it will be destructive of his life (more destructive than seeking peace) not to assume a warlike posture himself; so he will. Moreover, not only are actions destructive of one's life all forbidden by laws of nature; the connection runs the other way – all laws of nature are prohibitions of actions destructive of one's life. I shall not, however, make any use of this reverse connection.

The argument to one branch of the First Law in the alternative formulation, thus, runs from the assumption that no rebuffing has occurred to being prohibited from adopting a warlike posture, that is to say, to being required to adopt a peaceful – irenic – one. The rest of Subdivision 1 follows (the natural laws to be found there will be spelled out, following Hobbes's catalogue, later in this chapter). The argument to the second branch runs from the assumption that rebuffing has occurred to being prohibited from adopting a peaceful posture, that is to say, to being required to adopt a warlike one. The rest of Subdivision 2 follows.

Both arguments invite, indeed, demand some elaboration. What does rebuffing amount to, and how does it have the effect of switching people from one to the other of two mutually exclusive states? What are the grounds for holding that the states are mutually exclusive? What are the grounds for holding that in the one a warlike posture is destructive of one's life, while in the other a peaceful posture is?

That the postures are mutually exclusive may be treated as a matter of definition – Hobbes's definition. It is not perhaps entirely plausible.[7] Are there not postures not especially belligerent, not emphatically irenic, which people might take up – neutral postures? However, Hobbes does paint a picture of the State of Nature as one in which people are always precariously poised on the point of being destroyed, and whether they choose peace or war can make only at best a hair's breadth escape. The situation is meant to be one in which everyone has reason to be alarmed about every other one's motives. I think Hobbes's grounds for holding that in the situations assumed one posture or the other is self-destructive and excludes the other are broadly empirical. That is to say, he holds from his observations of men that were such a situation to exist, everyone in it would suspect any other of warlike intentions, hence, of being in a warlike posture, unless there were as obvious a commitment to peacemaking as is humanly possible; and if they are wrong in ascribing such a commitment, they expose themselves to destruction. Once out of the State of Nature, of course, it is reasonably safe for people to adopt an irenic posture and keep peace under the laws of an organized society, with the other members of the society.

A.P. Martinich has pointed out to me that Hobbes would not in principle regard it as possible to arrive at a universally quantified proposition (one about 'everyone') from observation, and Hobbes would not accept any empirical proposition as a scientific one. In a science, Hobbes held, we encounter only definitions and propositions following from definitions. My reference to observation at this point is, thus, not in keeping with Hobbes's philosophy of science, unless it can be argued that the definitions in a science may themselves reflect observation, with the system as a whole standing or falling by fitting or failing to fit empirical evidence. That would make Hobbes a precursor of the model theoretic view of science.[8] However that may be, I am not here trying to represent Hobbes's philosophy of science, but simply to reflect in my representation of his philosophy of natural law the uncompromisingly unsentimental observation of men with which the text of *Leviathan* surrounds the arguments about natural law.

Whether the proposition about the incompatibility with seeking peace of retaining an unabridged Right of Nature, which is brought in for the deduction of the Second Law, is empirical or not requires a little further argument. It might be taken as a logical truth that retaining an unabridged Right of Nature is equivalent to x's being in a warlike posture. Hobbes offers what seems to be an a priori assertion that anyone in a warlike posture (when this is not prohibited) has an unabridged Right of Nature; and vice versa.[9] But the proposition could also be taken to be a sociopsychological truth: So long as any person x fails to renounce her unabridged Right of Nature, she will be in the view of others in a warlike posture; and since she has not made herself clear on the point of renunciation she will, in fact, be in such a posture. The second interpretation is subtler and more interesting by itself; it also brings the proof of the Second Law fully in line with the proofs of the other laws on the point of depending on an empirical proposition. But on either interpretation the Second Law follows from the proposition about the incompatibility with seeking peace of retaining an unabridged Right of Nature, taken together with the prescription to seek peace.

Elaboration of Hobbes's Argument

How will the First Law, given both clauses, both the branch that says 'seek peace' and the branch that says 'prepare war,' work out? There is no difficulty in seeing how any agents at issue will in the absence of recent rebuffs be prescribed to seek peace. But suppose they seek peace yet are rebuffed. If the other people that they seek to make peace with are rational agents and they themselves have made it clear that they desire peace, they will not be rebuffed. But the other people may be irrational; or they may be misinformed, either about what rationality requires, obedience to the first clause of the First Law, or about the intentions of those who are seeking peace with them. The intentions may not be transparent; or even sufficiently translucent.[10] However the rebuff comes about, with a rebuff what is prescribed immediately shifts to the warlike posture.

Is that the end of the endeavour at peace? Hobbes could hardly have intended so. The agents' dispositions to seek peace must reset sooner or later, preferably sooner. The condition of being rebuffed must be understood to give way in time to a condition of not being rebuffed; as a first approximation, not being rebuffed may be taken to mean that the person in question, x, has not been rebuffed recently (or has recently been offered peace by another). That time can be made more precise by stipulation: Let it be 'not been rebuffed within the last twenty-four hours.' But, furthermore, let the condition of being rebuffed and, hence, unready to make peace also reset to the condition of not being rebuffed as soon as any other person makes an overture to x seeking peace.

This will still make peace-seeking, and peace-keeping as well, too fragile. Failure to obtain peace from one person, or even a second and a third, should not bring x's endeavour to an end. In an organized society, under a Sovereign, there will still be an occasional renegade to encounter; and in an organized society the peaceful posture must be robust enough to persist notwithstanding. Let being rebuffed mean, among other things, that x has been continually rebuffed by people that he has met within a twenty-four-hour period with whom he has taken an initiative in seeking peace; and also that he has not encountered, either, anyone taking an initiative in overtures of peace to him. In an organized society, under a Sovereign, it will be so unlikely to have anything of the sort happen that it may seem hardly worth mentioning; but Hobbes's support for an organized society has precisely to do with this improbability.

On the other hand, getting to an organized society from a situation in which no such organization is present may seem very difficult, in spite of the provisions for resetting being rebuffed and giving up the warlike posture. In Hobbes's state of nature, people deeply distrust one another, with very good reason; and it will be all too likely that any given agent will find no one among the people that she encounters in a twenty-four-hour period who is both rational enough and trustful enough (given inevitably imperfect information about x's intentions) to respond cooperatively to her overtures or to make an overture of her own. Moreover, getting one overture or one cooperative response will not be enough; a string of them must be accumulated before any real prospect of an organized society emerges. There will be difficulties about putting together a string of positive responses; and difficulties about holding it together in the face of strings of negative responses. But Hobbes does not hold that it will be easy to get to an organized society through a sequence of mutual disarmament among individual agents, or even easy to get to the stage of contemplating a general social contract. Most organized societies, perhaps all that have yet occurred in the world, begin not with a contract, but with a conquest.[11] (Hobbes's purpose in the social contract argument, I hold, is to show that since a contract must issue in an absolute Sovereign, people will be no better off under it than they are under a conqueror or the successor of a conqueror [*Leviathan*, chapter 20, par. 3]; hence they should reconcile themselves to the latter condition, in which they find themselves anyway.) But conquest can be built into 'not being rebuffed' – let the offer of a conqueror to spare x's life so long as x covenants to serve him (*Leviathan*, chapter 20, par. 10) be counted as an overture endeavouring peace. Thus, finally, 'being rebuffed' is to be taken to mean that x has been rebuffed by everyone that she has encountered within a twenty-four-hour period, having sought to have peace with each of those that she has encountered, and that she has not during the twenty-four-hour period succeeding had any overtures for peace from other people, including the offer of a conqueror to accept submission under a covenant. Let 'being refuffed' continue for x a further twenty-four hours. She will not be rebuffed again because she will make no overtures. But, then, at the end of that twenty-four-hour period, x's posture will reset to 'not being rebuffed,' and x will seek peace; and the posture will reset earlier if x receives an overture for peace.

I have been treating the First Law (in either formulation) as applying in the transition from the state of nature to organized society. Indeed, unless it applies the transition will never get under way. Moreover, it must apply in more than the sense of applying *in foro interno*, if this is taken to mean just being not opposed to seeking peace if the opportunity offers: It must mean actually making or accepting peacemaking overtures.

The same is true of the Second Law, about laying down the Right of Nature at least in large part. Is this application *in foro externo*? It is not yet an application in a settled framework that gives mutual assurance of the laws being upheld; without that settled framework they are not yet, at least on the peacekeeping side, fully laws (except in the perspective of God's authority, and God does not require unqualified obedience until the framework is settled). Yet the overtures made or accepted initiate an external, public application, required by the first branch of the two-branch First Law in the way of ventures toward getting the laws fully established *in foro externo*. Does the first branch then apply as a law in the state of nature? Not by itself, since if the ventures fail, the second branch calls for falling back on the Right of Nature. But in what sense is even the two-branch First Law a law in the state of nature?

Here Hobbes offers the alternatives, a theorem or disposition, the disposition of a rational agent, on the one hand, on the other, a law prescribed by God.[12] Taking him at his word as a believer, Hobbes would want us to choose both. Intentionally conforming to the overall prescription of the two-branch law will make no difference to the behaviour of rational agents unless there is a chance to get the transition out of the state of nature under way; the prescription at most just endorses what people will do anyway to defend themselves. The two-branch law may, through its first branch, make a difference if the chance of getting the transition under way offers itself. Can it in this respect (and in respect to the coordination between the two branches) be understood as a law laying down a certain obligation even on a purely secular approach? But then where is the authority that makes it a law? One answer to this question will be drawn in the next chapter from Hume's double theory of natural and moral obligation; another answer will be drawn in the chapter next but one succeeding that one from Copp's theory of choice by a society. Neither answer is Hobbes's answer; but if we set God aside, Hobbes's theory of the origin of sovereignty, especially the origin by institution (a social contract of the multitude) converges with Copp's reliance on social choice; and at least Hume's natural obligation is present in Hobbes's thinking: having the first subdivision of laws in force and heeding them is in everyone's self-interest.

Hobbes says (*Leviathan*, chap. 26, par. 8), 'The law of nature and the civil law contain each other, and are of equal extent.' He also holds that the Sovereign alone, as the authority behind the civil law, is to interpret them (chap. 26, par. 20f.). But the Sovereign is absolute; no subject can question the justice of the Sovereign's decisions. Does this mean that the Sovereign can interpret the civil laws – and hence the natural laws – just as the Sovereign pleases? If so, what is left logically of Hobbes's advocacy of the natural laws? But I think readers should go no farther than finding a striking paradox here; for it is clear, from the care with which Hobbes sets them forth and argues for them, that Hobbes is strongly attached to the natural laws with the meaning that he ascribes to them. So we may wonder how this is to be reconciled with giving the Sovereign complete liberty of interpretation; and maybe there is no perfectly satisfactory answer to this.

The notion of liberty of interpretation demands some pondering. I used to object to postmodernists that the sweeping liberty of interpretation which they championed would licence someone's offering a recipe for chicken noodle soup as an interpretation of 'Macbeth.' But this is unfair: It is not by the meaning of the term an interpretation at all. No more would be a Sovereign male monarch's offering as an interpretation of the law 'against Pride,' 'that no man by deed, word, countenance, or gesture, declare hatred or contempt of another,' liberty for himself to seize any of his subjects' women who attract him. So absurd interpretations, and with them a lot of self-serving interpretations, can be ruled out.

Still, is there not a lot of room left within the field of genuine interpretations for insensitive rulings, which, for example, refuse to count racist epithets as 'declarations of hatred or contempt' and would, thus, undermine social peace? There is. I think the way to deal with this is to say that Hobbes, in making the Sovereign absolute, with no appeal in justice against decisions laid down by the Sovereign, was ready to take the risk that the Sovereign's job would not be done well in order to make sure that it would be done somehow, in which connection it is crucial that the Sovereign's authority be unquestioned; it is a risk that has to be run to have the natural laws put into force. Hobbes is making no concessions in respect to the content of the natural laws as he understands them.

Reduction of Hobbes's System to One Branch
Aligned with St Thomas's Theory

Whatever the difficulties that arise on Hobbes's approach for getting from the state of nature to an organized society, his theory on this topic at least has the merit of confronting the topic and taking the difficulties that arise seriously (even if, as it may be, not quite seriously enough).[13] The attention that St Thomas gives to the Garden of Eden[14] is not really to the point, any more than discussion of communities of saints would be.[15] The characterological effects of the Fall might lead to a picture like Hobbes's; and some later medieval writers did advance in this direction. St Thomas, however, assumes throughout the exposition of his theory that he is dealing with people as they are ordinarily found in the world, as members of organized communities. This is a reasonable enough assumption, and only to be expected from such things as his best-known (circular) definition of a law as an ordinance of reason aimed at the Common Good, adopted by the community or by an authority representing the community, and promulgated. Hobbes can be brought into alliance with the assumption. The first subdivision of the doctrine of civil society, which has to do with laws that are heeded *in foro externo* once there is a civil society, fits the assumption perfectly. Moreover, the vanishing probability that in an organized society people in peace-seeking postures will be steadily rebuffed implies that the second subdivision of the doctrine will seldom, if ever, come into play there – where St Thomas might expect to find natural law being heeded to some extent. The result is that the laws upheld by Hobbes as having current force fall in with laws that St Thomas would recognize as such, with a minimum amount of challenge from the prescriptions in the second branch regarding a warlike posture.

Another, more trenchant way of dealing with the second branch, when Hobbes's laws and system are brought under natural law theory as traditionally conceived, would be just to drop it. St Thomas and the others might endorse limited measures of self-defence by agents disappointed in peace-seeking, but they would never go along with Hobbes's broad prescription to 'seek and use all helps and advantages of war.' Does Hobbes really mean this? Surely, for agents that are to seek peace again, this unlimited violence might well be counterproductive, destroying any possibility of the trust that must be postulated if peace-seeking gestures are to meet with peace-seeking responses. This consideration may well lead to making more of the licence aspect of the second part of the First Law than of the prescription aspect. The licence aspect is still there; Hobbes says 'may seek and use all helps and advantages of war.' Yet St Thomas and the others would not accept it that this is even licensed. There may in practice be little difference between, on the one hand, an agent's having such a licence, using it with discretion so as to minimize the damage to the prospects of peace, and, on the other hand, an agent's taking reasonable measures of self-defence without having the licence; but the difference in principle and possibilities remains. It seems best, consolidating Hobbes's laws and system with the traditional theory, to reject the second branch and admit that the traditional theory makes no satisfactory provision for getting from a state of nature or war to organized society. The recurrence of breakdowns in organized society in places like Lebanon, Cambodia, Bosnia, Rwanda, Kossovo, Sierra Leone, and the nightmares of ferocity accompanying them signal the significance of this omission; but in this exposition I shall make the omission notwithstanding.

If the second subdivision of Hobbes's system of natural laws for 'men in multitudes' drops out, then one could reformulate his system as assuming the presence of civil society (as he himself approaches doing, in his nomenclature for the whole division). Then one could put not being rebuffed and rebuffed aside, and set the system up as implying the prohibition of all warlike postures as undermining the thriving of organized society. The basic statement would then have to do not with being destructive of a person x's life, but with being destructive of his chances of living and living well ('commodiously') in a thriving community where others were doing likewise. However, though this moves beyond Hobbes's thinking to a core natural law theory that more fully reflects the thinking of St Thomas, it still too much suggests self-interested motivation. Better substitute for Hobbes's basic statement something more radically different, where what is at stake is having a happy, thriving community, and where x is forbidden to do anything unfavourable to having this.

How much justification is left to the project of fitting Hobbes's system into the system of received natural law theory if one-half of Hobbes's system has to be discarded, along with its shocking implications as to what rational agents are to do if they must remain in the state of nature? A system that we have to cut in half to give it a chance of fitting in may well seem a very different system. Yet, the project of inclusion remains reasonable. At the very least, one might say, the contrast between the organized society branch of the system and the state of nature branch shows vividly what difference organized society may make to civilized life – to Hobbes's 'commodious living' – and traditional natural law theorists need not dissent from the position that the state of nature may be as dangerous as Hobbes thinks. It is hard to maintain, keeping just the twentieth-century evidence in view, that Hobbes exaggerates the dangers. Traditional natural law theorists concentrate on organized society. But so, in net effect, does Hobbes. The second subdivision of Hobbes's system for men in multitudes is except for the second clause of the First Law, only a shadow edifice, which Hobbes himself does not develop point by point. The first subdivision, which he does develop, consists of laws that could figure in the general corpus of natural law on the received view; and Hobbes is quite explicit about their holding in organized society, which the received view postulates. In the argument laid out above (paralleled in the symbolic representation in Appendix 4.2), Hobbes's thought was opened up to unfold the second subdivision alongside the first; but now we can fold it up again, coming back to the first subdivision and the footing in organized society that Hobbes's main line of thought shares with St Thomas. What follows from the first branch of the First Law, with its picture of the laws holding in organized society, not only gets Hobbes's concentrated attention: In the coordination of the two branches, the first takes precedence for him over the second. What, in effect, Hobbes most strongly urges rational agents to do, if they find themselves in the state of nature, is get out of it as soon as they can.

Hobbes's Catalogue of Natural Laws Inviting Additions and Another Spirit

Thus, Hobbes and the natural laws that he presents do belong in the company of St Thomas and traditional natural law theory. His laws (taking the second clause of the First Law as not operating) fit into the received corpus. However, they form only a subset of the whole corpus. Each in turn is deduced from the tendency of the actions prohibited to undermine peace, and this conflict would be a good enough basis for adding other laws, if the full attractions of peace and commodious living in a thriving society are taken to figure in the basis. However, self-interest is the sole foundation for Hobbes's conception of peace and the laws essential to peace. This foundation does not extend to conveying their full moral attractions as conceived by St Thomas and others.

Hobbes sets aside the laws of nature that do not belong to 'the doctrine of civil society'; and so shall I. I shall also set aside the Fourteenth Law, 'Of Primogeniture, and first seizing,' though I shall return to the topic of this law when I come to discussing Locke's and Hume's views of private property. It is more specialized than the natural laws belonging to the corpus indispensable for carrying on 'civil society.'

The language in which Hobbes formulates and discusses the individual laws belonging to this corpus (so far as he does) is generally consistent with a broader basis for deduction that would include the mutual attachment that in a variety of ways is present in the fuller conception of the Common Good to be found in Rousseau and certainly in St Thomas. But the language does not actually reflect mutual attachment; and the corpus does not extend to laws that could be deduced and added only by bringing mutual attachment into the Common Good.

In part, what has to be done is to infuse the whole enlarged corpus, Hobbes's set of laws plus the additions, with the spirit of the additions, not simply by way of specifying further, more generous provisions, but by way of bringing every part of each rule under mutual attachment – rather than thinking first of making sure of one's self-interest, and then doing something for other people beyond that. Locke, in the *Second Treatise* (par. 6) says, 'Every one, as he is *bound to preserve himself*, and not to quit his station wilfully, so by the like reason, when his own preservation comes not in competition, ought he, as much as he can, *to preserve the rest of mankind*' (Locke's italics).

This can be read as having the effect of enjoining us to preserve others only when the cost to us is negligible. But Locke can also be read, going some distance toward mutual attachment and thus toward illustrating the spirit called for here, as enjoining us to preserve others unless doing so seriously jeopardizes our own preservation.

In part, what has to be done with Hobbes's corpus of laws is to enlarge it literally. I shall turn to St Thomas's catalogue(s) of virtues for clues about what rules to add to Hobbes's corpus. This accords with Hobbes's own claim to have provided in his laws of nature for all the virtues rightly recognized as such;[16] though I do not believe this claim, in particular as regards the aspects of the virtues that call for a spirit transcending self-interest. On the other hand, Hobbes may have some rules and virtues in mind that St Thomas does not. I shall not be bound to reject any of Hobbes's rules because St Thomas does not allow for them. Some of Hobbes's laws, like the Seventh, which, holding that 'in Revenges men respect only the future good,' permits punishment only as deterrence, may be more enlightened (in detail) than St Thomas would be.[17] Others – the Fifth, 'Mutual accommodation, or complaisance'; the Ninth, 'Against Pride'; the Tenth, 'Against Arrogance'; the Eleventh, 'Equity'; and the Twelfth, 'Equal use of things common' – manifest a remarkable tendency to insist on treating people equally, both formally and materially. I do not attribute this tendency to St Thomas, but I would incorporate its results as a morally attractive revision of St Thomas's corpus.

The first subdivision laws relating to civil society listed and proved by Hobbes are nineteen in number. They fall into two subsets, one bearing directly upon people in their daily dealings with other people, the other bearing upon procedures for settling disputes. All of them can be deduced from the First Law (in either formulation) by invoking in each case a premiss according to which conduct contrary to the Law in question implies a warlike posture in a situation where this posture is not appropriate and is prohibited by the First Law. Formalizing the deduction in each case would no doubt force into the light some considerations explaining just why the conduct in question led to a warlike posture, but, even in Appendix 4.2 below giving formal expression to Hobbes's system, I shall omit for present purposes carrying the formalization that far.

I proceed to list Hobbes's laws. Inevitably this is a bit boring, but it serves the purpose of making this chapter the main collecting point in this book for the laws of nature spelled out as such.

In the first subset of the first subdivision laws relating to civil society are to be found:

1 The First (the Fundamental) Law of Nature, as so named in *Leviathan* ('To seek peace'):[18] 'That every man ought to endeavour peace, as far as he has hope of obtaining it'

2 The Second Law ('Contract in way of peace'): 'That a man be willing, when others are so too, as far-forth as for peace and defence of himself he shall think it necessary, to lay down this right to all things, and be contented with so much liberty against other men, as he would allow other men against himself'

3 The Third Law ('Justice'): 'That men perform their covenants made'

4 The Fourth Law ('Gratitude'): 'That a man which receiveth benefit from another of mere grace endeavour that he which giveth it have no reasonable cause to repent him of his good will'

5 The Fifth Law ('Mutual accommodation, or Complaisance'): 'That every man strive to accommodate himself to the rest'

6 The Sixth Law ('Facility to Pardon'): 'That upon caution of the future time, a man ought to pardon the offences past of them that, repenting, desire it'

7 The Seventh Law ('That in Revenges men respect only the future good'): 'That in revenges (that is, retribution of evil for evil) men look not at the greatness of the evil past, but the greatness of the good to follow'

8 The Eighth Law ('Against Contumely'): 'That no man by deed, word, countenance, or gesture, declare hatred or contempt of another'

9 The Ninth Law ('Against Pride'): 'That every man acknowledge [every] other for his equal by nature'

10 The Tenth Law ('Against Arrogance'): 'That at the entrance into conditions of peace, no man require to reserve to himself any right which he is not content should be reserved to every one of the rest'

12 The Twelfth Law ('Equal use of things Common'): 'That such things as cannot be divided be enjoyed in common, if it can be; and if the quantity of the thing permit, without stint; otherwise proportionably to the number of them that have right'

The Twelfth Law invites being assigned to the second subset, dealing with procedures for settling disputes, as well as to the first. Hobbes sets it forth as an immediate corollary of the Eleventh Law ('Equity'): 'If a man be trusted to judge between man and man, ... he deal equally between them.' That clearly belongs to laws dealing with procedures, though the virtue may manifest an approach and a spirit that affects a person's dealings with others generally.

Other laws that belong to the subset dealing with procedures are

13 The Thirteenth Law ('Of Lot'): 'That ["for things ... that can neither be divided nor enjoyed in common"] the entire right (or else, making the use alternate, the first possession) be determined by lot'
14 The Fourteenth Law, which I am setting aside ('Of Primogeniture, and first seizing'), which explains in part (the part that has to do with 'natural lottery') what the Thirteenth Law means in its reference to 'lot:' 'Those things which cannot be enjoyed in common, nor divided, ought to be adjudged to the first possessor; and in some cases to the first-born, as acquired by lot'
15 The Fifteenth Law ('Of Mediators'): 'That all men that mediate peace be allowed safe conduct'
16 The Sixteenth Law ('Of Submission to Arbitrement'): 'That they that are at controversy, submit their right to the judgment of an arbitrator'
17 The Seventeenth Law ('No man is his own Judge'): 'No man is a fit arbitrator in his own cause'
18 The Eighteenth Law ('No man to be Judge, that has in him a natural cause of Partiality'): 'No man in any cause ought to be received for arbitrator, to whom greater profit, or honour, or pleasure apparently ariseth out of the victory of one party, than of the other'
19 The Nineteenth Law ('Of Witnesses'): 'In a controversy of *fact* [Hobbes's emphasis] the judge (being to give no more credit to one than to the other, if there be no other arguments) must give credit to a third, or to a third or fourth; or more.'

To these may be added another Law that Hobbes gives in 'A Review and Conclusion' at the end of *Leviathan*: 'That every man is bound by nature, as much as in him lieth, to protect in war the authority by which he is himself protected in time of peace.'

Enlargement and Another Spirit Taken from St Thomas's Treatment of Virtues

Questions arise immediately about whether this is a complete system of natural laws and about whether it is a consistent one. Clearly, it is not complete. Turning to St Thomas to enlarge it, I am supposing that it is not even complete in the sense of implying all the laws that belong to a satisfactory corpus, much less complete in the sense of setting forth explicitly all the laws that belong to it. The latter sort of completeness will not be present even with the enlarged system; and it seems out of reach, for one thing, because we cannot anticipate the whole variety of circumstances in which the laws are to apply, the same consideration that makes each particular law subject to unanticipated circumstances, and hence (though not only for this reason), incompletely formulated. I defer treating the question of consistency, which is best thought of as the issue of whether the system is in a reasonable sense quandary-free, until later.

How do the laws and virtues in Hobbes's corpus match up with the laws implied by St Thomas's catalogue(s) of virtues? It certainly must not be taken for granted that the terms mean the same even when they appear in both lists. St Thomas treats religion (devout observance of religion), honouring one's parents, loyalty to one's country, due respect and service to others, obedience to authorities, responsible punishment, sincerity, friendliness, liberality, *epieikeia* (see below), and gratitude all as aspects of justice.[19] They are all aspects of justice, in his view, because they all have to do with others – God or other people – and with obligations, more or less substantial, owed others. Hobbes takes a very narrow view of justice ('that men perform their covenants made'), which corresponds directly at most to part (the promise-keeping part) of what St Thomas means by 'sincerity' and excludes the other aspects even when they have more claim than 'friendliness' or 'liberality' or even 'gratitude' to be counted under justice as we now conceive it. Hobbes does not consider religion a virtue falling under justice. He does not treat *epieikeia*, the virtue (traditionally translated as 'equity') of dealing with the letter of the law in a spirit of being willing to make reasonable exceptions to it, at all; and what he does treat as 'equity,' which corresponds to distributive justice in St Thomas, Hobbes expressly holds should not be called 'justice,' regardless of its traditional standing as such. 'Equity' falls out of the concept of justice for Hobbes, along with the specific provisions ('equal use of things common' and 'lot') for what we would call just distribution. So do the procedural laws like those having to do with no one being an arbitrator in his own cause and with impartiality in judges.

It is true that since the foundation of organized society is justice in the sense of keeping covenants, either the covenant of every member with every other in the social contract, or the covenant of every member (or his ancestor) singly with a conqueror, and these covenants establish the ultimate political authority, 'obedience to authorities' can be teased out of Hobbes's position on justice by argument. But so, with a somewhat more elaborate argument, can a number of other virtues and laws on St Thomas's list. Failures in according respect to others, in enforcing the laws with due penalties, and failures in gratitude, too, will undermine peace and order; and hence, undermine, at least jeopardize, the keeping of the social contract. Hobbes covers failures to accord respect pretty adequately in the Eighth and Ninth Laws, against contumely and against pride respectively; and gratitude is called for in the Fourth Law. Maybe even religion, as a virtue, can be embraced by justice, since failure to keep up the religious practices ordained by the Sovereign would threaten the Sovereign's provisions for peace.

Of all the aspects that St Thomas finds in justice, the most important to him (measuring importance by the length of treatment) is religion, taken as the virtue of living up to one's obligation to serve and honour God.[20] Religion is not present at all in Hobbes's catalogue, though someone who gives full credit to Hobbes's professed theological beliefs could easily argue for adding it. I shall not add it; and, seeking to arrive at a secular version of natural law, I shall only note in passing that, at least in what religion calls for as practice in this life, it goes well beyond anything that is surely to be deduced from preserving one's life. It may, for example, call for self-sacrifice in order to maintain the true religion against attacks on its arrangements for worship and proselytization. How religion goes beyond self-preservation can be seen fully, however, only by associating it with charity (*caritas*, *agape*, loving kindness), a virtue which has a footing outside justice.[21]

I shall not press to have the rules associated with the virtue of religion included either in Hobbes's corpus, enlarged by the sort of argument just described, or in the corpus combining Hobbes's set of laws with those that are to be added following St Thomas. A secular natural law cannot make anything of religion as a virtue. So I set religion aside, noting that its absence along with the absence of the theological dimension may weaken the grip of the natural laws. Learning to abide by the laws in the context of a religion, not just a religion found in books, but a religion practiced, with moving ceremonies – and exhortations during the ceremonies reflecting a grand narrative about human destiny – may be more effective for more people (though, notoriously, it has been very imperfectly effective) than any arrangement for inculcating ethics so far arrived at under purely secular auspices. Certainly, it is likely to be more effective than university instruction in noncognitivism or even university instruction in applied ethics.

What is to be made of St Thomas's 'friendliness' and 'liberality' as possible additions to Hobbes's corpus? (I shall not here or with the other virtues to be treated in the following passage spell out the rules associated with the virtues; I take for granted that for each virtue there is a rule requiring its regular practice. Hobbes says specifically that 'a just man ... is he that taketh all the care he can that his actions may be all just';[22] the regularity that will emerge from this care has parallels in the practice of all the other virtues.) Hobbes's Fifth Law calls for mutual accommodation, which is at least an approximation to 'friendliness,' and perhaps something more, since Thomas makes a rather cool virtue of 'friendliness': 'In their ordinary dealings with others, people ought to be agreeable both in word and in act, so that each one observes the decencies [the proprieties] towards his fellow men' (*ST*, 2a2ae, Q.114, 1). That does not sound like much more than Hobbes's mutual accommodation. In the next article, Thomas cites a wonderful remark of Aristotle's, 'No one can put up with [a] gloomy or disagreeable man all day long,' and comments, 'Thus a person is bound by a certain natural debt in decency to get along amicably with others, except when for good cause there is need to be purposefully harsh.' That does not sound like much more than mutual accommodation either, though it makes a point (which Hobbes does not mention, but might accept) about keeping up a cheerful demeanour.

With liberality (generosity) and *epieikeia*, St Thomas puts himself beyond Hobbes's catalogue (as he does, even more comprehensively, with charity). Nothing in Hobbes suggests approval for being generous with money or other favours, though Hobbes admires generosity as a (rare) source of honourable conduct; and nothing suggests treating this as a virtue. Generosity may not be a virtue as indispensable to living together as friendliness (*ST*, 2a2ae, Q.114, 2), and the obligation ('the debt' or *debetum* at stake) is tenuous ('indebtedness in a very minor sense,' *ST*, 2a2ae, Q.117, 5), so it borders on being one of the virtues not all acts of which people are bound to perform by law (human law, resting on natural law) (*ST*, 1a2ae, Q.96, 3). Nevertheless, St Thomas holds that generosity is an aspect of justice, and therefore generosity is to some extent a matter of natural law.

The two principal instances of Thomas's virtue of 'piety' – honouring one's parents and loyalty to one's country – may well go beyond anything that Hobbes has in mind with his catalogue. Would Hobbes ask for any attachment to one's country beyond obedience, so long as obedience pays? However, loyalty could be brought onto the Hobbesian scene, though doing so may raise a question about the sufficiency of the motivations that Hobbes explicitly calls upon for the support of the laws and virtues that he treats. One might argue that loyalty, taken as a disposition that gives grounds for trust by other members of the community that they will not be deserted by anyone for whom a value-optimizing opportunity arises elsewhere, does supply some essential support to maintaining the community and with it peace and order.

An argument in Hobbes's perspective for honouring one's parents would have to be more contrived. Suppose they have become old and feeble. If one chooses not to support them, does this place a burden on other people? If it did, it would undermine peace and the contract to let the old folks shift for themselves. But does it? Other people may not be moved by the plight of someone else's parents any more than by the plight of their own. All the fit and active members of the community might combine to send Grandpapa and Granny out to sea or up into the mountains.

Epieikeia, as T.C. O'Brien convincingly argues in an appendix to his translation of *ST*, 2a2ae, QQ.101–2,[23] is for St Thomas more than being ready to make exceptions to a law when exceptions are required to carry out its purpose. *Epieikeia* may lead to making such exceptions, but it is a special virtue, and a special virtue is not needed to make exceptions; reasonable administration of each law taken singly would suffice. *Epieikeia* is the virtue of approaching the law in a properly flexible spirit, the spirit of not applying the law literally and rigidly at the cost of inhumane consequences for the people affected.[24] Thomas's discussion under Q.120 follows Aristotle rather than Christian Scripture; but several points of Scripture are in play: for example, 'Sabbath was made for man; and not man for the Sabbath' and 'The letter killeth, but the spirit giveth life.'

In Hobbes's perspective, though Hobbes himself does nothing to suggest that he has considered the matter, *epieikeia* might be argued for as indispensable to administering the system of laws without defeating the whole purpose of having a system. Applying the laws too rigidly would create resentment, and the resentment would build up to the point of rebellion. This again opens up the possibility that, without *epieikeia* and other provisions that spring more directly from mutual attachment and a disposition to spare other people unnecessary suffering than from arguments about the interest that everyone has in the maintenance of the system of laws, Hobbes's laws of nature would not suffice to keep the peace, and thus they would not suffice for his own purposes.

Thomas takes charity to be the virtue of adhering to 'the two great commandments,' to love God and to love one's neighbour as oneself. The two are intimately connected in his mind: The love of God impels us to love our fellow creatures, and what we love in our neighbors is the nature that God in creating them has imparted to them (*ST*, 2a2ae, Q.25, 1). Thus, love based on the communication of happiness to us by God is charity (*ST*, 2a2ae, Q.23, 1). We love God as the cause of our happiness; and love our neighbours as receiving together with us a share of happiness from Him (*ST*, 2a2ae, Q.26, 2). Since charity is directed toward God in the first instance, rather than to life with other people under a rule of reason (*ST*, 2a2ae, Q.23, 6), it is a theological virtue, and as such we might wonder whether it is to be associated with natural law at all. However, for St Thomas, charity infuses all the virtues, including all the virtues associated directly with the rules of reason that make up the corpus of natural law. There is no true virtue that is not ordered to God as the final good (*ST*, 2a2ae, Q.23, 7). Thus, charity is not only the most excellent of virtues (*ST*, 2a2ae, Q.23, 6), superior even to mercy, which is the chief virtue among those that relate directly to our neighbours rather than to God (*ST*, 2a2ae, Q.30, 4). Charity also is the form of all the virtues, since it supplies the proper end for every act of each of them (*ST*, 2a2ae, Q.23, 8). It is designed precisely to bring every part of each of these rules at once into relation with God and under mutual attachment in relation to other people.

If we disengage the love of one's neighbour from the love of God, as a secular version of natural law will do, we do not have to leave behind the community of human beings in which they recognize each other as neighbours. Charity implies as a rule, to be joined to the laws of nature, treating every other human being as a member of a community of all human beings, and doing so with loving kindness. A secular version of natural law can invoke a modified charity, without theological implications, in this connection; and if it could not, the virtue of mercy, which clearly does belong in St Thomas's view to the non-theological virtues, would serve. Chief of the virtues that relate to our neighbors, 'mercy takes precedence of other virtues, for it belongs to mercy to be bountiful to others, and what is more, to succor others in their wants' (*ST*,

2a2ae, Q.30, 4). We are far from Hobbes's perspective and system here; but the way has been prepared by the virtues of *epieikeia* and liberality, which have to do with the spirit in which adherents are to administer the laws of nature. They are to be generous with money and favours and as well sensitive, from instance to instance, in applying the laws, to the possibility that the laws will need modification if justice is to be done in the circumstances to the people involved. Charity directs sensitivity to the human consequences of applying the laws and insists on making in every instance those consequences as painless as can be and as productive of good for the people affected.

It is to charity that we may look, in the spirit of St Thomas even if we are not following the letter of his doctrine, for the prevention and cure of dissension. He does say that discord is contrary to the operation of charity, which 'directs many hearts together to one thing, which is chiefly the Divine good, secondarily, the good of our neighbour' (*ST*, 2a2ae, Q.37, 1). Given charity, some dissension will not start up because charitable people will be loath to pick quarrels with their friends. They will indeed take a charitable view of others and the purposes of others, friends or not. Much dissension that does occur will quickly be cured by compromise, since charitable people will be ready to recognize the reasonable demands of others and eager to have their own wishes in these respects accommodated. Any dissension that does persist will raise alarms about the dangers of embittered conflict; charitable people will redouble their efforts to limit the quarreling and reach some form of peaceful solution, for example, a temporary working agreement that will allow for further reflection, invention, and a renewed attempt to reach a meeting of minds through public deliberation. (Here we have been slipping into modern usage, which does not correspond to St Thomas's: He does not seem to have a place for charity in the sense just canvassed of being ready to believe the best of other people. Nor would he reserve, as we do, 'merciful' to attribute a virtue to someone in power dealing with a convicted criminal or a subordinate or to someone who has been offended dealing with the person who has offended her.)[25]

I am setting aside any extended treatment of the issue about the consistency of Hobbes's system of natural laws, whether or not embellished by the additions that I have drawn from St Thomas. Were I to take up this topic, I would hope to show that the system, whether or not embellished, is quandary-free in the sense claimed by St Thomas, that is to say, in the sense of never leading agents who have done all that the laws require into a choice-situation in which they are *perplexus simpliciter*, that is to say, forbidden to choose any of the options open to them. They may be *perplexus secundum quid*. They may find themselves both obliged to keep a promise and obliged not to keep it (say, because it has turned out very dramatically not to be in the public interest). But then perhaps they should not have made the promise in the first place. Or if they did, if they made the promise in good faith and with due attention at the time to the probabilities of future events, reasonable administration of the laws in the system combined with *epieikeia* will set the promise aside. Thus, the test of being quandary-free does not turn entirely on the formal structure of the system, but on the provisions that come with it for reasonable administration.

Appendix 4.1: Minute Scholarship on Hobbes's First Law

Let us return to the problem of identifying the First Law in the face of several conflicting tendencies in Hobbes's texts. At the beginning of chapter XIV of *Leviathan*, Hobbes says,

(D$_1$) 'A LAW OF NATURE, (*Lex Naturalis*,) is a Precept, or general Rule, found out by Reason, by which a man is forbidden to do, that, which is destructive of his life, or taketh away the means of preserving the same; and to omit, that, by which he thinketh it may be best preserved.' This invites being interpreted, in congruity with the further development of Hobbes's argument, as having two parts, one that forbids adopting or continuing in a warlike posture, when this is destructive of one's life, a second that forbids omitting to adopt or continue in a warlike posture when self-preservation is judged to call for this.

He says further, (D$_r$) 'RIGHT, consisteth in liberty to do, or to forbeare; Whereas LAW, determineth, and bindeth to one of them: so that Law, and Right, differ as much, as Obligation, and Liberty; which in one and the same matter are inconsistent.'

He goes on to say, (L$_p$) 'It is a precept, or general rule of Reason, *That every man, ought to endeavour Peace, as farre as he has hope of obtaining it; and when he cannot obtain it, that he may seek, and use, all helps and advantages of Warre.*'

The first Law of Nature in the Latin *De Cive* (ed. H. Warrender, Oxford: Clarendon Press, 1983, 100) is given as: (L$_c$) '*quaerendam esse pacem ubi haberi potest; ubi non potest, quaerendam esse belli auxilia,*' which corresponds better to the definition (D$_1$) of a Law of Nature given in Leviathan than the version of the first Law of Nature, called such, given in the English *De Cive* (ed. H. Warrender,

Oxford: Clarendon Press, 1983, 53), namely (L$_c$') *'That Peace is to be sought after where it may be found; and where not, there to provide our selves for helps of War.'*

Neither L$_p$ nor L$_c$' explicitly and unambiguously repeats in both parts anything corresponding to the gerundive of the passive periphrastic conjugation *quaerendam* repeated in the two parts of the Latin version, explicitly giving the same imperative force to both parts. The English version in *De Cive* does not repeat the imperative 'is to be sought.' In *Leviathan*, L$_p$ shifts from 'ought to endeavour' (Peace) to 'may seek, and use' and so is even further away than the English version in *De Cive* from the definition D$_1$ given just preceding L$_p$.

Hobbes goes on in *Leviathan* to say of 'the first branch' of L$_p$ that it 'containeth the first, and Fundamental Law of Nature; which is, (L$_?$) *to seek Peace, and follow it.* However one identifies the parts contemplated in the definition D$_1$ of a Law of Nature, L$_?$ does not on the face of it have those parts. Hobbes says that the second branch of L$_p$ contains 'the summe of the Right of Nature; which is, *By all means we can, to defend our selves.*' This on the face of it excludes from the First Law of Nature, renamed, both the second part of the first law in the Latin *De Cive* and the second part of the first law in the English *De Cive* as well as the second part of L$_p$, given just beforehand in *Leviathan*, not named a Law of Nature, though it falls under the definition (D$_1$) thereof.

The second branch 'containeth' the 'summe of the Right of Nature.' Is it identical with the Right, given that it presents the Right only in the company of the qualification about not being able to obtain peace? One might say the qualification blocks identification. On the other hand, the qualification, it is true, is basic and holds throughout the State of Nature. In the perspective of Hobbes's general rules of reason, which themselves hold throughout the State of Nature at least in *foro interno*, one will not encounter the Right in the absence of the qualification.

Is the second branch of L$_p$ simply a qualified permission, as the chief verb of the second branch, 'may,' suggests? But then L$_p$ as a whole would not be the sort of general rule of reason that would answer to the definition (D$_1$) of a Law of Nature. For according to that definition, a Law of Nature has two parts, each a prohibition, first of doing that which 'is destructive of [the agent's] life,' second of omitting to do, that by which the agent 'thinketh it may be best preserved.' Of the several formulas that Hobbes offers, the formula for the First Law given in the Latin version of *De Cive*, namely, L$_c$, answers best to the definition D$_1$ of the law of nature, and even improves on it slightly by repeating what we can regard as the imperative operator *quaerendam*. However, the formula in the English version of De Cive, L$_c$', comes close to D$_1$ if we take the imperative force of 'to be sought' in the first branch as carrying over to the second branch, as the imperative force of 'forbidden' carries over in the definition of the Law of Nature D_l from 'to do' in the first branch to 'to omit' in the second.

It would be a fallacy, something like a fallacy of 'conversational implicature,' to use Grice's terminology,[26] to substitute a permission, not so informative as a prescription on the same topic, even a permission qualified in the ways given, for a prescription. We are prescribed to seek peace; and prescribed, if we cannot obtain peace, to use the Right of Nature. It is true that the extent of the use is to be at the agent's discretion; and in a given instance he may not choose to be active in using it, at least for the time being. This discretion may account for Hobbes's use of 'may' in L_p. There is a little puzzle about having with the Right discretion to do or forbear and yet being forbidden to forbear (whenever it helps to use the Right actively). So, if there are two sides to every Right by definition, as Hobbes wants to insist, one side may be taken away, which he somehow overlooked.[27]

The little puzzle may help account for Hobbes's placing in the *Leviathan* the second branch outside what he there calls 'the first, and Fundamental Law of Nature.' There are other advantages to Hobbes in doing this: It is difficult to accept it that a benevolent God prescribes the unrestrained use of the Right of Nature in any circumstances; and equally anomalous to suppose that the authority which makes laws of the general rules of reason could in this case be the Sovereign, even invoked proleptically. For what is the Sovereign, with whom the State of Nature is superseded, doing laying down prescriptions for actions in the State of Nature? Nevertheless, imperative force bears as much on the Right of Nature in the second branch of the alternative formulation L_p as it does on the second branch of D_l; or, logically, it must so do if L_p is to be a general rule of reason of the sort that fits D_l.

A complication in matching the other formulas to the definition D_l of a Law of Nature lies in the fact that the formula of the definition does not on strict examination fall neatly into two parts, for two reasons. The phrase, 'or taketh away the means of preserving the same' (that is, one's life), is given under what the agent is forbidden to do; and there it may include on occasion refusing an offer of peace as an example of taking away the means of preservation. However, we might also think of the phrase as belonging under what the agent is forbidden to omit; on occasion, the means of preservation would be accepting an offer of peace. Suppose we put the phrase aside when we divide the formula of D_l into two parts, one concerning what the agent is forbidden to do, the other what he is forbidden to omit. (We can bring back the phrase twice over as a supplement to both the branches so obtained.) We could then read D_l, in line with the other two-part formulas, as having to do with a prescription to seek peace in the first part and with a qualified prescription to make use to the extent that one deems discreet of the Right of Nature in the second part. If we then choose to ignore Hobbes's own decision to identify the first branch of L_p only as the First Law, we have strong backing in the alignment of all the formulas with the definition D_l of a Law of Nature. We can identify L_p taken in both its branches and properly understood as aligned upon D_l and best modelled by L_c (the Latin formula) as the First Law of Nature.

There is, however, a further complication to be noted, a second reason standing in the way of dividing the formula of D_l neatly into two parts. Even if we set aside the phrase that can be assigned to either part, the intertranslatibility of prohibitions with prescriptions makes it impossible on the basis of the language alone to divide D_l unambiguously into a first part having to do with seeking peace and a second part having to do with using the Right of Nature if peace is not obtained. For, we can equally well say, first, it is forbidden to omit to renounce one's arms, when that takes away one's means of self-defence, just because that is destructive of one's life; and second, it is forbidden to omit to seek peace, when one thinks that so one's life may be best preserved. In other words, both parts (both the 'to do' part and the 'to omit' part) of D_l can be read as containing the two parts that figure in the other formulas.

Nevertheless, it is clear that Hobbes himself treats D_l as generating, in combination with assumptions spelled out in my language about not being rebuffed in seeking peace and being rebuffed, a First Law variously formulated as two distinct parts. (The formal expression in Appendix 4.2 following of Hobbes's system makes this clear.) The formulas L_c, $L_{c'}$, and L_p, all of which Hobbes gives as general rules of reason illustrating D_l as the definition of a Law of Nature, though anomalously he does not call L_p a Law of Nature, all clearly have two parts (L_c, which I take as the paradigm, most clearly). They all have two successive prescriptions where D_l has two successive prohibitions. Hobbes made too little of the intertranslatibility, we might say, when we go back from the prescriptions in the formulas to the prohibitions in the D_l definition. But the formulas do divide neatly. In effect in the move from the definition to the formulas Hobbes makes up his mind exactly what he wants to prohibit in one branch as against the other. So we can look upon the move as one in which Hobbes clarifies D_l and removes the ambiguity there.

Appendix 4.2: Hobbes's Axiomatic System Formally Expressed

Let us concentrate in formal expression upon Division II of Hobbes's doctrine, where the principle governing the natural laws of civil society is the two-branch First Law in the alternative formulation, *that every man ought to endeavour peace, as far as he has hope of obtaining it, and when he cannot obtain it, that he may seek and use all helps and advantages of war.* That two-branch law is reached by deduction from the basic statement about what a law of nature is, and this basic statement I symbolize in the following formula.

$$(\psi)(x)[C(\psi(x), Dx) \rightarrow F_1(\psi(x))]. \tag{1}$$

Here F_1 is an operator that combines with descriptions of states ascribed to persons to express prohibitions. We can read it 'Forbids as a matter of natural law' without prejudice to reformulating it as occasion might demand to exhibit the three features of a law (the **volk**, **wenn**, and **nono**) that I have in mind for full explicitness. ψ is a second-order variable ranging over descriptions of such states, while x is a variable ranging over persons. Dx is a propositional function that describes x as being in a state, D, brought about by himself, that is destructive of his life. C is a third-order predicate constant referring to something like a causal relation between x's being in ψ and x's thus being in a state destructive of his own life. Moving from the formula to (logical) English, we therefore get, 'For all predicates ψ and all persons x, if x's being in a state ψ brought about by himself is thus also in a state destructive of his life, then he is forbidden as a matter of natural law to be in such a state ψ.'

In my own first attempt to formulate (1), I fell into the trap set by the paradox of material implication, by giving a condition in the formula that itself took a conditional form. Knowing about the paradox is not enough to save one from the trap, and it turns out that it is not easy to escape the paradox without unduly complicating the formula and misrepresenting what I believe to be the intuitive simplicity of Hobbes's argument. In attempts to rescue me, Robert Causey has suggested a number of alternative formulations, one of them closely corresponding to my own sobered and revised thought of resorting to set theory:

$$(\psi)(x)(\psi \in \mathbf{D} \leftrightarrow F_1(\psi x)),$$

where **D** is the set of all states in which by his own doing a person x finds himself and which are destructive of his life. That turns out to be awkward for me to work with. Causey himself favours an approach that by-passes the second-order predicate calculus and relies on an axiom schema, $(x)((\psi(x) \rightarrow Dx) \rightarrow F_1[\psi(x)])$. Causey develops a formalized argument very elegantly on this basis, but the formalization is more complex than I myself could pretend to offer. (I have, however, sought his permission to reproduce it as a third appendix to this chapter: see below.) His discussion there brings out in a searching way the difficulty of escaping the paradox of material implication, which to me suggests, as others, too, have thought, that there is something wrong with material implication as a representation of the ordinary 'if-then' relation.) In (1) as it figures here I have taken up another of Causey's suggestions, which he brought forward in a renewed round of discussion, and which I have found easy to work with and which indeed lets most of the arguments as I originally formulated them stand.

We need two more symbols, and a couple of definitions, to proceed with the deduction from the basic statement (1). Wx means that x is adopting or persisting in a warlike posture. Ix (I for 'irenic') means that x is seeking peace, that is, adopting a posture in which x either seeks to escape from war to peace or seeks to maintain peace that has already been established. Finally, let $F_I(\psi i(x)) = M_I (\sim\psi(x))$ (M for '**muss**' – 'must' by definition. That is just a formality: $\sim$ is the symbol for 'not' and the prohibition of $\psi(x)$ can be rendered as the prescription of not-$\psi(x)$. More problematic is setting $Wx = \sim Ix$ by definition; for it is implausible to a degree that there should be no middle state in which people are neither visibly warlike nor visibly irenic. Yet, as I argue in the text of the chapter, the definition is faithful to Hobbes's thinking. Finally, in the formulation of the argument to (and within) Subdivision 1 we must not leave out of account Hobbes's intention that the prescription 'Seek Peace' [$M_I(Ix)$] is conditional on not being rebuffed. Let Rx mean 'x has been rebuffed,' a notion with all the complications and invitations to stipulation presented in the main text of the chapter.

Proceeding from (1), again,

$$(\psi)(x)[C(\psi(x), Dx) \rightarrow F_I (\psi(x))],$$

the argument in the first subdivision of the doctrine of civil society runs

$(x)[\sim Rx \rightarrow C(Wx, Dx)]$	(from observation)	(2)
$(x)[\sim Rx \rightarrow F_I(Wx)]$	(from 2 and 1)	(3)
$(x)[\sim Rx \rightarrow M_I(\sim Wx)]$	(from 3 and definition)	(4)
$(x)[\sim Rx \rightarrow M_I(Ix)]$	(from 4 and definition).	(5)

The other laws of nature that Hobbes gives, all in the first subdivision, now follow from invoking (5), in each case, together with an empirical proposition about the tendency of the conduct prohibited to undermine Ix, the seeking of peace. (5) is the first clause ('Seek Peace') of the First Law in the alternative formulation, with the clause reformulated to coordinate it as Hobbes intends with the second clause.

The revised argument in the second subdivision, which prescribes what to do when x has been rebuffed in his endeavour at peace, runs from (1) to

$$(x)[Rx \rightarrow C(\sim Wx, Dx)] \qquad \text{(from observation)} \qquad (2')$$

$$(x)[Rx \rightarrow F_1(\sim Wx)] \qquad \text{(from 2' and 1)} \qquad (3')$$

$$(x)[Rx \rightarrow M_1(Wx)] \qquad \text{(from 3' and definition).} \qquad (4')$$

(4') is the second clause ('Prepare War') of the First Law in the alternative formulation, with the clause reformulated to coordinate it as Hobbes intends with the first clause.

If the second branch of Hobbes's system of natural laws for 'men in multitudes' drops out, as it does when Hobbes describes how the laws underpin civil society, then there is no need to have the no-rebuffing assumption $\sim Rx$ coordinated with the rebuffing assumption Rx. One can put both assumptions aside and set the system up as implying the prohibition of all warlike postures because they undermine the thriving of organized society. Dx could now be interpreted not as meaning 'destructive of x's life,' but as destructive of his chances of living and living well ('commodiously') in a thriving community where others were doing likewise. However, moving beyond Hobbes's thinking to a core natural law theory that fully reflects the thinking of St Thomas, this still too much suggests a self-interested motivation for x; it would be better to substitute for Dx a proposition about the community, let us say $\sim H$, meaning 'The community will not be a happy, thriving one.' Then the basic statement (1) will look like this:

$$(\psi)(x)[C(\psi(x), \sim H) \rightarrow F_1(\psi(x))]. \qquad (1')$$

The second premiss in the argument to the first law (now, without further qualification, the first half only) might now become $(x)(Sx \rightarrow C(Wx, \sim H)$, where Sx means x is a member of an established community with a chance of thriving.

Appendix 4.3: Complications in the Formalization of Hobbes on 'Seeking Peace'
by Robert L. Causey

Braybrooke presents a formal reconstruction of some of Hobbes's arguments regarding war and peace. He and I discussed several possible formalizations before settling on the one presented in this chapter. This appendix explains some of the considerations which led to the final formalization.

The starting point of any formalization requires a formula that represents Hobbes's basic statement about what a natural law, a *lex naturalis*, is (given early in this chapter). The formula used in this chapter is (1), in which C represents some kind of causal relationship. None of the earlier formalizations used such a third-order predicate constant. Instead, they employed a subformula which was a conditional. I shall not review all of these earlier formulations, since their salient features can be represented by a couple of examples.

All of Braybrooke's formalizations have used a second-order quantifier. In (1) that quantifier is (ψ), where ψ is a second-order variable. To the extent possible, I have tried to avoid second-order variables. Thus, the present discussion begins with standard first-order predicate calculus augmented with two inter-definable deontic operators. Suppose that we have a suitable non-logical vocabulary *VOC* of basic predicates that is used to define all of the relevant predicates about persons and their states. Let $\psi(x)$ represent any *predicate*, with only the variable x occurring free, that can be expressed in terms of this basic vocabulary, and which is a predicate for a state of a person (a 'person state description'). Let F_1 and M_1 be deontic operators with the following interpretation: If ψ is any predicate denoting a state of a person x, then

$F_1[\psi(x)]$ means that $\psi(x)$ is forbidden as a matter of natural law,

and

$M_1[\psi(x)]$ means that $\psi(x)$ is prescribed (obligatory) as a matter of natural law.

Now let Dx be a specific predicate that has the intended interpretation: 'x is a person who is in a state D, brought about by himself, that is destructive of his life.' Let Wx be a specific predicate interpreted as 'person x is adopting or persisting in a warlike posture.' Let Ix mean: 'person x is seeking peace, i.e., adopting a posture in which x either seeks to escape from war to peace or seeks to maintain existing peace.' Let Rx mean: 'person x has recently been rebuffed in his endeavor at peace.' We assume the next two statements to be *definitional equivalences*. For any person state description $\psi(x)$, with the one free variable x,

$(x)(Wx \leftrightarrow \sim Ix)$, (Def1)

$(x)(F_1[\psi(x)] \leftrightarrow M_1[\sim\psi(x)])$. (Def2)

Since (Def1) and (Def2) assert definitional equivalences, they shall be used to justify substitutions based on the equivalences they state. Moreover, since F_1

and M_l are interdefinable, our logical language can be considered to use only one primitive deontic operator.

Let us now consider one of the previous derivations offered by Braybrooke. He formulated Hobbes's basic statement using second-order quantification over person state descriptions, $(P)(x)((Px \rightarrow Dx) \rightarrow F_l[Px])$, in which P ranges over those state descriptions. I changed this earlier formulation to

$$(x)((\psi(x) \rightarrow Dx) \rightarrow F_l[\psi(x)]). \tag{Ax1}$$

(Ax1) is an *axiom schema*, which is to be used as follows: Any instance of (Ax1) is an axiom, where an instance of (Ax1) is obtained by substituting for $\psi(x)$ in (Ax1) any well-formed expression with one free variable x, which is formulated in first-order predicate calculus using only predicates in the *VOC*. Of course, (Def2) is also a schema. Note that the manner in which (Ax1) is used prohibits the deontic operators from occurring in $\psi(x)$. This restriction on the form of allowable $\psi(x)$ expressions seems reasonable, given the historical context of Hobbes's argument. Moreover, my formulation of (Ax1) was intended to be a reconstruction of Braybrooke's earlier formulation which used the second-order quantifier. Presumably, the second-order variable P ranges over 'natural' properties of persons including, for example, psychological states and various kinds of actions. But there seems to be no reason why P should also range over properties with deontic components.

Following Braybrooke's earlier formulation, we now also state assumption

$$(x)(\sim Rx \rightarrow (Wx \rightarrow Dx)), \tag{Ax2}$$

which is based on 'observation' and supposed to have a status something like that of a scientific law. For now, we simply treat it as an axiom of a formal theory. By taking $\psi(x)$ to be Wx, we obtain this instance of (Ax1),

$$(x)((Wx \rightarrow Dx) \rightarrow F_l[Wx]) \tag{C1}$$

Let a be any individual constant of predicate calculus. We instantiate (C1) and (Ax2) with a, and then apply sentential calculus to obtain,

$$\sim Ra \rightarrow F_l[Wa]. \tag{C2}$$

From (Def2) one obtains,

$$F_l[Wa] \leftrightarrow M_l[\sim Wa]. \tag{C3}$$

From (C2) and (C3) one obtains,

$$\sim Ra \rightarrow M_1[\sim Wa]. \tag{C4}$$

Since (Def1) is a definitional equivalence, we substitute into the deontic context and obtain,

$$\sim Ra \rightarrow M_1[Ia]. \tag{C5}$$

Finally, since the constant a is arbitrary (that is, it did not occur in any premiss), we may perform a universal generalization to obtain the conclusion,

$$(x)(\sim Rx \rightarrow M_1[Ix]). \tag{C6}$$

(C6) is the same statement as the conclusion of the first derivation in this chapter. Thus, this conclusion can be derived using schemata – (Def2) and (Ax1) –, and it can likewise be derived using Braybrooke's earlier formulation with the second-order quantifier.

Notwithstanding all of this, (Ax1) is still problematic. If ψ is a totally vacuous predicate, say ρ, such that $\rho(a)$ is false for all persons a, then $(\rho(a) \rightarrow Da)$ is (vacuously) true for all persons a. Then, for any person a, it follows that $F_1[\rho(a)]$ is true. Suppose that $\rho(a)$ means: 'person a is taller than 100 metres and a is not taller than 100 metres.' Then, natural law forbids $\rho(a)$, for all persons a.

Perhaps 'natural law' *does* prohibit contradictions; at least no *practical difficulties* would appear to arise from prohibiting logically impossible states. Yet, other difficulties remain. Should natural law also prohibit states that are simply false for some people? If we allow this, as (Ax1) seems to, we obtain some surprising, and perhaps counterintuitive, results. For instance suppose that $\rho(a)$ means: 'person a is perfectly innocent.' Suppose, as a matter of fact, that $\rho(a)$ is false for some person a. Then $F_1[\rho(a)]$ is true by (Ax1), a somewhat surprising consequence. The result, $F_1[\rho(a)]$, would perhaps not be surprising if we could establish an analytic or nomological connection between perfect innocence of a and Da. The surprise results from the mere fact that a is not perfectly innocent.

One can trim away some of the surprising consequences of (Ax1) by reformulating Hobbes's basic statement in the form

$$(y)(\psi(y) \rightarrow Dy) \rightarrow (x)F_1[\psi(x)]. \tag{Bx1}$$

Suppose again that $\rho(a)$ is false for person a. It does *not* follow from this fact together with (Bx1) that $F_1[\rho(a)]$ is true. If ψ is a predicate which is false for *all* humans, then $\psi(x)$ is forbidden for *all* humans, but this consequence is perhaps acceptable. More importantly, if $(y)(\psi(y) \rightarrow Dy)$ is an analytic or nomological truth, then $\psi(x)$ is forbidden for all humans, which is a plausible result. However, (Bx1) does not yield quite the same derivations that result from (Ax1). Also, (Bx1) does not appear to be a correct interpretation of what Hobbes means by a *lex naturalis*, since his basic statement about this uses the expressions 'a man' and 'his life.' These expressions suggest that there is one quantifier, ranging over the domain of men (or, as we would have it, persons), with the scope in (Ax1) rather than two quantifiers with separate scopes as in (Bx1). For this reason alone, (Bx1) was omitted from further consideration.

Although (Bx1) was not used, it is heuristically valuable because it provides additional motivation to state some kind of analytic or nomological relationship between $\psi(y)$ and Dy. Yet, it is doubtful that Hobbes used our more modern concepts of analyticity and nomological connection. Instead of using those terms, let us just say that there should be a causal relationship between $\psi(y)$ and Dy. But there are well-known difficulties in representing causal relationships *merely* by conditional statements, especially material conditionals. Thus, if the basic statement about a *lex naturalis* does embody a causal relationship between $\psi(y)$ and Dy, then we should seek some other way to represent such a relationship in our formalization. But this is not the time or place to undertake an analysis of causation. Instead, we introduce a symbol to represent an unanalysed notion of the kind of causal relationship that Hobbes presumably had in mind. This leads to the following, in which the label (LN) indicates the basic statement about what a *lex naturalis* is:

$$(x)(C[\psi(x), Dx] \rightarrow F_1[\psi(x)]). \tag{LN}$$

(LN) corresponds to (1) in this chapter, with two differences. First, (LN) is an axiom schema, as is (Ax1). Second, in (LN) C is a metapredicate relating the syntactic forms $\psi(x)$ and Dx. Of course, $C[\psi(x), Dx]$ is intended to represent a causal relationship, just as it does in (1), where ψ is a second-order variable.

All of this is very interesting. But, in the end, I am inclined to be a little sceptical of modern reconstructions of old arguments, especially if these reconstructions are formulated in modern symbolic logic notation. Yet, attempts at such reconstructions can help to uncover subtle ambiguities and lapses of reasoning, which might otherwise go unnoticed. In the present attempt, the introduction of the unanalysed relation C can be criticised for sweeping the hard problem under the rug. At least its use has the pragmatic value of leaving an opening for further developments.

Chapter Five

David Hume: Natural Law Theorist and Moral Realist

Natural law theory founds moral judgments on what, given the nature of human beings and ever-present circumstances, enables people to live together in thriving communities. The cognitive features of moral judgments – the claims of literal truth for these judgments about these matters and the readiness to have the judgments stand or fall with the evidence for those claims (the two features by which Geoffrey Sayre-McCord defines moral realism)[1] – come front and centre with this characterization of natural law theory. Both what is good for human beings and what it is right and wrong for them to do are matters of fact implied by what is required for their thriving; and so it is reasonable to hold that natural law theory is a variety of moral realism. Michael Moore is an example of someone who holds this, maintaining that a natural law theorist must be a moral realist.[2] Moore is using 'natural law theorist' more broadly than I am; still, for him 'human nature natural law theory,' essentially the medieval natural law theory, shorn of certain excrescences, which is what I have in mind, falls under moral realism along with the other varieties of theory that Moore has in mind. So, if Hume is not a moral realist, he is not a natural law theorist. But I shall argue that Hume is a moral realist; and this is what I shall undertake to do, in the course of establishing that he is a natural law theorist, indeed, a human nature natural law theorist.

It may seem an exceeding paradox to call Hume a moral realist. Moore has told me he thinks so. J.L. Mackie looks upon him as an ultimate source for the error theory, and hence, in Sayre-McCord's classification, for the cognitivist variety of anti-realism. C.L. Stevenson has claimed Hume for the non-cognitivist variety. Simon Blackburn views Hume as a prototype both for projectivism and for quasi-realism,

Blackburn's program for reconciling projectivism with ordinary moral discourse.[3]

But it is paradox already to call Hume a natural law theorist. Against this stands not only the possible difficulty that he is not a moral realist, and therefore cannot be a natural law theorist, but also a refusal to even consider classing him as the latter, a refusal expressed in the flat-footed opinion of a Catholic natural law theorist like Robert George: 'Obviously, any theory of practical philosophical reasoning that merits identification with the practical philosophy of David Hume cannot plausibly be counted as a natural law theory.'[4] I think 'merits' is used ironically, or perhaps in the somewhat uncommon sense of 'meriting' severe condemnation. George is not to be rated as a close student of Hume. But Annette Baier, who certainly is to be so rated, says something subtler and perhaps for that reason all the more disconcerting, not in her later book about Hume, but in another place, where she treats Hume's calling the laws of justice 'laws of nature' as at most only half-serious, with Hume using that language 'arguing with and to some extent mocking the natural law tradition in ethics. He is keeping the terminology of this tradition but emptying it both of its theological implications and of its rationalist implications.'[5] But this, too, can be overcome if the emptying is treated not as an objection, but as a feature that makes of Hume's natural law theory an instance of the core theory – secular and empirical – with which I associate all my allied authors.

Hume's Natural Law: Empirical Basis, God Set Aside

It is certainly true that, traditionally, in the inheritance from medieval natural law theory, natural law comes with God. There is no God in Hume's laws of nature.[6] Nor does Hume suppose that they are discovered in the light of rational theology, 'the natural light' that a friend once teased him with lacking when he stumbled down the dark stairs to his cellar. Moreover, Hume certainly does not think that what he speaks of as laws of nature are discovered by reason apart from experience. Reflection on the relations of ideas, independently of 'norm-recognizing, correction-sensitive participation in a form of life, or practice'[7] does not show us that 'the measures of right and wrong are eternal laws, *obligatory* on every rational mind' (*Treatise*, 465).[8] If such independent reflection were (as Baier supposes) what traditional natural law theorists like St Thomas relied on, then in rejecting it Hume would be breaking away from the natural law tradition. However,

Thomas's position can accept it that 'law-discovery' does occur through 'participation in a form of life, or practice'; he holds that people must be educated to heed natural laws and assumes that both pupils and teachers are already members of a going community (*ST*, 1a2ae, Q.92, 1; also Q.97, 3). He accords as much weight as Hume to custom and to origin of some human laws in customs, along with the possibility of changing customs by human laws.[9] These certainly figure among the observations to be taken into account by reason in identifying laws, along with basic features of human nature and other circumstances of human life (*ST*, 1a2ae, Q.94, 2).

St Thomas extends the observations to biological function, a notion the abuse of which accounts for many doubtful features of traditional natural law theory, especially in application to sexual practices, as I noted at the outset of the present book. Hume does not invoke biological function. His doctrine is abbreviated (for the better) as a consequence. It is even more abbreviated than it needs to be as a consequence, since what Hume calls 'the three fundamental laws of nature,' are just those that concern *stability of possession, ... its transference by consent*, and *... the performance of promises*' (*Treatise*, 526). Other matters that figure in the traditional catalogue (for example, in Hobbes's catalogue, which is traditional so far as it goes) are not given the title of 'laws of nature,' though they are not denied it either, and the language of 'fundamental laws of nature' suggests that there are others not fundamental.[10]

Nevertheless, narrow as the scope of Hume's natural law theory may seem to be, given these considerations, the theory is on all fours with traditional natural law theory within that scope, both as to the content of the laws and as to the argument for them. Whatever is tongue in cheek about the passages in question, the distinctions between 'natural' and 'artificial,' which make one of them (*Treatise*, 484) a classic instance of philosophical illumination, are perfectly in accord with tradition respecting content and argument.[11] Hume says, 'Mankind is an inventive species; and where an invention is obvious and absolutely necessary, it may as properly be said to be natural as any thing that proceeds immediately from original principles, without the intervention of thought or reflection. Tho' the rules of justice be *artificial*, they are not *arbitrary*. Nor is the expression improper to call them *Laws of Nature*; if by natural we understand what is common to any species, or even if we confine it to mean what is inseparable from the species.' St Thomas would concur on both points: The laws of nature are common to all human beings and inseparable from their nature – that is to say, it is an essential part of their nature that they have the capacity to discover the laws of nature and (properly educated) the inclination to obey them (*ST*, 1a2ae, Q.94). But Hume has in effect amplified St Thomas's account to make it clear how discovery may come in the course of establishing a convention. Indeed, Hume outlines a model of how the discovery can come about in the course of purely practical activity, with vanishingly little recourse to explicit reflections of any kind.

Again, "Tis on the strict observance of those three laws, that the peace and security of human society entirely depend ... Society is absolutely necessary for the well-being of men; and these are as necessary to the support of society' (*Treatise*, 526). At the very end of the *Treatise*, when he is summing up his views, Hume says, 'The interest, on which justice is founded, is the greatest imaginable, and extends to all times and places. It cannot possibly be serv'd by any other invention. It is obvious, and discovers itself on the very first formation of society. All these causes render the rules of justice steadfast and immutable; at least, as immutable as human nature.' Far from being at bottom ironic, this accords and in effect is meant to accord with the a posteriori argument for natural laws, discussed in a preceding chapter, mentioned by Locke though not pursued by him: Without natural law, according to Locke, 'there would exist no religion, no society among men, no faith, and countless other disadvantages of this kind.'

Hume is forthcoming in a traditional way on human nature: Normal human beings exhibit at least limited benevolence and aim at rational consistency in their thought and behaviour. Reliance on normal human beings and their outlook establishes a deep connection with traditional natural law theory, without explicitly advertising the connection. For 'normal' here means what human beings naturally become and persist in being if they are not terrorized, excited by murderous demagogues, or psychologically damaged in other ways. It does not imply statistical prevalence in all circumstances: A whole population might be terrorized, and in that case it would not exhibit the normal features of human nature.

Hume is even more forthcoming on the circumstances, his famous circumstances of justice, not so dire as Hobbes's, but bracing enough. Indeed, the spelling out of these circumstances is an important way in which Hume helpfully amplifies received natural law in respect to the premisses about human nature and about circumstances. The laws of nature could not hold for human beings if they were uncontrollably ferocious or if they faced, not just scarcity, but irremediable insufficiency of provisions; the laws would not be necessary if human beings were saints or if provisions were abundant without effort.

If one must choose, it is better to think of Hume as a natural law theorist than as a proto-utilitarian. For though one can regard natural law theory as a systematization of what Sidgwick calls 'the morality of common sense,'[12] and a departure from this only in being more systematic, it is a modest systematization that (even in Hobbes's axiomatic system) does not make the radical departure characteristic of Sidgwick, and other utilitarians, from the plausible common sense project of 'making the people in group G as happy as possible' to the very different and weirdly implausible project of 'generating as much happiness in group G as possible regardless of its final distribution.' Hume gives no grounds for endorsing the latter project; he might well have resisted the suggestion that 'thriving' embraced only the former one.

Natural law, approached a posteriori, can find prescriptive force not in God but elsewhere, as Hume finds it. Hume ascribes to human nature another feature besides limited benevolence, a connected feature because it is the basis for acting upon benevolence and extending it beyond the limits of one's family and friends, namely, the capacity for humane feeling, which leads human beings, when their own interest is not in question, to rejoice in whatever is useful to other human beings, however remote in time and space, and to commiserate with them in whatever is harmful. So all (normal) human beings, Hume supposes, are moved by concern with their fellows, and in accordance with this concern, moved to support whatever is useful to them. That extended sentiment is the basic element in the (moral) prescriptive force of the laws of nature, felt by each human being individually, as an addition to the force with which they impinge upon her self-interest. But this element is reinforced by another. Other human beings, taking the part of humanity in both senses (the virtue; the species), stand behind the laws, ready to admonish and to sanction on their behalf, as they impinge on every individual person. Is this not prescriptive force enough? It is considerable force; and considerable enough so that we can dispense with the resort to God's will in this connection. For suppose we observe that there is this concert of human beings in support of certain laws of nature. It may be true that God's will favours and fosters the concert, but each of us needs go no further back than the concert to find a prescriptive force that will operate upon us even in those cases where we fail to be inclined individually to heed the laws. In some societies, at some times, the concert in support of the laws of nature may be brought about more by fear of God than by the inclination of humanity; and conceivably, in those cases, if religious belief weakens, the concert might dissolve. But Hume shows how it could be reconstituted on the basis of a sentiment that is already in the picture and the power of which could not be appreciated fully until the fear of God vanished.

Sentiments Correct or Incorrect; Judgments True or False

Does Hume's insisting on the place of sentiment in ethics cut him off from moral realism, that is to say, from meeting Sayre-McCord's two definitional conditions, of ascribing truth values to moral judgments and standing by some moral judgments as true? It is for Hume a matter of fact (as it is for Locke, Hobbes, and St Thomas) that human beings cannot have communities with those useful and agreeable features that we collect under the normative designation 'thriving' unless they heed the laws of nature. When we judge either that it is good for human beings to heed those laws or that they ought to heed them is our judgment literally true? Hume says many things that check us from saying so easily. At one stage (the *Treatise* stage) of Hume's thinking, he repudiated any role for reason in ethics, and though he did retreat from this repudiation later (in the *Inquiry*),[13] he never explicitly brought under reason the important tasks that he assigned early and late to 'the judgment and the understanding.' Hume repeats, in the first appendix to the *Inquiry*, the substance of his argument against looking upon reason as the source of moral distinctions. Furthermore, Hume talks in the *Inquiry* about our 'gilding or staining all natural objects with the colors borrowed from internal sentiment' (end of Appendix I). He asserts in the *Treatise* that 'our passions, volitions, and actions [cannot] be pronounced either true or false' (*Treatise*, 458); they are 'original facts and realities, complete in themselves, and implying no reference to other passions, volitions, and actions' (see also *Treatise*, 415).

Yet Hume at least approaches so close to using truth and falsity literally, by developing an analogy in ethics to the establishment of observational truths, that the distinction from not using them tends to vanish. Our utterances about good and evil express sentiments – in particular, the sentiment of humanity, in the *Treatise* founded upon sympathy or fellow-feeling, in the *Inquiry* something that absorbs fellow-feeling. But this sentiment can be correct or incorrect. To be correct, it must accord with the sentiment that a normal human being, looking upon human traits or social arrangements in a disinterested perspective, feels as instances of feeling the sentiment of humanity. Self-interest, or partiality for family and friends, may interfere both with our feeling this sentiment with appropriate force and with our being moved in accordance with the sentiment to the actions that it is appropriate and feasible for us to make. (Hume does not suppose that we always or even more often than not do act upon the sentiment.) But then we must defer under the pressure for consistency in moral discourse to the sentiment of people whose view is not in this instance distorted by self-interest or partiality. They can see how immediately agreeable a certain person is for manifesting certain virtues; and how useful to the people that he deals with it is for him to manifest other virtues, like justice, which are not always immediately agreeable or even in some single instances considered by themselves socially useful. Hume omits to give any phenomenological characterization of the sentiment; and instead defines it by its cognized object – what is agreeable or useful to our fellow human beings (or the reverse) – and by its double universality, felt by all (normal) human beings and extending to all of them. With minds and hearts unclouded by self-interest or partiality for family or friends, we feel for the sufferings of people long ago or on the other side of the planet; and correcting our judgments to take into account the distance, we find those sufferings a good deal more important than a transient scratch on one of our fingers (*Treatise*, 582–3; See also 416). Moreover, unless we are moved by humanity in these connections, we shall not appreciate the moral significance of the phenomena to be observed. Is not the sentiment functioning, not just under the auspices of cognition, but as an indispensable means to it, and as a vehicle for discovering and expressing information?[14]

These considerations supply for ethics at least an analogue of discourse in which truth and falsity contend with each other. So, if Hume is not literally a moral realist, he is a fellow traveller. Moreover, not too much should be made of the difference: We might interpret Hume by interpreting his analogy in accordance with a distinction like von Wright's between, first, rules having, like commands, no truth values, and, second, normative statements truly or falsely asserting the existence of rules.[15] Thus, Hume does surely hold that it is true that one fundamental law of nature, that is, one basic condition for having a thriving community, is stability of possession, and another is the keeping of promises. Moreover, Hume tells us, 'I cannot ... be more assured of any truth which I learn from reasoning and argument, than that personal merit consists entirely in the usefulness or agreeableness of qualities to the person himself possessed of them, or to others who have intercourse with him,' though in a rhetorical gesture of extravagant modesty, too extravagant to be taken literally, Hume throws the point away with his next breath.[16] Nor is this distinction utterly alien to the natural law tradition: On the contrary, it can be aligned with St Thomas's distinction between practical reason, which invokes the laws of nature to guide action, and speculative reason, to which I presume, though St Thomas does not say much about this,[17] may be assigned the task of identifying the laws of nature and their basis.

Hume presents at least an analogy to moral realism. Can he be said to go further? He certainly wants to insist upon the difference between judgments that spring from sentiments and judgments arrived at by reason alone, reflecting on the relations of ideas. I suppose he does this in part because he is so strongly concerned to establish an indispensable place for feeling in moral discourse. How could that discourse be moving if feeling did not have such a place? Aesthetic discourse is moving, too; and Hume insists on the parallels between our judgments of beauty and deformity, on the one hand, and of moral good and evil, on the other. In both cases, something is present that cannot be captured by propositions that, like those in geometry or logic or in the natural sciences, do not reflect sentiments on the part of the speaker. Yet to make this point, need moral judgments be severed from truth and falsity?

The strongest passages[18] in Hume, already cited, tending toward severance, about our 'passions, volitions, and actions' not being true or false because they are 'original facts and realities,' do not strictly speaking imply severance. For it may be admitted that 'passions, volitions, and actions' are not true or false, even if they may be appropriate or inappropriate. Something else respecting truth and falsity might, notwithstanding, be said of moral judgments. Is applying this distinction between feelings and judgments to speak more strictly than Hume intended? Perhaps so; but if so, that is because Hume's intentions on this point were not perfectly well-ordered. We can embellish the analogy already sketched with further points that culminate in adherence to truth and falsity for moral judgments.

Hume says we arrange in moral discourse to 'prevent contradictions' (*Treatise*, 581) and though this is not a sufficient condition for the presence of truth and falsity (since commands may contradict one another), it is a necessary condition. If we look upon emotions as action-guiding, we might well not wish to have emotions giving conflicting guidance either in the case of single persons or in situations in which the cooperation of several persons is called for. However, conceding this point only strengthens the argument for looking upon Hume as a moral realist. He certainly thinks of emotions (sentiments) as action-guiding; but, far from making conflicting guidance from emotions the ground for avoiding contradictions, he concentrates in his discussion on conflicts of judgments.

We aim in ordered moral discourse to extricate ourselves from conflicts between personal points of view and arrive at 'a concurrence of sentiments' and 'a stable judgment' (581). In the course of doing this, we 'correct our sentiments, or at least correct our language' (*Treatise*, 582), so that we speak another language, the language of 'general sentiment,' adhering to 'social and universal principles' (*Inquiry*, 96) and 'a general unalterable standard' (56). Speaking that other language, we 'say not ... that the character [of our servant] is more laudable' than that of Marcus Brutus long ago (*Treatise*, 582), just as we 'say not that [something] appears to us less beautiful' when it is at twenty paces' distance than when it is closer at hand. Are we not here dealing with judgments with a propositional content capable of truth or falsity? We can argue even closer to this result if we reflect that in eighteenth-century English, as in ours, the term 'sentiment' ranges over opinions as well as emotions.[19]

Sentiments lend themselves to expression in the verbal form, 'I feel that ...,' for example, 'I feel that this is good.' The form is even for us as much one of cognitive statements as of emotional expression. So it should be no surprise to find Hume actually saying that if by mistaking 'the true interests of mankind, ... any false opinion ... has been found to prevail, as soon as further experience and sounder reasoning have given us juster notions of human affairs, we retract our first sentiment and adjust anew the boundaries of moral good and evil' (*Inquiry*, 13). There is more than an analogy; Hume is a moral realist.

Perhaps it would be wise to concede that Hume's final tendency is not a settled one. It is, to be sure, the tendency that one reaches last only if one arranges the several tendencies in his discussion in a certain order. There are passages, which I have cited, in which he tends toward being an emotivist. There are other passages in which he refuses to join the moral realists (as I, following Sayre-McCord, have defined them) in calling moral judgments true or false, but in which he emphatically insists on distinguishing correct ones from ones that are incorrect. These are more numerous and more central. Should they bear more weight than the passages in which, after all, Hume speaks of true or false moral opinions?

The case for taking these last-mentioned passages as expressing Hume's final tendency does not depend, however, on accepting the arrangement that puts them last, which might be regarded as tendentious. It rests jointly upon their presence and on the strength of the analogy between correct or incorrect, as Hume treats these terms, and true or false, which the moral realists want to say instead. Hume is not just substituting terms, less common, but with much the same significance, for terms more commonly used. He is insisting upon the practice of correcting moral judgments; and he himself takes considerable pains to develop the analogy between this practice of correction with the practice of correction for judgments of perception. The analogy goes far enough to reduce to a vanishing point any difference between the use of 'correct' or 'incorrect' for moral judgments, taking into account all the aspects of the practice in which that use figures, and the use of 'true' or 'false' for moral judgments. So, I interpret Hume as moving toward moral realism in the passages on correctness and incorrectness, and on this ground I come down with final emphasis on the few passages in which he does literally express himself as a moral realist.

Another consideration, extraneous to Hume's text but integral to the present book, leads me to emphasize the aspects of Hume's theory that invite the appellation of moral realism. I agree with David Copp that truth and falsity do have an important place in current moral discourse; and I think that the modernized medieval natural law theory that I am presenting, with the assistance of Copp as well as my canonical authors, sits most comfortably with moral realism and truth or falsity. One can seize upon the few passages in which Hume does literally express himself as a moral realist as evidence that (even if it would be with certain reservations) he would agree to be comfortable himself. Locke, Rousseau, and St Thomas would make even less difficulty. About Hobbes I am not so sure, but I would stress that in his case the natural laws are presented as theorems of a science of politics: Truly, people must seek peace if they are to thrive.

Perhaps less hangs upon this than the philosophical controversy about moral realism suggests. Set aside the passages in which Hume literally expresses himself as a moral realist. Ignore Hobbes's view of the natural laws as theorems and emphasize his view of them as commands. Make the most of St Thomas's distinction between theoretical and practical reason. Let the moral judgments themselves – judgments approving this virtue or this action – be correct or incorrect depending on whether they are founded or not founded on the natural laws. Those laws themselves can be arrived at as indispensable by reasoning from observation. Shall we say that they are the correct laws – the right laws – if they are in fact indispensable? It might be enough to say that they are indispensable. At any rate, we do not need to say that they are true or false; they are rules, not statements. The whole system of natural laws, along with the action-guiding judgments founded upon them, can be presented as a system of imperatives (more properly, to invoke the definition of rules offered by me and my co-authors in *Logic on the Track of Social Change*, as a system of systems of imperatives). What is really vital is that the laws indispensable to thriving be identified and followed, not how they are to be fitted under practices of distinguishing truth from falsity.

Yet there is a difficulty that haunts this program. It may be impossible, accepting with Hume that there is a standard for correctness in moral judgments, to separate correctness from truth. No doubt one can say, 'R is a rule among the Ojibway,' without endorsing the rule; one can even consistently say, 'R is a current rule of my own society,' and go on immediately to condemn it as pointless at best and pernicious at worst. But can one say, 'R is a rule that answers to the standard of correctness for moral rules, namely, as something indispensable to people's thriving together,' and disavow any implication of imperative force? Yet the statement itself demands to be called true or false. One will not disavow the imperative force by calling it true. Indeed, one of the standard corrective moves made to keep up a moral rule is just to remind people in so many words that there is a moral rule that such and such be done. 'But that's cruelty; there's a rule against treating a child that way.' These considerations support a further, deeper reason for holding that Hume cannot stay with 'correct' or 'incorrect.' His thinking, indeed the thinking of anyone who takes into account how it must be true or false to say that a given rule is correct, the right rule, can come finally to rest only with true or false, thus, with moral realism rather than with an analogue, however close.

Disinterested Sentiment

In Hume's account, the whole apparatus of correction by the general unalterable standard sustains the view that in moral discourse truth and falsity are used literally, with truth sometimes achieved. But it is truth that does not stand alone; it is a truth that moves, movingly expressed. We may say that the analysis of a moral judgment of the form, 'That N has this trait is good' makes it something that implies, 'This trait causes in a normal human being who takes a fully informed and wholly disinterested view of it a favourable sentiment.' Hume gives us to understand that the analysis can be backed by a powerful theory as to what traits (and other objects of moral judgment) cause normal human beings taking such a view of them to have a favourable sentiment, namely, that the traits are either immediately agreeable or useful to the human beings affected. In the case of justice, the favourable sentiment arises from contemplating the operation of the general rules about property; approving the trait of justice depends on approving the rule that it exhibits conformity to. So, some moral judgments will have the form, 'The rule R ought to be obeyed.'

The presence of someone to whom it matters in a certain way whether the facts are thus rather than not thus is required for applying the moral epithets. But that certain way requires, besides a reaction in which the doubly universal sentiment figures and gets expressed in a proposition, the occurrence of the facts within a disinterested view in which intersubjective agreement may be expected; even those who are for the moment distracted by their private interest must defer to the disinterested view. The constraints upon moral judgments in Hume's case are very stringent, bringing into operation as they do 'an unalterable general standard.' Moreover, the range of things identified as good with correct moral judgment, along with the associated moral obligations, hang together in what Richard Boyd calls 'a homeostatic cluster' of values.[20] They all have to do with what is agreeable or useful to human beings and are desired because they really are so.[21] A systematic account of how they hang together can be given by natural law theory (as, for example, in Hobbes's axiomatic system of the laws of nature).

Hume's comment[22] that when with him we 'see that the distinction of vice and virtue is not founded merely on the relations of objects, nor is perceived by reason' this 'wou'd subvert all the vulgar systems of morality' suggests a break with tradition as well as with the thinking of plain people. But this comment is not conclusive; it is only a suggestion. Are 'vulgar' systems the ideas of ordinary people or the systems of inept philosophy? Against it we can set the point, strongly developed by Baier, that Hume was aiming to match his teaching to the practice, experience, and attitudes of ordinary, non-philosophical people rather than to received philosophical doctrines.[23] The common-place aspects of natural law may even help in this connection. Hume in the comment might well be mistaken about what people with received ideas were prepared to accept. Suppose they were asked, 'Would anything be good if its being one way or another mattered to nobody?' They might be ready to say, 'Yes,' imagining a world without the presence of human beings, though comforting themselves with the thought that how things were in that world would still matter to God (God carrying out a specialized duty that falls under the general back-up role assigned him by Berkeley). A secularized natural law theory would, of course, not have that recourse. It could not say, seriously intending the words used by Hume at the end of Appendix I to the *Inquiry*, 'The standard [of morality], arising from the internal frame and constitution of animals, is ultimately derived from that Supreme Will which bestowed on each being its peculiar nature and arranged the several classes and orders of existence.' But take out the Supreme Will, reference to which here seems to me no more than a rhetorical flourish, whether or not it is intentionally ironic as well. (Ironic or not, the statement as a whole, with the reference, is one more confirmation of Hume's working within the framework of natural law theory.) Do we not still have a basis for moral judgment as real as the basis for other judgments to which we properly attach truth instead of falsity?

Gilding and Staining: The Comparison with Secondary Qualities

The sentiment of humanity can be vivid and vigorous. It need not be, to do the work wanted of it in founding correct – true – moral judgments; and to make out the argument that I have mounted to justify treating Hume as both a moral realist and a natural law theorist. However, not everything that needs to be said about the relation of emotions (in the twentieth-century sense) to moral judgments can be founded on a cool sentiment; and not everything that Hume says about the relation can be thought to rest on a cool sentiment. There is a directness and intimacy about moral judgments on occasion that must be taken into account, and as well the way those judgments vary in strength, to the heights of indignation, for example, with the strength of the emotions expressed.[24] It is a stronger condemnation when it comes with stronger emotive force.

Can Hume accommodate judgments expressing direct, strong emotions without jeopardizing the application to those judgments (and hence to a comprehensive view of moral discourse) his apparatus of correctness and truth? It may be worthwhile to pause for a moment to explore this question, though I bypass it and stick to a path at a cooler elevation in the main argument of this book (and in the rapprochement that I effect between Natural Law Modernized and David Copp's theory).

Hume wants to contrast what would be the same truths and falsehoods for 'every rational, intelligent being' and opinions or judgments founded 'entirely on the particular fabric and constitution of the human species' (*Inquiry*, Sect. I, 4). Moral opinions and judgments essentially involve responses by human beings, given their 'particular fabric and constitution,' to the objects of those judgments. Moreover – and this is another point that Hume is making – those responses 'gild or stain' objects with colours that they would not have in the absence of the responses (*Inquiry*, end of Appendix I).[25] But neither of these points implies that the opinions or judgments in question are not true or false. 'If colours, sounds, tastes, and smells be merely [subjective] perceptions, nothing we can conceive is possest of a real, continu'd, and independent existence' (*Treatise*, 228).[26] Moreover, should a moral realist demand more than a basis universal to the species for intersubjective agreement upon moral facts? Or a basis more firmly rooted in the nature of things than colours (about which we truly or falsely say, 'This is green' or 'This is red')? The analogy with judgments of colour and other secondary qualities thus supplies another (though not strictly necessary) argument for holding that Hume attaches truth or falsity to moral judgments.

The analogy, though it is something authorized by Hume, is not something that he develops. In particular, Hume does not develop it in the direction of accommodating judgments recognizing and expressing greater vividness. Yet that direction is available: Colours may be specially intense (think of coming into a room decorated in brilliant gold and saturated ultramarine), and evoke a specially vigorous response. Likewise the spectacle of a specially noble and generous action will normally evoke specially vigorous admiration and approval (for example, an heiress renounces a great fortune in order to benefit people that she thinks more deserving). Similarly, a heinous crime (cutting off the hands of a village girl as rebels have done in Sierra Leone) will normally have an effect analogous to a specially garish colour or colour scheme, and evoke moral horror, and a judgment that expresses it.

Hume says that the moral sentiment 'is commonly ... soft and gentle' and that is all that his theory generally needs; but there are many cases – maybe commonly as many – in which it is a vigorous reaction.

The analogy with judgments of colour and other secondary qualities has been strongly contested and strongly defended.[27] I do not mean to take a strong position defending it myself, since it straddles (and hence may confuse) the distinction between the attitudes that we naively attach to rule-keeping and the attitudinal basis for endorsing the rules in a critical perspective.[28] I also think that the analogy limps a bit because of the absence of a special organ at work in moral perceptions, parallel to the eyes or ears, though perhaps we could fill out the analogy by likening the capacity to perceive vices and virtues to the *sensus communis* of medieval philosophy, to which was delegated the composition of perceptions arrived at by more than one dedicated sense organ operating at the same time. There are two further objections to the analogy that can be discussed with some advantage, since refuting them brings out some points of strength in Hume's theory.

One has to do with what is decried as the circularity, attributed to the 'sensibility theory' that some philosophers believe themselves to have inherited from Hume with the analogy of colour judgments, of defining good as whatever evokes a response identifying it as good.[29] Neither the analogy nor Hume's theory need bear this burden of circularity, however.[30] For Hume what is good is what is immediately agreeable or useful (and hence, agreeable in due course, after reflection). The responses in question are the responses of normal human beings (fully equipped with the capacity to feel in a disinterested perspective) to particular instances of agreeable or useful things: human traits or actions; policies (like the rules of justice). Even if the objects cannot be fully described without mentioning the fact that they do (given their other properties) evoke responses that express pleasure in encountering them, the goodness of the objects and the response that perceives them to have the property of goodness are two different things. It is the same as with the colours ascribed to coloured objects and the responses that ascribe them. The colours belong to the objects (in the ordinary conception or phenomenological one of colours and objects); the responses, to the persons making the ascriptions. Moreover, a vital point, in both cases the responses may be mistaken; it is not the response alone that confers the property, but the response under the relevant constraints – that the light be normal and the person's visual powers be in their normal state; that the sentiment be felt in a disinterested view.[31]

The other objection is one raised by Blackburn against the combination of the analogy with secondary qualities with the notion that the goodness of the objects is 'supervenient' upon their other properties. I need not go into the distinction that Blackburn invokes between supervenience and necessary connection farther than to say that supervenience opens up for Blackburn the logical possibility of there being worlds in which there are objects with the other properties that do not have the property of goodness. But what is Blackburn thinking of in this connection? The only relevant possible worlds are worlds in which human beings are present. A world is no doubt logically possible in which they are present, and on occasion exhibit what we would call and approve of as kindness, courage, or generosity, while no one among them responds to these things with pleasure and approval. But this would be something like having a world in which there were objects with the properties that would evoke colour judgments from people with normal vision, but no people with normal vision, only people blind or at least colour-blind. The absence of colour responses in such a world would not undermine the presence of observable colour in ours, along with colour responses. No more would the possibility of a world in which there were no people making moral judgments in response to the traits and actions that they observed undermine the presence of observable goodness in ours, along with moral responses.

The Scope of Hume's Natural Law Perspective: Some Further Points of Agreement and Disagreement with Annette Baier

Some further points relating Hume's doctrine to natural law theory can be made in the way of a series of comments on Annette Baier's book *A Progress of Sentiments*. Much influenced as I have been by this book, as well as by her other studies of Hume, have I come out at odds with her findings? Allowing for a little mutual adjustment, I do not think so. In Baier's last chapter, she ascribes to Hume an enlarged conception of reason and a broad conception of truth both of which harmonize with my argument and the two theses that it aims to uphold, the thesis about natural law and the thesis about moral realism. I have already noted that Baier makes of Hume's notion of sentiment the notion of something with intellectual content, indeed enough content to play the role in true judgments that moral realism requires. So do I.

A little adjustment may be needed in relation to the passage in which Baier asserts that rules play for Hume only a minor role in comparison to virtues. She makes of this an important point of difference from the sorts of ethics that do give prominence to rules. Natural law theory might be taken to offer an ethics limited to rules, or at any rate an ethics that puts so much emphasis on rules as to leave little room for virtues; and there may be some texts expounding natural law of which this is a fair description. If we go back to St Thomas, however, we find him discoursing on virtues at equal length with rules, maybe greater length; and his conception of rules as typically coming with exceptions not mentioned in the common formulas of rules, formulas short for the sake of efficiency, allows for repeated occasions on which people may exercise the special virtue of *epieikeia*, which is just the virtue of treating rules without rigidity, making exceptions when they are called for (*ST*, 2a2ae, Q.120). Hence, it converges with the faculty of judgment in what Baier pictures as Hume's final view of it, a preeminently discretionary faculty. Both certainly need to be exercised in exhibiting other virtues: For example, in withholding alms that benevolence would otherwise prompt one to give, when one sees that the alms will be dissipated (*Inquiry*).[32] This is *epieikeia* as well as judgment, because there is a rule to be made exception to; there is a rule for benevolence as well as a rule for every other virtue; it is something to be manifested in action on some occasions rather than others. We are not being benevolent when we give people who need help the go by in favour of helping people who have no need of help.

To be sure, the rule for a virtue is not always a construction as artificial as the three fundamental laws of nature. In an *ex tempore* rejoinder to the observations that I have just made, Baier has suggested that the rules associated with the natural virtues are not 'behavioral rules,' that is, not the same sort as the rules that come with justice, which must be set up to coordinate actions before virtues emerge along with the benefits of coordination. What Baier says in *A Progress of Sentiments* about Hume's opposition to rules is consistent with Hume's meaning to oppose having too many rules, including too many on topics that do not need to be regulated. Her citations (*PS*, 184 , to various passages in the *Treatise*) do not support a stronger interpretation of Hume's comments on rules (and maybe not even this one). On the other hand, Baier admits that there is room for more rules than Hume treats, though perhaps Hume would (rightly) resist the suggestion that all the rules needed are coordinative ('constitutive?') ones.[33]

No adjustment between us is needed in relation to Baier's acute observation that justice for Hume concerns only respect for people's external possessions and leaves out of account respect for their bodies or their lives. I find this observation startling, instructive, and well-founded. Alerted to the point, one immediately recognizes that Hume goes out of his way to confine the rule of justice to external possessions. We cannot be deprived, he says (*Treatise*, 487), too optimistically, of 'the internal satisfaction of our minds'; 'the external advantages of our body ... may be ravish'd from us,' but they are of no use to others (and so would not attract a rational consumer). (Hume was writing before the advances in our time toward medical cannibalization.) Only our external possessions are both things that can be taken from us and things that it is worthwhile for others to take. So, in Hume's view one gains nothing by injuring another person physically, apart at least from doing so in the course of taking external goods from him. In another passage (491), Hume recognizes that envy and revenge may lead to violence between persons, but he maintains that the occasions for envy and revenge are rare by comparison with the occasions for avidly seizing external goods in other people's hands. Once these occasions have been brought under the rule of justice, Hume holds, peace and social order will have been established. Killing other people or mugging them have been from time immemorial procedures of choice for gaining possession of the external goods in their hands; but these procedures are ruled out by justice only implicitly and (as Baier says, *PS*, 221) incidentally.

There is a lesson for my natural law thesis to be learned from this point, and that is that Hume's conception of natural law is even narrower than I have allowed above. For rules against interpersonal violence must be accounted among the first fundamental principles of natural law. Ruling assault and homicide out incidentally does not accord the subject enough importance and does not suffice to obtain an acceptable minimum of social order. We need a rule against killing out of envy and revenge; and though Hume does in a couple of passages treat murder as a crime (for example, *Treatise*, 467 and 468–9),[34] implying that a murderous disposition is a vice, he does not make it clear that it is a vice independent of its incidental connection with the security of property, or find a place under the natural vices and virtues to discuss it or its opposite (the name of which, if it is not to be 'justice,' is not readily supplied). But men kill each other for many other reasons as well. Hume passes over vanity in this connection much too quickly; wounded vanity is a prime motive for violence. So is the company and attentions of sexual partners; so is religion; so is ethnic hatred; and so is the desire for excitement, which leads to violence *pour le sport*, as with the Blue and Green factions at the games in ancient Constantinople, the football hooligans of modern Europe, and most depressing of all, the South Sea Islanders before Captain Cook came upon them. The South Sea Islanders, the most fortunate human beings that ever lived, had an idyllic climate and an abundance of food easily gathered, but they grew bored and so staged rather cruel wars against one another just to pass the time.

The best that can be said for Hume's reducing the account to be taken of the causes of violence to conflicts over external goods is that his naïveté in this connection was shared by Karl Marx. Do away with private property, given transcendence of Hume's circumstances of justice by the abundance that capitalism has made possible, and all conflict (along with all politics as we know it) will disappear. Tell me another. Baier's instruction on this point demands full acceptance; I am not sure that even she gives it as much weight as it deserves in bringing to light a staggering omission in Hume's theory. It is an omission that may not be reparable for Hume without more use of contractarian theory than Baier believes Hume intends. Recognizing not just the removal by the institution of property of an unnecessary source of conflict and the opening up with the institution of the opportunity to attain greater efficiency in producing goods, people renounce the means of protecting themselves against ever-present threats to their lives and freedom. Can they prudently do this without a government to make sure that others renounce the means, too?

I do not agree with one inference that Baier seems to draw from the limiting of justice to checking the love of gain in respect to private goods. Is 'every individual a gainer, on balancing the account' with justice, as Hume alleges (*Treatise*, 497)? Not only may some of the people who have to forego goods for the sake of justice in those instances that are not taken by themselves useful to them, or to the public, be ruined for life; some people will be in positions to make coups at the expense of others and get away with them scot free; for example, they may be movers and shakers in the savings and loan business. Baier sensibly questions (*PS*, 233) whether advanced age will lead many people to be tempted away from justice – how long can those approaching the end of their lives expect to enjoy their gains? But even here there may be exceptions, not only (as Baier allows) people thinking of their heirs. I thought that in the face of Baier's questioning I could save my long-cherished example of an elderly pirate, with just the time left to make one more cruise, only by shifting from justice (now limited in bearing to external goods) to some other artificial constructions that Hume supposes to be in everyone's interest, like the rules about modesty and chastity. But those rules do not apply with any stringency to men and they do not directly forbid kidnap[35] or rape, omissions from Hume's theory that some will think just about as staggering as the omission of directly forbidding murder.

Consider my elderly pirate, given the opportunity of seizing for a cruise around the Bay of Naples during his last two weeks on earth a luxurious yacht, with a number of cheerful entertainers of both sexes already on board, invited there by the present owner. Would that not be gain enough to tempt him? Such counterexamples might force Hume to qualify his position that the moral motive to justice presupposes for everybody self-interested returns, direct or indirect, on the whole range of instances that she faces; and that these suffice to motivate. However, would it not do well enough for Hume's purposes to argue that by and large justice was founded on self-interest though in some cases only moral pressure would succeed (if anything did) in eliciting conformity?

Baier makes two other interesting points, both of which have lessons to offer natural law theory. One is that the conventions respecting possession, exchange, and promises are not founded on fear of reprisal or provisions for punishment. I think this is true, and it fits a general conception of rules that I adhere to and would incorporate into natural law theory, namely, a conception that accepts rules as being associated with sanctions only when a need for sanctions has appeared, which is not the case with many rules (for example, the rules of language). But I would distinguish between sanctions and blocking operations. It seems to me that to get the idea of a rule people have to be taught some rules to begin with by blocking them from doing what the rules prohibit. We move a child to a safe distance from the fire, and move her again if she again wanders too close. As Baier reminded me face-to-face long ago, Hume says that we learn rules within families. It is by learning rules in this manner that people are prepared to generate the conventions that Baier refers to (*Inquiry*, 23). The rules or conventions need not be accompanied by sanctions (though under government this happens); but deviations from them will be checked by blocking operations, which may amount to no more than reminding someone about to seize a couple of coconuts that a neighbour picked them for his own eating, but might go so far as to put them out of reach.

The other point comes forward with the distinction that Baier makes between the condition that people might have been in before adopting the conventions and the condition that they would fall into were the conventions to lapse. Were the latter condition to continue, it might be much more miserable than the former condition, since people would have adapted themselves to the presence of the conventions; but it is the former condition that should count for Hume, though he is as Baier points out ambiguous on this point.[36] That is the relatively benign condition that permits an easy – non-contractarian! – transition to the conventions. I accept this; but would the condition of lapsed conventions continue? Would not people used to living under the conventions hasten to readopt them and get to them even more quickly than the first originators? Furthermore, if the community in which they used to live was successful to some degree, would not they have been habituated to some degree to the pursuit of the Common Good and have developed the appropriate motivations?

At the end of the *Inquiry*, Hume gives a nutshell synopsis of his position in ethics: 'The notion of morals implies some sentiment common to all mankind, which recommends the same object to general approbation, and makes men, or most men, agree in the same opinion or decision concerning it. It also implies some sentiment, so universal and comprehensive as to extend to all mankind, and render the actions and conduct, even of the persons the most remote, an object of applause and censure, according as they agree or disagree with that rule of right which is established. These two requisite circumstances belong alone to the sentiment of humanity here insisted on.' Given a community of people in which that sentiment was widespread, observance of that 'rule of right' would be assured, along, surely, with its prescriptive force. Hume does not require the sentiment to be paramount for anyone in every case: In some cases, one's own self-interest or one's partiality for one's family or friends will incline her to judge or act otherwise. But in those cases, other people will be in a position to take a disinterested view and base their judgments and actions on what humanity dictates. They will, among other things, correct attempts by people not in their position to judge or act otherwise. Thus, the system will be maintained, as cases change and people take turns to uphold it.

Hume implies that this is the normal situation, holding that it is normal for human beings to feel humanity in a way that makes it paramount in their dealings with each other when their partiality for themselves and the people that they specially favour is not at issue. Is this too optimistic? Does Hume allow enough for the depersonalizing effects of technology, which not only lead to people launching missiles against ships or cities that they cannot even see, but to communicating with their family, friends, and colleagues telephonically or electronically? Hume may have been assuming a necessary minimum of face-to-face experience of fellow-feeling; and the minimum may, in ways that Hume could not have expected, have by now been jeopardized.

Does Hume allow enough for the distortions of feeling that come in with persecuting religions, violent nationalisms, intransigent political parties, fanatic social movements? Distortions can come quietly: Small differences in culture or class outlook can make people uncomfortable with each other; and there have been villages where people of the same class and culture are haunted by suspicions, old grievances, and long-standing feuds between families. Philosophers writing on ethics are typically preoccupied (as Hume was himself) with the challenge that self-interest presents to other-regarding motivation – to humanity. On this point, I do not think that Hume was too sanguine; and the reflections on moral education in the next chapter will strengthen what may be deemed a strong position already.

In the world at large, however, the excesses of group feeling are far more destructive of ethics than the excesses of self-interest. In the face of these excesses, philosophers and moralists are arguing for a possibility of moral community that often fails to be realized, sometimes, it must seem, fails on every hand. Yet it would be important to argue for the possibility, even if at most times and at most places, the prospects of realizing it were bleak; and the argument is not entirely unrealistic, since at times and places, the possibility has been substantially realized. In the United States discrimination based on race or gender has been dramatically reduced in the last half century. It did not come as much of a surprise that a few weeks ago, just before I write, a jury in East Texas (which included a black man) convicted a white man of murdering a black. The rise of anthropology as a social science has made people in Western countries more conscious of ethnocentricism and more ashamed of exhibiting it. Most countries offer a mixed performance in respect to humanity at home or abroad, but some performances are less mixed than others: at the present day, those of Norway and the Netherlands, for example,[37] countries that rank at the top both in respect to their domestic Human Development Index and in respect to net development assistance given through their governments and through private charitable organizations to countries in need of economic aid.[38]

Chapter Six

From Private Property in Hume and Locke to the Universality of Natural Laws

The rules governing private property – in particular, the rules that are supposed to hold under 'property' in the narrow sense of estate – as Locke conceived them in the *Second Treatise* are demonstrably not natural laws universally valid in all societies; nor are they valid in a diachronic comparison with the sort of society that might develop from one in which they prevail. They are at best deductions or constructions suited only to particular circumstances, especially and perhaps uniquely the circumstances of a society of subsistence farmers with ample land, some of it still unclaimed (in Locke's case, disregarding the claims of the aborigines, North America with the frontier still open for settlement).[1] Even in such a society, differential accumulation may occur; and with differential accumulation the possibility, aggravated by inheritance, of oppressive conduct by more affluent property-owners emerges. Oppression is a real possibility even in a relatively poor society, since only a little advantage in resources may enable anyone to recruit and pay henchmen who will help oppress others.[2]

In other circumstances, the Common Good (the thriving of society in those circumstances) will call for modifications, on occasion far-reaching ones, in the rules for private property. If the farms are small ones, close to one another, what a given farmer does on his land may affect others substantially. The stench from a concentrated piggery, and the pollution that it causes in neighbouring streams, may greatly reduce the enjoyment of property by other farmers. (In principle, this might have been true in the circumstances that Locke presupposes, but he overlooks the possibility.) Moreover, over time, there may be some danger of subdividing the land into parcels too small for the farmers to support themselves and their families; or a danger of relegating some people to a landless condition. In such circumstances, can inheritance plausibly be left unregulated? In the *Second Treatise*, Locke does not even recall the way in which in principle the feudal system of property-holding forestalled the problem of landlessness, by assigning every man (woman, and child), not otherwise provided for in entitlements to land, a master responsible for meeting his needs.

In a society transformed into an industrial one, property rights may have to undergo even more drastic modifications. Some of them may occur while the transformation is going on, like the curtailment of expectations regarding the enjoyment of one's property that U.S. courts in the nineteenth century carried out in favour of more intensive exploitation of neighbouring properties.[3] Not only will there be more limitations on the use of property; the very things that are to be held as private property may well need sorting out. Is it sensible for a private person to own the steel industry of the entire country, or a fleet of ocean-going oil tankers? So much power and responsibility for employment and prosperity calls for control at least in part (in a larger part than private property by itself admits of) by agencies that exercise public authority. It will not be so anomalous, perhaps, for a corporation with private persons as shareholders to own the steel industry or fleets of ocean-going tankers; but the sort of property that they have, or at any rate their responsibility in law for their holdings, will be substantially modified. They will not have full responsibility, but only one that is limited to the amount of their investment. They will also, partly by voluntary renunciation, partly by regulation through corporate charters and other devices, have limited power over any physical property corresponding to their shares, property that will be mingled anyway with the physical property corresponding to the shares of others.

All of these points imply that Locke's thoughts on the acquisition of property and of its consequences omit to give reasonable attention to the complications arising. Nor is this omission wholly a matter of invoking, as he does, the coming-in of money as somehow sufficing to suspend the original conditions on acquisition, of not appropriating more than one can use and of leaving others enough and as good to acquire. The very least that someone who wants to make over Locke's theory of property for contemporary use would have to do is to reconsider and revise these conditions.[4] That is not my project here, however. I am concerned here simply to show how Locke's theory of property, as it stands, and Hume's theory combine to strengthen each other; and how even so combined for greater strength, they fall short of universality, yet just in falling short they raise a question that directs us behind them to other rules that may be more convincingly held to be universal.

In earlier chapters, I have cited examples of what my authors had in mind as natural laws; and it has been clear that every one of them considered that at least the most fundamental laws were universal. In one chapter, I even assembled, putting together Hobbes's catalogue with a catalogue from St Thomas, a pretty full collection of putatively universal natural laws. Hitherto, however, the most that I have done in the way of defending the claims of universality is report defences offered by the authors themselves. I have not tried in my own person to make out a defence. That is the business of this chapter.

Reflection on Locke's and Hume's doctrines of private property shows us the way at once to identifying universal natural laws and demonstrating their universality. Their doctrines offer a model for the discovery, not immediately of universal natural laws, but of laws that fit in with these in certain circumstances. Once they have discovered these laws, the people in those circumstances may not, and perhaps need not, look any further; they may, like Locke and Hume contemplating them, be under the illusion that they have arrived at universal laws. However, for us their doctrines open up a way to a comprehensive view of universal natural laws, first, as regards the more general laws that lie directly behind the special case of private property, and other cases calling for comparison with it, second, as regards all the others, which may be treated as means to keeping up the laws first uncovered. However, as regards the other laws, another argument demonstrating their universality emerges, which connects them directly with a rich notion of the Common Good; and this argument applies also (retrospectively, in my account) to the general laws behind private property. So, the demonstration will have a double strength.

Complementarity of Locke's and Hume's Doctrines Respecting Property

Locke's and Hume's doctrines respecting property are complementary. Without Hume's doctrine of the origin of the institution (or something like that doctrine) Locke's question about acquisition has to take for granted points that can be illuminated by convincing argument. Without Locke's doctrine of acquisition (or something equally convincing) Hume has (as he recognizes, without recognizing the extent of his weakness) only arbitrary criteria for assigning the property that the existence of the institution stands ready to guarantee.[5] Hume disregards how in the circumstances in which he pictures the institution of property originating an arbitrary criterion will not suit, and certainly not suit so well as Locke's criterion.

A good deal of the significance of this thesis of complementarity comes out most vividly only by reflecting on what Marx opposed and what Marx accepted under the head of justice. I shall want to say that Marx opposed a conception of justice associated with a doctrine of property exemplified by Locke's and Hume's doctrines combined and applied to an industrial society.[6] What I want to do here is argue for complementarity, not as representing what either philosopher had entirely in mind, but as making the best sense of what both have to say on private property given certain circumstances. The two doctrines could, of course, be complementary in respect to one giving answers to some questions on which the other is silent; and yet one could think of more adequate answers. I shall argue that in this case the answers coming from either side are so adequate for the circumstances presupposed that it is not easy to imagine undeniably superior alternatives. In this sense, the complementarity is a strong one.

Set some people in a woods and let them fend for themselves. They will provide for their food by gathering berries, perhaps acorns, sometimes by catching small game or fish. They will resist attempts by others to seize what they have gathered and caught. They do not need to have a theory of property to resist or even much experience of social life. (Though where did they come from, if they did not have experience of family life, or at any rate of reciprocal relations with some kind of caregivers as they grew up?) Locke's criterion of acquisition – mixing one's labour, the labour of gathering or catching, with the object that one is to ingest to meet one's needs – has its origin here, giving a non-arbitrary footing to the criterion for acquisition that Hume fails to appreciate. 'No body can deny but the nourishment is his' who ingests the acorns and the apples (Locke, *Second Treatise*, chap. V, par. 28.) With the consideration that a person must mix his labour with the land that he clears and farms serving as a bridge, the footing of the criterion is extended from provisions in hand to the land from which provisions for needs will be extracted. However, resisting attempts by others to take for themselves what one has gathered or caught does not by itself imply claims to property; nor would resisting the attempts of others to eject one from the land that one has cleared or to gather crops from it.

For there to be private property in these things there must be some intelligible ground, not just the fighting strength which can be brought to bear in the physical resistance, that will move others to desist from attempts to seize the things in question. In other words, there must be a rule or rules that assign the things; and people, mindful of the rule, must respect the assignments. There must be an institution of property.

The chief omission on Locke's side, which makes what Hume supplies complementary to Locke's doctrine, is, I hold, his failure to supply any explanation of how the institution of private property, as distinct from the criterion (or criteria) for acquisition, arises. One needs to call in something like Hume's doctrine respecting the origin of the institution to explain its presence, in particular its presence in the state of nature. Hume, in his *Treatise* (Book III, Part II, Section II), sets forth his theory of the origin of the institution of private property in a passage that is as brief as it is pregnant: 'I observe,' he says, speaking for someone in a situation in which the institution is about to arise, 'that it will be for my interest to leave another in the possession of his goods, *provided* [Hume's emphasis] he will act in the same manner with regard to me.' But he may be expected to do so, since 'he is sensible of a like interest in the regulation of his conduct.' When 'this common sense of interest is mutually expressed' and 'known to both,' a convention starts up, without any need for the 'interposition' of an explicit promise on either side. It starts up and keeps going, though perhaps not so quickly, as the implicit convention adopted by 'two men, who pull at the oars of a boat.' Nowadays, sophisticated commentators would bring in game theory; and treat the two agents adopting a convention about property (or about pulling at the oars) as playing an iterated game, each stage of which has the matrix of gains and losses of a Prisoner's Dilemma, in which cooperation according to the 'tit-for-tat' strategy succeeds better than any other and in favourable circumstances spreads through an entire population.[7]

What is Hume assuming about the agents or their possessions? Before the passage just cited he asserts that people would never have come to understand the advantages of having a society unless they had first experienced the advantages of being brought up in a family. This does not strictly imply that they had to have experience of something like the institution of private property while they were being brought up; and the passage just cited does not say anything about carrying over the idea of such an institution to the problem that adult agents, perhaps strangers to one another, confront. In a passage a few pages later (still in Book III, Part II, Section II), Hume does say that people get their first experience of justice (necessarily, on his approach, along with their first experience of private property) as children within their family circles. I think we can read the present passage as implying that the initial 'observation' that the observer will do better to leave the other in possession of his goods provided the other does likewise applies to the present case something learned in family life, and that connection with family life helps make the agent a more concrete and more intelligible person. On the other hand, I think we may also, equally well, read the present passage as having to do with rational agents about whom we make no further assumptions than that they have goods in hand and an interest in keeping them.

Of the goods in question Hume says nothing specific. They may be taken, since the argument applies equally well to all these things, to include not only the nuts and berries that the agents may have just gathered, or the day's catch of fish and game, but tracts of land that they are about to clear, or have cleared, with the crops that have been grown on them. (There would have been no precedent in infant experience within the family circle for claiming land to clear or cultivate, but maybe precedents would occur when the children grew old enough to support themselves.) Hume says (in the central brief and pregnant passage cited already) that the rule about 'stability of possession ... arises gradually,' and 'acquires force by a slow progression.' This gradual development might move from recognizing property in what people have severally gathered or caught (the berries, nuts, fish, and game) to recognizing it in land cleared and cultivated, perhaps by way of recognizing property in domesticated animals and birds. It might be gradual in other respects, too, spreading only in time, with many setbacks, from one part of the population to all others; and, again, only in time, with many setbacks, leading to a firmly settled social rule.

Hume contends that all this may happen without any explicit promise or even any explicit discussion. The institution of private property, thus, comes in as an adaptation of human nature, a nature manifesting neither (unlimited) ferocity nor saintliness, to the general circumstances of human life, circumstances manifesting neither abundance nor dearth. Instead of utter dearth, Hume assumes a scarcity that can be dealt with successfully by productive effort. The institution is established by people mindful of their common interest in having such an institution; then, once they have experience of it, and realize how much it benefits everybody, they approve of it on a disinterested view, and thus, the rules governing property acquire ethical significance, with adherence to them a virtue, specifically, the virtue of justice.

A state of nature like Hobbes's state of nature figures at least implicitly in Hume's account, but in Hume it is at most a transient prelude to there being (what corresponds to Locke's state of nature) an organized society of sorts, without a government, but with property at least tacitly recognized. There is a natural motive for recognizing and respecting property – self-interest, but that is not here a motive that works directly as a motivation for the single actions that fall under the laws. (Those single actions are not always even in the public interest.) The 'natural obligation' to obeying the laws of justice is founded on self-interest, directed at the overall operation of the rules, or put another way, on the mutual expectations of beneficial performance that are created by setting them up and maintaining them without exception. However, there arises as well a moral obligation to obey the laws: It is founded on a moral judgment that reflects the pleasure that fellow human beings feel on finding that obedience without exception to the laws advances the interest of the people affected.[8] To conform to the moral obligation is a moral virtue, but, again, it is so only as something presupposing the laws or conventions referred to. It is the virtue of justice – unlike benevolence, an artificial virtue. The virtue of allegiance is artificial, too. It presupposes an arrangement appointing some people to enforce justice, which is undermined by recurrent temptations to put short-run self-interest ahead of long-run benefits.

Does Locke's argument really need supplementation by Hume's, and is Hume's supplementation the most suitable? It might be denied that there has been any omission on Locke's part. For, it might be said, the institution arises simultaneously with the first acquisition.[9] True, the acquisition has to be recognized as legitimate by other people, when it has occurred; for we do not have an instance falling under the institution unless both the acquisitor and other people recognize that by separating the item acquired from the common store and (simultaneously) mixing his labour with it[10] the acquisitor now has a right to retain it (or to exchange it if he pleases). However, this recognition might come about straightaway consistently with Locke's position that, as with any idea, people would not have the idea of the institution prior to having relevant experiences. Suppose that N takes up an item of food not in the hands of any other person. Both he and M, who has observed him, reflect on the taking up and run through something like Locke's own argument for its being indispensable if the bounty of nature is to be put to human use. They may be held to arrive thus at the law of nature establishing private property in items thus acquired. The experience has called forth a certain train of reflection; that train of reflection ends with recognition both of the institution and of the criterion for acquisition. One might imagine the experience repeated again and again. Every time a person beholds what is to be interpreted as an instance of legitimate acquisition she is invariably led to a reflection ending in the recognition at once of its legitimacy and of the rule or rules (the institution) under which the items acquired now fall.

Yet that is not the only way in which human beings reasoning in the state of nature might, consistently with what Locke actually says, have arrived at the institution of private property; nor is it the most plausible way. Locke has at the very least omitted to consider an alternative way like the one described by Hume. Locke explicitly argues against there having to be agreement by all the other people with an interest in the bounty of nature consenting to the acquisition. One might extend his objections to there having to be a convention that everyone has fallen in with. But Hume himself explicitly denies that the institution of private property originates in an agreement; and the convention for which he does argue does not require for its beginnings universal conformity or readiness to conform, either.

If Locke fell back from relying on sequences of all-at-once recognitions of acquisition under the private property institution, he could allow for lots of people getting things wrong to begin with, failing to think through anything like his argument about acquisition, and some sequences, promising though they may be in respect to recognition at the beginning, or after a time, coming to nothing, because incomprehension creeps in. This is more Lockean, because it fits better his allowances (especially in the *Essays/Questions*) for widespread failure on the part of people to appreciate the laws of nature; it fits better, too, the general tendency of his opposition to innate ideas. Though, strictly speaking, the infallible sequences are not inconsistent with this opposition, it surely puts a great deal of strain on it to suppose that the relevant experiences immediately and infallibly trigger a robust conception of the law or laws relating to property.

The alternative account moves Locke closer to Hume, by incorporating precisely some of the features – for example, trial and error; gradual development – that make Hume's account of how the institution of private property arose, as distinct from the occurrence of recognized instances of acquisition, more convincing. The alternative account is equally consistent with what Locke has to say about the discovery of the laws of nature. Moreover, in keeping with what we know about the development of other complex social institutions, it explains how the discovery comes about gradually, with practice rather than in theory.[11] Once we come upon an instance of fully recognizing the legitimacy of an acquisition and the law of private property that it falls under, what does this recognition involve? If Locke, in the face of this question, had limited himself to saying, 'Recognition that there is a law of nature, laid down by God, obliging us to respect an item acquired under such and such conditions as legitimately acquired, and legitimately re-tained,' this would still leave out the purpose of the institution. To bring in the joint point and purpose of the institution, moreover, Locke would have to bring in more than the advantages of acquisition and retention for the owner. He would have to bring in the advantages for the owner of respecting the ownership of others, and for the others of respecting ownership on his part. But if this is brought into the recog-nition, then no substantial difference from Hume remains.

In Hume's view, though not in Locke's, the laws of property arrived at in the postulated circumstances are laws that need not have been enacted or promulgated by God. (I have consistently treated the re-ference to such enactment and promulgation as supererogatory, but some people will still miss it.)[12] Nor are they laws that have been adop-ted by an actual social choice on Copp's model, though they might well be an object of the hypothetical choice on which Copp ultimately re-lies, and they could be ratified by an actual choice perhaps generations after their origin. Hume might be taken to imply that they are laws of nature in a sense borrowed back from natural science: A society that fails to conform to them will not thrive. It could be held, in harmony with Hume and making use of a specific provision for laws originating as customs in St Thomas's doctrine (*ST*, 1a2ae, Q.97, 3), that they are examples of just such laws. Hume in his account of the origin of the laws of property gives a plausible picture of how customs of the sort may originate.

Universality, If Not of Locke's and Hume's Laws of Property, of Laws Implied

Are the laws of property universal laws, as both Locke and Hume sup-posed? One can understand how they would think that the search for natural laws in this connection would come to rest with the laws of private property. Consider that the model of discovery for natural laws might have two stages: In the first stage, people look for laws of one kind or another that fit their circumstances; and only for further purposes, which they may not have, including the purposes of theory looking for universal laws, would they move deliberately to a second stage, in which they would inquire in a thorough way whether the laws that they have discovered to fit their circumstances are universal. Locke and Hume did not work seriously in the second stage. I contend that it is evident that the laws of property, as they understood them, are not laws that hold for all people in all circumstances; in particular, they do not hold for all people in primitive circumstances. However plausible a beginning with people ready to be independent subsistence farmers may be, at the beginning things might have gone another way. There are, historically, quite different arrangements that are equally ancient, or even more so.

At the beginning, or perhaps even in reaction to disappointing previous experience with subsistence farming, people may have been hunter-gatherers. A band of hunter-gatherers might choose, instead of adhering to the laws of property, to pool the catch of any given day and let every member of the band help herself.[13] They might do this whether or not they had hunted singly or in cooperation. They could go further in communal arrangements – live together in one long-house, borrow their clothes from a common store (as is done in the Army, as was done in the Oneida Community, at least as regards dress-up clothes). My wife and her four sisters are continually passing dresses from one to the other, and since the populations of early villages were likely to be extended families, this example is perfectly pertinent. There is a story to tell, parallel to Locke's and Hume's story about private property, though not the same story, about how the communal arrangements develop, as people first discover laws that suitably apply within families and then extend them outside the families to villages and tribes and beyond.[14]

In my view, the hunter-gatherer society with its common pool of provisions invites being treated on an equal footing with the society of subsistence farmers. However, many people would think that there is a big obstacle to doing this. Many people (including Locke) would want to argue that setting up a society under these laws about private property can be uniquely recommended on the ground of being the path to optimal productivity. Would not a society that cared to have all its members thrive as well as possible be committed thereby to that path? Even Marx, who thought of capitalism as a necessary stage preparatory to socialism, would have endorsed the path. There are a number of things to be said about this suggestion.

In the first place, even if in the end the society to which the path leads is unambiguously more attractive, for a time at least the common-pool society of hunter-gatherers will bear comparison with the society of subsistence farmers and private property. Common-pool societies are certainly viable; indeed, they are of great antiquity. All that is required for the comparison that drives us behind the rules of private property to more general laws – to truly universal natural laws – is a society that for a time in some circumstances is viable – thriving to a comparable degree.

But in the second place, societies that do not go down the path of private property in provisions for needs may thrive in their own way and even enjoy affluence respecting the ability to meet their needs. Even in respect to life expectancy, they may do as well as societies of subsistence farmers and the industrial societies reached later on the path that begins there. Or do better.[15] Hunger, it is said, is less common among hunter-gatherer societies than in the agricultural societies around them. It is in those agricultural societies that cannibalism begins, and painful inequalities; and all of this comes with a lot of drudgery unknown in leisurely hunter-gatherer societies.[16]

Third, just what system of private property most favours movement on the optimal path remains to be identified: Is it, for example, to be one with life-tenancy or with inheritance, and if it is to be one with inheritance, how is that to be arranged? Fourth, at the end of the path lie, as we now all know, tremendous drawbacks respecting the destruction of the environment and the possibility of humankind bringing about its own destruction. Fifth, the more general rules reached through the comparison of societies will remain relevant as the basis for judging whether or not the arrangements reached at the end of the path are indeed optimal with respect to thriving. They apply to meeting needs at the end of the path as well as at the beginning.

Whatever universal laws apply to the common-pool society, as well as to the society that Locke and Hume had in mind of subsistence farming, would have to be more general than those of village pooling or of elementary private property. What would the laws applying to one set of circumstances have in common with the laws applying to the other set?

Locke's leading example, the ingestion of food, is in one way a very bad prototype for a general theory of acquisition, since in other cases (shelter, even clothing) provisions can be held in common and used turn by turn. In another way, however, it is an excellent prototype, because it zeroes in on the universal condition of meeting needs, namely, that people must be assured one way or another of being able to consume the provisions. Both with subsistence farming and with the common pool of the hunter-gatherers, there are arrangements that normally guarantee provisions for food from take up to actual ingestion, though the points of take up differ. There is a rule in force that no one who needs food shall be barred from all realistic opportunities to obtain it and to consume it once obtained.

Here is something more fundamental than the right of property to productive resources.[17] Under the common-pool system, everyone is assured of an opportunity to obtain provisions from the pool. To regiment the actual facts into something more picturesque, let us say everyone is assured of being able to reach into the common stewpot and to ingest what he takes from it, perhaps a rabbit's haunch or part of the haunch. He appropriates for his own consumption something from the common stewpot, and this is in accordance with a practice even more readily carried over from family life, one would think, than ascribing property to the hunter in what she has caught or to the gatherer in what she has collected. The assurance implies a second rule, that other people are to forbear from knocking the haunch from his hand, and from seizing it for themselves. So, the system of opportunities is surrounded by a system of forbearances.

Should there be a third rule under which everyone (or at least everyone old enough and able-bodied enough) to accomplish such things is to make a steady contribution to gathering the food? Some peoples do not insist upon this.[18] They may bear with an equanimity, surprising even to those among us who are not right-wing Republicans, having a significant number of able-bodied men spend their lives in gambling, but still living from the common pool. True, if other people were not together sufficiently productive, the tribe or village could not easily refrain from insisting that everyone who can work do so. Yet, I shall add the third rule, and hence, say more basic laws than any that Locke or Hume considered establish a threefold combination of (1) rules about opportunities, (2) rules about forbearances, and (3) rules about bearing one's share of productive effort.[19]

This same threefold combination applies to the situation of the subsistence farmers. They reciprocally forbear seizing the crops of other farmers or invading their land. The allotment of land and respect under the first rule for the allotment supplies the opportunities to provide for needs; and in favourable circumstances, those opportunities should suffice, given adequate productive effort as called for by the third rule on everybody's part, and the further application of the first rule to the producers' keeping their crops. The allotment of land associates the opportunities with the efforts. We may add, thinking that the thriving of the society should, if possible, imply the thriving of each member of the society, that when due effort does not suffice – when a farmer is struck by a flood or a tornado, for example – he can expect to receive aid from his fellows. This would, in the subsistence farmers' situation, be an instance of private charity. Or is it public, though public on the part of society rather than on the part of the government? It is something already provided for in the hunter-gatherer society by access to the daily common pool: Bad luck for one person in hunting or gathering one day would not debar her from access to the pool.

What do Locke and Hume respectively contribute, besides their contributions to a plausible model for the discovery of laws that fit some circumstances, to this generalized doctrine of the three-rule combination? Locke, by making ingestion crucial in the basic picture of appropriation, puts his finger on what the first rule, about opportunities to consume provisions for needs, must guarantee, with implied guarantees about opportunities to take up the provisions, whether from the common pool of what the band gathered and caught or from the natural commons from which goods have yet to be extracted. Locke also makes the bearing of the third rule, about productive effort, obvious by the prominence of the effort in his story. Hume, for his part, explicitly brings in, with the institution of private property, the second rule about leaving alone the goods in other people's hands, and supplies a justification for it, to begin with, as a matter of common interest, then as a matter of moral virtue. The justification relies, as Hume makes plain, on specific assumptions about human nature and circumstances. It is from these that he argues to the rules, which unlike Locke, Hume explicitly treats as morally attractive not necessarily case by case, but in their overall, exception-avoiding operation.

The first and second rules may seem better entrenched, along with the assumptions, than the third. Not only are there societies in which some people are productive and willing to share with those who make no effort. Can we not imagine circumstances in which there is no point in the third rule, because there is no scarcity (as Marx did, agreeing with Hume that there would be no need for justice then)? In this connection we must take scarcity as consistent with some effort being required: The coconuts may fall from the trees every day at lunchtime, but they still have to be picked up and cracked open. Why should people go in for the work of farming, a Bushman asks, 'When there are so many mongongo nuts in the world?' They are so plentiful in his country that thousands 'rot on the ground each year for want of picking.' But the nuts do have to be picked, and they have a hard shell, which entails some work to crack open.[20]

The three-rule combination, understood as something enabling all members of a society in which it applies to provide for their needs, goes beyond enabling the society as a whole to continue and prosper. A society might continue and prosper under an arrangement according to which land for subsistence farming was assigned in a yearly lottery that excluded (say) 5 per cent of the able-bodied population from having any land that year (and made little or no provision for people not able-bodied). A common-pool society might distribute food in a way so that individual members of the society had at best a fair chance to have provisions (they must, perhaps, race from a fixed starting point to reach a pot that does not contain enough for all). We could also imagine practices that accepted infringements of assignments actually made: The assignments might be only tentative, or the operative rule might differ from the official one. Libertarians might be found to present a Social Darwinist argument to the effect that marketing arrangements converging with the lotteries in results would incite greater personal efforts and, hence, greater overall output – allowing for a social surplus that private charities run by the privileged classes might use to erect opera houses and universities. Every year, a certain small percentage of the population might go to the wall, but the society as a whole would grow ever richer and more cultivated. We might even imagine combinations of motivations and circumstances that offered societies only the alternatives of running such Darwinist arrangements or of jeopardizing the lives of all their members by attaching humanitarian qualifications to the arrangements. It is not just chances of getting food that may thrust some people to the wall. Some societies have continued and prospered while they sacrificed the lives of some of their members in periodical rituals or in foolish wars.

A point made several times in the earlier chapters comes up again: Some specification going beyond continuing and prospering is required of what the Common Good attained by a thriving society is to amount to. It might well be a specification that builds in provisions for meeting every member's needs and provisions beyond that if feasible to allow every member commodious living – a productive and satisfying life. It will not suffice to have a principle that accepts societies as thriving no matter what drawbacks their mode of thriving has for people outside those societies. For their grisly rites, designed according to their religious beliefs to keep the universe from a 'daily threat of annihilation,' the Aztecs preferred to sacrifice not the lives of fellow citizens, but by thousands and even tens of thousands the lives of prisoners captured in wars waged just to capture such victims.[21] The general principle defining thriving must carry the qualification that the provisions and opportunities of no one outside the society should be reduced by the activities of the society in question to a level below that sought as minimal for members of that society.

This qualification, even though not laid out in so many words by St Thomas or other theorists, fits the Christian vision of all mankind as members of one community. Again, we come upon a point that belongs to any comprehensive understanding of the core of natural law theory, and to every system of that core, though Hobbes leaves it out. (Yet for Hobbes, sovereign states are in a state of nature and a solution to their woes is available to them – conquest or contract.) The qualification to the principle can also be argued for on the line that to ignore the effects of the activities of one's own society upon people outside it cannot be justified to them and therefore is bound to be deeply corrupting to the members inside. If they are so callous about people outside, will they not be liable to becoming callous about people inside, their fellow-citizens? (Compare similar arguments about the effects of tolerating callous treatment of animals of other species.) Such an argument may work even for people who do not respond to an argument maintaining directly that a system of ethics should be attractive (without granting special privileges) to all.

To sum up the preceding discussion, allowing as I have just done for less favourable cases, but taking as basic the case in which there is the wherewithal at the social level to meet everyone's needs: To make use of provisions for their needs, all members of the society must have a realistic opportunity to obtain them – to take the provisions up, I shall say – and consume them, in the case of food ingest them. Moreover, everyone in every society does have such needs. The points of take-up for the provisions may vary between societies: The common-pool society that I have described lies at one extreme, where the point of take-up occurs just before ingestion; the society of subsistence farmers lies an appreciable distance away; further yet, and closer to the other extreme, will be societies in which people must obtain credits in their banking accounts and arrange to have goods delivered them, perhaps from remote centres, by having their accounts debited for the charges. Though the points of take-up, and with them particular rules, including rules for rights, may thus vary from society to society, in every society there must be an assurance of opportunities to obtain and consume provisions that runs from the point of take-up to ingestion – final consumption. Rule (1) prescribes that there shall be such an assurance for everyone in the society. Besides the opportunities, however, if there might ever be an occasion for such protection, there needs to be a Rule (2) that prohibits everyone from interfering with the opportunities before or after taking up and before or after ingesting. (After ingesting? Consider, far-fetched though they may be, instances of induced vomiting or stomach-pumping.) Where are the opportunities and provisions to come from? Rule (3) prescribes that given the kinds of productive effort required everyone capable of doing so is to contribute to the effort. The three rules together may be taken to be consequences of a Principle of Primitive Equity, according to which all members of a given society are to be able to meet their needs.

Some societies may be fortunate enough to leave the Rules unobtrusive, as it were in abeyance. What the Rules call for is supplied, as in a society of saints, without question, spontaneously. Other societies, accepting the Principle of Primitive Equity and endeavoring to fulfill it, may aim at heeding the three Rules, but fall short, through inefficiency or want of resources. Do we not, however, have to consider societies that ignore the Principle of Primitive Equity and thus can treat the three Rules as irrelevant? But it is not so easy to have such a society. Doing without the Rules might mean the sort of chaos that Hobbes imputed to the State of Nature; there would not be a society at all. Alternatively, a set of unaggressive people, who did not have to deal with the limited scarcity that Hume explicitly assumes in the circumstances of justice might get along without subscribing to the Rules. However, they, like the society of saints, would be doing what the Rules called for – vanishingly little in their case; and as the formulation of Rule (2), which could be followed on this point by equally explicit phrasing in the formulation of the other two rules, expressly allows, the Rule may apply to them conditionally, so that should their situation change and limited scarcity prevail (or should their motivations change toward aggressiveness), it would make effective current demands on their conduct.

What is to be done in circumstances so desperate that some people must lose out regardless of the arrangements adopted to provide for needs, not to speak of commodious living? Hume writes these off as circumstances in which justice cannot hold, but we might consider solutions less drastic than abandoning justice altogether. The speed with which circumstances could be changed so that provisions could be made for everybody is one point to be considered in adopting temporary arrangements; minimization of the number of people denied sufficient provisions meanwhile is another.

More troubling than societies that struggle to fulfill the three Rules, but fall short, are societies, like those alluded to above, that disregard the Principle of Primitive Equity and the three Rules and accept without misgivings arrangements that succeed, and are intended to succeed, only in arriving at a statistical approximation to fulfilling the principle. (Maybe even if the society accepts the three-rule combination, it will not be able to do better than a statistical approximation.) Opportunities to take up provisions and opportunities to consume them exist, but the opportunities do not open up for everyone. Every year, under the arrangements of such a society, a proportion of its population is left to expire. Such a society is all too possible. It may exist, it may perpetuate itself, it may expand; it may achieve great things in technology, science, art, and philosophy. The cities of Greece and the Roman Empire, with their large slave populations, are examples. So the three Rules are not in force in all possible societies, even in all societies that have some claim to be called thriving. But that does not mean that, in force or not, the Rules do not hold. Here the normative force of natural law comes to the fore with the Principle of Primitive Equity; thriving without respecting the Principle and without giving everybody year in and year out, so long as it is possible, opportunities to meet their needs is not the sort of thriving wanted.

To return to the contention that private property in a society of subsistence farmers opens up a unique path to optimal productivity, I would point out that history warrants holding that there will be problems along the way about denying some people, perhaps many people, opportunities to thrive as persons. Suppose the land is parcelled out according to Locke's and Hume's doctrines of private property combined. Once there is no more land for the taking, the laws would be replaced by others, deduced as more suitable for the changed circumstances. Certainly, what to do about landless people will become a problem. Enserfdom, under a feudal system that imposes responsibilities for the welfare of serfs and vassals upon their superiors, may loom as a solution. However, this solution, insofar as it was a solution, had been breaking down for centuries (in Western Europe; Eastern Europe was not so lucky) before the time of either Locke or Hume. Another sort of solution emerged with the possibility of emigration to the frontier, in the New World, where primitive opportunities for appropriation could (for a while) still be found. But this emigration was even well into the nineteenth century very dangerous, since a large proportion of the emigrants perished at sea or succumbed to pestilence soon after they debarked. Furthermore, in many instances, it was forced emigration (the Highland Clearances; the transportation for trivial crimes of people to Australia), something that cannot easily be legitimized by Locke's and Hume's combined theory. Emigration reduced the practical dimensions of the problem of landless people, but there was no justification in the theory for the way in which the reduction was accomplished.

Nor could any justification be found there for the way in which the masses of landless (propertyless) people who stayed at home were treated. When Marx scorned capitalism as a system of slavery that did not even enable the slaves to earn a livelihood,[22] he may have exaggerated the degree to which the exploitation of people leaving the land for factory work was carried. Not every worker was forced to accept a subsistence wage for unconscionably long hours of work. Even when the conditions of factory work were very harsh, many people lived better by escaping rural poverty to work in factories.[23] Yet nothing in Locke's and Hume's combined theory of property stands against the reduction of every worker's wage to the subsistence level (or, temporarily, even below) and the increase of every worker's hours of works to the physiological limit (or, temporarily, even beyond). Taking justice under the received system of rules to be something like what Locke and Hume prescribed, carried forward to circumstances utterly unlike the primitive agrarian society that their prescriptions were designed to fit, Marx held that the concept of justice was obsolete. If this was an extravagance, and inconsistent with Marx's case against the exploitation of the propertyless class – the wage-slaves, when they were lucky enough to be in work – by an oppressive system that privileged the benefits redounding to propertyowners,[24] it also embodied an important insight. Moreover, this is not the whole of Marx's case against capitalism, which would be telling even if capitalism conformed to the threefold combination of Rules, yet failed to provide for many the chances to live full and satisfying lives.

As things have turned out, Marx's alternative, a system under which the threefold combination of Rules would be heeded in the course of carrying out democratic social planning, has not been tried enough or been successful enough when tried to inspire confidence. Moreover, where planned economies have been tried without effective democracy, they have had grave drawbacks, some of them horrifying. If, at times, they did manage to succeed in heeding the threefold combination of Rules, that only showed, like the deficiencies of capitalism, that the guarantees given by the Rules did not suffice to bring about or maintain an attractively thriving society. It does not show that the threefold guarantees are not necessary.

Something like private property – enough private property to sustain an effective market – may be necessary, too. A modern industrial society, unlike a band of hunter-gatherers, may thrive only with some form of the institution of private property. It would, one would think, have to be a substantially qualified form, however. Would it in particular have to be a form suited to a welfare state, in which the exploitation of the masses is limited by laws regulating the conditions of work, laws giving workers the right to organize, laws establishing social security arrangements, including unemployment insurance and pensions, laws providing for retraining as needed, even laws authorizing public provision of employment? The welfare state, at least in principle (in what it aims at), conforms to the three-rule combination. It does raise questions about redundancy, inefficiency, and even (in respect to economic incentives) cross-purposes. On the other hand, the case for any social system must do more than show that it conforms to the three-rule combination. That combination is a necessary – a universally necessary – condition of having a thriving society. To it must be added others, and for others with a similarly universal footing we must look further into what human beings require, not just to survive, but to thrive.

Universality on Topics beyond the Three-Rule Combination

However compelling the three-rule combination may be, it falls short of providing for all the conditions – even the minimal conditions – for good lives in a community thriving in a way that captures for its members substantially all the benefits of the Common Good. Where, it should be asked, are the provisions for enjoying family life (some sort of family life)? For everyone's having a chance to develop distinctive talents in satisfying ways? For the mutual commitment to the Common Good and the shared rejoicing about it described in the explication of that concept? For the charity, caring, and fellow-feeling that would go along with this mutual commitment? Having subsistence farmers help each other on a mutual insurance basis does not reach this far. Where, one might ask, are the provisions protecting life itself from the threat of death and the body from the threat of injury? Where is there any safeguard for personal liberty? These are surely moral topics that natural law should embrace. Moreover, we should seriously ask whether a society can be as assured of meeting the basic demands of the three-rule combination if it does not make life in the society agreeable in ways answering to these further topics.

It is certainly a very odd thing that Hume should set forth the natural laws of justice, on which he says the very existence of society depends, and not mention laws against murder or assault.[25] Though Hume does say, in another passage of the *Treatise*, that cruelty is 'the most detested of all the vices' (Book III, Part III, Section III), and wanton disregard for the pain of others or their death surely falls under cruelty, in the discussion of justice that he gives in the *Treatise* he is perhaps too much under the spell of his introductory review of what is at stake. There Hume dismisses attempts against the body as offering, compared to attempts to seize transferable goods, no prospect of gaining anything useful to the perpetrator. 'The external advantages of our body' (as distinct from 'the internal satisfaction of our minds ... may be ravish'd from us, but can be of no advantage to him who deprives us of them' (Book III, Part II, Section II). (Hume, of course, wrote before the age of organ transplants.)

Locke, though he gives little more attention than Hume to the security of life and limb, does make, as I have noted, a formulaic allowance for the protection of life in his technically extended definition of property (equating it with all that is 'one's own') as embracing 'life, liberty, and estate.' 'Life' and 'liberty' will do much, if not all, of the work required by 'security of life and limb.' Moreover, something could be made of the suggestion that the protection of liberty will imply some safeguards against physical threats to the body, whether they are threats of death or of injury. For is it not under such threats that the most obvious grounds appear for explaining how anyone alert to her own interest might lose her liberty? (If she loses it through persuasion, I am assuming, she will not have been alert to her own interest. I shall not pause to consider blackmail.)

To this suggestion, when we contemplate the three-rule combination, we may add two implications to be drawn from the third Rule, about productive effort. Insofar as the productive effort entails freedom of movement and freedom of choice, some protection of liberty follows from the third Rule. Even more clearly, and perhaps comprehensively, the third Rule will imply that the body be protected from any injury that would reduce its capacity for physical effort. Even small injuries, like the loss of a finger or a toe, might reasonably count here. They would amount to significant impairments even in a technologically advanced society: The loss of a finger would make typing more difficult; the loss of a toe might make using an accelerator or a brake pedal more tiring.

The three-rule combination can thus expand through implication to cover liberty (in part) and protection against assault. It can also expand, through implication, to include protection against assassination, and this by several routes. Nothing will deprive a person more surely of the capacity for productive effort on his own behalf, or on behalf of his family, than being killed. Why should one protect him against assault and let him be killed, even if the killing is efficient and poses no danger of physical injury short of death? Once we have built in a rule against assault, we might take it to preclude life-threatening assaults as well as more modest ones, and wish to use the notion of assault broadly. It will include any physical intervention in a person's life that threatens to kill her. Leaving her to starve to death in a locked room is a form of assault. Would putting poison in a discarded lover's soup be assault? Not in the colloquial sense of the term, perhaps, but the rule against assault, if it is to keep company with the third Rule requiring productive effort, should apply to debilitating poisons as well as to beatings. Furthermore, why should there be any fuss under the first Rule in the combination about having a person meet her needs, if her life is carelessly left in jeopardy? (I am setting aside without prejudice to the extension of natural law protections to strangers, cannibalism, practised, I think, much more often than not, on captives; and human sacrifice, sometimes practised upon consociates, but only as an aberration inspired by religion.)

There is another implication about liberty to be found in the three-rule combination. Slavery, whatever it might be in principle, in every historical instance has put the slaves under the arbitrary power of masters, subjecting them to corporal and even capital punishment, and harsh treatment in other respects, too. (This was true even of the slaves who became so by taking the route offered converting Christian boys in the Ottoman Empire to high office under the Sultan.) Thus, as an empirical matter, whether or not there is a strictly logical connection, slavery jeopardizes the protections afforded by the rules regarding homicide, assault, and avoidable shortfalls in the provision for needs. So, there is at least a strong practical argument from the three-rule combination, expanded by the implications noted previously, against slavery.

I am not arguing that the expansion, by implication, of the three-rule combination is the most natural way of arriving at protections for life and limb or liberty. If we care about liberty, we shall have to find a way of adding to what the three-rule combination implies a fourth rule giving fuller protection to liberty; and we might, just as plausibly or even more plausibly, have begun there as with rules for appropriating sooner or later the goods to be consumed in meeting people's needs. My point is not that the three-rule combination, once it has been discovered, is the best place to begin setting forth a full catalogue of natural laws, like the one to be obtained by combining Hobbes's catalogue with St Thomas's. It is, as it stands, not the best place, but only a distinctly more basic place than Locke's and Hume's combined theory of property, though it might be as good a place as any, if we added a rule about liberty. What the three-rule combination does, arrived at on the route through private property, is show what is in the heart – the core of cores – of natural law ethics (and here we might say of ethics in general), even if the combination does not give us a complete or even a balanced picture of the core of cores, or even of the rules that are to be found there.

It goes without saying that I have been working in this chapter under the assumption that an especially convincing way of getting to that core of cores consists, nevertheless, in beginning with Locke's and Hume's combined theory of property and asking what general principles stand at the same time behind that theory and a theory of communal property, like the one that fits the hunter-gatherer society with a daily common pool. They are principles anchored in basic human needs, but I am not here arguing directly from needs, but from the requirements of the Common Good – the indispensable conditions under which a society thrives and keeps on thriving.

The approach to these requirements by way of Locke's and Hume's theory of property is convincing partly because these two theories are compelling given the sorts of societies assumed in the two cases; but also partly because the approach occupies so much of the range of variation of rules for the final appropriation of vital necessities. It does that by occupying so much of the range of variation in distances between the take-up point and the point of final appropriation, or, to speak more precisely, by postulating at one end of the range arrangements with a minimal distance and at the other end of the range arrangements that can be taken to typify a remote distance. It cannot be said without further ado that the arrangements common in advanced industrial societies imply a remoter distance: We could count the take-up point as the point at which one produces cash or a credit card at the supermarket and gets food in exchange. We might go back to the contract (maybe drawn up years ago) under which a person, given his performance of certain services, acquires the entitlements realized by the cash or the credit card.

The hunters and gatherers in the one society help one another by contributing to the common pool of provisions. In describing the sort of society – the society of independent subsistence farmers – that Locke's and Hume's combined theory of property fits uniquely best, I was careful to note expectations regarding mutual aid to fellow-farmers struck by disaster. Yet this may seem to be no more than egoists or non-tuists would supply themselves in the way of social insurance.[26] The common-pool society itself might conceivably demand no more in respect to the motives of the people cooperating to fill the common pool, which can be thought of as giving daily insurance against bad luck in the hunting or gathering of any given person. Going to the hunter-gatherers from the society of independent subsistence farmers, that society might not seem at first sight to be a society that could be constituted entirely by egoists or non-tuists,[27] but reflection will bear out the suggestion that it might be.

A further reason for finding compelling the route to the core of cores from Locke's and Hume's combined theory of property emerges with this conception of a society composed entirely of egoists or non-tuists, but it is a reason that has to be dealt with very cautiously. The society of independent subsistence farmers can easily be thought of, giving unqualified weight to their 'independence,' as a society of egoists and non-tuists. To many, perhaps most, philosophers, rules that have a place even there will seem especially strongly entrenched because they demand (it seems) only the minimum in motivation.

Yet is it really a plausible minimum in motivation? It is treacherous, we shall find reason to believe in the treatment of moral education to follow in the next chapter, to think of this as the default point of departure, or the most conservative expectation about human motivation: That egoism or non-tuism is the minimum in motivation in either of these senses is nothing to be taken for granted. Moral education, going hand in hand with the development of persons, as described in a previous chapter, may be expected to produce people that already have social commitments not based on egoism or non-tuism.

Suppose, however, this plausible account of moral education and the development of persons is ignored. The minimum in motivation, as a point of departure, is taken to be egoism or non-tuism. The impression of deeper entrenchment for the three-rule combination will be reinforced by finding that the common-pool society may also be thought of as a society of this kind, too. So, the three-rule combination, which fits both societies whether or not they are composed of egoists and non-tuists, will fall in with the perennial philosophical project of founding ethics on enlightened self-interest, or at least of showing how far such a foundation would succeed.

We can accept this argument, but we should not be misled by it. The common-pool societies that we encounter in the world are far from consisting in membership entirely of egoists and non-tuists. Even real, historical societies of independent subsistence farmers have not been societies of this sort. They have been societies where the members joined in barn-raising, in building and maintaining churches and schools, in Masonic ceremonies, in husking-bees. Would egoists care about husking-bees, where people gather to perform work jointly just to have the fun of one another's company? And who are the people who gather there going to see? Neighbours, friends, uncles, aunts, cousins, grandparents, in-laws. Even in the society of independent subsistence farmers people will have families, and those families will extend through the generations from one household to another.

Through Locke and Hume we go back to the core of cores in natural law ethics; and we can argue to every other universal natural law as an implication of the core of cores or as a means of maintaining it – of keeping up the three-rule combination. Liberty is in part an implication, in part a means. Truth-telling and promise-keeping not only are means of making the rules in the core more useful; they are means of keeping up mutual trust and hence of maintaining the social system that rests on the three-rule combination. Yet the core of cores is richer in aspects answering to benefits and attachment than the three-rule combination by itself implies or suggests. We can also argue – indeed, it is more natural, to use this term lightly, to argue – for some natural laws directly from their attractions as ingredients of the core of cores, which is to say, directly from their presence in the realization of a rich Common Good.

The core of cores, in accordance with a sceptical treatment of assumptions about universal egoism, or even of universal egoism as a minimal point of departure in ethics, will reflect, from the bottom up, the assumption that the normal situation for human beings is living together in a community whose members are joined very extensively by ties of kinship and by friendships formed in joint activities. In this way, it will accord with a reasonable view of theory and practice in moral education and accord, too, with the full development of a rich notion of the Common Good, by supplying a favourable basis for such development.

With many of the aspects of the Common Good, to be achieved in its full development, the issue will be, not what universal moral rules are to safeguard these additional aspects, but what provisions will be most effective in achieving them. Those provisions will vary greatly from society to society, in part because of variations in culture, in part because of variations in wealth. Not every society, not every society that attains a rich and robust Common Good, will have a use for libraries, museums, opera houses, symphony halls, or universities; not every thriving society will be able to afford them. One might say, tentatively, though it is not a rule that much (if anything) has been made of in the tradition of natural law, that it is a universal rule that the people who decide about such things in every society should not miss opportunities to make provisions for the Common Good suited to the society in question. Sometimes these provisions will require action by public agencies; sometimes they might require simply that public authorities stand out of the way of spontaneous arrangements. The measures to be taken will not always, or even perhaps for the most part (at least after the minimal conditions for social peace and cooperation have been established), take the form of specific rules. Yet there are universal rules no more abstract than the ones in the three-rule combination to be added to it on the way to achieving a rich Common Good. They will be implied directly by the project of achieving such a Common Good, as well as by any assistance that they give to the narrow part of the core of cores that the three-rule combination constitutes. Rules about truth-telling and promise-keeping are among them; so are rules about family life, or at any rate about the upbringing of children, and an expandable rule giving fuller protection to liberty.

Hume has a place among his fundamental rules of justice for a rule prescribing that contracts be honoured, and he argues for giving it such a place by invoking the difficulties of economic cooperation in its absence. It is a cogent argument; and it exposes the unrealistic tendency of economic theory to concentrate upon momentary purchases in a market that clears maybe instantaneously, or at any rate only after a delay in which supply prices and demand prices are brought into coincidence, to the disregard of contracts and long-term cooperation. Long-term cooperation by means of contracts depends upon trust and increases trust; it is also the basis for developing friendly relations among buyers and sellers, and thus further increasing trust.

However, Hume's case for honouring contracts is too narrow to capture the full range and importance of promise-keeping. Promises bind in mutual trust not just economic agents, but friends and lovers. Turning out with the rest of the community to help in a good cause will in most instances, if not in all, rest on mutual promises: 'I'll be there to clean up the river bank, if you will be.' A natural law rule insisting on keeping promises will be better deduced from the aim of realizing the Common Good, fully conceived, than from narrow commercial considerations. So will a natural law rule requiring truth-telling. This is equally important in commercial connections, where buyers require information from sellers about the quality of the things that they are offered. Almost equally neglected in standard economic treatments of the market, the information at the disposal of sellers may call for augmentation. Sellers will often want to know something about the buyers' credit and other matters. Yet, again, what is at issue is so important to mutual trust, ramifying throughout the relations of members of the community, that the demand for truth-telling must be supposed to rest upon larger notions about the Common Good.

Given this richness of connections, it may be expected that different societies will have different rules regarding keeping promises and different rules regarding truth-telling, too. Must we not go behind them, as we went behind the rules regarding private property, to find any truly universal rules and rules that have more fundamental topics in view? My argument in this chapter seems to have moved in turn from one to another of at least three stages: one stage in which given the failures respecting universality of the rules of private property the more fundamental topics of opportunities and assurances for taking up provisions for meeting needs came into view; a second stage in which rules for other topics, in particular liberty, emerged as consequences of rules on these fundamental topics; a third stage that was introduced by associating with the pursuit of the Common Good a universal rule about seizing opportunities to advance it. Have we, contemplating rules about promises and truth-telling, begun to use the third stage just to collect some miscellaneous further rules that natural law theory would want to cover?

This is only an invidious description of what has been going on in the argument. The argument has been tied to the thriving of societies and their Common Good all along, anchored, as I have said, in meeting basic human needs, but arguing throughout – immediately – not so much from needs as from a generalized notion of thriving with the Common Good. The first business of the argument was to show how far one would get in specifying universal rules by rectifying the claims of Locke's and Hume's doctrines of private property; this, in the first stage, brought me back to the anchoring of the Common Good in meeting basic needs. Then, in the second stage, I considered what further rules were implied by the three basic rules discovered in the first stage, rules that had to be kept up if the three basic rules were to be fulfilled. Rules about promises and truth-telling have to be kept up for this reason, too: Schemes of cooperation that may be required to fulfill the three basic rules will fail if they cannot rest on promises and truth-telling; furthermore, the whole enterprise of keeping the society in question together may be jeopardized if people cannot trust one another to keep promises and tell the truth. Beyond these reasons, however, promises and truth-telling are morally valuable because they foster and manifest the mutual trust that will pervade a society that is fully attaining a rich Common Good. Thus, they call for making a direct connection of their own to the Common Good.

Promises and truth-telling require a shift of approach on other grounds. Locke's and Hume's rules of private property did not contain any core rule that could plausibly be attributed to all societies that attained the Common Good. I had to go behind them to reach such core rules – the three-rule combination. By contrast, both the rule about promise-keeping and the rule about truth-telling invite being treated as core rules. The exceptions to the core rules, no doubt, vary greatly from one society to another; but to every society may reasonably be attributed a core rule about keeping promises (perhaps given the condition that the promises in question meet certain tests for being taken seriously) and a core rule about truth-telling. Speculatively, one could perhaps imagine complex indirect arrangements for realizing trust and cooperation that dispensed with such rules. But in a simple sense of 'natural,' the most natural way of realizing the ends at stake with promises and truth-telling is just to have practices of promises and truth-telling. It would be difficult, maybe impossible, for people to learn a language without learning how to tell the truth in the course of it; and exchanges of promises make available in the clearest and simplest terms just what mutual expectations are at stake.

A rule giving fuller protection for liberty can rest on those larger notions about the Common Good, too. On an historical or anthropological view, however, the scope for liberty appears to vary enormously from one society to another. To allow for this, a descriptively universal rule applying in all societies might best be formulated as protecting the liberty to enjoy the benefits of one's status, where the status is something conferred by a given society. This, at the bottom of the range, where the scope for liberty is most limited, may not be much liberty, but we can perhaps assume that it is even there a status that in normal circumstances offers a livelihood. Then the rule will prohibit other people from interfering with the liberty of any given person to enjoy the benefits of her status, taking this enjoyment to be circumscribed under the rule to fall short of interfering with the status of others in her turn.

The rule about liberty can be a normative point of departure toward better rules. It is subject to expansion in several ways. It may expand by protecting people's opportunities to change their status for a status present in the same society, unchanged in regard to the schedule of statuses, with a greater scope for liberty. It may expand to cover the increased scope for liberty that may come in as one schedule of statuses gives way to another. Furthermore, it may go on expanding in this way, as the society in question approaches closer and closer to attaining the richest (or, to allow for different options in this connection, a richest) Common Good. At the limit the rule will grant (as Rawls's first principle would have it)[28] the maximum liberty to everyone that is compatible with equal liberty for others. However, this maximum must be understood to be constrained by expectations and commitments regarding cooperation in attaining the Common Good. Will liberty under the rule extend to the liberty to leave the society for another (or just to live in the woods)? This extension may not get much support in societies hard pressed to survive even when they are at peace; it will predictably get little or no support if the society to be left is under attack.

Generous views about liberty – including the liberty to leave – are likely to be associated with societies in the neighborhood of attaining a rich Common Good that are self-confident about their power to stay in the neighborhood. One may also expect to find only there full support for any rules associated with the virtue of charity (asserted by Locke in the *First Treatise*)[29] or with the virtues of gratitude, modesty, tact ('complaisance'), forgiveness, and nonvindictiveness (mentioned by Hobbes in his catalogue of natural laws).[30] Rules about these things will be so many rules about human beings playing their part in a society that in attaining a rich Common Good attains high levels of trust and mutual attachment.

Are we implying a distinction between a richer Common Good and a relatively impoverished one, the minimum that would make having a society worthwhile? That is far from obvious. Rules about these refined topics may come in very early, on the ground floor of what is required to keep a society going. At any rate, due caution in these matters suggests that every failure in a society's thriving may endanger its continuance. It is a striking aspect of Hobbes's doctrine that rules requiring forgiveness and gratitude (not just in inclination, but in expression) figure in his catalogue of natural laws. Like the others, they are moral theorems proved by the argument that if they are not adhered to there will be no peaceful social order. Hobbes is not, and is not to be thought of, as a great advocate of kindness; but with the case for these rules Hobbes is, in effect, making a case for there being no hope of keeping a peaceful society at all if its members do not treat one another with some kindness. Hence, however far away we may have come at the limit of expanded liberty from the three-rule combination, forgiveness and gratitude (along, very likely, with the other virtues mentioned) bring us back to the minimal conditions for having a society at all. They will, again, be conditions much easier to fulfill if the society in question is not composed wholly of egoists or non-tuists.

It is not part of my purpose in the present chapter to give anything like a complete list of the universal rules that natural law theory will want (sooner or later) to add to the three-rule combination. It has been, instead, my purpose to get some idea about just where – with just what rules or interpretations of rules – one is moving beyond minimal conditions of thriving and maintaining the Common Good to features that are no more than desirable additions, even if they are universally desirable additions, found only in societies attaining the Common Good at a high level of complexity. Surprisingly, if the present discussion is on the right track, it may be said that the transition occurs relatively late, only after substantial provision for brotherly and sisterly love. Without these things, the assurances of meeting basic needs under the three-rule combination weaken or maybe vanish. It may be true that universal rules on various topics go only part of the way toward the attainment of the Common Good, but that does not mean that the indispensable rules embrace only a minimal range of topics.

I suggested earlier that it might be regarded as a universal rule that the people who decide about provisions for the Common Good should not miss opportunities to make provisions suited to the society of which they are members. Put another way, the rule might require doing everything necessary to attain the Common Good that is currently feasible. Formally, such a rule covers all aspects of the Common Good. Does this conflict with the suggestion that, after a certain point, it is not so much rules that are to be relied on in attaining the Common Good as direct provisions (like libraries and opera houses)? We might make little of the objection that the comprehensive rule just cited is nothing but a tautological redescription of commitment to the Common Good. Once it is understood what the Common Good amounts to and what its function is in guiding personal conduct and social policy, inviting people to follow the comprehensive rule adds nothing to inviting people to aim at the Common Good. But we could say that the rule expresses the invitation; moreover, the rule might serve (as one of several options) as a basic axiom for axiomatizing the system of natural laws. The distinction between the aspects of the Common Good to be attained under the protection of universal rules and the aspects to be attained otherwise remains, but it has been, as it were, shifted down a level. The comprehensive rule covers all aspects, but some aspects are the business of more specific universal rules, while other aspects are not. Even if rules come in with the institutions of provision, these will not be universal rules, but specific rules for managing libraries or museums.

Natural law theory, before and after being modernized, has always claimed that it had in view moral rules that hold for every society and that actually govern the practices of societies that pursue, as successfully as they can, the Common Good. In this chapter, I have defended this claim and demonstrated its application to representative ingredients of the catalogue of natural laws outlined earlier. The defence and demonstration fall somewhat short of presenting the full evidence needed to extinguish every trace of doubt. That evidence may, in large part, remain to be collected. However, I believe that I have demonstrated that the claim is a robust and reasonable empirical hypothesis; and done something to guide the collection of further evidence. If I have not put every aspect of Natural Law Modernized beyond doubt, I think I have further strengthened the case for thinking that Natural Law Modernized has been a redoubtable contender in ethical theory all along, from St Thomas's time to our own.

Chapter Seven

With Us Still: Natural Law Theory Illustrated Today in the Work of David Copp

David Copp, in his ambitious attempt to produce a comprehensive ethical theory, *Morality, Normativity, and Society* (New York: Oxford University Press, 1995), does not once cite St Thomas. Copp mentions natural law only in passing, and then not as a variety of ethical theory, but as a position in the philosophy of law opposed to legal positivism.[1] All of this is in keeping with Copp's general omission to consider historic precedents for his combination of a 'standard-based theory' of moral propositions with a 'society-centered theory' of moral standards. Copp's combined theory amounts notwithstanding to a version of the same secular natural law theory that, I have been arguing, can be found embedded in a theological context in St Thomas (and in Hobbes and Locke as well) and, found dispensing with that context, in Hume. More of the theological context survives (curiously unperceived by Copp himself) in Copp's theory than does in Hume's, and for those who think natural law must have something to do with God this may be a special attraction. But leave the theological context aside. It must still come as something of a surprise to find the core of medieval natural law theory flourishing at the present day unperceived as such by an author who champions it. May its surprising presence in Copp's theory not signify that natural law theory is with us still, as much in the received ethics that Copp seeks to theorize as in any theory of the sort that he attempts? It is so familiar that, outside of Catholic circles, we look past it, and overlook it; but it is lying in wait all the while for theoretical attention.

Issues Dealt with in Copp's Combined Theory

In outline, Copp holds, under the 'standard-based theory,' that moral propositions (to the effect, say, that given actions are right or wrong)

are true or false in respect to implied claims that the actions accord or
fail to accord with justified moral standards. Oddly, given the central-
ity of the concept of a standard to his work, and the great care with
which he has worked out so many aspects of his argument, Copp is not
clear about what a standard is or how it might differ from a rule –
including the rule that makes it a standard. For example, if recruits to
the infantry must be five feet tall or taller, then there is a rule so
expressed that makes that height a standard; it is given effect as a standard by bringing about adherence to the rule.[2] Fortunately, for purposes of Copp's theory, the concept of a rule can be substituted for the
concept of a standard throughout;[3] and if a definition of a rule (which
Copp does not supply) is wanted, a robust definition can now easily be
supplied.[4] So, Copp's position is, in part (the standard-based part), that
moral propositions about, say, given actions being right or wrong are
true or false in respect to implied claims that the actions accord or fail
to accord with justified moral rules. This fits easily enough into the natural law theory that I have collected from the authors whom I treat,
though some little adjustments have to made in the case of Hume, as
we have seen, to accommodate Hume's tendency to avoid use of the
locutions 'true' or 'false' for moral judgments in favour of 'correct' or
'incorrect.'

The other chief part of Copp's position is his 'society-centered theory,' according to which a moral standard, that is to say, a moral rule, is
justified if it is a feature of a social moral code that would be adopted
in a rational choice by a given society, where it is recognized as something that would serve better than any other code – and better than not
having any code – primarily to meet the needs of the society. The
choice thus accords with natural law theory on the point of the a posteriori argument. The choice need not be unanimous, even though (in
Copp's view, as, speaking for natural law theory, in mine) a crucially
important consideration in meeting the needs of the society is meeting
the basic human needs of its members (the people who will be doing
the choosing), but justification requires that it should be nearly so. A
justified rule is not itself true, though it is the basis on which is erected
the truth of related moral propositions about the rightness or wrongness of actions, or, I might add, about the rightness or wrongness
of any object of moral judgment including personal character (rule-
abiding even in exemplifying virtues) and social policies.

I propose to combine both parts of Copp's position with the core natural law theory that I have been collecting from my chosen canonical authors. Thanks to Copp's care and sophistication in dealing with

current problems in ethical theory (metaethics) about internalism (externalism), cognitivism, moral realism, naturalism, and relativism, incorporating Copp in this way will automatically give me and the theory that I have been collecting robust state-of-the-art solutions to all these problems. Moreover, the fit between Copp's position and the collected theory, as they stand, goes far enough to automatically establish the collected theory as a serious candidate for being chosen instead of current rival theories like contractarianism or utilitarianism. The union of the two (with mutual improvements drawn from both sides) produces an even stronger candidate.

In this view of the union, I shall be assuming that either the additions to the collected theory brought in from Copp do not conflict with anything that the authors I have been treating would hold in assenting to the collected core theory; or if in one or another case they do, the additions do little violence to anything that these dissenting authors hold.

In ethics, the issue about internalism is the issue about whether when someone assents to a moral proposition about something being right or wrong she is by virtue of doing so acknowledging that it has normative force. Copp's position in his 'standard-based' theory, as he points out, is internalist, in respect to making normativity internal to moral propositions (with their logical reliance on justified moral rules); and internalist, also, in a way that more surely captures commitment by the person concerned in her own case, in respect to subscription to a moral rule, for example, the justified rule that underlies the present moral proposition. By subscribing to a rule as a moral one, a person commits himself to acting by it; and also to encouraging other people to act by it. Thus, the full normative force of a moral proposition comes from combining the reference to a justified moral rule with subscription to the rule as a moral one. Both parts of the combination fall under internalist conceptions of moral propositions.[5] However, the combination does not; Copp's position is externalist in allowing for a discrepancy between believing in a moral proposition and subscribing to the implied moral rule. Commonly, of course, the belief – 'This, being a case of fraud, is wrong' – and the subscription go together, along with actions motivated by the subscription; but, logically, in Copp's view, they stand or fall separately. One may believe, he wishes to say, in a moral proposition, and hence in the implication running to a justified rule, but not subscribe morally to the rule in question; and, of course, one may subscribe to a rule without (say, for want of information) seeing that a given moral proposition that relies on the rule is true.

Traditional theory (in the hands of St Thomas or of others) may not divide so neatly what is true or false in moral discourse from what is subscribed to or not subscribed to. In this respect, other authors with positions approximating Copp's, are more traditional, and more (I think) in keeping with ordinary usage – for one, Richmond Campbell, who offers a 'hybrid' theory of moral judgment, according to which in normal cases, the judgment has two functions, one 'to dispose the appraiser to act, feel, and generally be motivated in a morally appropriate way,' the other to represent 'this dispositional state, along with the norms that it embodies, as being justified or warranted.'[6]

Copp may oversimplify received moral discourse on these points. Yet he does offer at least the minimum of provision for both truth and subscription; and the fact the collected core theory could work effectively with that minimum is clarificatory. Copp's treatment of internalism and externalism is at least a first approximation to the full truth about these matters and one that highlights the chief points about them.

The issue about cognitivism is one that came up for extended discussion in the chapter on Hume, where it was held that Hume is (in the end) a moral realist, one who recognizes that moral propositions are true or false and that some of them are true. (Cognitivism has another branch, the rather bizarre 'error theory' put forward by the distinguished philosopher J.L. Mackie, which, like moral realism, breaks with non-cognitivism in accepting that moral propositions are true or false, but contends that all of them are false.[7]) Copp's position is cognitivist in respect to the truth values that it accords to moral propositions. However, the moral rules, the existence of which moral propositions entail, do not themselves have truth values; and this feature of the position gives a (limited) place in Copp's theory to non-cognitivism.

Copp does not make as much as he might have in his discussion of cognitivism versus non-cognitivism and of propositional approaches to ethical theory of what von Wright calls 'normative statements.'[8] These are propositions, parallel to the rules present in any situation, that do not themselves apply the rules to actions, but assert that the rules exist and that they are moral ones. They thus assert that the rules are justified, and since they are themselves propositions, not rules, they have truth values. Copp acknowledges as much, but he does not deal with the question whether these propositions contribute to the cognitivism of his theory.[9] To be sure, propositions asserting the existence of rocks and trumpet calls do not imply that rocks and trumpet calls have truth values; but there is more connection to truth in the case of moral rules, as I shall make clear in a moment.

Moreover, this point takes on a good deal of importance for Copp's claim that his position is a form of 'naturalism,' in which the rules are justified, or not, by empirical evidence as to their efficacy, operating together as a moral code, in enabling a society to meet its needs (its thriving by attainment of the Common Good, to use my language rather than Copp's) and, hence – as a further empirical fact – that it would be rational for the society to choose them.[10] The position is not just cognitivist, but (as Copp again maintains) realist, too, since it assumes at least some moral rules (including some familiar received rules) to belong to a justified social moral code, and to be known as belonging thereto.[11] Hence some moral propositions are currently true. They are true because they rest firmly on a code that has been (or would be) rationally chosen by a society that the code enables to thrive; and every rule that belongs to that code may be asserted in the other sort of propositions, the normative statements, to have a naturalistic or empirical connection with meeting the needs that must be met for the society to thrive.

At the same time, however, Copp's position allows for a certain relativism, just as I have allowed for a certain relativism in the collected theory: In principle, different moral codes, perhaps very different moral codes, might be justified for different societies. Not only may there be different ways of thriving in different circumstances: In Canada, one thrives by taking up cross-country skiing; in the Bahamas, by taking up scuba-diving. Even in similar circumstances, different societies may thrive in different ways – not in some cases by activity in sports, but by engrossment in music, in the theatre, in the tea ceremony, and in flower-arranging. It is possible, though not particularly plausible, that these differences come with basic differences in moral codes. In practice, as Copp thinks likely, and as traditional natural law theory has held, the codes will almost certainly be found to contain some of the same rules.[12] Moreover, it remains open to natural law theory to show that all these codes can be brought under the same general rules as deductions or constructions suited to the different circumstances of the societies surveyed. If that is so, relativism fades out as a possible point of difference between the collected theory and the collected theory incorporating Copp's position.

This escape from relativism is also encouraged by concentrating at the social or community level on meeting the needs of the members of the community (consistently with providing for its survival when that survival is useful to its members). Copp does in effect end up doing this. His distinction between needs and values (made much of at the personal level) would have complicated matters for him had he seriously carried it forward to the level of social choice.[13] A person may balance her needs against her values when on occasion provision for the one conflicts with provision for the other. But what would 'balancing' social needs against social values amount to, if it is to be done democratically, but a host of problems aggravated by bringing values as well as needs into the picture? Since this a move toward generating social choices out of variable personal preference orderings, the problems would be aggravated, among other things, in a way that connects with the problems of social choice theory, which otherwise Copp can set aside in a very successful passage.[14] Copp transposes his scheme of rational choice respecting needs, values, and (mere) preferences from the personal to the social level; but in the course of doing so he sets social – transpersonal – values and preferences aside as not making so much difference on the social level.[15] Thus, I shall speak of looking for a code that best meets the needs of society when a code is to be socially chosen. Then, though social needs (the needs of a society) are not identical with the needs of the persons who belong to the society, meeting the needs of the persons concerned is of crucial importance among the social needs.[16]

Among Copp's achievements are some welcome additions to the collected natural law theory:

1 An illuminating distinction between moral propositions and moral rules put forward with the thesis that the truth of the first depends on the presence of a justified case of the second
2 A careful explication of how the justification of a moral rule or of a set of moral rules (a social moral code) may depend upon a rational social choice, at least if it is insisted that justification must include making them binding
3 A careful explication of how this, in turn, depends on having a conception (which Copp takes care to supply) of what a society is that supports ascribing choices as well as rules to it
4 A theory of rational choice that, extended from persons to societies, explains what it is for a society to make a rational choice.

On the last two points, what Copp has to say is that a society is a population of human beings in which one generation after another usually enlists new members by birth. The new members grow up to take part in interactions with other members of the society in the pursuit of material necessities and other things, and, in the course of a moral education as they are growing up, expectably come to heed various persisting rules governing these interactions. In these respects combined, the society supplies a framework for its members' lives, which no larger grouping of human beings does by answering to the same combined features, even if the society is not characterized by unity or solidarity.[17] Such a society can be said to make a choice when the members of it are nearly unanimous in the preferences that they express when a choice is called for about a given set of options in social policy.[18]

The additions on these points and others are ones that the collected natural law theory can accommodate, and might even invite. I said above that Copp's application of the distinction between internalism and externalism did not seem radically inconsistent with the collected core natural law theory.

The invitation is stronger than this point about at least rough consistency on internalism versus externalism and other points suggest. St Thomas, for example, means to make an important distinction between speculative (theoretical) reasoning and practical reasoning. The criterion that he offers for making the distinction is that practical reasoning falls under the rule to seek good and shun evil, taking this not so much as a source for the content of specific rules, but as a criterion for sorting out moral rules from other objects of reasoning, and setting up the perspective and orientation in which the search for rules is to be initiated.[19] (Hobbes follows him in offering a rule, though not the same rule, as the criterion; in Hobbes's case, it is 'Seek peace.') Hence, it is a mark of practical reasoning that such reasoning has to do with moral rules.

Insistence, with Copp, on the fact that the rules do not have truth values helps define the sphere of practical reasoning. Moreover, the sharpness of the distinction is not lost by recognizing the parallel propositions to the effect that the rules involved exist, that is, are justified. For basic connections in the reasoning still run from rule to rule: If one rule prohibits an action A, then one may infer that there is a rule prohibiting another action B, when B has as an inevitable consequence (or maybe even just a highly probable consequence) the doing of A. One has, of course, to go over the basic features of the source rule (see above, chap. 2) – the **volk, wenn,** and **nono** components – to make sure that they fully cover the corresponding elements of the rule inferred.

The distinction between the spheres of theoretical reasoning and of practical reasoning becomes clearer, moreover, when we consider Copp's allowances for non-cognitivism. Not being vehicles of truth values, rules cannot be for Copp direct expressions of knowledge. Nor can subscription to any of the rules, with the entailed commitment to adhere to it, be pre-empted, as it were, by propositional reasoning. It may be incongruous, even illogical by the standards of deontic logic, not to subscribe to a given rule when one subscribes to a more general one under which the more specific one falls. But subscription requires in every case an act of faith – a commitment – in which the person concerned brings his outlook and intentions into line with the rule or the set of rules in question.[20]

Copp's Theory Complemented and Strengthened by the Core Natural Law Theory

On other points, secular natural law theory in the version that I have collected and brought forward not only complements Copp's theory, but makes good some of its defects by supplying:

1 Attention to compassion and care, characteristic of the canonical authors (except Hobbes), where Copp omits entirely to consider what in human psychology would motivate moral subscription of any kind, including in particular moral subscription to justified moral rules[21]
2 A means of distinguishing a moral code from other sets of rules (for example, the rules of logic), which, in spite of his explicit intentions, Copp omits to give; the means, present in St Thomas's treatment of justice as a general virtue, has to do with how people treat each other in respect to their welfare, indeed in not making sense (as the rules of logic do) in applications in which such treatment is not at issue (or at least presupposed)[22]
3 A clearer position as to why a backing in social choice may be required for a standard – it is evidently required as a substitute for God's authority; if we are not to take natural laws as commandments by God, traditionally thought indispensable to making them

binding (see, for example, Locke), they must be binding on some other basis and being commanded by society (by the community, according to St Thomas, speaking of human law) is the most likely one.

Copp defines a person's moral code (92) as an exhaustive and non-redundant set of rules – all of which that person subscribes to morally, wanting them to be current in her society, with conformity by herself and all others who belong to it, and negative responses to nonconformity. This fits a code that consists of the rules of logic and a code that consists of the rules of personal hygiene. One may subscribe to these rules as moral standards, too: Contrary to what Copp says (85), we may well care whether people in distant parts of our society follow rules of hygiene since (at the very least) we may care whether they pose a danger of infection to other people. We may also well care to assert that 'people who make logical mistakes deserve ... negative responses.' Lapses in logic undermine rational discourse in the community – or discourse just between you and me, if you continually contradict yourself or deduce something from affirming a consequent. Any member of a given society might well want to have other members observe rules about logic as well as about hygiene, and thus desire the currency of both. One could also contrive to say that both sets of rules have to do with dealing with other people. But Copp resists treating them as moral rules; and though this is plausible, especially in the case of the rules of logic, he provides no reason for not applying his definition of a moral code to include them. One needs to say something about the direct impact of actions coming under the moral code upon the welfare of specifiable other people; and making no sense otherwise.

Copp's use of the term 'justified' is unfortunate for his technical purposes, since for him it goes beyond the ordinary sense of being established as appropriate to include being binding. There is no puzzle about why if a rule is to be 'binding,' one may ask for the authority on which it rests and, hence, look for a choice by the authority. If this does not give enough credit to custom and tacit consent, it is nevertheless a wholly familiar move. Why must a code be chosen in order to be 'justified'? Why has not one said all that is required to make out a code as justified when one shows how heeding it contributes (better than other codes) to the good of the society in question, including the welfare of the people belonging to the society? Thus, justification may be covered by a theory, as Copp acknowledges,[23] that is society-centred, since the theory has to do with effectively meeting the needs of a society, but does not require a social choice. If the issue of bindingness is deferred, this is also a natural way of reading the justification supplied by the secular natural law theory that I have collected in the present book from my canonical authors.

St Thomas's conception of rules, specifically the natural laws, accords better than Copp's with ordinary language ways of speaking and thinking, in which instances of language that carry truth value do not neatly divide off from instances that do not. In *ST* 1a2ae, Q.94, 4, for instance, St Thomas says that 'in respect to particular conclusions come to by the practical reason there is no general unanimity about what is true or right.' Note the use of 'true.' Immediately thereafter, in the course of producing an example of such particular conclusions (which in the next article, Q.94, 5, he will identify with 'secondary precepts'), as it happens, one on which he does report unanimity, he says, 'All hold that it is true and right that we should act intelligently' (that is to say, in accord with reason). Thus, for St Thomas, the utterance 'We should act intelligently' both expresses a rule and has a truth value. This means, I think, that we need not contemplate his somehow presupposing a parallel, speculative science of ethics in which there is a proposition asserting the existence of every rule that the practical reason brings to light and expresses as a rule.[24] Richmond Campbell's account of moral judgments is closer to this position than Copp's.[25] The practical reason does the job of establishing the existence of a rule at once with laying it down and calling for heeding it.

This approach not only abstains from forcing a distinction that ordinary language does not make. It fits better than Copp's approach with the fact that the expression of rules in declarative sentences invites the ascription of truth values. This invitation is offered not only by declarative sentences containing prescriptive locutions – 'We should act intelligently.' It is offered even more strongly (as von Wright explicitly noted)[26] by declarative sentences (commonly used in and out of the law) that express rules without using any distinctively prescriptive locutions – 'Every able-bodied male citizen keeps the firearm issued him by the Army at his home.'

Normally, as Copp admits, expressing belief in a moral proposition ('This is fraud and it is wrong') goes hand in hand with expressing some commitment to upholding the implied rule, both comprehensively and in this very instance, where refraining from the action oneself may be called for, along with obstructing others from doing it, and reproaching them if they do. It may simply beg the question about whether the commitment is logically implied to dismiss the meaning normally conveyed as a matter of 'conversational implicature,' as Copp does.[27] Nor does Copp's distinction figure historically in the sources of the collected natural law theory, so far as I know. Nevertheless, as I said earlier, it is far from clear that sticking with ordinary language on these points is an unequivocal advantage. Copp's neat division between moral propositions (with truth value) and rules or standards (without truth value) extricates the main business of ethical theory from perennial confusions. It might stand alone if one did not insist on reconciling it with truth-claiming features of moral discourse in ordinary language and explain (as one can by reference to these features) why theorists have wished, in effect, to complicate Copp's scheme by making other places for truth.

Still, just what is to be done on Copp's approach about propositions asserting the existence of justified rules? Copp himself puts them in his category of 'type-two normative propositions,' true if and only if they imply and rest on justified rules or standards.[28] (Type-one normative propositions rest on rules, but without implying that they are justified ones; they may simply be current.)

Type-two normative propositions of this sort asserting the existence of justified rules, not just implying their existence, but at the same time implying the rightness of adopting them, involve Copp in a good deal of trouble, first, as he admits, in an infinite regress, since no rule can be accepted as justified beyond question unless one can cite a rule superior to it that does the justifying. Once we have in hand the basic moral proposition that a given action is right because it falls under a justified rule R, we may ask how is R justified (or why is it right to adopt R?); and the answer, according to Copp, must be that it falls under a superior justified rule R'. But what justifies R' (or why is it right to adopt R')? It must fall under a justified rule R" superior to it. And so on. Copp thinks that he need not worry about the infinite regress because in his view a rule may be justified in status even if no one has completely 'verified' its status by doing the impossible, going through 'an infinite sequence of events of justification' (Copp, 42–3).

But he does need to worry. Even if we accept it that we are never really going to know whether the rules at issue in type-two normative propositions are justified, the infinite regress in their justification involves Copp in a second difficulty – an uncomfortable dilemma in which he is found to be admitting, on the one hand, that there is no sufficient condition that finishes the job of justifying any rule, and maintaining, on the other hand, that it suffices to justify a rule to have it answer to the needs (and values, so far as these are admitted into the terms of choice) of a society that rationally chooses the rule to be part of its moral code.[29]

One way to escape from the dilemma is to get rid of the infinite regress, maintaining that it suffices to justify a rule for it to have certain empirical properties ('natural' properties, as demanded by ethical naturalism), namely, answering to the needs of a society and being chosen (in the appropriate circumstances) by the society that has those needs.[30] One stops there, as Copp himself intends (with part of his mind, in the more important part of his work).

This is Copp trimmed, but still Copp (it is Copp still with a problem, to be treated below, about the significance of social choosing). However, it requires abandoning the assimilation of the propositions in question to type-two normative propositions (since having the 'natural' properties referred to is not the same thing as implying that there is a justified rule other than itself on which it depends). But do they not have normative significance even so? How can one say, 'It is a justified rule that one ought not to embezzle,' without conveying some normative significance? In normal or paradigm cases, one cannot. The issue now is whether the normative significance has to be treated in the same way as the normative significance of type-two normative propositions ('Taking one's employer's money is wrong'). I think not. Suppose one says that the normative significance of asserting that a rule is justified is to call attention to its place in moral discourse as the basis for type-two normative propositions, a place that it obtains because it figures in a moral code that meets the needs of the society in question. Simultaneously, such an assertion serves to call attention to the crucial importance of people subscribing to it and acting accordingly. Call such a proposition a 'type-three normative proposition.' There is nothing arbitrary about doing so, if such propositions have a key – a systematic – part to play in well-ordered moral discourse; and they do.

On at least one point secular natural law theory and Copp's theory can be improved at the same time and that is by introducing an explicit non-circular definition of rules. St Thomas's most famous definition is circular: 'A certain ordinance of reason for the Common Good, made by him who has care of the community, and promulgated' (*ST*, 1a2ae,

Q.90, 4). It is circular because it refers essentially to 'an ordinance of reason.' St Thomas does not develop the alternative definition that is foreshadowed in his brief description in a neighbouring passage (Q.90, 1) of rules as inducing people to act or restraining them from doing so. Copp's characterization (of a 'standard,' for which, given, as I have noted, his licence for doing so, I have been systematically reading 'a rule') is curiously loose and indirect: '(1) A standard is not a proposition, but (2) it specifies that certain conditions are to be met by things of a certain category, perhaps under certain conditions, and (3) it is something to which things (the things in question) can conform or fail to conform and with which (if the thing in question is an agent) an agent can comply or fail to comply. These three characteristics are individually necessary and jointly sufficient for something to be a standard' (19).

This does not become much less loose or indirect when we substitute 'rule.' No matter: We may substitute for the characterization the clear, robust, non-circular definition of rules available in *Logic on the Track of Social Change* (by me and my collaborators). There rules are reduced to prohibitions, and prohibitions are defined as systems of operations (physical or verbal, in either case sometimes manifest, often latent) that are intended to block actions of a specified type. To ascribe a rule to a society is to say that such a system is operative there, upheld, to use the language of subscription, by general subscription of the members of the society. Abbreviated representations of rules, the kind commonly encountered in applications of rules, for example, 'Embezzling is forbidden,' may be regarded as asserting the existence of such systems of operations, and as true or false accordingly. When the representations imply that the rule represented is justified, the assertions are true if and only if the systems are justified. (This corresponds to what Copp says about the truth of statements asserting the existence of a justified standard.)[31]

The Relation of Justification to Bindingness

Because it will clarify the relation between the content of natural laws and the authority to be ascribed to them in secular natural law theory by contrast with a theistic one, it will be useful for the purposes of the present book to explore further Copp's position on justification and bindingness.

In traditional natural law theory, for example, in Locke, God binds human beings to act one way rather than another by His choice of the moral rules and the will that He expresses in the choice. With Copp, as with Hume, God vanishes, but in Copp's case we have more of an equivalence to the presence of divine choice than may seem at first sight.

Let us distinguish from Copp's usage 'justified' in a sense (I think the ordinary sense) that does not imply being rooted in an authoritative choice, divine or otherwise. The term so understood applies both to choices and to rules (no doubt along with certain other objects of choice). A choice is justified in this sense even if does not rely on a rule at all, or at any rate any rule more specific than to behave rationally in the use of resources; in the face of an unprecedented problem, the agent takes actions as well suited as any available to her to deal with the problem. But a choice may be justified by appeal to a specific rule. The rule itself may be justified by the hardships that following it forestalls or by the benefits that following it obtains.

We have, in Copp's account, a code that is justified (ordinary sense) just because it answers the needs of a given society (say, ours) better than any other code; and a rational choice by that society of the code, which survives screening against alternatives. Where is the bindingness in this picture? It comes partly from the choice by society, which expresses the will of the society enforced by appropriate means, just as God's choice in the traditional picture expresses His will and readiness to enforce and partly from the fact that it is a rational choice, made without illusions and with full information fully digested (which is true of God's choice as well). Yet the bindingness also rests in part on the fact that the code has the character of answering the needs and, hence, is a suitable object of choice for the society. On this point, too, there is a parallel with the reliance on God. One theological tradition says that it is not God's choosing that makes what He chooses good; He chooses what he does because it is good. (This implies that we can tell what is good independently, which is like telling whether a code is justified [ordinary sense].) Ultimately, Copp's account comes to rest on a hypothetical choice.[32] The choice is one that the society would make, that is to say, the members of the society would support with near unanimity, knowing that the code meets its needs. The effect of this is to put even more weight on the code's being justified [ordinary sense], but notably it does retain for the account a place for an authoritative choice.

As compared with going back to God for the choice, there is more than one advantage in coming to rest on having the choice of the code being made by the society. God does not will the natural law because it answers His needs. Moreover, the society does not, like God, invite being ascribed omnipotence, which a theological tradition (voluntarism) opposed to the one cited a few sentences back took to embrace being able to make things good simply by choosing them.

There is a bindingness – a self-bindingness – that comes person by person from subscribing to the code as a moral standard.[33] If we follow Hume, who portrays moral obligation as a matter of recognizing, person by person, on a disinterested view, the social benefits of keeping up morality, we could dispense with tracing bindingness further, to any sort of authoritative choice, if not God's choice, then at least society's. It is true that concurrence in these personal subscriptions can be looked upon as an analogue to social choice, as Copp conceives of it, expressing nearly unanimous favour for having the code as the social moral code. However, we might wonder about the relation between the support that the majority in near-unanimous favour gives person by person to the social choice of the code and any moral subscriptions to the code on their part. Copp says that person by person, they prefer this code as a social option; but do their preferences have the same meaning as the choices of Rousseau's citizens, who give their opinion of what is in 'the interest of the State'?[34] Copp does not seem to say. The Rousseauian picture seems to fit Copp's intentions best (though Copp does not mention Rousseau); and it does (by virtue of the commitments of the citizens to the underlying social contract) entail personal moral subscriptions. (Indeed, it entails these for the outvoted minority, because the minority have reason to think that in the event their opinions turned out not to be in accordance with the probably correct identification of the Common Good by the General Will.)

However, Copp does not, I think, quite get to the point of implying personal subscriptions on the part of the persons engaged in the social choice of a moral code. He explains what he calls 'epistemically justified' reasons for their making the choice;[35] but he does not require them to have those reasons; he does not explain or even stipulate what their motivations are to be. Would there be an incongruity if the subscriptions were not forthcoming once the code had been chosen for the society in question? Perhaps not. We might take Copp's position to be that if by nearly unanimous support from the people belonging to the society, no matter what the grounds they have person by person, the society did choose the moral code that best met its needs, it would be rational to do so. Copp says, 'A code's being a social moral code [M] implies that it is generally morally subscribed to by the members of the society.'[36] Does this imply that any person who, understanding this proposition, prefers M to be the social moral code must himself at the moment of choosing the code morally subscribe to M or even just subscribe to it?[37] Not quite. He might wait to see how the social choice turns out. Or he could intend to free ride on the code if it does become the social moral code; or he could prefer it because of the eloquence with which it is expressed, because it has been presented in a certain type-face or because a voice tells him to prefer it.

The theory of rational choice thus backs having such a code, according to Copp, even if nearly unanimous support, were it to be forthcoming in fact (or hypothetically), would not imply nearly unanimous subscription by the people taking part in the choice, but would rest instead on incongruous grounds. Copp wheels into place all the evidence that the code in question is the most suitable, and he makes sure that the members of the society know this and know that the issue before them is whether the code is to be chosen as the social moral code for their society. But, perhaps from an excess of zeal regarding the avoidance of begging any moral questions, Copp does not explicitly and firmly require that people choosing the code do so on the grounds of its suitability. Thus, I expect unintentionally, he leaves room for a sort of social voluntarism.

Copp may be assuming, without specifying that he is doing so, that each person who prefers M to be the social moral code is at least ready to subscribe to it morally. Or he may be assuming, again without specifying that he is doing so (in line with Rousseau, though Copp does not mention Rousseau) that to count in the social preference or choice of a social moral code a person's preference for M must be based on the fact that M answers to the needs of the society in question. Either of these assumptions would make the reliance on the social preference or choice more plausible. However, the latter assumption, about a person's preference being based on the service of the code to needs, increases the weight on justification [ordinary sense] relatively to the choice. The former assumption seems to beg questions in the way that Copp seems to be trying to avoid in a passage on 'societal moral values,'[38] though the bearing of this passage on the character assumed for personal subscriptions is not entirely clear. A 'societal moral value' implies there being a moral standard 'shared with near unanimity by the members of a society'; and Copp means to set such values aside in the justificatory choice. Yet, if the members do share a moral standard with near unanimity, will this not count with them, choosing individually the moral code that they want for society and themselves? That is one way in which people may be led to insist on a code that protects liberty and autonomy, not to speak of securing the public goods features of the Common Good.

Thus, with the room that he may have left for voluntaristic social choice, Copp falls somewhat short of explaining how justification in his sense rests on a plausible rational choice. And short, too, in other respects. Asking only for near unanimity leaves open the possibility of choosing a moral code with oppressive consequences for the minority. Nor is this the only point on which Copp begs moral questions more than he intends to in making out how the choice of a moral code can be rational.

The agents taking part in the social choice are supposed to look upon the candidate codes, setting aside any moral values that may be ascribed to the society as a whole, and any preferences so ascribed, simply in terms of the degree to which the codes meet the needs of the society, including the need to have its population continue to exist and the need to maintain a fruitful system of cooperation. These needs imply that by and large the basic needs of the people belonging to the population have to be met. Whether this is done or not is an issue of fact. Yet it is also an issue of moral value. One might argue that it would not be at all plausible to invoke a rational social choice as the basis for justifying a moral code if it was not a moral choice specifically giving moral weight to people's basic needs, even if meeting these needs were no more than biological and psychological preconditions of their leading morally attractive lives. Copp, however, gives a morally richer account of basic needs than this, because he lays down as a criterion for what is to count as a basic need that meeting it is required 'to avoid impairment of [people's] capacity to have and to pursue the satisfaction of values,'[39] that is to say, a certain liberty or autonomy;[40] and this is a moral value. If the code did not advance this value it would not be a candidate for rational social choice, and hence, it could not be justified.

There is no objection in my view to having the personal moral value of liberty or autonomy built into the social choice; indeed, with my notion of the thriving together of people in a thriving society, I am committed to begging the question of justifying a moral code in some such way. Nor, though I do not think it necessary for bindingness to go beyond a Humean consensus on a social moral code that promotes thriving better than any other, do I object to adding a provision for a rational social choice, whether or not the choice is in some aspect question-begging. This can be looked upon as an option for natural law theory, both the one collected from the canonical authors that I have been treating and the one unifying this collected theory with Copp's. Bringing God back into the picture is a further option. Let the people who think that the theory is strengthened by adopting either of these options adopt them, so long as they recognize that for others bindingness, along with justification, can be supplied without using means so controversial.

Chapter Eight

Moral Education

The Common Good, as specified in an earlier chapter, consists of public goods, in the economists' technical sense, some of which are goods answering specially to the interests of people with public spirit and communal feeling. The motivations of people in whom such feeling reaches the pitch of wholehearted commitment to the Common Good far transcend the motivations of rational egoists, not to speak of the motivations displayed in the cruelty that human beings often practise upon one another, both person to person and en masse. Does that make the availability of the transcendent motivations an extravagant expectation? There are some general reasons for pessimism on this point, besides the calamities that continually pile on top of one another in history. Some philosophers have thought that human beings are not in natural impulse inclined to do good, though they may allow, with the ancient Chinese philosopher Xun Zi (310–219 BC), that people properly trained under social rules may acquire the habit of doing good.[1] In Xun Zi's view, the habit once inculcated seems to be capable of persisting apart from the regime of rules under which it was inculcated. But other philosophers may insist, with Hobbes, that the habit will persist only under a regime of rules that is with reasonable efficiency enforced. Hobbes is less optimistic in this respect than Xun Zi, but still optimistic to a degree, since he believes human beings can (if not by contract, then through conquest and submission to conquest) successfully set up and maintain regimes of rules under which they will exhibit virtuous habits. Moreover, Hobbes, in spite of standing with Xun Zi in respect to natural impulses as being, if not evil (since in the state of nature they are not evil), at least not inclined immediately toward practising civilized virtues, explicitly holds, as

Xun Zi holds at most by implication, that human beings have natural tendencies, that is to say, dispositions to give effect to the natural laws, hence to set up a regime of rules under which those virtues can be practised.

Is optimism with regard to maintaining such a regime once set up well-founded? The corpus of natural laws, identified as the set of settled social rules that a society must abide by to thrive (or at least as one such set), might not be laws that any society could keep up for any appreciable length of time. Maybe no society could even succeed in setting them up. If people had to set them up in the circumstances that Hobbes envisages for the social contract, they may not get set up, because the contract cannot be achieved.[2] If people did set them up, defections might begin immediately, as rational choice theorists might argue from the temptations of free-riding. Once started, the defections might spread more or less rapidly through the population, until Hobbes's state of nature returned.

If this were true, the honour of being the set of laws under which a society could thrive would be a rather empty honour, at best (if we are thinking of a society thriving for an appreciable length of time) a hypothetical honour; and the project of natural law theory would lose a good deal of its attractions. However, I think there is no reason to be quite so pessimistic. Events in the twentieth century in places like Lebanon and Bosnia, where people who had lived as friends and neighbours turned bloodthirsty enemies overnight, show that a tolerable regime of rules may be frighteningly and astonishingly fragile. Nevertheless, even there thriving societies persisted for the time of a generation or more; and elsewhere (say, in Denmark, not a violent country in modern times) they have persisted for many generations.

Moreover, to the general reasons for pessimism about the availability of suitable motivations there may be opposed general reasons for optimism.

In this chapter, I shall argue, first, that human motivations are such as not only to invite the inculcation of the natural laws, but also to rise, duly fostered in happy circumstances, to the pitch of wholehearted commitment to the complex and mutually sustained Common Good defined for the core theory presented in this book. The attractions of rational egoism, such as they are, do not stand in the way of cooperation under the natural laws; nor does rational egoism have such a persistent presence as to limit that cooperation short of genuine humanity and mutual attachment. A hypothesis more favored than otherwise by current psychological evidence would hold that the natural development of infants into persons (which parallels in its early stages the development of untrained animals into participants in systems of human–animal interaction) goes in the direction of communal feeling rather than in the direction of rational egoism. It is, on this hypothesis, selfishness and rational egoism that are anomalies needing explanation. And (according to a further hypothesis) they are to be explained by failures in systems of interaction, that is to say, failures in patterns of group membership. So, by having perverse patterns supplant favourable ones is the even more frightening pathology of excessive commitment – fanaticism in imposing the will of one's own group, religious, ethnic, nationalist, or partisan in some other way, upon outsiders.[3]

I shall argue, second, that the rules need not be so rigid or so repressive as to defeat their purpose. How are people to learn to heed the rules and practise the virtues that the Common Good calls for? Even more to the point, how are they to learn these things without becoming perhaps as much disaffected as committed? This problem is not absent from the teaching of virtues, but it presents itself most acutely when approached on the side of rules, for rules are inevitably constraints upon people's desires and actions, and those constraints are often more exactingly defined than the general examples of virtue. It will not do as much good as the natural law theorist would want done to have people's motivations escape rational egoism, if their humane and generous impulses are subjected to narrow, rigid repression, whether in family circles or outside. But this, too, is a difficulty that is more manageable than it looks at first sight.

Combined, my two arguments will thoroughly vindicate the contention of natural law theory that the natural laws fall in with the natural inclinations of human beings. This contention itself has a double aspect: (1) the assumption that there is a set of laws, heeding which will enable human beings to thrive together in thriving communities and which, thus, afford human beings benefits that they will find congenial when they are living under them, and (2) the assumption that motivations inclining human beings to adopt the natural laws and commit themselves to heeding them can be installed by some straightforward process of moral education, given people's initial motivational capacities. Keeping the first aspect of the basic contention in place, the two arguments of this chapter concentrate on the second aspect.

Rational Egoism as an Obstacle to Whole-Hearted Commitment to the Common Good

A complete ethics, with due provision for mutual commitment transcending the demand that others be able to make a productive contribution to a society of mutual advantage, cannot be founded on rational egoism. Maybe question-begging is inescapable in ethics – we have to assume, to get moral discourse going, some concern with the welfare of other human beings; striving to avoid question-begging about this concern may cut us off from ethics itself. Yet a question that can be answered remains, the question that I began with. Where, if it is present, does the commitment and its wholeheartedness come from? The party that wants to found ethics on rational egoism asks this, without any conviction that it can be answered, or even needs to be, as a question about how the commitment can be added to rational egoism as something that goes beyond egoism. The party that does not believe in rational egoism as a foundation for ethics thinks that the question needs to be answered, but may understand it in the same way, assuming that rational egoism is at the very least the default case of (mature) human motivation and that we need an explanation of how anything more generous in motivation appears. (The grimmer of the two pictures of moral education to be laid out below is consistent with this view.) It is not rational egoism, however, that comes first or serves as the default case. Rational egoism is a second-comer, deriving from natural human motivation by degeneration and shrinkage.

By 'natural human motivation' I do not mean motivation unshaped by training. Natural human motivation is trained motivation that comes about in the course of forming persons. We cannot have normal human beings without having persons formed by training; assuming that rational egoists are persons, we cannot even have rational egoists. Human beings become persons by being enlisted by their parents in systems of social interaction for each of which there is a common purpose and a Common Good. In favourable cases, these systems, which we may regard as approximately equivalent to what Xun Zi, along with Confucius (551–479 BC) and Mencius (371–289 BC), had in mind in insisting upon the importance of ritual, and the common goods realized in these systems harmonize and fall into a harmonious pattern with the common goods of more comprehensive systems.

Other animals become persons, so far as they do, in the same way. Since the systems are in their case simpler and less various I shall begin with animals, following Vicki Hearne's discussion in her richly challenging book *Adam's Task*.[4] Hearne's approach to animal training may be only one among several. Moreover, animals are so plastic (as are human infants) that they can be trained to do all sorts of things. So, maybe it is not remarkable, in the way of being surprisingly hard to do, that they can be trained to do the things that Hearne trains them to do. However, I am not concerned to show that Hearne's is the only way that animals can be trained. Nor am I concerned to show that what she trains them to do are the only sorts of things that they can be trained to do. What is remarkable is not that Hearne trains animals to do certain things, but that in the course of being trained to do these things they become persons, or something near to being persons, in a way that serves as a model for how human beings become persons. The systems of interaction constituted stage by stage by a human trainer and an animal under training (a domestic animal, a dog or a horse) take form in one or another of a small number of well-defined games (fetching, tracking, jumping a series of successively higher fences), and continue to operate in these forms, though they may develop further, and there is some generalization of the behavior learned in them to other contexts.

Importing from Kenneth Kaye[5] a distinction between four stages of personal development, which Hearne does not use herself, we may say that in the first stage of training the object is to capture the animal's attention for longer and longer periods, and to direct the operants and responses that the animal furnishes from his innate repertoire into patterns suited to the turns that the animal must take as he plays the game with the trainer. A dog naturally inclines to run this way and that to inspect various interesting things; the trainer seeks to concentrate the dog's attention on the object to be fetched, at first an object that the trainer drops right at hand, then stage by stage an object that she throws out, farther and farther away, finally one that she has placed out of sight. This first stage becomes quite quickly a second stage of shared intentions, in which the dog aims, like the trainer, to have the object retrieved that the trainer throws out. Then a third stage supervenes: The shared intentions are caught up in a shared memory. When the trainer, about to leave the house, takes up the target object or the tracking harness, the dog takes this as a sign that a game which they have learned together is about to begin anew. Or the dog may take the initiative and signify that it is (in his view) time for a game by bringing the object or the harness to the trainer and trying thereby to induce her to leave her desk (where she is writing a book about how dogs and humans communicate with each other).

Does a dog ever reach a fourth stage for which some people (including Kenneth Kaye) would reserve the term 'language,' in which, to communicate with the trainer, the dog produces a conventional signal that he has hitherto learned only to comprehend, or comprehends a conventional signal coming from the trainer that the dog has hitherto learned only to produce? That is not so clear; and this is crucial for the issue of personhood, that is to say, for how much claim to personhood the dog can reasonably be allowed. The succession of stages from one to four parallels the order of considerations that determine personhood. Given stages one and two, the communications between animals and trainers in stage three, based on shared memory as well as sharable (and shared) intentions meet basic criteria for communication among persons. They, therefore, imply that by these criteria the participants on both sides – the animals as well as the trainers – are persons. More stringent demands respecting personhood would invoke the criteria of stage four; and here, not making the rich and ever-expanding use of conventional language that falls within the power even of children, other animals are at a disadvantage.

Yet trained animals seem to have at least a foothold in stage four. Moreover, it may be injudicious to put so much weight on full development there. What animals accomplish with their foothold in stage four may meet criteria for personhood that are not just more elementary, but more impressive. Hearne offers arresting evidence for accepting the games that a dog and his trainer learn to play together as language games – forms of joint activity in which they are mutually communicative participants. They are games of a form that different players – different pairings of animals and trainers – can instantiate; but with each animal the trainer learns a game particular to the two of them and engages in a particular conversation. In this conversation, Hearne holds, the trainer and the animal acknowledge each other's personhood; and the two thus join to acknowledge and create a shared social space – the space for jointly carrying out a ritual.

Even if the ritual is notably ceremonious, the conversation that goes on in this space is a limited conversation, not very rich perhaps in any connection, and limited even when it is most specific by the form and purpose of the game that animal and trainer jointly aim at playing. Yet it is enough, in Hearne's view, to make the animals interlocutors that demand respect as agents of some dignity with serious things to say

and responsibilities to exercise that call morally for matching seriousness and responsibility on the part of the trainers. Within the forms of
their games, trained animals exhibit care for the other participants and
trust in them; and the care and trust generalize, even if the specifics of
communication do not, beyond the games. On both sides, the participation exemplifies for Hearne the thesis that 'talking entails care and
care-taking'[6] – with the participants taking care to 'mean what they
say,' but also taking care in the sense of mutual concern for each
other's performance and well-being. They take care not to set each
other tasks beyond their powers – the rider will not put her horse at a
fence much too high for the horse to clear; the dog will bring the ball
back and drop it within what he and his master have agreed is a feasible range. They comfort each other for failures that could not have
been prevented. They become upset when the other shows signs of
being too feeble through ill-health to carry on the game or ritual.

In the references to comforting, I am going beyond what Hearne herself reports, though Hearne does give an example of a horse running a
jump course when her rider was in too much pain to control her, in
effect controlling herself as she allowed for his frailty; and another
example of a rider (herself) demonstrating confidence in a horse that
had stumbled to her knees and now faced another fence to jump.[7]
Comforting coming from the human side is no doubt more plausible
(at least to people who know dogs and horses no better than I). But if a
trainer had a bad fall during a tracking exercise, might not the dog
pause and show some concern, or come back to do so?

I am also, in speaking of rituals, going beyond what Confucius and
Mencius and Xun Zi say. Their examples have to do with presenting
gifts, in particular with presenting gifts to a member of the opposite
sex or receiving gifts in such a connection, with hosts and guests
exchanging courtesies, with waiting upon a prince or a wise man, with
getting married, with burying the dead and conducting memorial services.[8] How to do these things, of course, has to be learned; and hence,
they are learned in the course of moral education. But they are not the
elementary forms of joint activity illustrated by tracking exercises and
horsemanship; or in human cases, the forms corresponding to these.
These elementary forms, if they belong to the extension of the term at
all, are rituals some distance away in range. On the other hand, some
of the classical examples do have to do with family life; and both
Mencius and Xun Zi, treating the aspect of *Li* that makes it a virtue
associated with rituals as well as the rituals themselves, stress the

importance of showing due respect for one's father or elder brother. This parallels the respect that the dog or horse shows his mistress or trainer and emerges in the course of small-scale, face-to-face, domestic forms of interaction; I say, of rituals.

Infant human beings follow much the same path as the dogs and horses: They become persons – sociable beings – through the rituals of interaction with mentors. These need not be parents or other grown-ups; they may be, very early, the infants' peers, and these may be in some respects more effective mentors.[9] At the beginning, the infant must operate on the basis of an innate repertoire of operants and responses; the parent, like the trainer, begins by ascribing to these operants and responses significance (intentions) that strictly speaking they do not entail. Their ascriptions continually outstrip their pupils' actual capacity. But this 'presumption' – anthropomorphizing the infants – is pedagogically indispensable, as on Hearne's account it is in training other animals. The parent, like the trainer, sets the system up (the pattern of interaction, in arrangements for eating, exercise, play, and sleep) and incorporates the pupil more and more fully into it until the pupil becomes an equal partner – which does not mean that the development ends, just that from that point it becomes a development in which both make substantial contributions. Each looks to the other to assume the responsibility for contributions; each is concerned that the other continues to be capable of exercising the responsibility. Wherever sustained, cooperative interaction occurs, we can expect to find mutual concern developing for each participant's performance and well-being.

To care in mutual concern for each other's performance and well-being puts both pupils and teachers – animals and trainers – outside of egoism in their relations with each other; but both are outside of egoism in their commitment as well. A trained dog will ignore temptations and disregard discomfort in the resolute pursuit of his part in a tracking enterprise; a horse will resolve to undertake a jump of frightening height, at the very limit of her capacity.[10]

Were the animals ever a sort of egoists – egoists before training? It is true that training as Hearne practises it involves 'correction,' which she would distinguish from punishment, though it is sometimes similarly forceful, and may even, as noted in an earlier chapter of the present book, take the same form. Going along with the training, are the animals just operating egoistically under a calculus of physical pleasure or physical pain? This may be doubted, not just because there is a certain extravagance in supposing that dogs calculate pleasures and pains (it borders on extravagance to suppose this of human beings in ordinary connections), but because the pleasure and the pain come with the company and the talk of the trainer, and above all, with the development of a common purpose with the trainer and, thus, a common good. It qualifies as such by being a public good: Neither benefits from it at the expense of cutting the other off from the benefit in any part. Even if the calculus did operate, any simple calculus of this kind is left behind when the animal emerges at a higher stage as a trained and committed participant in a game with a purpose that the animal shares with the trainer. Either one must say that in the game the animal ignores pleasure and pain in favour of that purpose, or one must say that in the game the animal heeds only pleasure and pain of a higher sort – moral pleasure and moral pain, which come respectively from living up to the shared purpose-oriented standard for the activity or lapsing from it.

Children, like dogs and horses, can normally rely on commitments forthcoming from their mentors in return for the commitments that they make themselves. If Kate desists from throwing her porridge upon the floor, she will be left to eat it in peace; it will be supplied in due quantity at due times. If Frank stays out of the street, the walk to the park will continue. Morever, when things are working well, the commitments lead to the achievement of common goods – the Common Good of each joint activity or ritual: Both mother and child act with the object of having the child regularly fed under a form of civility that both respect; both father and child act with the object of walking to the park and doing so in decent order and safety. So, in both cases, the commitments to each other are commitments to the Common Good. It may be an error to think of commitments to the Common Good preceding the development of mutual concern and love – humanity; the commitments and the sentiments no doubt develop hand in hand. But it may be a worse error to think of rational egoism as established before any form of self-interested cooperation is and of commitments to the Common Good being confined in the first instance to such cooperation, with any mutual concern and love following only as a grace flowering within the charmed circle of mutually beneficial cooperators.[11] Human beings who have been enlisted in the sort of moral education that I am describing rise beyond any narrow rationality. Their choices are rational only if the choices reflect concerns for others, which moral education builds into their utility functions, solving the problem of cooperation, as it were, without pausing at any stage where the problem is raised under the auspices of egoism.

Do accounts of moral development, like Piaget's or Kohlberg's, beginning in a stage of egocentricism (Piaget) upset this conception of moral development through induction in language games with common purposes? 'Egocentricism' is not, in fact, at all the same thing as egoism or selfishness. It is 'the inability to infer the visual, affective, or cognitive perspective of another, insofar as these [sic] perspectives are undifferentiated from one's own';[12] or, otherwise expressed, 'the inability to distinguish between the objective and the subjective, between what is psychical and internal and what is physical and external.'[13] Neither Piaget nor Kohlberg is rigidly committed to there being any primordial stage in which egoism predominates.[14] As a minimum, we could insist that accounts, like that of Nancy Eisenberg, which do make egoism (though perhaps not rational egoism) primordial, do not tell the whole story. Side by side with egoistic tendencies there are, at least as early as these can be distinguished, tendencies to subscribe to common purposes.[15] It may just be the case that for children (as for some philosophers) it is more difficult initially to articulate these tendencies than the egoistic ones. (They are more complicated; to articulate them on the present account one has to go by way of articulating the common purposes that are implicit in the games.)

Children do not want to be left out of activities that others find interesting. Children insist that they can 'help,' so that they won't be left out. Though in Daniel Lapsley's review there is, curiously, only minimal reference to what I am making so much of here, the cooperative aspects and effects of learning social practices (and along with them suitable forms of language), he does pick up this point about joining in social practices by helping.[16] Not enough, however, seems to have been made of it by the psychologists. Children have helping parts to play in the common purposes of arrangements for eating, exercise, play, and sleep. The parts, and the rules indispensable for achieving the common purposes, become even more salient in the more sophisticated joint activities of dish-washing or gardening. To make an effective contribution to the common purpose of dish-washing, the child must learn the rule of not wiping dishes that have not yet been washed; to the common purpose of gardening, that weeds (so designated by the very rule at issue) are to be pulled up, but not the infant flowers and vegetables. Are these not beginnings on the project that will lead in time to understanding that certain rules – the basic rules of natural law – must be accepted if the common purpose – the Common Good – of a community that is seeking, along with its members, to thrive is to be achieved?

The choice of enlistment in joint activities is a choice that is initially, for the most part, made for children by their parents, as trainers make the choice for other animals. I read in an autobiography that I have long since otherwise forgotten that the author's parents moved from Connecticut to Boston when he was two; he says that he decided to go along with them. In time, the children will face decisions about joining groups, which they are to make on their own. But, again, the decision to join may be based more on a desire not to be left out than on a calculation of net personal benefits.[17] When it is based on such a calculation, the motivation normally changes in the course of participation. Personal development resumes on this new branch; by learning to take part in the system of interaction distinctive of the group, the new member learns what is expected of him and what he may expect from others in their collaborative efforts. Obtaining the Common Good of the group without shirking, without letting the others down, becomes the new member's prime motivation.

If the normal development of infants into persons takes a course like the one that I have just been describing, then selfishness is an anomaly that stands in more need of explaining than do mutual concern and commitment. What happened to selfish persons – what was so abnormal and defective in their development or experience that led to their being so twisted? Or led, in the case of rational egoists, to their being, with their greater sophistication, so narrow in outlook and so shrunken in spirit? These, it seems to me, are the right questions, even if the point of departure for the shrinking cannot reasonably be supposed to be people selflessly cooperative.

Not only is willingness to cooperate commonly found side by side with self-striving. A sensible upbringing will cultivate personal independence as well as cooperativeness, sometimes at the same time (as when a child taking part in a joint enterprise is asked to say what she wants), sometimes at different times (as when a child is encouraged to develop a capacity to amuse himself). Moreover, to be prepared for the larger world outside her initial intimate milieus, the child must be prepared to defend herself against exploitation by others. (Elinor Ostrom points out that empirical studies of strategies for repeated games show that people who are prepared to cooperate no matter what may be expected to lose out and are, not surprisingly, very rare.)[18]

The point of departure, however, is not a person who is bifurcated between being sociable and being self-striving. The point of departure is whatever approximation to a duly balanced combination of independence and cooperativeness has been achieved in the particular case. The independence will be an independence that has a cast reflecting the development of cooperativeness, something that in a number of persons may be expected to extend much farther in commitment to the Common Good than Hume's 'limited generosity.' It is not necessary to maintain that all cases will be of this kind; for my purposes, it is only necessary to maintain that they will be common enough if things go reasonably right in the formation of persons, for moral education to culminate in strong persistent support for the natural laws and the Common Good. [19]

One may expect, I think, to find that selfish people, and rational egoists, suffered some failures in group affiliation as they were growing up. The family was not close-knit enough to act together repeatedly for group purposes; it may have broken up early in the egoist's childhood, or from the beginning had only a vestigial presence. No church captured the child or his family for its activities. No Boy Scout troop or drum and bugle corps enrolled him. High school may have been large and impersonal, leaving many students out of group activities and untouched by school spirit. University may have been no more congenial. At work, the size of the workforce, the absence of a labour union, and continual turnover of personnel may have precluded identification with the company and its aims or with fellow-workers and theirs. The egoist may seldom or never have had any experience, while growing up, of being caught up for a time in the activity and purposes of a group or team and of having her purposes assimilated to those of the group. Or if this did happen early on, in later life she lost touch with the groups to which she had been attached; and the circumstances of her life supplied no other groups to take their place. By the testimony of many writers, this is a common experience in modern society, that is to say, in *Gesellschaft*; and it occurs even in the absence of adversity, indeed, in prosperous *Gesellschaften* able to afford their members a high standard of living. People move out of their family circles, but do not find brotherhoods, sisterhoods, fellowships at work, where the disciplinary aspects of bureaucracy (given great weight by Weber,[20] and portrayed in the direst terms by Foucault)[21] combine with the unremitting pressure of the market to discourage people from feeling community with others. The church supplies it for some; and sometimes modes of recreation do, but many people fall outside their reach.

Moralists must guard against humanity and the commitment to the Common Good being supplanted by rational egoism, but they do not have to argue for supplementing egoism. They do not have to bring in humanity, as it were, from outside to supplement rational egoism. We have commitment to the Common Good (to various common goods, in the innumerable social practices, loosely or not so loosely defined, of various groups) already, in language and the practices in which language is embodied, and with it we have humanity, at least in relation to fellow members of these groups. The theorists of egoism need to argue for shrinkage – for putting the Common Good and commitments to it aside, even if their project is to see whether it can be got back. And if they claim (as David Gauthier does)[22] that the project of 'reconstructing' ethics on this basis will throw light on the relation of self-interest to ethics – by showing how far they run hand in hand – we may admit that a useful lesson may be in prospect. It is a lesson applicable, perhaps, to rescuing from their degenerate condition people who have, in fact, become rational egoists. Yet we must not allow the lesson and its light to blind us to the unnaturalness of this proceeding. Certainly, we must not lightly concede that the reconstruction captures everything sound in ethics in a firmer grasp.

Rigidity and Repressiveness of Rules Standing in the Way of Their Inculcation

In some cases, in happy circumstances, the cooperative games or rituals in which children develop commitments to cooperation and concern with fellow cooperants will generalize without trouble, first from the simplest initial rituals (which begin between mothers and babies immediately or almost immediately after birth) to complex rituals involving the whole family and household (consider, for example, the daily schedule that assigns everyone tasks and allows everyone to meet the obligations of school and work). Generalization may continue outside the family, to brotherhoods, sisterhoods, fellowships, modest in preoccupations and ambitions, sometimes not so modest: classroom projects at school, clubs, and teams, projects involving the whole school; church activities, with a diverse range of affiliated organizations; Scouts; neighbourhood associations; good government movements; political parties; the Sierra Club; bowling leagues. Bureaucracy (by supplanting them) and the market (insofar as it fosters egoism) work against these things, but they have not yet crowded them out.

The rituals may be generalized without trouble. They may be established at each stage without trouble, or with only a minimum, certainly, without any explicit attention to modes of instruction or to making a choice between modes. Yet sooner or later in the course of development such attention may be called for. It may be started up when development psychologists get to work on childhood. It is surely very likely to be called for when the generalization of rituals moves beyond families, neighbourhoods, one's home town, to rituals in which strangers – strangers, even if they are fellow citizens – will be taking part. A specific issue has arisen in ethical theory, in the *Auseinandersetzung* between virtue ethics and the ethics of rules. Is ethics better taught by example, by examples of practising the virtues, as virtue theorists incline to think, or by promulgating and inculcating rules, which may seem to be the approach relied upon in the natural law tradition?

Now, it may be well to give teaching by example a large part in moral education, indeed, as large a part as possible. Teaching by example does not lend itself as readily to intrusion and repression – to thwarting the will of the pupil – as teaching by rules. Yet, it is hard to see how it could be the only approach, just as it is hard to see how an ethics could be exclusively an ethics of virtues without any rules. Is there not a rule for every virtue, generally a set of rules? It is a virtue to be generous (what St Thomas calls 'liberal'), but as a matter of rule one will not be practicing the virtue if what one gives away belongs to someone else (*ST*, 2a2ae, Q.117, 5). Every virtue is ascribed, as Hobbes carefully explains in the case of the virtue of justice, not on the basis of any one instance, but on the basis of a regular pattern kept up over an unending number of instances.[23] A person who is just is not a person who honours her contracts in one instance; she does it time after time, that is to say, regularly. Similarly, one must convey to children that the examples of virtues given them are to be followed time after time, that is to say, as a matter of rule.

Moreover, from the very beginning of moral education, both teaching by examples and teaching by rules are present together. Preston, let us say inadvertently, bangs his twin Warren in the face with the back of a saucepan; Warren cries out from shock and pain; their mother comforts him. That is teaching by example. Preston seizes Warren's plastic salamander, though he already has one of his own; his father takes it back and returns it to Warren. That is teaching by rules, I think, even if the father does not say something like, 'That's Warren's salamander, not yours; you must let Warren keep it.' So it would be teaching by rules if the mother said to Preston in the saucepan incident, 'You hurt Warren; you must comfort him.' If she then showed how the comfort was to be given, we have a case in which teaching by example and teaching by rules both play a part.

St Thomas teaches that we could hardly do without rules, even if we all steadily inclined to act for the best. Too few of us are wise enough to judge just what we should do by directly assessing the circumstances as they change before us.[24] Rules enable us to make the best use of the limited amount of wisdom available[25] not just in giving us guidance when right action expresses straightforward conformity with the rule, but also (I add, as a gloss) when we must make an exception, for then the rule focuses our thought. It leads us to ask, is this an exception that accords with the purpose of the rule, in this instance better than the (received, formulated) rule itself? Is it an exception in which other considerations override that purpose?

We do not all steadily incline to act for the best. The inclinations that we do have may run counter to the Common Good, and hence need to be checked. Rules, with the sanctions attending them, play for St Thomas an important part in forestalling deviations both in the short-run control of adult behaviour and, in the long run, advance perspective of moral education.[26]

Is this not a disappointingly unattractive picture of morality and moral education? Let us not be deceived by the smooth formulation alluding to 'the sanctions attending' the rules. St Thomas is not especially enthusiastic about the retributive aspect of punishment; on the contrary, his treatment of punishment is oriented in the main toward the future, deterrent aspects. However, he holds that without punishment to enforce the rules – fear or force – we cannot have enough morality in this world and he does not, so far as I know, bar whatever punishment is efficient, maybe flogging, maybe something even more medieval, branding, cutting off a hand or an ear. But is not the insistence on rules repugnant already, before we bring punishment in? Will not rules make morality rigid to the point of being mechanical, and as a mechanism imposed on human beings, a straightjacket for their freedom? Punishment redoubles the presence of repression. Rules are inescapably constraints; they easily multiply beyond necessity; and even the necessary ones may be burdensome. It is the great attraction of anarchism that (at least in some versions) it proposes to reduce rules to a minimum or even to eliminate them.[27] The impression of rigidity can be mitigated, however, by recalling that St Thomas is thinking of rules as typically even in their most efficient formulation as rules with exceptions, some known (though it may not be efficient to mention even these), some as yet unknown, because the circumstances that call for them have not yet been encountered.[28] There is even, as we have seen and St Thomas emphasizes, the special virtue, mentioned in the previous chapter, concerned with making exceptions – *epieikeia* – which encourages us to judge and act in accordance with what the spirit of the rule, rather than the letter, requires.[29]

What can be done to remove or dilute the repressiveness (an aspect of rules that may persist in standard cases, even if exceptions are allowed)? The rules do not impede good will and spontaneity on the part of the saints, who adhere to the Common Good with no thought of avoiding any punishments imposed under the rules. Saints hardly need to be told about the rules at all (except perhaps – a problem that St Thomas does not take up – for purposes of coordination in doing the good for everybody that they always individually seek). Certainly, saints transcend in motivation any influence from punishment. But how do they do this? In particular, how, if they begin as children learning morality on the same pattern as everyone else, how do they get beyond feeling the rules as constraints backed by punishments? The picture that St Thomas gives, of moral education as an education in rules, is a picture that raises suspicions about constraints and sanctions operating not to encourage and facilitate the rise to sainthood, but operating, on the contrary, to obstruct it. Punishment and the threat of punishment induce fear, and they are meant to do so. Perhaps fear can with time and practice change into glad adherence, but when it does, is this not a lucky accident? Fear seems the wrong way to go about reaching glad adherence. Is it not, for one thing, likely to create resentment and hostility to the rules? Will it not often, at best, lead to resigned acceptance, resting solely on a cautious regard for one's skin, rather than expressing a spontaneously good will?

These difficulties all appear to be aggravated, furthermore, by the advanced understanding of rules offered by my colleagues and me in *Logic on the Track of Social Change*,[30] which among other things makes all rules reducible to prohibitions, the elementary model for teaching them being physical blocking. The baby tries once more to drop her porridge onto the floor; mother intervenes, grasps the baby's wrist, and firmly redirects the laden spoon to the baby's mouth or back to her dish. The toddler begins wandering into the street; father intervenes, grasps him by the shoulders and lifts him back onto the sidewalk. These interventions, which certainly look like heavy-handed exercises of authority, redouble again the part that physical repression has in the picture of moral education that we have before us. They look like negative reinforcements to be assimilated to the negative reinforcements that rules once established and associated with punishment involve. Hence, they may seem to have no acceptable part in enlightened education, not merely because negative reinforcements are distasteful, but also because they are not even effective (if B.F. Skinner, on this point at least, a prototype of moral and philosophical enlightenment, is right).[31] Moreover, such interventions are even, in a way, more repressive than the punishments that may come along with rules. For the punishments will generally just be threatened, leaving people free to make up their minds about whether they will risk or undergo them. But here we have people's (little people's, but still people's) freedom directly circumscribed in a way that interferes with the most basic and narrowly defined freedom, freedom of movement (which Hobbes treated as basically definitive of the concept).[32] This should trouble us; and I shall not be able to extinguish the trouble.

Even so, reduction to prohibitions is a good way of understanding rules. It avoids incorporating into the logic of rules a paradox parallel to the paradox of material implication according to which from a contradiction every proposition whatever can be inferred. The parallel in the logic of rules is perhaps even more unsettling: Given a contradiction between rules, one may infer, in standard deontic logic, that everything is permitted, indeed prescribed. (Alternatively, if one has the leisure to do so, one just suspends the use of logic until the situation clears up.) If rules are all at bottom prohibitions, however, all that the most thoroughgoing conflict will amount to will be a quandary, in which one finds oneself prohibited from doing any of the actions that offer themselves as possibilities. That, of course, is not a comfortable position to be in; but it is a position that is logically perfectly in order, with no absurdities to infer about everything, every action in every connection, now being permitted, something that we might regard as demolishing the whole of whatever system of morality we might have on hand.

Reduction to prohibitions is also a good way of understanding rules just because it permits us to use the notion of physical blocking in the elementary model for teaching rules. People learn rules from observing others being blocked, not necessarily physically or even verbally blocked; or just from observing others heed the rules; or just from being told what the rules are. One says, 'No!' when doing the wrong thing impends; or, more subtly and more positively, one demonstrates the right thing (the correct pronunciation; courteously giving way). (Thus, blocking, subtly extended, becomes a feature of learning by example, something that virtue ethics specially advocates.) Yet, physical blocking associated with some rule or other will, we may expect, be found somewhere in the beginnings of everyone's rule-learning history. Physical blocking, moreover, is always available as an alternative to whatever means are actually used to teach a rule or to bring about conformity to it. This seems to me to give us as simple and convincing an analysis of the nature of rules as we can hope to get, coming to non-circular rest on concrete physical facts and ostensive definition.[33]

In *Logic on the Track of Social Change*, my co-authors and I, let me remind the reader, use a logic of rules in which the standard formula for a rule has three components: **volk**, specifying the people to whom the rule applies; **wenn**, specifying the conditions under which it applies to them; and **nono**, specifying the action prohibited.[34] For a given rule, the system may be entirely latent, in the sense that though blocking operations might be forthcoming if the rule is violated, they are not actually forthcoming, because the rule is never violated, or because violations are infrequent and go unobserved or unchallenged. Even for a rule in which blocking operations do occur from time to time, relevant blocking operations remain latent in other cases, often the majority of cases. (If we join to overt blocking operations by other people, silent checks that people apply to themselves, no doubt there are many more blocking operations than might first seem; but even these checks will in many cases be latent, since people who have fully internalized a rule simply do not think of violating it. You do not notice that you have dropped your wallet under the table; I reach down, pick it up, and return it to you, without considering for a moment whether I could contrive to pocket it.)

Blocking – grasping the baby's forearm or turning the toddler around – often involves physical force. However – and here is the beginning of the tendency of this definition to mitigate the appearance of repression in teaching and maintaining rules – blocking is not to be confused with physical force exerted in the course of negative sanctions, that is to say, punishment. The blocking may, indeed, be accompanied by a show of anger, even of punitive force on the part of the parent who spanks Junior as she pulls Junior away from the street. (He has tried getting into the street all too many times this very day.) Even then the force, exerted in the course of teaching, may be as much 'correction' as punishment.[35] But anger may be wholly absent. The parent may kiss or cuddle the child as she carries him away, or just carry him away without comment. If the child makes a mistake in grammar or pronunciation, the parent or teacher simply gives the correct form, and may do so jokingly. The teaching of rules begins to look very different if we move to corrections of this sort: The corrections are now at least as much positive reinforcements as they are negative ones.

Too little, it now seems to me, was made in *Logic on the Track of Social Change* of positive reinforcements. Not only mild and loving corrections need to be considered; but the whole array of rewards, beginning with expressions of approval. ('That's a good boy!' when the child has washed his hands before the meal.) If full allowance is made for positive reinforcements to the observance of rules, inculcating rules will seem at no great disadvantage in comparison with inculcating virtues by examples. The examples of virtues will sometimes be set without admonitions of any kind to follow them and without corrections if they are not followed. But this is far, one might think, from being the only case, or even the most common one. Teaching virtues through examples may be as constraining in technique as teaching rules. Moreover, unless the pupil is given a rule about what aspect of the example to follow, will she not suffer some epistemological uncertainty and anguish about what she is supposed to do? She might welcome the explicit instruction conveyed by a rule, whether it is a rule about how the example is to be followed or any other rule.

The term 'rule' is sometimes used to imply, in distinction from mere conventions among other things, being accompanied by negative sanctions. This usage very likely arises from a confusion between punishment and correction; and it does not match the breadth of the ordinary use of the term, which leads us to speak easily of 'rules of language.'[36] Only if people cannot be counted on to abide by a rule (in the broad sense) is it reasonable to attach sanctions to it. When it is reasonable to attach them as eventualities, the sanctions represent an economy of attention and of forcible actions. In principle, the authority that is the source of a rule could stand over recalcitrants and block them – if necessary, physically block them – from doing the prohibited actions. Instead, the authority announces that sanctions are attached to the rule, and enforces the sanctions often enough to deter most of the people tempted to flout the rule from giving way to the temptation.[37]

In any case, the conception of rules in view, when it is fully appreciated, introduces a sweeping mitigation of the initial picture of rules that can be gathered from St Thomas and others, which takes rules to be inculcated by negative sanctions or the threat of them. Inculcation, like maintenance, may proceed with minimal use of negative sanctions. Possibly there will no need to use them at all; and this, once the distinction between correction and punishment is recognized, is not a utopian possibility, which could be realized only by saints. People may be tempted to flout the rules; people may flout them. But mild corrections, which presumably are still available, may suffice to keep the temptations and lapses under control.

St Thomas, contemplating human beings in their fallen condition, emphasizes the imperfections of the pupils as the cause that makes resort to punishment necessary. Human beings are commonly fractious to begin with; and though St Thomas does not make the distinction between the physical blocking used in teaching and the force brought to bear in punishments, I think he would say that children, even when they have learned protonorms by being judiciously and systematically blocked, will persist in trying to deviate when they imagine they can get away with it, and will have to be checked by the threat of punishment, sometimes carried out. From this they learn a further lesson: Even if no one is present who blocks them in a specific instance, they cannot generally expect to get away with behaviour that deviates from the protonorm, now transformed into a rule, without suffering for it. For some pupils, fractious throughout life, perhaps even after the age of forty, when aggressive male criminals are said to lose their belligerence, the rules and their sanctions must be in place to keep this expectation fresh and constantly in mind. We can think of such people as never entirely completing their moral education.

If there are, in a given jurisdiction, a lot of such people about, the picture of morality and moral education that is called for certainly tends to exhibit the rigidity and repressiveness that we began by finding repugnant. At this point, however, it should be clear that a whole range of pictures is consistent with a natural law theory like St Thomas's. Inculcation to the point of internalization may be reached more or less successfully on a number of different routes. We may be lucky – with care, we may assure ourselves of being lucky – in having relatively few people who have to be punished during their early moral education; in having those few invite punishment infrequently, and only in relatively early stages; in having adults who have, at most, to be reminded now and then that negative sanctions can be brought in to back the rules that on some rare occasions they contemplate flouting. We may be even luckier and be able to get along with mild corrections and no punishment at all. Even if, as St Thomas may not have sufficiently considered, bringing in sanctions during moral education can be counterproductive, because they are more likely to arouse resentment and hostility than to induce internalization and glad adherence, sanctions may not be counterproductive if used sparingly. Even if, in detail, they are, if they are used rarely, other processes in which negative sanctions are not present may overwhelm them in effect. The processes in question may fit Laurence Thomas's account of how parents 'affirm' their children's identity and character;[38] given such affirmation, children can learn moral lessons even from occasional displays of parental anger. The resulting community may be mild in outlook and harmonious in conduct.

The grimmer, more repressive community at the other end of the range no doubt to some degree represents a failure of moral education. Certainly, it runs what we could agree with Laurence Thomas are horrible dangers of producing much less than fully committed moral agents. Even so we should not lightly concede that moral education could not succeed in a way close to St Thomas's expectations, with a heavy emphasis from an early stage (if not from the very earliest) on rules and sanctions.

We would no doubt prefer a minimal use of punishment, which at least for the sorts of persons we would prefer to be and prefer to have around is unpleasant to administer. Yet are the grounds for apprehending that reliance on punishment is counterproductive conclusive grounds? Are there no causal mechanisms by which, in time, human beings come to internalize rules and gladly adhere to them, even if they have been taught them with heavy doses of punishment? It is easy to sketch one: In time, the pupils understand that it is too painful to continue defying the rules; they resign themselves to conforming. But then conforming becomes habitual. Indeed, whether they recognize that they would be happier if they cease resenting having to conform or simply because the habit of conformity becomes a paramount feature of self-identification, they become uncomfortable doing or trying to do anything else but conform. A community in which internalization was deep and widespread, even on this basis, is a community that could maintain morality for most people, after a certain age, with a minimum use of punishment. It would differ from the more attractive one pictured a moment ago in having a relatively repugnant process of moral education. This would be an important difference, especially if the unhappiness caused the pupils, and lingering perhaps throughout life, resentment and a sense of defeat that could have been avoided, fractious as the pupils might have been. Nevertheless, the process might in other respects be successful enough as a process of moral education. Grown up and accustomed to the rules, the people who came through this process might recognize that the rules were conditions for their own thriving and their community's, and on that basis be ready to give the rules their reasoned consent.

The grimmer picture, moreover, has something reassuring to tell us about the extent of impatience and intractability that is consistent with the internalization of moral rules. In this connection, it may help us face with some assurance deeper problems about these obstacles. The child is to become not only ready and glad to conform; the child is to apply the rules responsibly, with discretion. The child cannot do that without achieving substantial personal independence, with a sense of her own identity. How is she going to do this, without asserting herself in opposition to her parents? She resists their instruction not just out of moral backwardness, but in order to assert her independence. And they seek to have her conform, not just out of conscientious care to induce in her habits of good conduct, but to assert their own wills and maintain tolerable order in the household. Even these remarks hardly suggest how deep and inevitable the conflict between child and parent, moral pupil and moral teacher, may be. The child competes with one parent for the attention of the other; and this can clearly be a matter of distress, even if it is not coloured by the sexual impulses of the Electra and Oedipus complexes.[39] Yet, wonderfully, somehow, moral education often succeeds, not just in producing conformity, but in producing persons independent enough to exercise discretion responsibly. 'Affirmation' is often strong enough to override all the conflicts and complications. The child understands that occasional punishments, even expressions of anger, signify love and care for her, as the devastating alternative of abandoning the child would not.[40]

Fragility of Moral Motivations

In desperate circumstances, rule observance and the communal feeling that encourages the pursuit under the natural laws of the Common Good may break down into egoism. At any rate, motivations may shrink in that direction. There is a Newfoundland story about a fleet of fishing schooners getting caught in a pack of ice, with sinking so imminent that the men in the crews scramble out of the ships onto the ice. They are going to try to make their way to land by jumping from one ice floe to another. But there is not room on many of the floes for more than one man at a time. The men, all friends of long-standing from the same outports, are quite ruthless in jostling others aside to get onto the next floes. This is not egoism. Do they have any choice? Each of them has a family back in port that is liable to starve if he does not get home. There is no time to draw lots to see who would get the best-guaranteed opportunities to escape.

Similarly, moral shrinking goes no further than to families first in most of the people who have prepared for household self-sufficiency, sometimes armed self-sufficiency, on one pretext or another, like the threat of nuclear war or the once supposedly impending disaster in Y2K. Yet, for any bachelors who are making these preparations, does the shrinking not go all the way, as with people forced from their homes and separated from their families during the disasters of war?

If there are opportunities for cooperation in spite of the breakdown or displacement of normal relationships, people habituated to pursuing the Common Good with communal feeling may, in effect, fall back on the approaches to building trust and reputations for trustworthiness through (guardedly) cooperative strategies that Ostrom attributes to rational agents dealing, in effect, with strangers.[41] Ostrom allows for people learning norms through socialization;[42] and she refers to 'substantial evidence ... that humans inherit a strong capacity to learn reciprocity norms and social rules that enhance the opportunities to gain benefits from ... social dilemmas.'[43] However, Ostrom assumes no special advantages from moral education. The rational agents that she describes may be thought of as adopting strategies that agents with a good moral education would adopt as a mode of dealing with other people with whom they did not have established patterns of cooperation and from whom they had no immediate reason to expect brotherly, or perhaps even humane feeling. Once again, rational egoism turns out to be the result of moral shrinkage, though this time there is no need to suppose that it is a fundamental shrinkage of character or personality.

Rule observance and communal feeling may break away from the morality of natural law into something worse than egoism, into just what Hobbes, thinking about the English Civil War and perhaps even more about the wars of religion on the Continent, feared most: group fanaticism. Then nothing that the advancement of the group seems to call for will seem out of bounds as something to be done to defend the group, advance its purposes, and affirm its glory, all at the expense of other groups. Massacres, like those in Rwanda or Bosnia (by the Serbs at Srebrnica), follow.[44] The fanatics become monsters, though just a little while ago they were like us reasonable people with humane sentiments, and they may become so again. The most urgent problem of practical morality is not to restrain egoism, but to safeguard ordinary human beings like us from becoming monsters of fanaticism. The path to attachment to the natural law is not simple or unique; and the attachment may seem firmly anchored at the mean between rational egoism and group fanaticism, yet, disturbingly, all too often it has turned out to be quick and easy for people to cut loose from the anchor.

We might wonder, which path of moral education, the one that fits the grim picture, with lots of use of harsh punishments, or the one that fits the tender-minded approach, relying on soft corrections, leads more dependably to commitments and motivations that are proof against breakdown situations. Very possibly it depends on the sort of breakdown situation that is in question. Some writers have said that liberal-minded people with tender upbringings did not do so well in the Nazi concentration camps as people who had been toughened by physically dangerous struggle outside (for example, members of the Communist Party).[45] Other observers are not so hard on liberals as such; they are inclined rather to emphasize the vulnerability of prisoners who had no strong convictions of any kind, political or otherwise.[46] There may be an analogy with military discipline. The discipline of the Prussian infantry under Frederick the Great was very harsh – no Sans Souci for them; but they did well in battle. Even today, discipline in the Brigade of Guards and in the U.S. Marines is notably severe; but in some breakdown situations, I expect, they would afford more reliable protection than troops, like Dutch troops, who at least at one time, were allowed their choice of hairstyles and even the right to strike. (In Srebrnica, Dutch troops were not willing to risk annihilation by the Serbs to protect the Bosnian Muslims in their charge. Had they been willing, their annihilation would have provoked massive intervention by the NATO powers; but had they been willing, they might not have been annihilated – the Serbs might have had enough sense to back off and forego the intended massacre.)[47] In other breakdown situations, maybe tender-minded training has better results. People with such training may have in greater proportion than people with a grimmer training resisted the clamour to deal with the Tutsis or Muslims, whom they had been living with peacefully and cooperatively, as if they no longer had any claims to humane treatment. But this is a subject on which philosophy needs to turn to scientific psychology; it is one more instance of philosophers thinking up interesting problems that they do not have the facts to answer, and I fear, one more instance where the psychologists have not collected the facts.[48]

Chapter Nine

Epilogue: The Lasting Strength of Natural Law Theory in Jurisprudence

To cut a convincing figure again in jurisprudence – to which I turn in this final chapter, an epilogue to the main argument of the book – natural law theory, by which I mean and shall mean as I have meant throughout the book, traditional natural law theory, basically the theory of St Thomas combined with the theories of the modern authors that I have treated, must be made convincing again in ethics. Otherwise, it can hardly make much of the traditional claim that to be genuine laws must accord with this ethics. A number of things need to be done about the theory on the side of ethics: Retire God to at most a role speaking offstage; disambiguate the concept of the Common Good in a way that makes some headway toward reconciling aggregative and distributive considerations;[1] prune away doubtful features regarding contraception, abortion, and other matters (including the subordination of women, even slavery); establish a corpus of rules that apply in every culture in spite of present variations in convention. I believe that I have done these things, or at least made substantial headway toward doing them, in the preceding chapters.

Why should one want to do them? My view is that reviving traditional natural law theory in a selective way offers the best hope of making plain the attachment of ethics to human needs; and to mutual consideration, beginning with basic needs and expanding to other concerns. These are not attractions that will move philosophers who wish to keep open for rational agents the option of rejecting concern for others (maybe even of concern for themselves); but that is an option, I believe, that must be left behind if one is to cross the gap (which a convincing natural law theory must fully allow for) between 'is' and 'ought' in order to take up in a defensibly comprehensive ethics a commitment to 'ought.'

It is one thing, however, to restore the cogency and strength of the theory as an account of ethics backing with an effective justification the right moral prescriptions, including the right moral prescriptions for what is to be made into laws. It is quite another thing to make the theory count, as it traditionally aspired to do, on the jurisprudential side. On its jurisprudential side, where natural law theory maintains that laws are not even to be reckoned as laws if they do not conform to the moral prescriptions which it stands by, the theory is by general reckoning a lost cause.

Nuance this position as one likes, the definition of law that it implies seems irremediably at odds with the way that the term 'law' is used, by lawyers and everybody else; and ill-adapted for application to the phenomena. It seems equivalent to insisting on using the terms 'man' or 'soldier' as honorifics, refusing to apply them to anyone who runs from danger. But we know that many who have been enrolled in the army, indeed many who have been put through recruit training, will prove faint-hearted in battle. Are they not, in a plain and useful sense, soldiers, too, just not very good ones? Traditional natural law theory seems in an even worse position with respect to the definition of 'law' than this. One might imagine using 'ship,' too, as an honorific, to apply only to vessels that were seaworthy; but ordinary language seems to have settled otherwise, rejecting any analogy with 'man' or 'soldier' in having honorific uses. Not only does common observation tell us that all sorts of rules, some in accord with refined moral prescriptions, some dramatically opposed, are generally accounted to be laws. Common observation tells us that this is what in ordinary language they are called, without (it appears) any complication from an additional familiar honorific use. On this point, what does natural law theory offer in contention with what may be called the Positivist Descriptive Criterion but terminological confusion? It is confusion, moreover, that natural law theory can avoid and still lay down its ethical prescriptions, including its prescriptions for morally acceptable law. Whatever its merits as an ethical theory, will this entirely superfluous baggage about what is to be identified and described as laws not just unbalance the merits and cast them into the shade?

The Positivist Descriptive Criterion says that the laws in any observed system of laws are such just by being enacted by the procedures accepted in the system. (I take enactment to be more fundamental than being established by precedent, since where there are provisions for enactment, laws can always be enacted to displace any precedent; and I waive any treatment of customary law, with whatever difficulties customary law may cause positivists.) They may be good laws; they may be evil laws; they are laws all the same if the procedures have made them laws. Natural law theory not only seems bent on blinding people to these matters; it also (since it wishes to denounce the evil laws and refuse to endorse obligations to obey them) ties itself into knots dealing with them. On the one hand, it has to recognize that what are called 'laws' in a given system may conflict with natural law; on the other hand, it withdraws the recognition, saying with St Thomas, that 'unjust laws' are not really laws at all. Is this anything more than double-talk?

A Kind Invitation to Desist from Terminological Folly

A typical current assessment of the traditional natural law position in this regard can be found in one of the chapters contributed by Jeffrie Murphy to his and Jules Coleman's book on the philosophy of law. Murphy quotes St Thomas's definition of law (to be found in *Summa Theologiae*, 1a2ae, Q.90, 4), attaching (from 1a2ae, Q.93, 3; Q.95, 2) some points that St Thomas makes in elaboration: 'Law is nothing else than an ordinance of reason for the Common Good, promulgated by him who has the care of the community ... Human law has the nature of law in so far as it partakes of right reason ... So far as it deviates from reason, it is called unjust law and has the nature, not of law, but of violence ... Such are acts of violence rather than laws because, as Augustine says, a law that is not just seems to be no law at all.' Murphy comments:

> What seems to be happening here is that the concept of ideal or morally good law is seen as part of the moral order; from this correct insight, a careless slide is made into identifying law itself with a part of morality ... He is committed to the claim that an evil or unjust law is no law at all, that legal requirements must, as a matter of definition, require only conduct that is morally permissible. A dramatic and decisive counterexample to this view ... is the obvious existence of legal rules that clear thinking would force us to acknowledge as laws even if we believed them to be morally evil. Suppose, for example, that you believe that it is morally wrong for the state to eliminate all considerations of fault in granting legal divorces. Surely you could not reasonably conclude from this that all those persons in a 'no-fault' state who claim to be legally divorced are

really not divorced at all but are still legally married. You may think that these laws are unworthy of your respect (because they are, in your judgment, evil or irrational laws), but what is gained in saying that they are not laws at all?[2]

In a more recent book in which natural law has a prominent place, Lloyd L. Weinreb says much the same thing: 'Although [the arguments for deontological natural law in] its various formulations have important points to make, they establish nothing that is not compatible with legal positivism and contained less misleadingly within it. The persistence of natural law in its present guise is ... a puzzle.'[3] Weinreb continues: 'Defenders of natural law have no difficulty establishing that law and morality generally coincide in fact, over a broad range. (Nor do positivists disagree.) The difficulty has been to establish, within strictly deontological bounds, that there is a necessary connection between them, which makes it correct to say that law, as such, has an inherent moral dimension. There are simply too many examples of a law that is, or is thought to be, inconsistent with generally accepted moral principles ... If natural law requires us to deny that such laws are immoral or, contrary to the habits of ordinary speech, to deny that they are laws, it puts too great a strain on common sense.'[4]

This is what positivists say about the issue respecting the Descriptive Criterion. But nowadays writers sympathetic to natural law theory are inclined to join them. David Richards, whom Weinreb reckons as a natural law theorist, thinks of himself as offering a 'methodological natural law theory,' but on the issue raised by the Positivist Descriptive Criterion, he repudiates traditional natural law theory.[5] John Finnis would dearly like to jettison the traditional claim that unjust law is not genuine law; and he insists, accordingly, much more on the passages in which St Thomas uses 'law' varying over bad laws as well as good ones than on the passages in which St Thomas defies the Descriptive Criterion.[6] Philip Soper, sympathetic to natural law theory in other respects, says that at its worst, natural law theory can be reduced to 'a slogan invented by positivists' for ascription to natural law theorists, namely, 'that unjust law is not law.'[7] Soper says that the slogan 'distorts the natural law insight,' and to leave natural law theory there 'is to start and stop a theory in a single sentence.'[8] The slogan fails 'to identify law apart from ... moral inquiry into justice.'[9] Yet Soper himself in this passage goes along with reducing natural law theory to the slogan far enough to maintain that 'natural law theories are hardly theories at all.'[10] Thus, one might conclude, they have nothing to offer as a useful alternative to the Positivist Criterion.

Are these comments really credible on close inspection? Five pages later, Soper quotes St Thomas's definition of law, and to (I expect) the astonishment of anyone coming straight to this passage from the one that I just cited, asserts that 'with a slight modification of the usual interpretation, this formulation conveys the essence of the theory of law' which Soper is himself maintaining.[11] Murphy portrays St Thomas as a simpleton who failed to recognize that what is enacted as law may conflict with what he regards as law properly so called; Weinreb (in these passages) implies the same of every champion of the theory. St Thomas (as Finnis insists) did not fail to recognize such discrepancies; Murphy, for his part, has lost sight of his own quotation from St Thomas, in which the recognition is explicit. Nevertheless, may we not think of Murphy and Weinreb as joining to offer St Thomas and other champions what appears to be a straightforward invitation, kind, if a trifle condescending, to terminological clarification? Leave natural law prescriptions out when deciding whether something is a law or not; bring them in, if you wish, to distinguish between good laws and evil ones.

Balking at the Kind Invitation

Yet St Thomas could, I think reasonably, refuse to accept the terminological invitation; so, I think, can current champions of traditional natural law theory like Finnis. This is so in spite of the fact that the invitation can be strengthened by insisting that legal theorists who stand by the Criterion against traditional natural law theory – let us call them Basic Positivists – may be perfectly ready to join natural law theorists in the project of making sure that only laws which accord with M*, the moral rules upheld by traditional natural law theory, get into the statute books or stay there. Basic Positivists may be allies in this project, furthermore, whether or not they take the natural law view that the rules in M* can be established as moral truths holding for everyone.[12] They could, for example – though there is nothing in legal positivism that requires this – take an emotive-imperative view of the rules in M*. For all these people, traditional natural law theorists and Basic Positivists among them, one might say, it is just the fact that some things purporting to be laws have been given the force of law that makes them urgent subjects of remedy. Again, why not simply call them laws, but denounce them as bad ones?

The issue drawn between traditional natural law theory and Basic Positivism respecting the Criterion is not a neatly determinable one. The honours in the end must be divided between the two camps; and even those, I among them, who in the end will find it more convenient to come to rest in the positivist camp, will have grounds for treating with more respect than is common nowadays those who refuse to the end to acknowledge laws as fully such that fit the Criterion yet are at odds with M*. On the issue raised against traditional natural law theory by the Criterion, which is whether enactment suffices to determine what is to be described as a law, a full survey of the evidence that bears upon the issue will give the natural law theorists strength enough so that they can reasonably refuse to accept the Criterion as originally conceived, that is to say, narrowly enough to exclude any implication that moral considerations come into enactment, or into anything else necessary to establish something as a law. It is, to be sure, a strength that can be finally vindicated only by finding prescriptive strength on the ethical side of natural law theory; but it is still an advance over current assessments of the issue to see that if traditional natural law theory can make good its claims to be a sound and useful guide to moral prescriptions,[13] then its descriptive claims convincingly go beyond what as it stands the terminological invitation contemplates.[14]

The Criterion itself, to be reasonable, must be more elastic than the Positivists acknowledge in putting it forward. Either the Positivist Descriptive Criterion is too narrow, taking an arbitrarily restricted view of what it means for a law to be enacted or established, and traditional natural law theory offers a reasonable way of filling out the general description of a law; or the Positivist Criterion, amplified to take full account of what it means for a law to be enacted and established, consorts better with natural law theory than it does with, what we may suppose, taking the Criterion at face value was originally intended with it. The term 'enactment' by itself turns out to have enough elasticity to prevent the issue about the Positivist Criterion from being settled out of hand to the discredit of natural law theory.

Enactment goes further in the overall process of establishing laws than seems at first sight. But the argument on the natural law side about the Criterion does not depend on the elasticity of 'enactment' alone; it brings in stages of secure establishment that come after enactment, in the broadest sense. When we consider the whole length of the process of establishing laws, a narrow Criterion will turn out to be descriptively inadequate. It captures what is currently accepted and enforced as law over the whole range of jurisdictions; it does not capture, the natural law theorists may insist, what in any jurisdiction can be described as law fully established and fully realized, free of legislative, and in this respect free of legal defects.

Throughout I shall be concentrating, with the Positivist Criterion, upon enactment and the law-establishing process of which enactment, taken more or less narrowly, is the initial stage. The debate in which legal positivism has sought to overturn – to dismiss – natural law theory has often touched on other topics as well – for example, legal authority, the nature of legal obligation and its general relation to moral obligation, the obligation to obey laws defensible in intention but imperfect in formulation, the praise or blame to be meted out for obeying the law, the character of judicial reasoning, the difference between rules and commands. I shall come no closer to treating these other topics, many, maybe all of which will furnish further and subtler reasons for crediting natural law theory with important insights, than to come within sight of obligation and political authority when I treat, as the last stop on the path that begins with enactment, the legitimacy of regimes. I shall keep to a narrow path that leads from enactment to further stages of the law-establishing process. This will enable me to maintain, returning to an issue settled prematurely in the minds of many, that there is something substantial to be said for traditional natural law theory even when it is most nakedly exposed to positivist objections.[15]

Sooner or later advocates of traditional natural law theory may be persuaded to retreat on the issue about the Criterion – to retreat in terminology, or at least to make concessions for temporary purposes and particular inquiries. Nevertheless, they can properly refuse to countenance such concessions until the descriptive strength of its position has been acknowledged. Even then, though less will be at stake for either side in the concessions, it may be a toss-up whether to make them or not. Either way, more will have to be said, for example, about conflicting interpretations of law and judicial discretion, to give an adequate definition of law. At best, on the path that I am taking, traditional natural law theory may get only to the beginnings, and somewhat shaky beginnings, of an adequate definition – and hence, no further than that in making a necessary connection between their moral prescriptions and what is to be described as law. Yet the current terminological invitation, offered by Murphy or Weinreb or others, is premature.

Basic Response to the Invitation: Law and Enactment Cannot Be Disconnected from Secure Establishment; Enactment and Secure Establishment Cannot Be Disconnected from M*

It is a basic thesis of traditional natural law theory that once people understand what is at stake for them in M* they will adhere to it. This is not happenstance. Natural law theory holds that given the nature of human beings and given the circumstances in which they find themselves, M* consists of the rules that they must adhere to in order to flourish together. Moreover, they are biologically constituted as rational animals – we would say, nowadays, 'programmed' – to discover this fact. It will give at least a partial representation of this position to treat it as implying a number of empirical hypotheses (deeply entrenched in what has been discovered about human beings as a natural kind): (H_f) Flourishing together implies adherence to M*; (H_p) Human beings are programmed to discover (H_f); (H_u) Once human beings discover H_f they will adhere to it; (H_a) Human beings do adhere to M*, that is to say, acknowledge its claims to moral truth, and insist, so far as they are able to, that any rules which they are to obey accord with it.[16] Subtler versions of the last three hypotheses, allowing as those do not for an unequal distribution of discovery and adherence between 'followers' and 'opinion leaders,'[17] could easily be supplied and would do the same service. I shall work, however, with the hypotheses as given; and concentrate upon H_a, indeed make the most of H_a alone, calling in the other hypotheses, in particular H_f, only as a means that theorists in the natural law camp might use to resolve results not neatly determinable.

Assuming H_a, traditional natural law theorists may hold that even if legal positivists correctly describe with their criterion what over the whole range of jurisdictions may be currently – for the time being – accepted and enforced as law, they leave out of account something that is essential to making laws securely established, namely, that laws which conflict with M* are continually liable to upset, in particular liable on rational grounds centrally relevant to the law-making process. The natural law theorists do not have to bring forward the whole of M* to make this point. Confining themselves to the most egregious conflicts with M* – points on which there is conflict with rules that have wide support outside natural law theory as well as inside it, they may leave any further features of the Common Good aside, and bring forward only conflicts with everybody's interest in respect (say) to meeting needs for food or for security of life and limb. They can leave the morality of some laws unsettled – for example, laws relating to the legality of divorce (Murphy's example, above) or laws giving a licence to kill in order 'to repel a felonious entry into ... one's house.'[18] They can still maintain that accordance with M* on the points cited is indispensable to secure establishment.

How real is the liability to upset, given a conflict with M* even in its most obvious parts? What can 'secure establishment' mean, in the face of what (in instances like slavery or the subordination of women) have amounted to the persistence over centuries of laws that we would now regard as impossible for natural law theory to defend? The uncomfortable facts here cannot be denied. I mean to give them full attention, taking into account the complexity and uncertainty of political processes as well as persistent ignorance and prejudice on the part of people engaged in such processes (when they have been permitted to engage in them). However, the point at issue with the meaning of 'secure establishment' can be seen more easily if we run for a while with the additional assumption (call it 'D') that we have democratic procedures with agents who not only as H_a says, adhere to M*, but are rational and well-informed and have to deal with one simple (binary) issue at a time, that is, 'Yes' or 'No' on the issue of ratifying a single specified project of law. The case for the traditional natural law position on accordance with M* is at its strongest with this assumption. As I dismantle the assumption, step by step, the case will weaken; but I shall argue that even at the end, where nothing remains of democratic procedures, the case does not fade out entirely, indeed, does not even fade out so far as to leave the issue about the Criterion neatly determinable against traditional natural law theory. Under this assumption, D, with its constitutional implications, we can say that projects of law that conflict with M* on the points cited, should they happen to get through earlier stages of the law-establishing process, are liable to be quickly overturned by popular demand. Has even their 'enactment' come to an end if they have not faced this test? It took a long time, and many strange vicissitudes, as Arthur P. Monahan has shown,[19] for consent to gain the weight with adherents of natural law that we would now give it; but in respect to the issue of secure establishment we might claim that consent is logically embedded in natural law theory from the beginning. What is law, St Thomas tells us, is enacted by the people for the Common Good or by a prince who has their Common Good in view;[20] but the Common Good, achieved by laws reflecting

M*, is what people adhering to M* will insist on choosing if they are rational, fully informed, and given a chance to choose. Thus, traditional natural law theorists might not just withstand the siege laid against them by Basic Positivists operating from the Descriptive Criterion; traditional natural law theorists might sortie and capture the Basic Positivists' position on procedures, in part capitalizing on what elasticity there may be in the concept of enactment, in part seizing the opportunity to connect enactment with further stages in the law-establishing process.

Either the procedures of enactment would not have come to an end until the people who are to be subject to the law have been given an unambiguous opportunity to reject the projected law, or further stages in the law-establishing process remain in which this opportunity will figure. No doubt the notion of enactment has stretched beyond the intentions of Basic Positivists, or has given way to a larger conception, which the Criterion as they intended it did not embrace, of the law-establishing process. Yet, so far as the point remains one of deciding what, given the received usage of the term 'law' and given the phenomena to which it is to be applied, shall be the definition of law, it turns out, within the limits of the present assumptions, of D added to H_a, to be something that might as reasonably be settled, by using 'enactment' in a larger sense or by replacing it with the term 'law-establishing process,' in favour of traditional natural law theory rather than a point obviously won at the outset by the Basic Positivists.

This point about procedures would be irresistible even within the confines of the term 'enactment' if the present assumptions were embodied in a model (DM) of democracy, direct or representative, under which it was prescribed that every act of the legislature should (say, within one month of passing) be put by itself, as a single issue, to the electorate for ratification. However, the point is nearly as strong if we relax the prescription to requiring that a ratification vote be taken if within a given period (say, three years) citizens petition for one. Do we lose much by relaxing the prescription further, and striking out the limit of three years for taking the initiative? Then by petition, followed by an unfavourable vote, the law in question could be overturned at any time, even if meanwhile it is treated within the legal system as both enacted and established. Its establishment would fall short of having the thorough backing, both in rational argument and (given what I am at the moment assuming) in observable consent, that it would have if the procedures had been carried through ratification.

Secure Establishment with Imperfect Democratic Enactment

In the real world – in history – the claim that unless the law-establishing process goes far enough to bring about accordance with natural law (with M*) the process does not suffice to securely establish laws must mean less than the connection just made out, even at its most relaxed. It can be said for the claim is that there is a tendency for people to demand a say about the laws that they are to be subject to. It can be said, further, that where the demand is heeded another tendency will operate, as the people in question become better informed and more fully habituated to the terms of discussion;[21] given H_a, they will insist on accordance with M*, at any rate in its more obvious parts.

H_a, adherence by human beings generally to M*, of course, in spite of the backing that it gets from the other hypotheses, may itself be questioned, and the questions will press in the more strongly the more imperfectly it is translated into legislation. H_a risks more the more of M* that we take into account: It risks little if we consider cases in which everyone's interests are flouted (maybe everyone's except the ruler's); it risks a bit more if we bring in any aspect of the Common Good with which M* is concerned that transcends personal interests; it risks a lot if we bring in the whole of the Common Good, and with it the whole of what traditional natural law theory would want to put into M*. Even with the whole of M* brought in, the hypothesis would not be absurd, difficult as it may be to confirm or falsify, provided the theory has been circumspect enough to keep to a transcultural core of rules in identifying M*. Moreover, the main empirical difficulty with the hypothesis may be, not that people do not typically seek a Common Good that answers so far as it goes to M*, but that they do not go far enough with it to include human beings outside their own ethnic or religious groups. Let us persist in assuming H_a for the time being.

H_a notwithstanding, procedures in the real world will not fulfil the model DM, even at its most relaxed. They often amount, nevertheless, to significant approximations to fulfilment. The initiative is a standard feature of the procedures in some American state governments; there are also provisions for referenda. Occasionally, in general elections, the issue about a given law becomes salient enough for candidates to take a stand on it; clear linkage may follow between favour for the law and the fate of enough candidates for office to change the political party in power; and the party may on these occasions follow through with the mandate given it.

The procedures, looked upon as devices for producing mandates, are not as such reliable. Not to speak of the difficulties raised by Arrow and the school of social choice theory, consider the ambiguity of votes for candidates who take positions on several issues at once.[22] The voters may not be informed enough anyway, or rational enough, to give mandates that accord with their interests or with the Common Good. They may fail to press for such mandates; or even press for, and give, mandates that are contrary to M*. (Sometimes they may reasonably think that it will be less trouble to go along, at least for the time being, ` with a law at odds with M* than to try to upset it; and in doing this they may be giving weight and respect to procedures that in the given instance they think have miscarried.)

Here the Basic Positivist case for defining and describing law in accordance with a narrow Criterion increases in strength. Basic Positivists may well maintain that it is methodologically best more often than not to treat as established laws laws that have been duly enacted short of being passed upon by the electorate as a whole, and are already being applied in the courts. May it not still turn out that the electorate will invoke against these supposed laws some device that gives them a late-operating chance for intervening in enactment or for overturning what up to that point was accepted as fully enacted? The Basic Positivist may acknowledge that the electorate may indeed, do so, but hold that such future events are too rare and too uncertain to carry any substantial weight in determining what is here and now the law.

A reasonable natural law theorist may be strongly inclined to go along. A reasonable natural law theorist should go along if the question is narrowly one of identifying what over the whole range of observable jurisdictions currently – that is to say, for the time being – may be accepted and enforced as law. Should she do so, however, without first driving home the point that enactment, certainly enactment opening up into the larger process of law establishment, turns out to be a matter of degree which prevents an out-of-hand resolution, with a narrow conception of enactment, of the definitional and descriptive issue respecting the Positivist Criterion? Or without making the second point that it is only from defects in procedures as well as defects in information that this situation comes about?

Properly marshalled, the thrust of natural law theory here – and it is a powerful thrust – can be to say that these are defects which a fully satisfactory descriptive theory of the law must recognize as such. Whether they work out to this end or not, the procedures in question –

here, democratic procedures – are conceived under the purpose of giving the people subject to the laws the final say in whether they are to be
accepted. When we know that what the legislature has enacted runs
square against what the electorate as a whole would accept, were it
given a full opportunity to express its views, we have reason to say
that were the procedures to work to an end, those (putative) enactments would not stand as law. They would not stand because, in the
end, assuming H_a, people would see that they conflict with M*, and act
to remove the conflict. Nor is this an idle counterfactual gesture: The
condition about opportunity is often substantially met, with the results
predicted. If the procedures, though in intention democratic and supported for this reason, are so imperfect that enactments conflicting
with M* on obvious points can persist even for generations without
effective challenge, then natural law theory is ready to charge that
there are defects in the procedures and describe what in upshot they
amount to.

Beyond Democratic Enactment: The Legitimacy of Regimes

What is to be said of cases in which the procedures are not democratic?
Although St Thomas allows for democratic procedures (laws are to be
enacted either by the people or by their vicegerent), his language
shows that he regards it as the normal case that the laws should be
enacted by a prince, by 'him who has the care of the community.'[23] We
can agree with Weinreb that it would outrage 'the habits of ordinary
speech' to claim that only laws that result from democratic procedures
are genuine. Is this, at last, a juncture at which natural law theory must
in reason accept, if it has not accepted before, the Positivist Criterion
on the issue of immediate, if superficial description? Is it not the criterion most suitable for general use covering all regimes? I am taking
expansion of the notion of enactment to the point at which under democratic procedures it brings into operation the larger law-establishing
process as a point won, but this leaves the Positivist Criterion (and
should leave it) as operating without any general implication that the
law-establishing process will be democratic.

There is still something to be said about secure establishment before
these concessions take effect, this time something about the legitimacy
of regimes that legislate against people's interests and other aspects of
the Common Good in ways that the people subject to the legislation in
question would predictably reject if they had the opportunity, under

democratic procedures, to do so. A prince who legislates in ways contrary to natural law is, in St Thomas's view, betraying his responsibility to the community.[24] Furthermore, the legislation in question is so far null and void, in St Thomas's view, that no one is obliged to obey it (in some cases, for example, if it prohibits the practice of true religion, there is no option but to defy it).[25] This at least opens the way to justifying rebellion (a way actually taken by Locke).[26] It also brings advocacy of democracy into play again.

Traditional natural law theory does not imply that only a democratic regime is legitimate. It does, however, withhold legitimacy from regimes that legislate with results that run contrary to those that democratic procedures would enable people to reach, and predictably would reach if they were fully informed and fully attached to M*. A prince who does conform in legislation to his responsibility to the community and its Common Good enacts perfectly genuine laws. But St Thomas is, in effect, committed to democracy if, whether as a transitory stage between an unenlightened autocracy and an enlightened one or as a permanent provision, it is the only practical way of achieving laws that accord with the Common Good, and procedures suited to producing securely established laws.

Underneath the issue about whether laws are to be defined and described by the Positivist Criterion, therefore, there lies, on the natural law side, a position about the legitimacy of democracy, which whether or not a legal theorist wishes to accept it, is again far from making (wrongheadedly) a trivial verbal point. The issue about definition, as we have seen, itself has a dimension connecting enactment with the law-establishing process and with secure establishment, a dimension attention to which natural law theory does more to safeguard than Basic Positivism; but now it appears that secure establishment connects further with a position on the legitimacy of regimes. It is a position that can rally powerful moral arguments and at the same time seriously contend in descriptive strength. Regimes that are not regarded as legitimate by the people subject to them often have a lot going against them; in particular, they dare not put their laws to the test of fully informed consent by the people whose conduct the laws are to regulate. The acceptance and enforcement of the laws must rest then on force, on fraud by the rulers, or on mistakes that the rulers and the ruled share about the content of M* and the extent to which legislation has conformed to M*.

Sophisticated positivists shy away from force.[27] Can they be any happier about falling back on fraud or mistakes, considerations that (I imagine) tell in every lawyer's eyes against legality, as the foundation of laws? Another argument – family of arguments – for natural law jurisprudence surfaces here, which I shall not pursue: that the Positivist Criterion fails to take as full account as natural law theory of considerations internal to legality. My present point is that if people living under an undemocratic regime do (in accordance with H_a) adhere to M*, then they will consent to laws that conflict with it only if one or another of these legally indefensible considerations inhibit their protests. The considerations would go a long way to explaining the discrepancy between what is currently accepted and enforced as laws and what H_a would be expected to lead to, if H_a is true.

The Status of Laws without General Adherence to M*

Not everyone at all times can be expected to adhere to M*, even if we put aside situations of scarcity so desperate that all social ties break down in favour of *sauve qui peut*. The argument just given, in its last stage, which abandoned any assumption about the presence of democracy, allowed for the possibility that a prince might legislate contrary to M*, and he might do so either by mistake or by selfish intention. So might a minority coalition, and if such a coalition were powerful enough and selfish enough, it might deliberately oppress the rest of the population. The argument just given, in its last stage, applies again to such a coalition. Indeed, it has in effect already been implied, since princes do not succeed in oppression as single persons, but only as heads of coalitions.[28] Nor, it might be added, will they succeed in oppression if they do not conform in some degree with M* in the legislation that they lay down, for their regimes cannot continue without giving the people subject to them some protection for life and limb, and some guarantee of provisions for needs.[29]

Could there not, however, be majority coalitions that deviated from the non-discriminatory rules of M* to impose discriminatory enactments upon minorities? There certainly could be; sometimes there are. H_a, the empirical hypothesis that people adhere to M*, is not the only hypothesis in the field. On the other line of argument that briefly surfaced above, I could maintain that mere force exerted by a majority was no better a foundation for laws than mere force exerted by a minority. Keeping to the narrow path of the present argument, all that I wish to say at this point is that H_a is not to be discredited out of hand. There are a number of powerful considerations that work upon majorities, once at least the legislative process has been opened to the influence of majorities, in favour of their adhering to M* – among them the cost and the uncertainty of maintaining oppression, but also the endeavours of politicians to recruit support from minorities. Hence, we typically find nothing like a naked repudiation of M*, but at worst claims that the minorities have forfeited any right to non-discriminatory treatment by undermining valid institutions and traditions, by being shiftless or determined free riders, or by failing somehow to achieve fully adult or even fully human status. These may be tributes paid by vice to virtue, but they are nonetheless significant for that. Moreover, they are claims that invite, and succumb to, insistence upon contrary evidence. Full information, combined with constraints on public postures in democracy, and the psychological difficulties of professing given moral beliefs while disavowing them in one's heart tend to bring about adherence to M*. No doubt other conditions for acting on moral conviction, indeed, for having morally enlightened convictions, need to be added, like the absence of desperate material scarcity.

Assessment of the Case, Weakening Stage by Stage, for the Basic Response

Looking back at the stages of the case just made out for holding that laws depend in enactment and secure establishment (taken together) on accordance with M*, Basic Positivists would note, and natural law theorists would have to admit, that as one stage succeeds another, the grounds for holding this grow weaker and weaker. Even at their strongest, the grounds may well be thought to be inadequate to explain crucial aspects of what counts as a law – the discretion given judges, for example, especially when there would be controversy about what M* implies, or the weight to be given precedents in the interpretation of M*. But these are aspects that Basic Positivists, too, must attend to in the definition of law; and natural law theorists may be in as good a position as they are to add an account of those aspects to the definition of law, if they can make a beginning at the definition in their own way.

Can the natural law theorists say anything better than that the grounds on which they must rely in this connection do not fade out altogether? Even if Basic Positivists conceded this point, they might well go on to maintain that whether or not H_a, the empirical hypothesis about adherence to M*, was true, there were so many complications in the way of obtaining adherence in legislation that the tendency for what is enacted as law to accord with M* is often very feeble; and this alone makes bringing M* into the definition of 'law' inconvenient. I am inclined to agree. Basic Positivists might go on, though without my company, to say that the feebleness of the observed tendency counts against H_a; and that the doubtfulness of H_a is an additional reason for falling back on the Positivist Descriptive Criterion, eliminating any reference to M* that may have been insinuated, as the basis for defining and describing laws.

The natural law theorists may reply that 'not fading out altogether' is an assessment better replaced by 'still substantial even in the most unfavourable circumstances.' They might suggest that if the stages had been taken in the reverse order, beginning with the most problematic and ending with the least so, the overall impression would have been quite different. They may say that the stage-by-stage review of the grounds for their traditional claim, so far as H_a can produce such grounds, has at the very least shown, whatever the order of stages, that the issue between them and the Basic Positivists is not neatly determinable. It is only by balancing considerations that one can come to a judgment agreeing with one side or the other, either on the observed tendency for laws to accord with M* or on people's adherence to M*.

The frequency with which accordance with M* is to be observed remains contestable. Frequency alone, the natural law theorists might go on to say, cannot determine the issue anyway. Suppose the art of shipbuilding had progressed no further than to make seaworthy ships once in ten times, so that most ships were not seaworthy; in nine cases out of ten, what were launched as ships capsized as soon as they left the stocks or as soon as they put to sea. It would nevertheless be indispensable to understanding what a ship was to understand that it was useless as such if it was not seaworthy. ('A ship is safe in harbor; but that is not what a ship is for.')[30] Similarly, it may be maintained on behalf of traditional natural law theory that even if attempts at laws very frequently fail to accord with M*, this accordance, with the consequences enabling human beings to flourish together (hypothesis H_f) is what laws will exhibit in the end as people cease to make mistakes in design – in enactment (unless they are prevented from rectifying deviations imposed upon them).

This functional argument for natural law theory is a different argument from the one that I have been making. I bring in (H_f) here only as something that would sway traditional natural law theorists and lead them to persevere in the claims about enactment and secure establishment in the face of evidence that leads Basic Positivists to decide, on balance, to resolve the indeterminacy in the contrary way. Nor, given the belief of traditional natural law theorists in the truth of H_f, the hypothesis about flourishing only under M^*, is this just wishful thinking. If H_f is true (if accordance with H_f is analogous to what has to be done to make a ship seaworthy), then it is reasonable to think that, sooner or later, its truth will be generally recognized; and that along with adherence to M^*, H_a, projects of making laws will fall into line with it. Where the Basic Positivists are preoccupied with short-run considerations, traditional natural law theorists see mixed results from a long-run endeavour that is favoured – in a vector of increasing moral enlightenment running from the more problematical stages to the less problematic ones – by the nature of things.

The Ultimate – Prescriptive – Resources of Natural Law Theory

On the point of secure establishment, there could be a sort of theory of the law that made the point relatively to various sets of moral rules M_1, M_2, M_3 ... that is, those sets that various societies at various times took to be ultimate. Weinreb sees this possibility, but holds that if natural law theorists took it up they would have given in to the legal positivists.[31] Would it not be just as plausible to hold the reverse, to hold at any rate that anyone who took it up was closer to the natural law camp than to the positivist one? Imagine a class of theorists who allow their reference to the moral principles to which laws must conform to be securely established to be relativized in this way. Given a suitably broad conception of enactment and reference to further stages of the law-establishing process, they might still claim to have captured, for relativized quasi-natural law theory, the Positivist Criterion, arguing that in enactment, or if not in enactment, in those further stages of establishing what is law, some M_i will inevitably enter, given full opportunity to insist on legitimacy.

However, natural law theory does stand by the uniqueness of M^*, claiming substantial current knowledge of its content, and traditionally relying on the fact that this content, insofar as it involves the basic rules indispensable for a thriving society, consists of commonplaces, to which all human beings may be expected to agree. In a departure from tradition that would have astonished past philosophers and most of our forebears, philosophers or not, the commonplaces or at least the possibility of agreeing upon them have become controversial. Unsettled by the controversy, one might be prompted to ask of traditional natural law theory, more promptly and urgently perhaps than whether it has any descriptive strength, 'Does it have any prescriptive strength?' In the foregoing account of its descriptive strength, I have assumed or hypothesized some prescriptive strength; and the case for the descriptive strength has been one – just as natural law theorists would insist – that stands or falls with its prescriptive strength, with M* embracing intuitively convincing moral rules and justifying them in a convincing way.

Traditional natural law theory, represented by Natural Law Modernized, may claim, with a judiciously and circumspectly selected M*, to represent at least the core of morality, and argue that in spite of cultural differences in history and in the present world the core holds in every culture, because in every culture human beings have some of the same needs and face circumstances that in some respects create the same problems about meeting those needs. To cite, again, among the simplest and most basic needs, two: the need for security of life and limb; the need for food. Answering to the first is a rule prohibiting assault; answering to the second is a rule prohibiting interference with the consumption of assigned provisions. People may be mindful enough of the prohibitions to heed them without having legislated them or even formulated them.

Different cultures will qualify the prohibitions in different ways. Some will not regard sparing the rod in dealing with children as ruled out by any prohibition, others will; some will run armies in which officers are allowed to knock soldiers about, others will strictly prohibit army officers from laying a finger upon their men. In assigning provisions for food, some cultures will assign provisions under a right of acquiring private property; others will not recognize such a right and consider that it is a point at which a barrier to interference is set up. Some forms of assault, in some connections, we may nevertheless expect are prohibited in every culture; this is a commonplace, and natural law theorists assume that it is a commonplace. It is not a commonplace to express the point by saying that a core rule in M* will cover them, as a core rule in M* will cover forms of interference with the consumption of food that are prohibited in every culture. To get to the core rules, take all the heads of exception recognized anywhere in the whole range of cultures to the basic prohibition, in the one case of assault, in the other of interference with consumption of food, and combine the basic prohibition with the shared subsets of heads of exception.[32]

The same needs come up as aspects of the Common Good, first as matters to be safeguarded by further social arrangements, so that help from others is forthcoming when members of the community run out (let us suppose through no fault of their own) of food or find themselves in danger of assault; second, as matters respecting which social arrangements (not necessarily governmental arrangements) are valued by members of the community as means of accomplishing their own humane purposes regarding other members (maybe regarding other members of the world community). Commonplaces again, as traditional natural law theorists would expect them to be; but again, a technical notion helps show just what is at issue. The arrangements in question are public goods in the technical sense of being goods that any member can benefit from without taking anything away from the benefits which the goods make available to others; but so were the core rules prohibiting assault and interference with the consumption of food.[33]

Let M* contain rules on all these points. If it contains no more, it will certainly fall short of settling all moral controversies, though it should not be rejected on that account, in the absence of more comprehensive bodies of rules more widely accepted. In some controversies – those about distributive justice, for example – it may be possible to get no further toward general agreement than simply to limit the range of acceptable arrangements, short of favouring any of a number of proposals within the range. An arrangement under which one person lives an abundant life while everybody else leads a miserable short one would be ruled out; whether anything like Rawls's Difference Principle should be upheld after basic needs have been met would be left open. In other controversies, even this much headway may prove impossible; but in some cases (for example, controversies about genetic engineering) the difficulty may come, not so much from defects in the representation that M* gives to the core of received morality, as from the fact that the issues fall outside the former bounds of human powers and, hence, outside the bounds of morality as traditionally conceived.

As a position on certain moral prescriptions Natural Law Modernized can be formulated and advocated quite independently of its claim to contribute to descriptive jurisprudence by entering through the notions of enactment and beyond enactment of secure establishment into the very definition of what is to count as a law. Yet its position in ethics becomes more convincing the more weight is given to its empirical hypotheses about what people, duly informed and unintimidated, will demand of laws. So far as it goes, evidence for these is not just evidence that the prescriptions of natural law are practicable; it is evidence that traditional natural law theory specially requires, because it holds that human beings do discover the prescriptions and what is at stake for them in the prescriptions, and that they act accordingly. Can human beings flourish without as much attention to their needs and to public goods as the ethical attractions of natural law theory implies? Do human beings continually – imperfectly it may be, but still continually – exhibit this much attention? In particular, do they exhibit it when they are making (or unmaking) laws? So far as they do, traditional natural law theory makes a persuasive connection between what it holds laws ought to be and what it holds laws will be, in the end, once they become securely established.[34]

APPENDIX

Natural Law in Philosophical Traditions outside the Christian West

Asking how far the rules falling under natural law are recognized in societies other than our own is a familiar question, and one that I have touched upon more than once in the body of this book. Less familiar, but at least equally interesting, is the question whether the perspective and theory of natural law, in the present case of Natural Law Modernized, can be found in the theories worked up in other societies, that is to say, in other philosophical traditions. To produce the beginnings of an answer to this question, one of my junior colleagues, Michael McLendon, explores the teachings of Ibn Khaldun. (He first, at my suggestion, undertook to treat Maimonides as well. However, though Maimonides could be said to adhere to the natural laws themselves, he turned out to hold that the laws were divinely revealed to an elite only, who had to teach them to the rest of humankind. This elitism is not a feature of Natural Law Modernized, or of its medieval source in St Thomas.) Moving further away from the Christian West, another junior colleague Xiusheng Liu explores the affinities with Natural Law Modernized manifested in classical Chinese philosophy. The upshot, I think, is a sort of corroboration of Natural Law Modernized, since if it is right about there being universal moral rules indispensable to having societies thrive, and readily discoverable by the human beings who must heed them, one should not be astonished to have philosophers everywhere arrive at these views; and it seems that they do.

Appendix Part 1

Ibn Khaldun Modernized

By Michael McLendon

Natural Law need not be viewed as a transcendental code of right and wrong, but simply a set of rules, discoverable through practical reason, which best help human beings attain their desired ends.[1] As has been shown throughout the book, this conception of natural law, known as Natural Law Modernized, can be found in natural lawyers from St Thomas Aquinas to Jean-Jacques Rousseau. Despite the religious or metaphysical pretensions of some philosophers, practical reason and the ethical processes described by Natural Law Modernized lie at heart of almost every theory of natural law. That Natural Law Modernized can accommodate almost every natural lawyer in the western canon of political philosophy since Aquinas is in itself an impressive accomplishment. More impressive, however, is the ability of Natural Law Modernized to extend beyond the West. The political and ethical thought of Ibn Khaldun, one of the great intellectuals of the medieval Muslim world, can also be shown to be consonant with much of Natural Law Modernized, both in terms of the privileged yet modest role he affords reason and his rejection of metaphysics or rational theology. In addition, much of Ibn Khaldun's thought is amenable to the improvements made to the theory derived from David Copp's 'society-centered theory' as put forth in *Morality, Normativity, and Society*.

The Life of Ibn Khaldun

Abd-ar-Rahman Abu Zayd ibn Muhammad ibn Muhammad ibn Khaldun (hereafter referred to as Ibn Khaldun) was born in 1332 to an aristocratic family in Tunis. As a consequence of his well-to-do background, young Ibn Khaldun received, relative to his contemporaries, a first-rate education. He was very well schooled in the Koran, the Hadith, and, thanks to the Moors, was quite familiar with the writings of Aristotle. Politically and socially, Ibn Khaldun enjoyed a distinguished life as a statesman, jurist, and scholar in northwest Africa, Spain, and Egypt until his death in 1406. Intellectually, his greatest accomplishment was a history of the Arabs and the Berbers entitled *A Universal History*. Although most of *A Universal History*, the actual history Ibn Khaldun recorded, has been ignored in the West, the introduction or prolegomena, Book I of the work, has won Ibn Khaldun the praise of scholars in both West and East. In the prolegomena, now known as the *Muqaddimah*, Ibn Khaldun outlines a science of history that was unprecedented in its sophistication and use of empirical social science.

Perhaps because Ibn Khaldun wrote at a time when the Muslim civilization was in decline, he was preoccupied with discovering the inner laws of history that governed the rise and fall of a society. While most Muslim scholars worked within either a scholastic or Platonic framework, Ibn Khaldun stands out among Muslim medieval intellectuals by rejecting these philosophical approaches in favor of a natural science approach, although he borrowed much from Muslim theology, metaphysics and epistemology.[2] At bottom, Ibn Khaldun was a committed social scientist who sought, through empirical analysis, to discover the hidden laws of cause and effect which underlie the workings of society. He was, in Isaiah Berlin's words, a true hedgehog who believed he had discovered the true law governing history. Rather than search for the eternal verities, Ibn Khaldun was concerned with a more practical, down to earth question: How does the social world work?

In so doing, Ibn Khaldun was the first political theorist to articulate a sociology of history. Both eastern and western scholars have not been hesitant to acknowledge Ibn Khaldun's achievement here. As early as 1917, the *Muqaddimah* was called one of the earliest attempts at sociology, pre-dating Auguste Comte, who is widely credited as being the father of sociology, by several hundred years.[3] Moreover, Ibn Khaldun's attempts to understand the character of a people through their physical environment led to him being called 'ein arabischer Montesquieu' by a nineteenth-century German scholar.[4] The *Muqaddimah* also makes impressive contributions to political economy and economics in general, ones that go unrivaled until Adam Smith appears in the eighteenth century. Ibn Khaldun's 'list of firsts' is truly remarkable, and it would not be difficult to continue in this vein for several pages. If Europe had known of Ibn Khaldun before the early nineteenth century,[5] it probably would not be too much of a stretch to call him the father of the Enlightenment. Whatever the case, as we will see, it is Ibn Khaldun's commitment to the empiricism that Enlightenment thinkers were so taken with that makes him compatible with Natural Law Modernized.

Ibn Khaldun's Political Thought: A Deductive Ethics

The starting point of Ibn Khaldun's political thought ought to sound familiar to students of modern English political philosophy. According to Ibn Khaldun, humans are social animals. By social, Ibn Khaldun does not mean social in the Aristotelian sense that humans only develop properly and flourish in a society. Rather, Ibn Khaldun's theory of sociality refers to the need to live in a society to insure self-preservation, and is thus far more reminiscent of the social contract tradition found in Grotius, Hobbes, Locke, and others. Like Aquinas and John Locke, Ibn Khaldun claims that God instilled in humans a desire for self-preservation.[6] To enable humans to sustain themselves, Ibn Khaldun (and Locke) argue that God inserted in humans the ability to reason, or as stated in the *Muqaddimah*, an experimental intellect.[7] Through reason or the experimental intellect, which is somewhat analogus to practical reason in Aristotle, humans learn what they must do to survive. According to Ibn Khaldun, the experimental intellect teaches humans that they must cooperate and place themselves under a ruler,[8] and, again anticipating Locke, that God gave to humans the earth and everything in it as a means for self-preservation.[9] It is worth noting that Ibn Khaldun is here basically describing government as arising from the state of nature, although he does not make use of the term. Nevertheless, he is clearly detailing how and why individuals in a pre-political society come to place themselves under the authority of a government.

In somewhat of a Hobbesian twist, however, Ibn Khaldun argues that achieving cooperation is complicated by the fact that human nature is not wholly predisposed towards such behavior. 'Aggressiveness,' Ibn Khaldun avers, 'is natural in living human beings.'[10] Humans, alas, are born to be social, but not every aspect of their nature is conducive to sociality. Moreover, to compound matters, the problems that aggressiveness causes for attempts at cooperation are aggravated by the fact that humans are fundamentally equal. By equal, Ibn Khaldun does not mean political or social equality, but equality in terms of physical vulnerability. Since humans can make weapons, a weaker individual may kill a stronger one without too much trouble.[11] The unfortunate consequence of this equality is that humans left to themselves will never reach peace and stability naturally. The strongest will never be able to impose order on the weakest for the simple reason that the strongest can still be toppled by the weakest. Thomas Hobbes later elaborated on this point in his description of the state of nature. According to Hobbes, there was no natural occurring stability in the state of nature because one 'needeth little force to the taking away of a man's life'[12] and 'the weakest has strength to kill the strongest, either by secret machination, or by confederacy with others that are in the same danger with himself.'[13] Given their agreement on this point, both Ibn Khaldun and Hobbes argue for the establishment of a ruling authority that has the power to restrain natural aggressiveness and the injustices it will inevitably cause, although Ibn Khaldun's ruling authority differs on important points from Hobbes's almighty Leviathan.

Here, Ibn Khaldun most closely conforms to Natural Law Modernized. For Ibn Khaldun, individuals are born with certain desires, self-preservation, and certain circumstances, a world provided by God to sustain oneself and a natural aggressiveness which leads to destructive conflict. Through reason or experimental intellect, by which Ibn Khaldun means reflecting upon one's empirical observations, individuals figure out how to best preserve themselves, which is by cooperating with one another and putting themselves under the subjection of royal authority. Thus, all the primary ingredients of Natural Law Modernized are in place: given desires or needs, certain circumstances which hinder one's abilities to meet those needs, and rules derived from practical reason or experimental intellect, which allow one to overcome those hindrances and meet their needs. Thus far, the only gulf that separates Ibn Khaldun from the Natural Law Modernized is vocabulary. Although Ibn Khaldun is conceptually in accord with his European natural law counterparts, he never uses such terms as state of nature or laws of nature.

To be sure, although he makes use of the basic ethical conception of natural law modernized, Ibn Khaldun could do more to flesh out his state of nature and his laws of nature, if I may import those terms to his theory. The only laws of nature of which Ibn Khaldun speaks are the need for cooperation, right to private property and not to force an individual to labour (Ibn Khaldun was plainly cognizant of the interrelations between economic misfortune and political decline),[14] the need to sustain group feeling or *asabiyah* (which will be discussed shortly), and the need for a sovereign. Clearly, if the state of nature is populated by aggressive human beings, then there must be a whole host of practical rules or laws of nature to be adopted to neutralize natural aggressiveness and everything else that might undermine efforts at cooperation and the reservoir of group feeling which re-channels aggressiveness outside the community. Hobbes, whose notions of human nature and human interaction are somewhat similar to Ibn Khaldun's, came up with over nineteen laws of nature to combat threats to social cooperation, and that, as shown in chapter 4 of the present book, is a very incomplete list. Ibn Khaldun, conversely, lists only a few such laws; laws that are much broader and more general than those of Hobbes and could be elaborated upon and broken down into more particular rules. In any case, it should be quite clear that the basic structure of Natural Law Modernized can be found in Ibn Khaldun.

Before Ibn Khaldun is drafted into the Natural Law Modernized camp, however, we must consider other aspects of his political thought that might be at odds with the theory. One of these aspects is Ibn Khaldun's belief that physical environment has a lot to do with the development of society. Here, Ibn Khaldun departs from the English social contract tradition and takes a turn towards Montesquieu and Rousseau. According to Ibn Khaldun, climate very much shapes the character of a population.[15] For example, societies closest to the equator tend to produce peoples who have a healthy moral sense and are intellectually well developed. Those societies farther from the equator, such as South Africa or the Slavs, conversely, tend to have less developed morals and intellects. These societies and its inhabitants, Ibn Khaldun contends, are less evolved and have more in common with animals than with humans. In a similar vein, Ibn Khaldun also remarks that abundance or scarcity of food in a region also has an important effect on the character of a people. Those who have access to lots of food tend to become fat and corrupt, and develop a stupid and intemperate character.

Although these views are somewhat politically incorrect and certainly out of place in contemporary times, the importance of climate and character of a people can be of some use to Natural Law Modernized. Not all peoples and societies, it must be acknowledged, are the same. Societies with different climates or different economies, as will be demonstrated shortly, will produce citizens with different virtues and vices – with different characters. Thus, two societies that share the same goals and values will likely have to adopt different rules or laws of nature to attain the same goal as their circumstances will undoubtedly differ. Because reason in Natural Law Modernized is instrumental, the theory is flexible enough to accommodate this differences in the content of the laws of nature without being reduced to relativism. Universal laws still apply in Natural Law Modernized, though they are not always realized in the same manner. Ibn Khaldun, of course, makes no such arguments. Nonetheless, Natural Law Modernized is compatible with Ibn Khaldun's views concerning climate, and can even improve itself because of them.

The Bedouin Culture and Asabiyah

The most famous part of Ibn Khaldun's political thought is the distinction between Bedouin cultures and sedentary cultures. Making use of this distinction, Ibn Khaldun charts the rise and fall of civilizations, and identifies the laws which govern the cycles of political change. As we shall soon see, accommodating this part of Ibn Khaldun's theory to Natural Law Modernized presents some thorny problems.

According to Ibn Khaldun, early societies, or Bedouin societies, are essentially nomadic tribes that closely resemble a family. Although they are drawn together through the necessity of cooperation, Bedouins come to share an affectionate 'group feeling,' known as *asabiyah*, which unites them and creates a powerful social bond. *Asabiyah* unites Bedouin tribes so strongly that they treat each others as blood relatives. If one member of the tribe gets hurt, everyone in the tribe feels an intense grief. As for character traits, Ibn Khaldun's Bedouins are slightly more developed than *l'homme sauvage* Rousseau describes in *The Second Discourse*. Unlike Rousseau's *l'homme sauvage*, Bedouins have mastered some primitive occupations, such as farming and animal husbandry.[16] However, like Rousseau's *l'homme sauvage*, Bedouins are lacking in many traits that today are considered essential to humanity. Most important of these missing traits is self-consciousness, which renders Bedouins unable to distinguish between good and evil. Moral life, as a consequence, is extremely limited.

However, like Rousseau with *l'homme sauvage*, Ibn Khaldun identifies a number of admirable traits Bedouins possess precisely because of their lack of both personal and cultural development. For example, because Bedouins are not economically advanced and live in relative scarcity, their consumption habits are quite moderate and they are economically self-reliant. Moreover, the limited moral life and the brutal conditions under which Bedouins live make them excellent soldiers. Constantly having to fend off the attacks of rival tribes, Bedouins come to have extraordinary amounts of courage and bravery.[17] Put together, courage, *asabiyah*, and limited moral life lead to Bedouins developing hardy souls, in soldiers to be feared. These Bedouin traits, in fact, are so useful to a people that they help pave the way for the development of civilized society. Successful Bedouin tribes who have moderate consumption habits, are able to defend themselves militarily, and sustain *asabiyah* are able to produce enough surplus goods to enable them to quit nomadic life and settle down into civilized societies.

Once settled into communities, the Bedouin lifestyle slowly evolves into a sedentary lifestyle. Fueled by moderation, security, and *asabiyah*, sedentary societies develop in all sorts of ways. Over time, the population grows larger and larger, and most importantly, more sophisticated and efficient means of production begin to develop. Sedentary societies thus come to accumulate more and more wealth. In the process, however, the Bedouin traits responsible for the growth of the community slowly disintegrate and come to be replaced by corrupt sedentary values. According to Ibn Khaldun, the excess wealth created in a sedentary society causes rulers and citizens alike to become greedy and overcome by hedonistic desires. Such traits are actually encouraged in sedentary societies, as commercial life rewards the unscrupulous behavior of business men and others who are able to take advantage of the economic arrangements. Those who possess worthy qualities, such as teachers and religious folks, increasingly find themselves sliding down the ladder of social status.[18] As a consequence, *asabiyah*, the powerful group feeling that unites the society, slowly erodes to the point where open hostility exists between citizens.[19]

Moreover, luxury eats away at the courage and bravery of the citizenry, which forces society to hire mercenaries in order to protect itself against foreign invasion. Armies cost money, and taxes rise, which results in a decline of production. This process, Ibn Khaldun argues, begins to feed off itself, as taxes keep rising to pay for a mercenary army that becomes increasingly important for a ruler trying to hold on to power. Production, as a result, continues to dwindle as more and more resources are used to sustain an army, which becomes more and more necessary as society declines. The mercenary army is soon asked to defend society against disgruntled citizens as well as external enemies. As the mercenary army becomes more important to the ruler, the more he alienates the people who brought him to power. Without loyal followers, which mercenary armies most certainly are not, the ruler's position becomes more and more untenable.

Eventually, the corruption of society reaches a breaking point, and the ruling regime becomes too vulnerable and is in time replaced by another ruling dynasty. Ibn Khaldun estimates that this decline takes three generations, which last about forty years each.[20] Once complete, Ibn Khaldun contends that the whole process will start over again. A new ruling dynasty will become strong because of its commitment to primitive Bedouin values. However, as society develops under this new regime, it too will turn its back on its Bedouin roots and become corrupted by its own successes and appetite for wealth, and will also be overthrown and replaced. Ultimately, then, the wealthier a society gets, the less capable it is of sustaining itself: 'The greater their (sedentary civilization) luxury and the easier life they enjoy, the closer they are to extinction.'[21] According to Ibn Khaldun, these are the cycles of political history, and they go on indefinitely.

Fitting this aspect of Ibn Khaldun's theory into Natural Law Modernized is somewhat problematic. By defending a cyclical theory of political change, Ibn Khaldun greatly diminishes the role of human agency. According to Ibn Khaldun, the character of the individual is more or less determined by their location within the cycles of political change. Those who live in times of political renewal will probably be loyal, courageous, and temperate, while those who live in periods of political decline will most likely be lazy, materialistic, and greedy. The springboard of human action is thus not reason, but rather the forces and laws of history that govern society and in turn human behavior. Although at the beginning of society it is reason which induces individuals to seek the cooperation of others, the role of reason, strangely enough, significantly diminishes in importance in Ibn Khaldun's sociology of history once society has been established.

It is possible to argue that appeals to reason and empirically discoverable maxims might be of great help managing the cycles of politics. Indeed, Polybius and Cicero, who also held cyclical theories of political change, proposed solutions (for example, Polybius's mixed regime) for slowing down or managing political cycles, solutions that come from an empirically oriented practical reason. Reason, however, plays only a marginal role in Ibn Khaldun's attempts to manage the cycles of political change. Like Polybius and Cicero, Ibn Khaldun also thinks it is possible to slow down or manage the cycles of political regimes. But for Ibn Khaldun, it is revelation and not reason which is the most reliable method for such management of history. Although he is perfectly open to the existence of secular states and does not morally judge such states, Ibn Khaldun believes that religious states were much more effective at maintaining *asayibah*, creating better laws, and making better citizens.[22] Thus, Ibn Khaldun does not rule out a limited role of reason in his sociology of history, but he certainly prefers religion to legislation based on reason as the best means available with which to improve the governance of society, or more specifically, to moderate the cycles of political change. Both of these moves clearly take him away from both the letter and spirit of Natural Law Modernized.

This, however, is not to say that Natural Law Modernized is without response. Although Ibn Khaldun's belief that historical laws are determinants of human behaviour will leave an unresolved tension with Natural Law Modernized, his endorsement of religion is of much less consequence to our theory. In contending that the Muslim religion is useful for preserving *asabiyah* and managing the cycles of politics, Ibn Khaldun is actually making a utilitarian argument that is based on reason. Although he is appealing to religion, he is not appealing to it in the sense that it is a metaphysically sanctioned authority that must be adhered to or serious consequences will result. Instead, he utilizes religion much in the way Machiavelli uses religion as a means for the prince to remain strong, Rousseau uses civil religion to insure a healthy general will, and Tocqueville uses religion to temper the excesses of democracy.[23] Thus, Ibn Khaldun's reliance on religion in this instance can be reduced to empirical reason, and does not offend the fundamental principles of Natural Law Modernized.

The Role of God and Metaphysics in Ibn Khaldun's Thought

A broader inquiry into Ibn Khaldun's religious views would also confirm that there is nothing in the *Muqaddimah* that would conflict with the secular orienta-

tion of Natural Law Modernized. Ibn Khaldun, in fact, is as distrustful of rational theology[24] as most self-proclaimed agnostics. At first glance, this might not
seem to be the case. Although celebrated by scholars of medieval political
thought for his pioneering empirical outlook, most of those same scholars
understand that the Muslim religion was extremely important to Ibn Khaldun.
In the words of one notable Ibn Khaldun scholar, 'Ibn Khaldun was not only a
Muslim, but as almost every page of the *Muqaddimah* bears witness, a Muslim
jurist and theologian ... for him religion was far and away the most important
thing in life.'[25] Indeed, the *Muqaddimah* is saturated with references to the
Koran. Fortunately, besides Ibn Khaldun's belief, mentioned in the third part of
this article, that religious communities are more enduring than secular ones,
his theological beliefs can be reconciled with the core of both his empiricism
and Natural Law Modernized.

Like most medieval intellectuals, Ibn Khaldun was very concerned with
squaring his religious beliefs with his scientific and epistemological views. In
trying to make room for both in his political thought, Ibn Khaldun came to the
conclusion that the only thing standing in the way of his being able to simultaneously commit himself to the Muslim religion and empirical science was the
speculative metaphysics inherited from the ancient Greeks.[26] Following al-
Ghazali, Ibn Khaldun furiously assaulted the Neo-Platonists (at the time
known as Neo-Hanbalists) as well as the scholasticism of al-Farabi, Ibn Rushd
(Averroes) and Ibn Sina (Avicenna) that the Neo-Hanbalists displaced as the
leading philosophical school in fourteenth century Islamic philosophy.[27] The
crux of Ibn Khaldun's attack on rational theology (metaphysics) and speculative philosophy is quite simple and surprisingly modern. In short, Ibn Khaldun argued that rational theology (metaphysics) is too removed from
experience to be capable of empirical demonstration. Rational theology, he
realized, could neither prove God exists, nor provide unassailable first principles, nor could it show the way to happiness – all of which fall outside the
scope of its speculative methodology.

For Ibn Khaldun, however, the failure of rational theology to provide reliable knowledge could lead to very dangerous consequences. Unlike a great
many contemporary theorists, who hold that the inability of rational theology
to demonstrate its claims merely renders its appeals useless, Ibn Khaldun des-
perately wanted to make room for the Muslim religion in his thought. Failed
attempts to establish metaphysical truths, he argued, resulted in the undermining of all religious claims. In trying to prove knowledge of the heavens and
failing, speculative metaphysics casts doubt on the entire religious enterprise
itself. As such, Ibn Khaldun concluded that 'the harm they [metaphysics and
speculative philosophy] can do to religion is great.'[28] And religion, it is not to

be forgotten, can be a very useful resource for a society trying to manage the vicissitudes of political life.

For religion to thrive, therefore, it must be kept well out of the reach of philosophy.[29] Human intellect can be useful, but only when it solves problems that it can solve and should solve. Rather than try to prove that God created the universe or God must exist, Ibn Khaldun maintained that intellectuals should primarily engage in empirical inquiries and simply be contented that certain questions lie outside the scope of reason and properly belong to religion and theology. If intellectuals try to mix reason and religion, they will end up undermining the latter.

Although Ibn Khaldun's mistrust of rational theology puts him at odds with many of the leading intellectual figures in medieval Islamic thought, it fits in very nicely with Natural Law Modernized. Like Ibn Khaldun, Natural Law Modernized also seeks to reduce reason to a more instrumental and practical role; for it too recognizes that trying to prove the existence of first principles through reason is a futile project. Natural Law Modernized, moreover, would have little trouble purging God from Ibn Khaldun's thought without causing any major disruption to his theory. Ibn Khaldun's own rejection of rational theology makes this task much easier. For the most part, the role of God in Ibn Khaldun's thought is one of creator of the universe; Ibn Khaldun subscribes to a sort of deism. For Ibn Khaldun, God does not interact in human affairs and is only responsible for placing in humans the ability to reason and desire to preserve themselves. However, it would be extremely plausible to treat the traits and desires of humans, as well as their circumstances and conditions, as bald empirical facts. Ascribing religious origins to the empirical assessments that humans have the capacity to reason and the desire to survive adds nothing to Ibn Khaldun's argument.[30] Indeed, there is no reason to think that a quick survey of human nature and the condition of the physical world, conducted by the staunchest of agnostics, would not result in the same empirical assessments as Ibn Khaldun's, that is, that humans desire self-preservation and must cooperate to survive. In assigning God such an overarching role in the universe, Ibn Khaldun greatly diminishes God's explanatory power. To borrow from Spinoza,[31] by making God explain everything in the universe, Ibn Khaldun actually winds up making God unnecessary for explaining anything.

As demonstrated earlier in this appendix, religion is mostly discussed in utilitarian terms in the *Muqaddimah*. Thus, God can be removed so easily from Ibn Khaldun's political thought because Ibn Khaldun himself thought God was incapable of empirical or logical demonstration. As a result, the logic guiding Ibn Khaldun's program rests almost entirely on empirical reasoning, and religion, consequently, can be reduced to such empiricism.

Ibn Khaldun and David Copp's Society-Centered Theory

The final part of this appendix will attempt to reconcile Ibn Khaldun with the improvements made to the Natural Law Modernized through David Copp's society-centred theory argued for in *Morality, Normativity, and Society*. Copp helps refine natural law in four primary ways: through his distinction between moral propositions and standards, his improved definition of a society, his convincing demonstration of the existence of a social rational choice and, finally, his understanding that different societies will require different rules or natural laws for effective governance. As with the core principles of Natural Law Modernized, Ibn Khaldun can be shown to be compatible with Copp's refinements to the theory.

First, there is good reason to think that Ibn Khaldun's thought could profit from Copp's distinction between moral propositions and standards, as might the authors who comprise Natural Law Modernized.[32] According to Copp, the standards, that is to say, the norms and rules that have currency in a given society need not have currency elsewhere; and even when they do, they are not to be afforded the status of capital T truth. However, some standards are justified; they are standards that members of a society would together rationally choose as meeting the needs of the society. Moral propositions are asserted in reference to a standard, and can have the status of truth only if the standard is justified. For example, a society may have a standard of internal harmony. From this standard, it can be deduced that threats of physical harm may undermine internal harmony, and are thus to be condemned in moral propositions: for example, 'It is wrong to make such threats because to do so goes against the standard of internal harmony.'

In the *Muqaddimah*, Copp's distinction can be found at work on some level, although Ibn Khaldun, like other philosophers with some affinity to Natural Law Modernized, fails to achieve Copp's clarity and analytic rigor. There are obvious identifiable standards present in Ibn Khaldun's descriptions of societies, be they Bedouin or sedentary. According to Ibn Khaldun, the reason individuals join societies is to ensure self-preservation. In Copp's terminology, self-preservation would serve as the standard for society. Given Ibn Khaldun's belief that self-preservation is best sustained through the establishment of a sedentary society,[33] moral propositions that rest on that establishment of a standard would include all aspects of a Bedouin society that successfully lead to a sedentary society. In the case of Ibn Khaldun, moral propositions taken to be true include those endorsing *asabiyah*, courage, and moderate consumption habits. As for established sedentary societies, the goal is to sustain the society against decline. The same moral propositions, *asabiyah*, and so forth, would also be taken to be true. Thus, Copp's distinction operates, if somewhat crudely, in the *Muqaddimah*.

There is also good reason to think that Ibn Khaldun would go along with Copp's second improvement to Natural Law Modernized; an upgraded definition of society. Copp's definition includes the following five criteria: (1) is multigenerational and extended through time, (2) membership is not a matter of choice, (3) members of a society interact among others in activities directed at securing the material necessities and priorities of life prescribed by the culture, (4) interaction among members is governed by a system of rules that are at least implicitly accepted by the populace, and (5) society provides the framework for its members' lives.[34]

With regard to the first criterion, Ibn Khaldun's political regimes tend to last three generations of forty years,[35] which certainly seems to coincide with Copp's requirement that societies be multi-generational. The second criterion, that membership is not a matter of choice, might be slightly problematic for Ibn Khaldun because he, like the English social contract tradition, argues that people discover through their reason that it is a good idea to join a society and cooperate with others. Thus, there is some choice going on, although it would seem that once an individual is a member of a society, be it Bedouin or sedentary, his or her offspring would also be a member of that society. Nowhere does Ibn Khaldun argue that each member of a society must choose to live in a society. The third criterion, that members of society interact with others in activities directed at securing the material necessities and priorities of life prescribed by the culture, also could be made to fit in nicely with Ibn Khaldun. Ibn Khaldun argues that Bedouin communities come to exist to insure self-preservation and thrive because they are extremely effective at cultivating character traits in their members that promote that goal. Political decline occurs for Ibn Khaldun when sedentary cultures adopt values that undermine the traits, *asabiyah*, courage, and so forth, which contribute to the success of a society. Thus, he is at least implicitly aware of this third requirement of Copp.

The fourth criterion is also implicitly accepted by Ibn Khaldun. For him, Bedouin societies operate so well and are able to mutate into sedentary or civilized societies because their members join because they know they need to cooperate to survive and internalize this belief. It is this internalization which leads to *asabiyah*, the strong group feeling that unites Bedouins. Thus, Bedouins are more than implicitly aware of the rules that bind them; they primarily define themselves by that very bond. Similarly, sedentary cultures decline because the growing appetite for wealth amongst the rulers and the populace undercut the rules and traits that allowed the society to thrive in the first place. In particular, as the ruler becomes more dependent upon mercenaries to control society, the original members are quite aware that the rules or terms of their joining the society have been violated, and they undermine the ruling authority. Finally, the fifth part of Copp's definition of a society, that society provide the framework for its members' lives, would probably also be acceptable to Ibn Khaldun. Ibn Khaldun, remember, is probably the world's first sociologist. In his thought, society is responsible for shaping the character and personality of the citizens. For example, Bedouins are loyal, moderate in appetites, and fiercely courageous, while civilized individuals in sedentary cultures tend to be overcome with greed and hedonistic desires. There are no free-floating atoms in the *Muqaddimah*.

Ibn Khaldun's commitment to sociology would also leave him well-disposed to embracing Copp's belief that a social unit as a whole can make a rational decision. By this, Copp simply means that it is possible for individuals in a society to realize that they share certain ends, and that they can adopt rules as a collective group to help realize those ends. Ibn Khaldun's description of how society gets formed (as with the Anglo social contract theorists), in fact, seems to be a good example of the phenomenon that Copp describes. Individuals who live in a pre-political society realize they must cooperate with one another if they are to up their chances of survival; they make a collective decision to cooperate because they collectively share the belief or value that life is better than death. This realization, in fact, is so powerful that it leads to the development of *asabiyah*, which is so intense that it does more than make possible a collective rational choice; it makes a veritable one out of many. Along the same lines, Ibn Khaldun argues that societies decline because they are unable to make a collective rational choice. Individual greed becomes so destructive that the government and the individual citizens are unable to perceive their collective interests and act with a unified voice. Ibn Khaldun endorses religious rule as a method for slowing down the cycles of politics for the very reason that it keeps the citizens unified and concentrated on the same goals.

Finally, Copp's point that different societies might require different rules, is also consistent with Ibn Khaldun's thought and with Natural Law Modernized. Although Ibn Khaldun is a committed Muslim, he is perfectly accepting of non-Muslim cultures and is unwilling to morally judge those cultures.[36] His only claim is that religious cultures are more successful in sustaining *asabiyah*. Presumably, if a secular culture could find a way to sustain *asabiyah* without religion, then Ibn Khaldun would have to accept that state as useful and legitimate. As has been suggested, the *Muqaddimah* is primarily a work of sociology and history. While Ibn Khaldun makes appeals to the wisdom of the precepts of the *Koran*, for the most part he discusses them in terms of their utility for ensuring peace and prosperity. In this sense, Ibn Khaldun is very open to the idea that different cultures might require different rules in order to thrive.

Moreover, Ibn Khaldun's belief that the climate influences personal character also would speak to his acceptance of Copp's position here. If individuals develop differently in different cultures, it would make sense that they would require different rules to satisfy their desires and needs. For example, individuals from cultures shaped by colder climates, for example, might be more aggressive than individuals residing in warmer climates, and hence would need different natural laws in order to satisfy, say, the basic desire for self-preservation. While cultures in colder climates might adopt rules that seek to harmonize the public, the warmer climate might adopt rules to make them more aggressive in order to fend off the attacks of foreign invaders. Therefore, in almost all respects, Ibn Khaldun's political thought is not only compatible with Copp's society-centered theory, but could derive obvious benefit from Copp's precise and finely drawn distinctions as well.

Conclusion

Natural Law Modernized has been successful in identifying a core system of ethics in thinkers as diverse as St Thomas and Rousseau. Setting aside their religious beliefs, many theistic philosophers still offer a cogent ethical system that is capable of providing the elusive 'ought' necessary for a properly functioning ethics. Natural Law Modernized, moreover, can make a claim to universal appeal, as its fundamental beliefs also show up in non-Western philosophers. Ibn Khaldun, one of the great treasures of Islamic political thought, is testament to this fact.

Appendix Part 2

Natural Law in Classical Chinese Philosophy

By Xiusheng Liu

Traditionally, natural law as conceived (for example) by St Thomas Aquinas is a set of norms governing human behaviors, moral, social, or political. It has at least two essential features. First, it derives its validity from a superhuman legislator inherently, namely, God; and therefore, second, it is binding everywhere and always. While preserving the universal validity of natural law, modern natural law theorists like Thomas Hobbes, implicitly or explicitly, make the effort to limit the role of the superhuman power by stressing the empirical requirements of peace and order among human beings. Contemporary natural law theorists such as David Braybrooke try to revitalize natural law theory by retiring the superhuman power to at most a role speaking off-stage and appealing to the concept of Common Good and the idea of human attachment through humanity. Thus, there should be a broader definition of natural law. Natural law accordingly is a set of moral, social, and political norms which (1) have universal validity among human beings, and (2) are given either by God or by nature, including human nature and the nature of society.[1]

Does Chinese philosophical tradition contain the idea of natural law? Although ancient Chinese philosophers defend the universality of moral, social, and political principles, a negative answer might still be given based on the fact that Chinese tradition does not have the transcendental idea of God that can serve as the foundation of natural law. It is true that Chinese tradition does not have the idea of God, but it does not follow that Chinese tradition does not ever, even for a short period, have any idea of a superhuman power. Moreover, the universal validity of natural law, according to some modern and contemporary natural law theorists, can be grounded in human nature or the nature of society. Following the broader definition of natural law, I contend that Chinese philosophical tradition contains the idea of natural law, although it might be disputable as to whether natural law in Chinese philosophy falls in with the Western traditional version, that is, the Thomistic version. It is fairly safe to say that Taoism is a form of natural law theory. But I do not hesitate to call Confucianism or Mohism a natural law theory. Students of Chinese philosophy would not find it hard to bring out the strong similarities between Confucius (551–479 BC) and Aristotle (384–322 BC) or St Thomas (1225–74), between Mencius (371–289 BC) and David Hume (1711–76), between Xun Zi (fl. 300–230 BC) and Hobbes (1588–1679), and between Mo Zi (fl. 480–400 BC) and Jean-Jacques Rousseau (1712–78), in spite of their significant differences, one of which is that some of them lived about two thousand years apart (like Mo Zi and Rousseau).

Since Chinese tradition does not have the idea of God or any other (lasting) idea of transcendental superhuman power with universal authority, the main stream of natural law in Chinese tradition focuses its attention on essential human perspectives, that is, it is based on a notion of human nature or a notion of the nature of society. Harmony between social and individual life, proper arrangements of social and political order, reasonable distribution of goods to meet individual and social needs, and so on are not just problems to which natural law needs to supply with answers but also grounds on which natural law stands. In that sense, Chinese natural law finds itself close in doctrine to the practical aspects of Western natural law tradition, and closer to contemporary (modernized) Western natural law theory.

In what follows I shall write up accounts on how far natural law theory can be found in classical Chinese philosophy. In doing so I shall concentrate on the foundational issues of such a theory, such as its ground, its fundamental principles, and its universality. I start with Pre-Confucian and Confucian concepts of Tian and Ming, then go to Confucius' concept of humanity, which lays the ground for the Confucian notion of natural law. Next is Mencius's concept of human nature as the foundation of natural law. After that I take up Xun Zi's notion of needs and the derivation of the principles of *Li*. Lastly, I consider Mo Zi's theory of universal love and his concept of the general will.

Tian, *Ming*, and Natural Law

Chinese tradition does not continually invoke a transcendental idea of a superhuman power, which plays an essential role in traditional natural law theory in St Thomas and thereafter. But it does not follow that Chinese tradition does not ever contain some form of superhuman power, which in some way legislates for social and individual life. *Tian* (Heaven) was once considered such a power, although it is much less powerful than God and it only co-exists with humanity. As found in different classical texts, *Tian* is sometimes called *Tian-Di* (Lord of Heaven) or *Shang-Di* (Lord on High).[2]

Tian has five meanings in Chinese philosophy. (1) It is the material heaven, the counterpart of earth, as in Zhuang Zi. (2) It is nature, as in Xun Zi and Zhuang Zi. (3) It means fate or destiny, referring to things that humans cannot do anything but accept, as in Confucius, Mencius, and Xun Zi. (4) It is the set of objectively valid moral and political principles, as in Confucius, Mencius, and Neo-Confucianism. (5) It is a superhuman power, which has its own will and legislates for humans, as in Mo Zi, and, mostly, in pre-Confucian literature.[3] Confucius and (sometimes) Mencius also speak of *Tian* in the last sense, but they believe that *Tian* should not be considered a factor to prevent human beings from making efforts to practice their own moral principles. Critics of Chinese philosophy often confuse those five meanings of *Tian*. Some scholars even go so far as to compare *Tian* to God.

Ming literally means fate, destiny, order, ordinance, or decree. Like *Tian*, it has different meanings in Chinese philosophy. However, only the following two are significant: first, it is what, as natural phenomena, is beyond human control. In that sense, *Ming* is the same as *Tian* in the third of the above five meanings. Mencius says, 'That which is done when no one does it is due to *Tian*; that which comes about when no one brings about is due to *Ming*' (*Meng Zi*, 5A6). Second, *Ming* refers to the providence of heaven, or the mandate of heaven. In that sense, it is sometimes called *Tian-Ming* or *Tian-Dao*; and it corresponds to *Tian* in its last, that is, the fifth, meaning above. As the superhuman power (the divine legislator) of all things, *Tian* has human beings carry out its will through giving them orders, which are *Ming* in the second sense.[4]

Tian in all its five meanings has had a great influence on the development of Chinese philosophy and especially in moral and political thought. But it is only in the last sense, that is, as a superhuman power, that *Tian*, when joined by *Ming* in the second sense, more or less plays the role of God as in the traditional Western natural law theory. That is, it is *Tian*'s will that human beings as well as any other beings live or exist according to laws it dictates. If everything, including human beings, lives or exists accordingly, harmony will be the result. If not, punishment and disaster will follow. That idea can be found in many pre-Confucian texts, some of which are seen as classics by Confucius and other Confucians. In the *Book of Odes* (*BO*), for example, poems about both *Tian* and *Ming* occur quite often. One of those reads: '*Tian* creates the teeming multitude; / As there are things, there are their specific principles' (*BO*, ode no. 260, 'The Teeming Multitude').[5] Another reads, 'No need to know what it was like,/ No need to know what it is like,/All that is needed is to follow the decree of Lord' (*BO*, ode no 241, 'Huang Yi').[6] Still another reads, '*Tian-Ming*

(The Mandate of Heaven), / How beautiful and unceasing'! (*BO*, ode no. 267, 'Tian-Ming').[7] In the *Book of Shang*, passages can be found about why the decree of *Tian* should be observed.[8] One of them reads, 'I fear the punishment of Lord on High [*Shang-Di*], so I behave according to its principles.'[9]

Tian and *Ming*, when interpreted properly, do indeed provide a foundation for a concept of natural law. For they account for the universal validity of moral and political laws and the laws by which natural things abide. With the dawn of the Confucian period, that idea of natural law is quickly naturalized and humanized by Confucianism and Taoism. The naturalized and humanized natural law theory in Chinese philosophy has a fairly 'modern' or even 'contemporary' outlook to Western philosophers, for it turns away from *Tian* and *Ming* (in their narrow transcendental meanings); and turns to the idea of human nature or the idea of the common good or the idea of necessary arrangements of social institutions or the idea of harmony between human and nature. That is, essentially human and non-theological perspectives somehow replace *Tian* and *Ming* to serve as the foundation of natural law.

The transition from the superhumanly founded idea of natural law to the humanized and naturalized natural law is in no sense a sudden change. *Tian-Di* (Lord of Heaven) or *Shang-Di* (Lord on High) never dominates in Chinese philosophy even in pre-Confucian times. Coexistence with it is a fundamental philosophical concern about real and worldly human life. In *Zuo Zhuan*, a pre-Confucian text, we find these passages: 'If you listen to the common people, your nation will thrive; if you listen to *Shen* [gods], your nation will perish.' '*Tian-Dao* [the Way of *Tian*] is far away, but the way of human beings is close at hand.'[10] Passages like those can also be found in other texts such as *Guo Yu*.[11] The idea that there is a superhuman power behind natural law is marginalized after that transition, but its influence does not go away quickly. Some superhuman elements can still be found in Confucius, Mo Zi, and Mencius. I now examine the humanized and naturalized idea of natural law. *Tian* and *Ming* remain very important notions, but, unless indicated otherwise, they are not used in the sense of a superhuman power. *Tian* may have any of the five meanings defined above except for the last one. Similarly, unless otherwise indicated, *Ming* no longer means the decree of the Lord. It simply refers to that which, as natural phenomena, is beyond human control.

Tian Humanized and Naturalized

Tian is humanized and naturalized in Taoism. For Taoism, everything has its own *Tao*. *Tao* can be understood as the highest principle or law or the way things are. It certainly includes the laws of nature. *Tian* has its own *Tao*, and so do human beings, in a different way.[12] And the *Tao* of *Tian* and the *Tao* of human beings unite under the *Tao* itself, which is a completely naturalistic concept. Lao Zi (fl. 580–500 BC) says that *Tao* is the mother of the universe, and that '*Tao* is great. *Tian* is Great. Earth is great. And man is Great. There are four great things in the universe, and man is one of them. Man models himself after Earth. Earth models itself after Heaven [*Tian*]. Heaven models itself after *Tao*. And *Tao* models itself after nature' (*Dao De Jing*, Chap. 25).[13]

Zhuang Zi (fl. 360–280 BC) emphasizes that *Tian* is nature, and that the *Tao* of *Tian* means to let nature take its own course. He agrees with Lao Zi on that *Tian* and man unite under *Tao*. He also agrees with Lao Zi in making the distinction between *Tian* and human. What is *Tian*? What is human? Zhuang Zi says, 'A horse or a cow has four feet. That is *Tian*. Put a halter around the horse's head and put a string through the cow's nose, that is human.'[14] That which comes about naturally is because of *Tian*, and that which comes about through human effort is because of humans. Authentic life is to discard human and to identify oneself with *Tao*, that is, nature (*Tian*). Zhuang Zi says, 'Don't let human destroy nature. Don't let wisdom destroy *Ming*.'[15] The Taoist highest moral and political principle thus is *Wu-Wei*, that is, don't do anything contrary to the workings of nature (*Tian*). What are the workings of nature? *Tao* or nature itself. But Taoists do not think we can have knowledge of *Tao*, or knowledge of the laws of nature. For they believe that the best knowledge is no knowledge at all. That line of thinking does not seem to promise application in moral and political activity. Taoism ends up advocating a passive way of life: no conscious human effort is valuable, so do nothing but following nature (*Tian*).

The dominating idea of natural law can be found in Confucianism, which also honors a humanized and naturalized concept of *Tian*. As pointed out above, humanistic concern is already an important element in Chinese philosophy in pre-Confucian times. But it is Confucius who turns that humanistic spirit into the strongest driving force in Chinese philosophy. As a figure of the transitional period, Confucius speaks of *Tian* as a purposive master of all things. He often associates *Tian* with *Ming*. He says, 'At fifty, I knew the decrees of Heaven (*Tian-Ming*)' (*Analects*, 2: 4). At another occasion, he says, 'If the *Tao* I hold is to advance, it is *Ming*. If it is to fall to the ground, it is also *Ming*' (*Analects*, 14: 38). Confucius, however, never associates *Tian* with *Di* (God or Lord). That indicates that an anthropocentric *Tian* in Confucius has replaced the theocentric *Tian*. *Tian-Ming* is not something that human efforts can change, but that does not prevent human beings from making efforts to practice *Tao*, for doing so is the requirement of humanity (*Ren*) and righteousness (*Yi*).[16] Confucius says that he does not murmur against *Tian* when not succeeding in practicing *Tao* (*Analects*, 14: 27); he just does it, regardless of the result. *Tian* is thus no longer the central concern of Confucius, for it only serves to honor humanity in a very important sense. Confucius tells people to stay away from any non-human factors. When asked about wisdom, Confucius says, 'Devote yourself earnestly to the duties due to human beings, and respect spiritual beings but keep them at a distance. This may be called wisdom' (*Analects*, 6: 20). Another passage in the *Analects* reads, 'Ji Luo asked about serving the spirits of the dead. The master said, "While you are not able to serve human beings, how can you serve the spirits of the dead?" Ji Luo added, "I venture to ask about death?" He was answered, "While you do not know life, how can you know death?"' (*Analects*, 9: 11) From the *Analects* we know that 'Confucius never discussed non-natural phenomena, mysterious power, promiscuity, and gods' (7: 20). *Tian* and *Ming*, maybe in form, is still the foundation of the idea of natural law, but they do not really play the role God plays in the Western tradition. Confucius's primary concern is a good society based on good government and harmonious human relations, in which humanity is honored. To that end, he offers a moral and political theory, which includes a set of rules (*Li*) and virtues centered on the highest virtue of humanity (*Ren*). In order to support that theory, he even goes so far as to associate *Tian* with human nature (*xing*). 'What *Tian* has conferred (*Tian-Ming*) is called [human] nature (*xing*).'[17] *Tian* then loses its transcendental meaning. It is brought down from heaven right to where human beings stand. That statement indicates the completion of the humanization of *Tian*, and it takes the mainstream of Chinese philosophy to a new stage. Mencius and Neo-Confucians all take that idea as one of the central themes of moral and political philosophy. The idea of natural law switches its foundation from a purposive *Tian* to human beings and society.

Mencius occasionally speaks of *Tian* as the master of all things (*Meng Zi*, 5A5; 6B15). But more often and more importantly he considers *Tian* as the universal objectivity of moral and political laws. In that regard, he associates, following Confucius, *Tian* with human nature (*xing*). 'One who exerts his heart (mind, feelings, mental constitution, etc.) knows one's nature. One who knows one's nature, knows *Tian*. To preserve one's mind and to nourish one's nature is the way to serve *Tian*' (*Meng Zi*, 7A1).[18] The idea of the unity (coincidence, oneness) of *Tian* and human nature, a major theme of Chinese philosophy, is held by key philosophers one way or another. Chief among them include Dong Zhongshu (179–104 BC), Zhang Zai (1020–77), Cheng Hao (1032–85), and Cheng Yi (1033–1107), Zhu Xi (1130–1200), Wang Shouren (1472–1529), and Wang Fuzhi (1619–92).[19] Neo-Confucianism goes so far as to identify *Tian* with *li* (logos, the principles of morals), as well as *Tian* with human nature. *Tian* as a superhuman power behind natural law now entirely drops out of the picture. Its place is taken by human beings who are by nature capable of moral perfectibility.

Xun Zi speaks of *Tian* as nothing but nature. He agrees with Taoism on the division between *Tian* and human, but criticizes it for allowing human beings to do nothing but following nature. He agrees with Mencius on the perfectibility of human beings, but criticizes him for claiming that *Tian* establishes *ren xing* (human nature) as goodness. Xun Zi says, 'The course of *Tian* is constant: it does not survive because of the actions of a Yao [, a benevolent king]; it does not perish because of the actions of a Jie [, a tyrant]. If you respond to the constancy of *Tian's* course with a good government, there will be good fortune; if you respond to it with disorder, there will be misfortune. If you strengthen the basic undertakings and moderate expenditures, *Tian* cannot impoverish you. If your nourishment is complete and your movements accord with the season, then *Tian* cannot afflict you with illness. If you practice *Tao* single-mindedly, then *Tian* cannot bring about calamity.'[20]

According to Xun Zi, one who knows the division between *Tian* and human can be a 'perfect human.' Although human beings are not supposed to 'compete with *Tian* in its work,' they can make the best use of *Tian*. '*Tian* has its seasons; Earth its resources; and mankind its government.'[21] 'How can glorifying *Tian* and contemplating it be as good as tending its creatures and regulating them? How can obeying *Tian* and singing it hymns of praise be better than regulating what *Tian* has mandated and using it?'[22] Human beings become the centre of all things, and the only basis of moral principles, laws, and government.

While all major philosophers by his time had turned to a humanized and naturalized notion of *Tian*, Mo Zi, the founder of Mohism, remodeled *Tian* and posed a notion of the will of *Tian* to serve as the basis of moral and political principles. According to him, *Tian* has its own will, and it dictates the principles for human life.[23] 'Those who obey the will of *Tian* love universally and benefit each other, and will surely obtain rewards. Those who oppose the will of *Tian* set themselves apart from each other, hate each other, and injure each other, and will surely incur punishment.'[24] It might seem that for Mo Zi *Tian* is not yet naturalized and humanized. However, that is not entirely true. *Tian* in pre-Confucian times is not just the master of goodness but also, sometimes, the source of evil. By contrast, Mo Zi's notion of *Tian* has an ethical human face. For the content of the will of *Tian* is universal love.[25] Furthermore, Mo Zi holds against the idea of *Ming*. According to him, *Tian* rewards or punishes by reviewing one's action, but since everyone has free will it is up to the individual to make the choice of action. This is incompatible with the idea of *Ming*, for which 'choice' is a meaningless term because an individual's course of life is predetermined. 'The fatalists say: When *Ming* (fate) decrees that the country shall be wealthy, it will be wealthy. When it decrees that it shall be poor, it will be poor ... When it decrees that the country shall be orderly, it will be orderly. When it decrees that it shall be chaotic, it will be chaotic ... [If that is true, then] what is the use of exerting strong effort? ... The fatalists are against humanity (*Ren*).'[26]

Confucius: Humanity and Natural Law

Joseph Needham and Hu Shi, among others, focus their attention on *Li* (for principles and rules,) or *Jing* (for the constant standards) in explicating Chinese natural law.[27] There is no doubt that both *Li* and *Jing* contain some laws of nature. However, none of them can exhaust the richness of the idea of natural law in Chinese philosophy. As in the Western tradition, natural law theory covers an understanding of human nature, an explanation of the nature of society, a set of principles or virtues directing human actions, and so on. Any comprehensive account of the idea of natural law in classical Chinese philosophy has to include all those points. Such comprehensive accounts need to be given of Confucius, Mencius, Xun Zi, and Mo Zi.

The heart of mainstream Chinese philosophy is the idea of humanity (*Ren*), just as humanity is a central concept for Hume's natural law theory. The concept of humanity exists before Confucius, but it is Confucius who first philosophizes it and makes it the central theme in moral and political philosophy. What does Confucius mean by the virtue of humanity? Confucius says that humanity is human-loving (*Analects*, 7: 22). He also says that humanity is human (*The Doctrine of the Mean*, chapter 20). The character of humanity (*Ren*) in Chinese is formed from human (*ren*) and two (*er*). That suggests that humanity has something to do with human beings as a group. Humanity thus is a definitional element of human beings as social beings. It essentially refers to fellow feelings such as sympathy.[28] Principles of humanity exist wherever human beings exist. Humanity is also love of fellow beings. But it is not universal love – *agape* – found in Christianity or some modern philosophers. Nor is it romantic love – *eros*. It is closer in meaning to Aristotle's concept *philia*, or Hume's concept of humanity. Confucius says that the best model of love can be found in loving a father or a brother or a friend. It has its roots in natural feelings, so it starts from a family and then extends to others.

Humanity is a special virtue, along with all other special virtues such as propriety, wisdom, etc. It is also a general virtue, and as such it is the unity and the source of all special virtues.[29] (See St Thomas speaking of justice as a general virtue as well as a special virtue.) As the unity of the virtues, humanity is the basic virtue in which all special virtues are rooted. And the principles of humanity are the most basic principles of human nature, by which all human activities achieve their integrity through integrating motivations and actions. It is hard to characterize the unifying force of humanity from a moral psychological point of view in texts earlier than *Meng Zi*. There are, however, passages in the *Analects* that give some hints for explaining the unity thesis. According to one of such passages, Confucius said to his student Zeng Shen, 'Shen, my *Tao* (doctrine) is that of an all-pervading unity.' When asked about what Confucius meant, Zeng Shen said, 'The doctrine of our master is *Zhong* and *Shu*, nothing more' (*Analects*, 4: 15).

What do these two words, *Zhong* and *Shu*, mean? How do they fit together to form the 'all-pervading unity'? There are a few different answers to those questions.[30] It seems to me that the interpretation given by Fung Yu-Lan and Zhang Dainian is the most plausible one. *Zhong* and *Shu* are two virtues. Confucius says, 'The person of humanity is one who, desiring to sustain himself, sustains others, and desiring to develop himself, develops others' (*Analects*, 6: 28).[31] There Confucius is defining *Zhong*: 'Do to others as one would do to oneself.' When asked about humanity, Confucius says, 'Do not do to others as one would not like to have it done to oneself' (*Analects*, 12: 2). There Confucius is defining *Shu*. *Zhong* and *Shu* together amount to humanity. That is to say, humanity necessarily leads to the adoption of *Zhong* and *Shu*. On the other hand, practicing *Zhong* and *Shu* is practicing humanity. As such humanity is the one thread passing through Confucius' doctrine. The virtue of humanity, that is, love of fellow beings stabilized by the rules of *Zhong* and *Shu*, is the ground of all special virtues and principles concerning human actions.

Although Confucius is not so systematic as Mencius or Xun Zi, we can still see the general organization of his system. The virtue of humanity is the most general standard. Then less general standards follow. Chief among them are standards such as *Zhong, Shu, Xin* (fidelity, truthfulness), *Xiao* (filial piety), *Di* (fraternity), *Yong* (courage), *Zhi* (wisdom), *Li* (propriety), *Yi* (righteousness), *Zhong-Yong* (mean), *Gong* (earnestness), *Kuan* (liberality), *Min* (diligence), *Hui* (generosity), *Jian* (frugality), *Sheng* (sageness), etc. Each of those Chinese characters expresses a virtue or a specific rule (*gui fan*).[32] As Zhang Dainian has observed, however, those standards are not well organized into one coherent framework.[33]

An important feature of Confucius' system is that it does not distinguish legal matters from moral ones. Generally, Chinese natural law tradition focuses more on the moral side of the coin; and it relatively neglects the coin's another side – the legal side. But that does not mean that Chinese natural law overlooks legal rules altogether. An examination of *Li* may tell why. *Li* as a virtue is propriety. But it is also the name for all rules, principles, rites, and so forth. The

Chinese character '*Li*' originally refers only to ritual ceremonies. But even before Confucius's time while *Li* is not yet a philosophical concept, its scope of application had expanded to include laws as well as rules, arrangements, conventions, customary codes, orders, and forms. It denotes all standardized codes of behavior, legal or social. It describes 'good form' not just in temple or at court, but everywhere. And it sets norms for every daily action of any significance.[34] It is Confucius who first gives *Li* a philosophical and moral significance by relating it to humanity.

Li as a general name is used before Confucius, but not in the way we see it today. From a historical point of view, the concept of humanity in Confucius summarizes, generalizes, and philosophizes *Li*, that is, the existing rules, principles, rites, and etc. But it does not follow that *Li* is more fundamental than humanity. For from a justificatory point of view, humanity is the philosophical ground of *Li*. In that way *Li* reflects and actualizes humanity. Since humanity is the unity of all virtues, all rules corresponding to those virtues are included in *Li*. (Again, see St Thomas's treatment of justice as a general virtue.) Confucius says that all human actions should be restrained by the rules of *Li*. '*Ren* is to subdue one's self and return to *Li* ... To practice *Ren* depends on oneself. Does it depend on others? ... Do not look at what is contrary to *Li*; do not listen to what is contrary to *Li*; do not speak what is contrary to *Li*; and do not make any move which is contrary to *Li*' (*Analects*, 7: 1). However, not all rules, principles, or rites included in *Li* can be considered laws of nature, for *Li* is too broad. Yet those that are direct inferences from the principle of humanity, such as 'Be truthful to friends' or 'Show filial piety to parents,' are certainly laws of nature according to Confucius.

For Confucius laws of nature are not just moral laws, they are also principles of government. That leads critics to say that Confucius moralizes politics.[35] When asked about government, Confucius says, 'To govern (*zheng*) is to rectify (*zheng*). If you lead the people by being rectified yourself, who will dare not to be rectified?' (*Analects*, 12: 17). Rectify by what means? Not by punishment but by fostering virtues (standards of actions) and *Li* (the core of which is laws of nature). 'Lead the people with governmental measures and regulate them by punishments, they will avoid wrong-doing but will have no sense of honor and shame. Lead them with virtues and regulate them by *Li* (principles of propriety), they will have a sense of shame and, moreover, set themselves right' (*Analects*, 2: 3).

Confucius believes that every one has the capacity for humanity, and the capacity for knowing and obeying the laws of nature. So if people set themselves right, an ideal society will be the result. In *Li Ji: Li Yun*, a Confucian classic, a passage reads,

When the Great Doctrine prevails, all under heaven will work for the Common Good. The virtuous will be elected to office, and the able be given responsibility. Faithfulness will be in constant practice and harmony will rule. Consequently mankind will not only love their own parents and give care to their own children. All the aged will be provided for, and all the young employed in work. Infants will be fathered; widows and widowers, the fatherless and the unmarried, the disabled and the sick will all be cared for. Men will have their duties, and women their home. No goods will go to waste, nor need they be stored for only private possession. No energy should be retained in one's own body, nor used for only personal gain. Thieving and disorders cease; so the gates of the houses are never closed. That state is called the Great Commonwealth (*Da Tong*).[36]

The authors of that book attribute that passage to Confucius. That is doubtful. But it is certain that the passage reflects Confucian moral and political ideal.

It seems that Confucius sometimes contrasts the right (*Yi*) and the good (*li*). He says, 'The superior person understands the right; the inferior person understands the good' (*Analects*, 4: 16). He also says, 'One who acts only out of interest will be much murmured against' (4: 12). He again says, 'The superior person holds the right to be of highest importance' (17: 23). Most critics thus identify Confucius with Kant in dealing with the relation between the right and the good.[37] That identification is unsupported. When Confucius speaks against the good, he is against private interest when it is in conflict with moral principles. He never speaks against the common good. One of Confucius's political principles is 'To promote utilities considered as such by the common people' (20: 2). As shown above, Confucius's ideal society is one in which the Common Good is promoted greatly, protected properly and distributed fairly. It is a mistake to draw the conclusion that, for Confucius, the good (private or common) plays no role in morality because it is the opposite of the right. I would defend Zhang Dainian's interpretation of Confucius.[38] According to Zhang, the right is consistent with the Common Good, and it is supposed to protect and to promote the Common Good. The right is irrelevant to private good if private good does not go against the Common Good. When private good is in conflict with the right, and thus in conflict with the Common Good, the right takes priority. Confucius says, 'Wealth and honor obtained through unrighteousness are but floating clouds to me' (7: 15). Confucius, however, does not go so far as to identify the right with the Common Good or any part of it, as Mo Zi does. Mencius and Neo-Confucians apparently misinterpret Confucius, consciously or unconsciously, to hold the right against the good.

Natural law theory in Confucius is rich, but sketchy. It lays the groundwork in many senses. It presents a philosophical understanding of humanity, which becomes the major thesis of Confucianism and Chinese civilization for the next more than two thousand years. It sets up a system of virtues (standards) for human actions, which is honored by almost all philosophers after him. It offers a philosophical theory of *Li* (propriety), which contains rules of human actions (the core of them consists of the laws of nature). It honours the harmony between the good and the right, and pays due attention to the common good. It turns human efforts from worshipping *Tian* back to concerning human beings themselves, and thus enforces the already practical spirit of Chinese philosophy. Two important philosophers in the classical period, namely, Mencius and Xun Zi, inherit the Confucian tradition. But they respectively develop that tradition with different emphases. Mencius stresses *Ren* (humanity), while Xun Zi accents *Li*.

Mencius: Human Nature and Natural Law

Mencius speaks of *Tian* in at least three senses. First, *Tian* is a superhuman power that governs all things. That meaning of *Tian*, however, does not play any significant role. Second, *Tian* refers to that which goes beyond human control. In that sense, *Tian* and *Ming* have the same meaning. 'That which is done when no one does it is due to *Tian*; that which comes about when no one brings about is due to *Ming*' (*Meng Zi*, 5A6). Third, *Tian*, when associated with *xing* (human nature), has a moral meaning. 'One who exerts his heart (mind, feelings, mental constitution, etc.) knows one's nature. One who knows one's nature, knows *Tian*. To preserve one's mind and to nourish one's nature is the way to serve *Tian*' (7A1). The third meaning of *Tian* is essential to Mencius, for it is in that sense that Mencius lays the ground of moral philosophy in his theory of human nature. In the Western natural law tradition, Hume tries to ground the laws of nature in human nature and essential human circumstances. Hume and Mencius are surprisingly similar in doctrine on this point and others.

Confucius meaningfully speaks of human nature in the *Analects* only once. There he says, 'By nature humans are alike. Through practice they become far apart' (*Analects*, 17: 2). That saying may have not had much influence on Mencius. In *The Doctrine of the Mean*, a passage reads, 'What *Tian* has conferred is called [human] nature.' That statement captures the spirit of Mencius's view of human nature. There are different interpretations of his notion of human nature. Some claim that *Ren* (humanity), *Yi* (true judgment, righteousness), *Li* (propriety), and *Zhi* (wisdom or knowledge) are human nature. Others claim that the beginnings (*duans*) of *Ren*, *Yi*, *Li*, and *Zhi* are human nature. The feeling of sympathy is the beginning of *Ren*. The feeling of shame and dislike is the beginning of *Yi*. The feeling of deference and compliance (reverence and respect) is the beginning of *Li*. And the feeling of approbation and disapprobation is the beginning of *Zhi*. Both interpretations are problematic. Mencius says that human nature is 'that which gives rise to the differences between human beings and other animals' (*Meng Zi*, 4B19; 7A16).[39] The mere phenomenological differences between human beings and other animals are not human nature. They are simply the manifestations and effects of human nature. *Ren*, *Yi*, *Li*, and *Zhi* and the beginnings of them are mere phenomenological differences; they cannot be human nature. What is 'that which gives rise to' those differences? 'The capacity possessed by human beings without having been acquired by learning is *liang neng*, and the knowledge possessed by them without deliberation is *liang zhi*' (7A15). '*Liang*' means 'original,' 'innate,' and 'good' (7A15; 6A8; 6A17; 3B1; 7A9). '*Neng*' means 'capacity.' To use a modern British philosophical term, '*liang neng*' is something similar to 'moral sense.'[40] '*Zhi*' in this context has been commonly translated as 'knowledge.' That translation is not wrong; but it is misleading. For '*zhi*' can also mean '[moral] consciousness' and, especially in this context, 'the capacity to know or to be conscious of.' So '*liang zhi*' characteristically means the capacity to have moral knowledge or moral consciousness. 'Moral sense' – in its cognitive interpretation – also has that meaning. In short, '*liang neng*' and '*liang zhi*' – roughly moral sense – are human nature. They are that which give rise to the differences between human beings and other animals.

How do '*liang neng*' and '*liang zhi*' connect to the four *duans* and the four virtues, namely, *Ren*, *Yi*, *Li*, and *Zhi*? Human nature is the capacity for *Ren*, *Yi*, *Li*, and *Zhi*, that is, moral sense, or more accurately for Mencius, 'human' sense. Mencius believes that to practice *Ren* is a naturalistic process: it has '*liang neng*' and '*liang zhi*' as its ground, has the four *duans* as its starting point, and has *Ren*, *Yi*, *Li*, and *Zhi* in the full sense as its completion.[41] As Zhang Dainian has pointed out, there are at least the following three ways of using the term '*ren xing*,' i.e. human nature.[42] First, it means that which human beings are born with. Gao Zi, for example, holds that view. Second, it means that which makes 'human beings' human. Mencius holds this view. Third, it refers to a holistic and cosmological view of the nature of the universe and human beings. This is the view of Zhu Xi and Zhang Zai. Mencius's view of human nature converges with that of Western philosophers like Aristotle and Hume in important ways. Human nature refers to the characteristic capacity of human beings. It is wrong for one to say that Mencius does not have a concept of human nature, and that '*ren-xing*' in *Meng Zi* cannot be translated as 'human nature.'[43]

Confucius talks about *xin*, but not in a systematic way. Mencius is the first philosopher who systematically deals with *xin* in moral philosophy.[44] '*Xin*' has many meanings in Mencius. It can mean emotion, feeling, mind, or heart (both biological and cultural) and so on. To stress one important meaning of *xin*, Mencius contrasts it with the senses of hearing and seeing. He says that, 'to *xin* belong the functions of thinking and reflecting (*si*)' (*Meng Zi*, 6A15).[45] It is clear that *xin* has the functions of thinking, feeling, judging, and so on. Most importantly, Mencius treats *xin* as the 'home' of human nature. Mencius says, 'what belongs by nature to human beings is [the '*liang neng*' and '*liang zhi*' of] *Ren*, *Yi*, *Li*, and *Zhi*. They are rooted in *xin*' (7A21).[46] He also says that '*Ren* is *xin*' (6A11). Interpreting Mencius, Zhu Xi says that '*xin* commands [human] nature and emotions.'[47] This is why Mencius claims that, 'One who exerts one's *xin* knows one's nature' (6A1). He also says, 'All things are complete in us' (6A4). There 'things' refers to 'moral' actions, rules and suchlike. Again he says that 'Everyone can be a Yao or Shun' – who were morally perfect (6B2). Briefly, human nature is '*liang neng*' and '*liang zhi*' – together, moral sense; and they are rooted in *xin*. If *xin* is cultivated properly, so will be human nature. Mencius claims that human nature is good. 'If you allow people to follow their feelings, they will be able to do good. That is what I mean by saying that human nature is good' (*Meng Zi*, 6A6). Zhu Xi interprets feelings as motions of human nature,[48] that is, feelings are the emerging and unfolding of human nature.

Mencius's moral theory is more systematic than that of Confucius. Before I give a picture of the system, however, interpretations of the key virtues are necessary. To cite again: 'The feeling of sympathy is the beginning of *Ren*; the feeling of shame and dislike that of *Yi*; the feeling of deference and compliance (or reverence and respect) that of *Li*; and the feeling of approbation and disapprobation that of *Zhi*.' (*Meng Zi*, 2A6)

Ren has to do with the kind of natural feeling of sympathy and love. Confucius already makes that clear. But it is Mencius who first says that sympathy is only the beginning of *Ren*. Fully developed *Ren* is something more than sympathy or natural love. Mencius says, 'Every one has some thing that one cannot bear. Extend that feeling to that which one bears, *Ren* will be the result' (*Meng Zi*, 7B31). Zhu Xi's interpretation of those statements is this: every one in principle has the feeling of sympathy. However, he may not be able to (or not be able consistently to) extend that feeling to people from a general point of view when blinded by self-interest. If he makes the effort consistently to extend sympathy to not just those who are close to him but also those who are not, *Ren* will be the result.[49] It follows that *Ren* is stable or consistent sympathy or love. That reminds us of Hume's move from the principle of sympathy to the principle of humanity. In the *Treatise*, Hume says that morality is founded on the most general principle of human nature – the principle of sympathy. (Hume uses the term 'principle' more freely than we do today. It can mean a rule or a feature of human nature or a mental quality.) But he soon finds that the principle of sympathy is not sufficiently general to ground morality. There are at least two problems with sympathy. (1) Let x and y stand for individual persons, and z for a context. Then x's sympathy towards y may vary as y changes in position or outlook or as z changes. (2) Sympathy as a psychological mechanism functions well only if 'our own person is not the object of any passion, nor is there any thing, that fixes our attention on ourselves.'[50] In the second *Enquiry*, Hume moves one step forward. He claims that the principle of humanity is the most general principle of human nature, which grounds morality. However, he does not simply abandon the principle of sympathy. He incorporates it into the principle of humanity. For Hume, humanity is corrected sympathy, that is, to use Hume's language, sympathy stabilized by correct judgments, which are not themselves the sources constitutive of morality. Because of the similarity between Mencius and Hume, I consider humanity the best fitting translation for *Ren*.[51]

Kwong-loi Shun sees *Yi* as (1) 'a quality of actions' and (2) 'an attribute of a person.'[52] As a quality of action, *Yi* 'refers to what is fitting or proper to do.'[53] Some examples of *Yi* are actions that follow *Li*, rules and principles; and some other examples show that actions falling under *Yi* can go beyond the constraints of *Li*, that is, *Yi* is more important than *Li*. As an attribute of a person, *Yi* has to do with a firm commitment to some ethical standards, which, according to Shun, differ from social standards. Ethical standards are about appropriate character, and social standards are about what is socially (that is, externally) recognized as such. 'The commitment involves having disdain for, and regarding oneself as being potentially tainted by, what falls below [ethical] standards ... It also involves to some degree a capacity to judge in accordance with such standards.'[54] Following that interpretation of *Yi*, Shun draws these contrasts between *Ren* and *Yi*. He says, 'We may infer that jen [*Ren*] emphasizes an affective concern for others, both not wanting to harm others ... and not being able to bear the suffering of others ... On the other hand, yi [*Yi*] emphasizes a strictness with oneself, a commitment to abide by certain ethical standards that involves both not acquiring things by improper means and not accepting others' improper treatment of oneself.'[55] Briefly, Shun seems to be suggesting that *Ren* emphasizes how to treat others, and *Yi* emphasizes how to treat oneself. I contend that Shun misrepresents the relation between *Ren* and *Yi*. And his mistake is due to his inaccurate interpretation of *Yi*.

Mencius says, '*Ren* is human heart, and *Yi* is human path' (*Meng Zi*, 6A11). He again says that '*Ren* is the safe home of human beings, and *Yi* is the right path' (4A11). 'To live in *Ren* and to go by *Yi* are sufficient for one to be a person of greatness' (7A33). What does Mencius try to imply by those metaphors? In the *Analects* Confucius sees *Ren* as the supreme virtue, the unity of the virtues. Mencius not only inherits but also develops that idea. He offers a moral psychological account for that unity. As Chen Chun says, *Ren* is the complete virtue of *xin* (the mind/heart); and, taken totally, it includes all virtues and principles.[56] That is, *Ren* is the foundation of all virtues and principles. The principle of *Ren* is the most basic principle of human nature, by which all human activities achieve their integrity through integrating motivations and actions. Given that interpretation of *Ren*, we know that *Yi* cannot be anything that has no intrinsic connection with *Ren*. The way Shun treats the relation between *Ren* and *Yi* seems to suggest that those two are not intrinsically related. Given the fact, as Shun also observes, that Mencius on the one hand frequently associates *Yi* with specific moral actions or non-actions such as to respect an elder or not to accept office in a corrupt government and, on the other, frequently relates *Yi* to general moral considerations, it seems clear that *Yi* is the medium between *Ren* and the practice of *Ren*, that is, between humanity (morality) and moral practice. What is the medium between *Ren* and the practice of *Ren*? It is (true moral) judgments. Thus, the most plausible interpretation of *Yi* is that it is (true moral) judgments. Now those metaphors at the beginning can be deciphered. *Ren* is in a most important sense the source and the root of morality, thus it is the home of moral agency. *Yi* consists in (true) moral judgments, which lead the moral agent to moral action; thus it is the path from the home to 'the working field.'

In moral practice, when faced with a specific situation, *xin* (the mind/heart) needs to make a judgment about what is right and appropriate to do based on *Ren*. *Ren* as a defining principle of mankind is then tied up with and applied to a specific situation. *Yi* is that judgment. That is why it is said that '*Yi* is appropriateness and fitness' (*The Doctrine of the Mean*, chap. 20). Zhu Xi says that *Yi* is the judgment about how *Ren* is applied in a concrete case.[57] Chen Chun says that *Yi* is the judgment of *xin*.[58] Ma Zhenduo interprets *Yi* as moral judgment.[59] According to Chung-ying Cheng's account, a person of *Yi* is able to make appropriate moral judgment in particular situations.[60] Shun, at one point, comes very close to the conclusion that *Yi* is (true) judgment, although he never makes it quite all the way to this view. There he says that *Yi* involves 'to some degree a capacity to judge' in accordance with ethical standards.

A judgment can be either true or false. Mencius is fully aware of that. He says that, 'A great person never follows the *Yi* which is not really *Yi*' (4B6). That is to say, a great person is able to distinguish true moral judgments (*Yi*) from false ones, and he follows only the true judgments. However, Mencius, as well as Confucius, characteristically uses *Yi* as true judgment. 'One who sees *Yi* and does not act accordingly lacks courage' (*Analects*, 2: 24). There *Yi* can only be true judgment.[61]

Is Shun's interpretation of *Yi* – (1) 'a quality of actions' and (2) 'an attribute of a person' – simply wrong? No. *Yi* is indeed used in those meanings, as found in *Meng Zi*. However, those meanings are derivative. Since *Yi* characteristically refers to true judgment, so it is derivately used to mean whatever is right – a right action, a right rule. It is also derivatively used to characterize a person who does the right thing. Therefore, it is not wrong to translate *Yi* as rightness or righteousness. But *Yi* is basically true judgment. Chung-ying Cheng says that *Yi* 'justifies the morality of human action' and that *Yi* 'makes virtue virtuous.'[62] That is wrong. *Yi* itself does not 'make' things moral. It is from humanity (*Ren*) rather than *Yi* that the root of morality is found. *Yi's* justificatory force comes ultimately from humanity.

Confucius speaks of *Li* as a virtue and the name of all rules, principles, laws, and rites. Mencius also talks about *Li* as a virtue (propriety) and as specific rules. For Mencius, *Li* has its beginning in the feeling of respect and compliance. Mencius inherits Confucius' view: 'Respectfulness, without the rules of propriety (*Li*), becomes laborious bustle; carefulness, without the rules of propriety, becomes timidity; boldness, without the rules of propriety, becomes insubordination; straightforwardness, without the rules of propriety, becomes rudeness' (*Analects*, 8:2).[63] Mencius considers *Li* as external constraints on actions, and *Yi* as internal constraints.[64] He believes that when *Li* and *Yi* are in conflict, *Yi* takes priority (*Meng Zi*, 4B6).

Zhi is a central concept in *The Great Learning*. It can be translated as knowledge or wisdom. It is also a virtue to have wisdom or knowledge. *Zhi* has a relatively broad meaning in Confucius. Confucius says, 'Without knowing (*zhi*) *Ming*, it is impossible to be a gentleman. Without knowing *Li*, it is impossible for the character to be established. Without knowing the force of words, it is impossible to know a person' (*Analects*, 20: 3). So *Zhi* has *Ming*, human being, and *Tian* as its objects, which are pretty much everything in the universe. However, Confucius gives more emphasis on moral knowledge. That tendency in Confucius is fully developed by Mencius. Although occasionally speaking of *Zhi* as knowledge of nature,[65] Mencius characteristically uses *Zhi* to refer to moral knowledge and consciousness. He says, 'The feeling of approbation and disapprobation is the beginning of Zhi' (*Meng Zi*, 2A6). Interpreting that claim, Zhu Xi says, 'Approbation (*shi*) means to know what is the right and to believe it is the right. Disapprobation (*fei*) means to know what is wrong and to believe it is the wrong' (*Si Shu*, 237). Confucius says that *Zhi* benefits *Ren* (humanity), that is, *Zhi* nurtures humanity. *Zhi* as knowledge or wisdom prepares the way for and facilitates humanity.[66]

Confucius's system is this: as the supreme principle of morality, humanity (*Ren*) is the unity of the virtues. *Li* is the actualization of *Ren*. Influenced by Confucius, Mencius first offers the four-virtue framework of his moral system, that is, *Ren*, *Yi*, *Li*, and *Zhi*. *Ren*, *Yi*, *Li*, and *Zhi* have their roots in human nature, which is '*liang neng*' and '*liang zhi*.' Their starting points are certain kinds of feelings, which are the emerging and unfolding of human nature, *xing*. *Ren*, *Yi*, *Li*, and *Zhi* respectively start with the feelings of sympathy, shame, respect, and approval. Mencius believes that *Ren* is the unity of the virtues. As pointed out above, *Ren* as a special virtue is simply one virtue among others; but as a general virtue, it is the unity of the virtues. Chen Chun says, 'Taken totally, it is called *Ren*, but *Yi*, *Li*, and *Zhi* are included in it.'[67] He also says, '*Ren* is the complete virtue of *xin*. It includes and controls the four virtues.'[68] The practice of humanity (*Ren*) requires all virtues and in particular *Yi*, *Li*, and *Zhi* to be in full operation and cooperation. As Chen Chun says, 'in the operation of the creative principle of *Ren*, respect and deference, which are the restraint ... of *Li*, are already beginning to form. In respect and deference ... a judgment (*Yi*), and a determination of its truth value (*Zhi*) are already beginning to form.'[69] Mencius says that without the regard to *Ren* in the first place, those rules (*Li*), judgments (*Yi*), and knowledge (*Zhi*) would not even obtain. (To cite Hume, we would not have moral language – even if we had, it would not make sense to us – without the basic principle of human nature.)[70] Chen Chun says, 'If one can practice *Ren*, all virtues will follow.'[71]

With the four-virtue framework of the *Ren* system, Mencius's Natural Law theory presents moral standards well organized around the center of humanity. There are two sets of standards. The first of those is: *Xiao* (filial piety), *Di* (fraternity), *Zhong* (loyalty), and *Xin* (truthfulness) (*Meng Zi*, 1A5).[72] Those standards, as Zhang Dainian says, are natural preliminary standards (virtues).[73] They are basic, although not as systematically important as *Ren*, *Yi*, *Li*, and *Zhi*. A second set of those standards is specific guides of human relations. There are five such guides. 'There should be affection between father and son. There should be righteousness between king and minister. There should be distinctive functions between husband and wife. There should be a proper order between old and young. There should be truthfulness between friends' (*Meng Zi*, 3A4).[74]

Mencius advances the idea of humane government (*Ren-Zheng*) put forward by Confucius. A humane government is also called 'a commiserating government' or 'a kingly government.' That political idea is based on Mencius's view that human nature is good. Mencius says, 'Every one has a heart which cannot bear to see the sufferings of others. The early kings had that commiserating heart, thereby had likewise a commiserating government' (*Meng Zi*, 2A6).[75] He distinguishes two kinds of rulers, namely, *wang* and *ba*. A *wang* rules by virtue, while a *ba* rules by force. 'He who, using force, makes a pretense to *Ren* is a *ba* ... He who, using virtue, practices *Ren* is a *wang* ... When one subdues people by force, they do not submit to him in their hearts but only outwardly, because they have insufficient strength to resist. But when one gains followers by virtue, they are pleased in their hearts and will submit of themselves as did the seventy disciples to Confucius' (2A3). That political idea is an extension of Confucius's idea that to govern is to rectify according to virtues. 'To govern (*zheng*) is to rectify (*zheng*). If you lead the people by being rectified yourself, who will dare not to be rectified?' (*Analects*, 12: 17). Mencius is surprisingly revolutionary. He maintains that if a ruler lacks the moral qualities to be a *wang*, the people have the right to overthrow that ruler and even to put him to death. He once says that to kill a ruler of no moral character is not a crime of regicide, because if a ruler does not practice a humane government, he is no longer a ruler according to the doctrine of the rectification of names (*Meng Zi*, 2B8). Mencius sounds pretty much like John Locke on that point. '[In a state] the people are the most important; the spirits of the land and grain (guardians of territory) are the next; the ruler is of slight importance' (7B14). Mencius is so idealistic as to rest government on a ruler's moral character. That may be because of his view that human nature is good. Mencius once sadly admits that his doctrine is not practicable in his time. Xun Zi criticizes him vigorously by saying that it is rules of law (*Li*) rather than moral character that serve as the ground of government. Xun Zi claims that human nature is evil (I shall discuss this in detail in the next section).

Based on the idea of government of *Ren*, Mencius says that a *wang* (benevolent ruler) does all he can for the welfare and benefit of the people. Specific measures that Mencius details include the following: First, government is supposed to protect people's normal agrarian activities. 'If the seasons of husbandry be not interfered with, the grain will be more than can be eaten. If close nets are not allowed to enter the pools and ponds, the fishes and turtles will be more than can be consumed. If the axes and bills enter the hills and forests only at the proper time, the wood will be more than can be used' (1A1).[76] Second, a government is supposed to make sure that people own adequate property, for without adequate property they will do anything, illegal or immoral, to satisfy their own self-interest. Only after adequate property is owned can people live in a thriving and orderly society (1A7).[77] Third, the most important way for government to secure people's adequate property is the equal distribution of land. Mencius even calls for remodeling the ancient system of land to make sure that people will have a commodious life as well as a thriving state (1A3; 3A3).[78] Fourth, a government should establish educational institutions (schools) to inculcate human relations such as filial and fraternal duties (1A3; 3A3).[79]

With so much attention to the Common Good, Mencius, however, surprisingly makes some deontological claims against the good (interest, or utility) in favour of the right (*Ren-Yi*, morality). We practice *Ren*, *Yi*, *Li*, and *Zhi* for they are what make us human beings. 'One is not a human without the feeling of sympathy. One is not a human without the feeling of shame and dislike. One is not a human without the feeling of deference and compliance. One is not a human without the feeling of approbation and disapprobation' (2A6).[80] Once King Hui of Liang asks Mencius what specific goods (profits, utilities) his counsel would bring. Mencius replies, 'Why must your Majesty talk about goods? What I am provided with are counsels to *Ren* and *Yi*, and those are my only topics' (1A1). He believes that if everyone, from the king to high officials and from low officials to common people, talks about goods (interest) from their own point of view, the entire state will be endangered. For in that case moral and political standards (principles, rules, laws, and virtues) – that is, *Ren-Yi* – by which social order is maintained will be destroyed (1A1; 6B4). It is moral laws (the right) that take priority over specific goods (the good).[81] As Liang Qichao points out, Mencius holds morality against not just self-interest but also public interest, for he maintains that interest, private or public, cannot serve to motivate proper human actions, only moral considerations themselves can serve such a purpose.[82] To have a full picture of Mencius's moral philosophy, we need to understand Mencius's above deontological position with reference to his strong advocacy that the Common Good, proper political regulations, fair distribution of land, and public education should be the central concern of a ruler of *Ren*. We also need to understand his position with reference to his claim that moral considerations require some basic livelihood (physical goods) being satisfied first (1A7).

Mencius is very close in doctrine to Hume in grounding natural law on a notion of human nature. He is also very close to Hume in seeing the importance of the feeling of sympathy and the principle of humanity. Mencius develops Confucius' notion of *Ren*, but fails to pay sufficient attention to *Li*. Given Hume's system of natural law, Mencius's system does not appear fully developed in important respects. Mencius relies so much on the assumption that human nature is good that he does not even consider self-interest playing any significant role in moral considerations. That is where he departs from Confucius; that is also where he loses his comparison to Hume. Xun Zi criticizes Mencius's assumption about human nature and his neglect of the importance of *Li*. Mencius is idealistic, but Xun Zi is very realistic.

Xun Zi: Social Needs and Natural Law

Both *Ren* and *Li* are essential concepts in the *Analects*. Confucius sees *Ren* as the root of *Li*, and *Li* as the actualization of *Ren*. He accents two aspects of moral and political life. First, to practice Ren depends on oneself and not others; second, social and individual behavior must be regulated by *Li*. Mencius inherits and develops the first aspect by claiming that human nature is good and that if one makes the effort to cultivate oneself, one will be a person of *Ren*. Xun Zi, on the other hand, inherits and develops the second aspect of Confucius by claiming that human nature is evil and that human behavior must be regulated by *Li*, or there will be no peace in society. In what follows I explicate Xun Zi's view of natural law, which is surprisingly similar to Hobbes's system.

Although noting that human beings have an *in foro interno* capacity for good not manifested in the state of nature, Hobbes speaks of human nature as evil by observing, what he calls, 'the Felicity of this life.'[83] 'Felicity is a continuall progresse of the desire, from one object to another; the attaining of the former, being still but the way to the later. The cause whereof is, That the object of man's desire, is not to enjoy once onely, and for one instant of time; but to assure for ever, the way of his future desire.'[84] Hobbes lists those desires and inclinations; chief among them include the desire for power, the love for competition and contention, the desire for ease and sensual delight, and so on. Xun Zi says,

> Human nature is evil ... Now the nature of human beings is such that they are born with a desire of gain. Following that desire will cause aggressiveness and greedy tendencies to grow and courtesy and deference to disappear. Human beings are born with feelings of envy and hatred. Following those feelings will cause violence and crime to develop and integrity and truthfulness to perish. Human beings are born with the desires of ears and eyes, which are fond of sounds and colors. Following those desires will result in dissolute and wanton behavior and cause *Li*, *Yi*, proper form, and natural order to perish. Therefore to follow human nature and human feelings will inevitably result in strife and rapacity, combine with rebellion and disorder and end in violence.[85]

Xun Zi even depicts a state of nature, which is also very similar to what Hobbes pictures as a state of nature. Hobbes says that the state of nature, since there is no common power to keep people all in awe, amounts to the war of all with all. 'Where there is no common Power, there is no Law, no Injustice. Force and Fraud, are in warre the two Cardinall vertues.'[86] Xun Zi notes, 'Let us imagine a state where we do away with the authority of kings, do without the transforming influence of the rules of propriety (*Li*) and righteousness (*Yi*), discard the order provided by the laws and rectitude, do without the constraints of penal laws and punishments. How would people in that state deal with each other? In such a state the strong would inflict harm on the weak; the many would tyrannize the few and wrest their possessions from them; and the perversity and disorder would quickly ensure their mutual destruction.'[87]

Xun Zi's view that human nature is evil[88] is based on the distinction he makes between what he calls nature (*xing*) and what he calls conscious exertion or acquired character (*wei*, or culture, as Fung Yu-Lan translates it).[89] 'What cannot be gained by learning and cannot be mastered by application yet is found in human beings is properly termed human nature, *xing*. What must be learned before a human being can do it and what a human being must apply himself to before he can master it yet is found in human beings is properly called acquired character.'[90] Human nature and conscious exertion are, however, closely related. 'Nature is the root and beginning, the raw materials and original constitution. Acquired character is the form and order, the development and completion. If there were no nature, there would be nothing for conscious exertion to improve; if there were no conscious exertion, nature could not be refined.'[91]

It seems that Mencius and Xun Zi are at two opposite poles. Mencius says that human nature is good. His arguments are based on the fact that human beings have the feelings of sympathy, shame, respect, approbation, and so on. But Mencius fails to recognize (or pay due attention to) another part of the story, namely, that human beings also have the feelings of envy, hatred, and so forth. That part is picked up by Xun Zi who, however, fails to recognize (or pay due attention to) the good aspect of human nature. To conclude that Mencius and Xun Zi are at two opposite poles is too quick, because Xun Zi's definition of human nature is subtly different from that of Mencius. Xun Zi relates, 'Mencius says that human nature is good for human beings can learn. That is not true ... It, however, shows that Mencius does not understand the division between nature and acquired character. Human nature is what is original and complete (*tian zhi jiu ye*). It cannot be learned, nor can it be worked for.'[92] In 'Rectifying the Names' Xun Zi again repeats the point about original completeness. Yet Mencius says that human beings are born with the beginning of *Ren*, the beginning of *Yi*, the beginning of *Li*, and the beginning of *Zhi*. 'Beginning' implies 'incomplete.' For Mencius complete *Ren*, *Yi*, *Li*, and *Zhi* can only be attained through conscious learning or exertion, that is, they are acquired character, although their beginnings are innate. According to Xun Zi's definitions of nature and acquired character, Mencius cannot draw the conclusion that human nature is good. On the other hand, the desire for gain or power and the feeling of envy or hatred are originally complete in human beings, that is, they are already in human beings without being attained through learning. Thus, human nature is evil. Xun Zi's line of argument against Mencius presupposes that Mencius claims human nature to be composed of *Ren, Yi, Li,* and *Zhi* in the full sense. But Mencius never makes that claim. He does not even claim the beginnings of *Ren, Yi, Li,* and *Zhi* to be human nature. As pointed out, Mencius sees human nature as composed of '*liang neng*' and '*liang zhi*,' that is, the capacities (potentialities) for *Ren, Yi, Li,* and *Zhi*.[93] Mencius claims that those capacities will be developed into fully fledged *Ren, Yi, Li,* and *Zhi* if they are properly cultivated. That is why human nature is good. Xun Zi and Mencius characterize 'human nature' differently, and thus Xun Zi's criticism of Mencius misses the point.[94] It would be unwarranted to conclude that Mencius and Xun Zi are at two opposite poles with regard to their views of human nature or their moral theories,[95] although we have to admit that they adopt very different approaches.

Mencius says that human beings are born with the beginnings of *Ren, Yi, Li,* and *Zhi*. So for Mencius to bring up rules of propriety (*Li*) and rules of righteousness (*Yi*) is to cultivate human character. Xun Zi says that human nature is evil. How does Xun Zi explain the origin of the rules of *Li* and *Yi*? He says,

> It is the case that nature is given: it is not something that can be learned or something that requires application to master. The rules of *Li* and *Yi* are creations of the sages. They are things that people must study to be able to follow them and to which they must apply themselves before having the ability to fulfill their precepts.[96]

> All rules of *Li* and *Yi* are created from the acquired character of the sages, not from human nature. When a potter shapes the clay to create the vessel, which is the creation of the acquired character of the potter and not the product of anything inherent in his nature ... The sage learns from practice, and he accumulates his thoughts and ideas. He then creates the rules of *Li* and *Yi*. This is how laws and standards arise. This being the case: *Li, Yi,* laws, and standards are the creation of the acquired character of the sage and not the product of human nature.[97]

The question is: Can human beings acquire any character that they do not have in any form, for example, its beginning (*duan*), in their nature? Xun Zi believes that all human beings, a sage or a petty person, share the same nature. 'The nature human beings share is one and the same whether they be a Yao and Shun [who were morally perfect] or a Jie and Robber Zhi [who were evil]. The sages and the petty human beings share one and the same nature.'[98] If there is not any form of *Li* or *Yi* in human nature, the sages as well as the petty people equally do not possess it. Do the sages themselves create *Li* and *Yi* out of nothing? Remember, sages are not God. Xun Zi's view would be problematic without further explanation.

Mencius says human beings have the potentiality (capacity) for good. Hobbes, who believes that human nature will be expressed in evil ways unless regulated, says that human beings have a disposition toward obeying the laws of nature (justice), which are with them *in foro interno* even before they organize. Natural interest plus natural rationality leads to contracts, from which rules of justice and morality arise. Those contracts thus allow human beings to have rules *in foro externo* as well as *in foro interno*.[99] In order to account for the origin of *Li* and *Yi*, Xun Zi has to allow, at least, human beings to have the capacity for *Li* and *Yi*. Regardless of their seemingly tremendous differences, Xun Zi and Mencius run parallel at that point. Like Aristotle who distinguishes capacity from ability, Xun Zi does so as well when talking about human potentiality for moral perfection. 'It is true that anyone in the street has the capacity (*ke*) to become a Yu [who was morally perfect]. But it does not follow that everyone in the street has the ability (*neng*) to become a Yu.'[100] What is the difference between capacity and ability? Xun Zi answers that question by examples. 'Human beings are capable of traveling by foot the width of the whole world, yet there is no one who is able to do so. The artisan, carpenter, farmer, and trader are capable of practicing each other's business, yet they are not able to do so. Accordingly, capacity does not necessarily imply ability. But not having ability does not imply not having capacity. Capacity is very different from ability.'[101] It is obvious that, for Xun Zi, capacity is potentiality, and ability actuality.

It is now clear that Xun Zi implies, among other things, that human beings are not born with the ability for the good when he says that human nature is evil. But he does not deny that human beings are born with the capacity for the good. (That brings him very close to Mencius.) Human abilities for the good can only be acquired through practicing and learning, that is, *wei*.[102] Mencius speaks of the capacity for moral knowledge and moral practice; so does Xun Zi. Xun Zi says, 'Anyone in the street can become a Yu. Yu became a sage-king because he practiced humanity, righteousness, law, and rectitude. That shows that humanity, righteousness, law, and rectitude can be known and practiced. Since anyone in the street has the capacity to know humanity, righteousness, law, and rectitude, and also has the capacity to practice them, anyone can become a Yu.'[103] Human beings are different from any other animal beings on earth precisely because they are capable of living a moral life. Xun Zi says that in the clearest language.[104]

Human beings have not just the capacity for morality and moral knowledge but also natural rationality. That brings Xun Zi even closer to Hobbes. One important aspect of natural rationality is that human beings can recognize or even make social distinctions and divisions, including social classes (*bian*). (I shall specify this point below.) Another important aspect is that human beings can make judgments, which direct their activities. Xun Zi says, 'What human nature manifests as liking and disliking, delight and anger, and joy and sorrow is called feelings (or emotions, *qing*). The mind's choosing among those feelings is called judgment (*lu*). Putting judgments into action is called conscious exertion (*wei*).'[105] Conscious exertion leads to *Li* and *Yi*. It is natural rationality that takes human beings out of narrow self-interest.

Human beings are by nature selfish; they, however, have the capacity for morality and moral knowledge; and they have natural rationality, which can take them out of narrow self-interest. Those three conditions lead Xun Zi to a more promising account than his simple reference to the sages for the origin of *Li* (propriety) and *Yi* (righteousness). This time, he appeals to social needs.

Human beings have many desires. Not all of them can be approved and satisfied. That, however, does not mean that we need to rid ourselves of desires. For the occurrence of desires does not depend on their objects' first being obtainable.[106] Desires can only be guided and moderated by our minds in considering the scarcity of goods. The rules of *Li* (propriety) arise from the need of harmonizing desires and goods:

> How did the rules of *Li* arise? Human beings are born with desires. If those desires are not met, their satisfaction will be sought. To seek their satisfaction without constraints results in contention and fighting, which lead to disorder. Disorder means that things are out of control. The ancient benevolent kings abhorred such disorder, so they established the rules of propriety and righteousness to put things in order. By those rules desires were regulated and nurtured, needs were disciplined and met. Those rules were so fashioned that with their constraints desires would never want for goods and goods would never be exhausted by desires. That was how the rules of propriety arose – they came from the tension and balance between goods and desires.[107]

Mencius claims human nature to be good, so *Ren* and *Li* arise from following natural feelings and desires. Here 'following' presupposes self-cultivation. Xun Zi sees human nature as evil, so *Li* and *Yi* do not arise from simply following natural feelings and desires. Those feelings and desires, instead, need to be controlled and transformed (*hua*).[108] Here 'controlling or transforming' presupposes self-cultivation as well. Both the 'following' process and the 'controlling or transforming' process presuppose that human beings have the capacity for morality and the capacity for moral perfection.

Confucius emphasizes both *Ren* and *Li*. Mencius stresses *Ren* or *Ren-Yi*. Xun Zi, on the other hand, mostly accents *Li* or *Li-Yi*. It does not follow, however, that Xun Zi does not pay attention to *Ren*. He once even says that for a sage king *Ren* takes priority over *Li*.[109] Xun Zi accents *Li* because he believes that only *Li* can set constraints from outside on selfish human desires. The practice of *Ren*, as Confucius says, depends on one's self, so *Ren* cannot effectively control human conduct from outside. Xun Zi says, 'The rules of *Li* are that whereby a person's character is rectified ... Without rules of *Li* how could one's character be rectified!'[110] Xun Zi often associates *Li* with laws (*fa*).[111] According to him, when study (learning) has been perfected in *Li*, it has come to its terminus. For *Li* contains fundamental laws of social distinctions and fundamental guiding rules of behaviour. Xun Zi sees rules of *Li* providing the highest standards of human behaviours:

> If the blackened marking line is set true, it is impossible to be deceived about what is straight and what is crooked. If the balance is hung true, it is impossible to be fooled about what is lightness or what is heaviness. If the compass and square are adjusted true, it is impossible to be cheated about what is a square and what is a round. So too, if a gentleman is thoroughly acquainted with *Li*, he cannot be manipulated about what is fraud and what is pretense. The marking line is the highest standard of straightness. The balance is the highest standard of equalness. The compass and the square are the highest standard of squareness and roundness. So too, rules of *Li* are the highest standards of the way of human (*Tao*).[112]

Li is immensely important. It provides the footing human beings tread on. Without that footing human beings stumble and fall, sink and drown. Xun Zi repeatedly says, 'One would not be able to live without *Li*; an undertaking would not be accomplished without *Li*; and a nation would have no peace without *Li*.'[113] It is rare that Mencius, however, associates *Li* with specific rules. He stresses moral judgment. Confucius, as pointed out, does give *Li* a central role in his system. He once says that one should not look at, or listen to, or talk about, or act upon that which is contrary to *Li* (*Analects*, 12:1). But for Confucius, to constrain one's desires by *Li* is the way to become a person of *Ren*. Thus he is actually paying more attention to the cultivation of one's character (for example, humanity, *Ren*).[114] Although he takes self-cultivation seriously, Xun Zi has a much broader perspective in mind: He accents *Li* because *Li* is a necessary condition for peace and thriving of a society. Peace and thriving, according to Xun Zi, start with social distinctions and divisions. *Li* is to set constraints (*jie*) and to make distinctions (*fen*).[115]

The theory of social distinctions and divisions (*fen*) plays a central part in Xun Zi's moral and political philosophy. It is also the ground of *Li* in an important sense. Human beings are capable of organized social life (*neng qun*). They are not as strong as bulls; nor are they as fast as horses. But bulls and horses are used by human beings. Why so? Because human beings live an organized social life, but bulls and horses do not. An organized social life is stronger than any life in separation:

> Why can human beings live an organized social life? Because they know the distinctions and divisions in society. How can social distinctions and divisions be carried out? Through righteousness (*Yi*). Peace arises from social distinctions and divisions when regulated by *Yi*; unity and solidarity arises from peace; great power arises from unity and solidarity; and strength arises from great power. When strong, human beings can dominate nature ... So human beings could not live without society; society ends up nothing but contention and fighting without social distinctions and divisions; contention and fighting lead to disorder; disorder leads to society's disintegration; disintegration leads to weakness; and once weak, human beings will not be able to dominate nature ... Therefore, human beings cannot abandon *Li* and *Yi* for an instant.[116]

Like Confucius, Xun Zi claims that a central function of *Li* is to bring peace, that is, *Li* is established to meet the need for peace in society. For there would be no secure and commodious life without peace. Xun Zi observes that distinctions between things are one of the most important feature of the universe. 'All things are present together in universe; but they have different forms.'[117] Human beings are classified and divided in different groups and classes. In order to live in a peaceful society, people have to recognize the social distinctions and divisions:

> To be as honored as the Son of Heaven (*Tian-Zi*) and to be as wealthy by possessing the whole world – that desire is shared by every one alike. But if every one gives free rein to one's desires, the result would be impossible to endure, and the material goods of the whole world would be inadequate to satisfy them. Accordingly, the ancient Kings act to control human desires and to distribute goods by *Li* and *Yi*. Observed therewith are differences in status between the noble and the base, disparities between the

privileges of age and youth, and the division of the wise from the stupid, the able from the incapable. Human beings then perform their duties of their station in life and to receive their dues ... That is the way (*Tao*) to make the whole populace live together in harmony and unity.[118]

Human beings are distinct from other beings because they have, among other things, natural rationality. Because of natural rationality humans have *bian*. '*Bian*' refers to human ability to recognize distinctions between things, especially social distinctions and divisions, and the ability to incorporate those distinctions into social behavior codes.[119] 'Animals and birds have parents and offspring, but they do not have consistent and socialized love between father and son. Animals and birds have differences between male and female, but they do not have consistent and socialized separation of sexes.'[120] Thus, *bian* is essential to the way of human. Because of bian, social distinctions and divisions are recognized; based on social distinctions and divisions, *Li* is established.

Ren provides a unifying perspective for Confucius's system; so does it for Mencius's system. The conceptual unity of Xun Zi's system needs to be examined. Antonio S. Cua argues for what he calls 'the completion thesis.'[121] According to that thesis, 'As an ideal way of life, *Tao* provides a unifying perspective for evaluating human life as a whole. In this sense *Tao* is basically a holistic thesis.'[122] Xun Zi speaks of *Tao* in many different ways. The following three, however, are important. First, influenced by Taoism, he speaks of *Tao* as natural patterns (*logos*) by which things in universe change. He says, '*Tian* has a constant *Tao*.'[123] *Tao* in that sense cannot be the unifying force of human activities or the unifying perspective for a moral system. Second, *Tao* is used as a value-free term. It is purely epistemological. A good translation of it may be 'truth.' Xun Zi says: 'In the doctrine grounded on utility, *Tao* ends up with calculation of profit. In the doctrine grounded on human desires, *Tao* ends up with seeking satisfaction. In the doctrine grounded on law, *Tao* ends up with making legal intrigues ... Each of those doctrines includes but one single corner of *Tao*. However, *Tao* itself is unchangeable in its form yet embraces varying perspectives and embodies constant changes. One corner is insufficient to ground it.'[124]

It is clear that *Tao* as used in the above passage is value-neutral. It is in that sense that Xun Zi repeatedly says that *Tao* is 'the standard' (*quan* or *heng*).[125] The notion of truth of any system cannot be the unifying perspective of that system. Third, *Tao* is a moral term. It is no longer value free. There *Tao* specifically refers to *Tao* of human beings (*ren tao*). When talking about *Tao* of early Kings, Xun Zi says, '*Tao* is not *Tao* of *Tian* or *Tao* of Earth. It is *Tao* of human beings, *Tao* of the sages.'[126] *Tao* of human beings is the primary use of *Tao* in

Xun Zi. A passage in 'The Great Compendium' reads that only when *Ren, Yi,* and *Li* have been fully understood is one a person of *Tao*.[127] Cua takes that passage as evidence for 'the completion thesis,' the view that *Tao* is the unifying perspective for Xun Zi's system.[128]

There are, however, at least two problems with Cua's view. First, as Han Yu says in 'An Investigation of *Tao*' (*yuan dao*), *Tao* is purely formal (*xu wei*). It has no content. That is why any substantial use of '*Tao*' takes the form of '*Tao* of something' – *Tao* of *Tian*, *Tao* of *Earth*, and so on. A bare term '*Tao*' is empty. In the above passage, *Tao* is not used in a general sense. It characteristically refers to *Tao* of human beings. Therefore, Cua cannot draw a general conclusion to say that *Tao* is the unifying perspective for Xun Zi. The only inference from that passage Cua can draw has to be this: *Tao* of human beings is the unifying perspective. Second, to say that *Tao* of human beings provides unity for Xun Zi's system, however, is at best inaccurate. For '*Tao* of human beings' is still too general, or too formal. '*Tao* of human beings' in Confucius is *Ren*. So is it in Mencius. Cua is mistaken for not going further to account for what is '*Tao* of human beings' in Xun Zi. 'What is the unifying perspective of Xun Zi's system' is then the same question as 'what is '*Tao* of human beings' in Xun Zi.' One view is that it is *Ren*. That view may have some evidence:

> *Ren* is the manifestation of love, thus it is expressed in one's treatment of relatives. *Yi* is the manifestation of natural order (*li*), thus it is practical. *Li* is the manifestation of measured moderation, thus it leads to completion (success). *Ren* is like the village where one dwells; *Yi* like the gate to one's dwelling. Where *Ren* is not the village where one dwells, there is no *Ren*. Where *Yi* is not the gate through which one proceeds, there is no *Yi* ... Only after one dwells with *Ren* and proceeds through *Yi* is one truly a person of *Ren*. Only after one practice *Yi* according to *Li* is one truly a person of *Yi*. Only when one regulates with *Li*, returning to the root [*Ren*] and perfecting the branch, is one truly a person of *Li*.[129]

It is fair to say that Xun Zi sometimes takes an equivocal attitude on the importance of *Ren*. As a master of Confucianism, he is heavily influenced by Mencius and, in particular, Confucius. So he sometimes, as in that passage, seems to be giving *Ren* the central place. However, that conclusion is too quick. Although Xun Zi admits that human beings have the capacity for *Ren* and *Yi*, he claims human nature to be evil. *Ren* can only be nurtured by *Li*. He actually centers his moral and political thought on *Li*, for *Li* is more basic than *Ren*. '*Tao* of human beings' is the unifying force of human activities. What is '*Tao* of human beings?' Xun Zi says, '*Li* is the extreme of *Tao* of humans.'[130] He also says that

Li is 'the extreme of virtues.'[131] Neither *Tao* nor *Ren* is the unifying perspective for Xun Zi's system. *Li* serves as such a perspective.

Mencius is a deontologist. For him, the right takes precedence over the good unconditionally, because he sets the good and the right at opposite poles. Xun Zi does not agree with Mencius. He says that the good and the right are two sides of one coin. The right is supposed to regulate the good; but it is not supposed to rid of the desires for the good: 'A sense of the right and a desire for the good are both possessed by human beings. Although they were unable to get rid of the desires for the good in people, Yao and Shun [two ancient sage Kings] nonetheless were able to educate them not to allow their desire for the good to triumph over their sense of the right. Although they were unable to get rid of people's sense of the right, Jie and Zhou [two ancient evil Kings] could nonetheless cause their desire for the good to conquer their sense of the right. Thus, a well-ordered society will be the result if people's desire for the good is effectively regulated by the right; and social chaos will be the result if people's desire is not regulated.'[132] Xun Zi, within this framework of the right and the good, advocates the moral and political principle of 'maximize good, minimize harm.'[133] He, however, is not an utilitarian, precisely because of his unique characterization of the relationship between the right and the good. Partially because of his emphasis on the good (and partially because of his thesis of human nature as evil), Xun Zi has been treated unfairly by later Confucians, especially by Neo-Confucians. It is my judgment that Xun Zi actually has a deeper understanding than Mencius of human society in terms of the right and the good.

Xun Zi's view about a ruler, however, is similar to that of Mencius. As pointed out, Mencius distinguishes between a *wang* and a *ba*. The former is a king who rules by virtue, and the latter a king who rules by force. Mencius believes that only a *wang* is morally acceptable and thus a real king. So does Xun Zi. He says that the responsibility to rule a country is the heaviest therefore only the strongest person can take it. That person has to be the ablest to make social distinctions and divisions in society and has to be the ablest to bring harmony in society. Who could be such a person? Only a *wang* (sage king).[134] Like Hobbes, Xun Zi says that a king (or sovereignty) has the absolute power. However, that presupposes that the king rules by virtue. Unlike Hobbes, Xun Zi believes that if a king does not observe rules of *Li* or govern by virtue or promote people's interest, common people have the right to remove him, even through revolution.[135] Hobbes believes that once a sovereign is established, citizens have to obey it unconditionally. The sovereignty may happen to promote people's interest, but it does not necessarily need to do so. Revolution is never allowed.

Mo Zi: the General Will and Natural Law

Mo Zi lived later than Confucius, but earlier than both Mencius and Xun Zi. He was the founder of Mohism, which was as influential as Confucianism in ancient times. I put him after Mencius and Xun Zi not for chronological but for doctrinal reasons. The contrasts between Mohism and Confucianism run very deep. Actually Mohism is in many regards a refutation of Confucianism. Interestingly, Mo Zi, different from any other major classical philosophers, seems making a sort of religious and transcendental claim for the validity of moral and political principles. He talks about *Tian-Zhi* (the will of heaven) and the existence of spirits. Those ideas were already outdated in his time. A closer analysis, however, suggests that those seemingly superhuman and supernatural claims are really claims about human beings themselves.

Like Confucians, Mo Zi speaks of *Ren* and *Yi*. What he means by those terms, however, are very different. Confucianism claims that love starts from a family setting and then extends to non-family members, to society. Thus love for one's father and love for a countryman are different; love for the king and love for a minister are different. That is to say, love is differentiated according to different family and social relationships. Mo Zi calls that kind of love partiality (*bian*), as opposing to universal love (*jan*) – love being equally and unconditionally extended to any human being. According to Mo Zi, the lack of universal love gives rise to various evils.

> The sage who gives peace to the world should know the origin of disorder. What is the origin? It is the lack of love for one another (universal love) ... If a son loves himself and not his father, he would then seek gain at the expense of his father. If a younger brother loves himself and not his elder brother, he would then seek gain at the expense of his brother. If a minister loves himself and not his emperor, he would then seek gain at the expense of his emperor. All those are what are called disorder. If the father shows no affection to the son, if the elder brother shows no affection to his younger brother, and if the emperor shows no affection to the minister, disorder is the result ... All the disorder is due to the lack of love for one another (universal love). A robber loves his own house but not that of the other, so he robs it to enrich his own house. A thief loves himself but not the other person, so he steals from that person to enrich himself ... All the disorder is due to the lack of love for one another.[136]

What brings the greatest harm to the world? Big states attacking small ones, big families overthrowing small ones, the strong oppressing the weak, the many harrying the few, the cunning deceiving the stupid, the eminent lording it over the humble – those are harmful to the world. So too are rulers who are not generous, minister who are not loyal ... What is the origin of all those harms? Do they come about from loving each other and trying to benefit each other? Surely not ... Do they come from universality or partiality? Surely partiality.[137]

Partiality in love, according to Mo Zi, is precisely the origin of social evils. For partial love, for example, self-interest, leads people to fight over property and other material goods. For Mo Zi, the solution to social disorder is universal love: 'If people were to regard the countries of others as they regard their own, then who would raise up his country to attack the country of another? If people were to regard the cities of others as they regard their own, then who would raise up his city to attack the city of another? It would be like attacking his own. If people were to regard the families of others as they regard their own, then who would raise up his family to overthrow that of another? It would be like overthrowing his own.'[138] Thus, universal love is the solution to the problems partial love causes.

Although Mo Zi appeals to *Tian-Zhi* (the will of heaven, which I shall specify below) for the validity of his principle of universal love, he also offers a utilitarian basis for it. Mo Zi says that any doctrine, any social and political principle must meet some standards. What are those standards? Mo Zi gives the three-standard formula, that is, any doctrine or social and political principle must be (1) historically well-founded; (2) socially examined; and (3) practically profitable. For any moral and political principle, its basis is to be found in the undertakings of the ancient sage kings. Its acceptability is to be examined against the experience of the people. It has to be put into law and governmental measures to test whether it brings about benefits (utilities) to the nation and the people. The most important of the three is the last, that is, the practical benefit standard. Mo Zi says, 'It is the business of the benevolent person to seek to promote what is beneficial to the world, to eliminate what is harmful, and to provide a standard for the world. Whatever benefits people he will carry out; whatever does not he will leave alone.'[139] Universal love brings peace, order, and security of property in a society, thus it is a great beneficial doctrine.[140]

Mo Zi is the first philosopher to define *Yi* (the right) in terms of *li* (the good). He says that what is the right (righteousness) is what is the good (public goods or social utilities). Utility for Mo Zi is exclusively social (general). That is why the central standard in his three-standard formula is based on 'the benefits (utilities) of the nation and the people.' The highest utility, according Mo Zi, is the thriving of a country.[141] There are three great worries of the people that arise from the poverty of a country. 'The hungry cannot be fed, the cold cannot be clothed, and the tired cannot get rest.' There is also another set of worries arising from the lack of moral and political codes. 'The strong plunder the weak, the many oppress the few, the clever deceive the stupid, and the honored disdain the humble.'[142] The highest utility is a commodious and moral life and a flourishing society in which all those worries are healed.

Mo Zi, however, is a radical utilitarian. He says that a thing should not be done if it does not bring about concrete profit (li). Confucianism considers music as essential to human life, but Mo Zi is against it. He does not think that a society should put its efforts – financial or labour – on music while the common people do not have enough food to survive. Confucianism considers proper funeral ceremony as important. Again, Mo Zi is against it. He does not think people should put any more money and labor on funeral above the minimal need. He even goes so far as to denounce many human feelings as useless, and thus to be suppressed.[143] He also says that private interest should be limited to the minimal level of life necessities. Anything beyond that limit should be sacrificed for the common good.[144] Mohism is criticized by Confucianism. Xun Zi, for example, says that, 'Mo Zi is blinded by utility and insensible to the value of good form.'[145]

Of the origin of political society, Mo Zi turns to a notion similar to, again, Hobbes's notion of the state of nature:

> In the days of old when there were no government and law everyone observed nothing but his own standard of right (Yi). As people's standards were different, one person had one standard, two had two different standards ... The bigger the population was, the more the standards existed. Everyone held his own standard and despised that of any other; what followed was mutual destruction. As a result, father and son, elder brother and younger brother became enemies and were estranged from each other, for they were unable to reach any agreement. Everyone worked for the disadvantage of the others. Just like water and fire, they could not get along, hating one another like poison. Surplus energy was not spent for mutual aid; surplus wealth was allowed rot without sharing; excellent ideas (Tao) were kept secret and not revealed. Chaos was the only order when human beings lived together like beasts.[146]

The solution to these evils is a general agreement on what is the right standard.[147] Although both Mo Zi and Xun Zi have a notion of the state of nature, which are both similar to that of Hobbes, they pose different reasons for the necessity of a political society. For Xun Zi, only a political society can be characterized by unity and solidarity. Thus, only a political society can have the power to dominate and make the best use of nature to produce the necessary goods for human life. For Mo Zi, only in a political society can people reach a general agreement on what is the right (*Yi*), which in turn governs the society.

Mo Zi advocates a theory of general agreement in sorting out the governing principles of *Yi* (righteousness). There are three chapters in Mo Zi entitled '*Shang Tong*'; *Tong* means 'to identify' or 'identification,' and *shang* means 'the superior' or 'to advocate' or 'advocating.' '*Shang Tong*' can be translated as 'to identify one's *Yi* with that of one's superior' or 'to advocate a general agreement on what is the right.' Many critics believe that Mo Zi uses '*Shang Tong*' only in the first sense. That is wrong. Mo Zi uses it in both senses, as Liang Qichao suggests.[148] On the one hand, Mo Zi does indeed say, 'The chaos came about because of the absence of rulers and leaders. Therefore the most virtuous and able person was selected and set up as the Son of Heaven (emperor) ... When the rulers were all installed, the Son of Heaven proclaimed the principle of his rule to the people of the world, saying 'Upon hearing of good or evil, one shall report to one's superior. What the superior considers right, all shall consider right; what the superior considers wrong, all shall consider wrong. To identify (*Tong*) oneself with one's superior and not to form cliques on the lower levels.'[149]

On the other hand, Mo Zi accents that the function of the rulers is to identify all the *Yis* of the world, that is, to advocate the general agreement on what is the right. '*Shang Tong*' is used in both senses. To advocate the general agreement, according to Mo Zi, is for the rulers to take into consideration 'the real perspectives of the common people.'[150] In the second sense, the concept of '*Shang Tong*' is similar to the social contract theory as found in, among others, Rousseau. Mo Zi actually uses the term of contract (*yue*) to explain the establishment of the relation between the emperor and the people.[151] Mo Zi claims that the general agreement of *Yi* has to be reached among all people. He also holds that once an agreement is established, everyone must be forced to identify one's *Yi* with the general agreement, which is also the *Yi* of the Son of Heaven (the highest ruler, the sovereignty).[152] That makes him even more similar to Rousseau, for the latter claims that after the sovereignty is established, every member of the society must, if necessary, be forced to support the agreement in order to be free.

Mo Zi says that the will of heaven (*Tian-Zhi*) is behind the general agreement on the right and the universal love. In other words, the validity of all moral and political principles is founded on the will of heaven, just as the validity of all moral and political principles in Christianity is founded on God's will. According to Mo Zi, everyone has incentives to obey the will of heaven. 'One who obeys the will of heaven, loving all humans universally and working for their benefit, will surely win reward. But one who disobeys the will of heaven, showing partiality and hatred and working to the disadvantage of others, will surely incur punishment.'[153] What is *Tian's* (Heaven's) will? Universal love, righteousness, and the common good.

Both Fung Yu-lan and Liang Qichao claim that Mo Zi is very religious. Liang explicitly says that Mo Zi's doctrine is very close to that of Christianity.[154] I would defend Qian Mu's position, according to which the notion of *Tian-Zhi* is not essential to Mo Zi's doctrine; thus Mo Zi is not essentially religious (*The Complete Work of Mr. Qian Tsin-si*, Vol. 6, 35). Upon close analysis, we find that the will of heaven is actually what Rousseau would call the general will. According to Rousseau, the general will is formed from the wills of the people. It aims at what is in everyone's interest. Although claiming the will of heaven (*Tian*), Mo Zi does not believe people's fate is determined by *Tian*. He has argued that it is human efforts rather than any superhuman power that determines human fate. And according to Mo Zi, all human efforts aim at the public goods. Mo Zi's notion of *Tian* is different from any transcendental notion of superhuman power; and the will of *Tian* is the reflection of the wills of the people. He says that *Tian* and human beings desire the same thing.[155] Mo Zi gives an example of the will of heaven: 'Why would *Tian* desire *Yi* (righteousness)? In the world, where there is *Yi* there is life; where there is no *Yi* there is death. Where there is *Yi* there is wealth; where there is no *Yi* there is disorder.'[156] *Tian* desires *Yi* because humans desire *Yi*. *Tian* also desires, as has been said, universal love, government, and order because individuals commonly desire them. The will of *Tian* then combines the wills of people; that is, it is the general will.

Concluding Observations

I make a few observations in concluding this essay

Observation 1

Does Chinese philosophical tradition contain the idea of natural law? If natural law is defined broadly, then the answer is yes. The broader definition is the following: natural law is a set of moral, social, and political norms which (1) have universal validity among human beings, that is, must be heeded by any flourishing individual and any thriving society, and (2) are given either by God or by nature, including human nature and the nature of society. Classical Chinese philosophers I have discussed in this paper all believe that there exists a set of universal principles, which must be observed by any flourishing society and individual. The difference between Chinese philosophers from their Western counterparts lies in the fact that Chinese philosophers do not appeal to God for the universal validity of natural law. Confucius finds the ground of natural law in his notion of humanity. Mencius finds it in human nature; Xun Zi finds it in social needs; and Mo Zi finds it in the general will. There are some obvious similarities between Confucius and Aristotle or St Thomas, between Mencius and Hume, between Xun Zi and Hobbes, and between Mo Zi and Rousseau.

Observation 2

Concerning the relation between individuals and society, most Chinese philosophers are against individualism, the view that it is individual that is the center of social life and that the value of individual is above the value of society. Western natural law theorists such as Hobbes and Locke are in one way or another individualists. Confucianism says that only a flourishing society can bring up flourishing individuals and only flourishing individuals can contribute to a flourishing society. The relation between individuals and society is harmonized by a holistic value of individuals and society. The theory of self-cultivation serves as the bridge between individuals and society:

> The ancients who wished to illustrate illustrious virtue throughout the world, first ordered well their own states. Wishing to order well their own states, they first regulated their families. Wishing to regulate their families, they first cultivated their persons. Wishing to cultivate their persons, they first rectified their hearts (*xin*). Wishing to rectify their hearts, they first sought to be sincere in their thoughts. Wishing to be sincere in their thoughts, they first extended to the utmost their knowledge. Such extension of knowledge lay in the investigation of things. Things being investigated, knowledge became complete. Their knowledge being complete, their thoughts were sincere. Their thoughts being sincere, their hearts were then rectified. Their hearts being rectified, their persons were cultivated. Their persons being cultivated, their families were regulated. Their families being regulated, their states were rightly governed. Their states being rightly governed, the whole world was made peaceful and happy. (*The Great Learning*)[157]

Observation 3

Chinese civilization is basically non-religious. It does not produce a native religion of its own. Later Taoists put some of their mysterious doctrines into practice, but they are never widely accepted. After being introduced into China, Buddhism incorporates some native Chinese doctrines to form a relatively independent religion, Chinese Buddhism. Chinese Buddhism, however, did not produce significant influence until much later in history. As a matter of fact, Chinese Buddhism has never been fully accepted by Confucian thinkers in history. For the purpose of this essay, I shall not go to the details about the relevance of Chinese Buddhism to natural law theory.[158]

Notes

1 Did Medieval Natural Law Die Out?

1 Sigmund Freud, in *Introductory Lectures on Psychoanalysis*, trans. J. Strachey (New York: Liveright, 1966), 316, says, 'Sexual activity [is] perverse if it has given up the aim of reproduction and pursues the attainment of pleasure as an aim independent of it.' He is in part just reporting prevailing opinion; but he associates the distinction with 'the breach and turning-point in the development of sexual life,' which 'lies in its becoming subordinate to the purposes of reproduction.'

2 In his recent book, *Aquinas: Moral, Political, and Legal Theory* (Oxford: Oxford University Press, 1998), 143–54.

3 Robert P. George and Patrick Lee, 'What Sex Can Be,' in George's *In Defense of Natural Law* (Oxford: Clarendon Press, 1999), 161–83, 170.

4 Ibid., 181.

5 Along with Pope John Paul II. George and Lee, 'What Sex Can Be,' 161 and note.

6 Ibid., 179.

7 I repudiate the passages in St Thomas's *Summa Theologiae* slighting women, including *ST*, 2a2ae, Q.156, 1, which declares women (most women) weaker in temperament than men and hence less resistant to temptation; 2a2ae, Q.163, 4, in a series of ruminations on a literal reading of the story of the Fall in the Garden of Eden, which says that the man was more perfect than the woman, and so far his sin would have been more grievous, though in this case the woman's sin was more grievous because it came from being 'puffed up with pride' to defy God's will; 2a2ae, Q.70, 3, which says that women's evidence (like that of children and imbeciles) may through 'a defect in the reason' be less reliable than men's; and *ST*, 1a, Q.92, 1, 2, 3,

which holds that the procedure used to create the woman in *Genesis* was appropriate as giving her less dignity than the man and putting her under his authority.

8 George, in fact, invokes the now happily past disagreement about slavery as a parallel to the present disagreement about abortion and homosexuality, which he holds requires patience on the part of the morally enlightened, but which he hopes will eventually be resolved according to his principles (219). In granting George and his allies readiness to accept the equality of women, I am relying chiefly on the absence of evidence to the contrary. They do not argue for the view, traditional in natural law theory, for the subordination of women. I may be being too generous. Searching George's works for references to women, I have found only two, in which the equality of women is mentioned as a consideration that Rawls and Judith Thomson take to favour a pro-choice view of abortion. The consideration drops out of sight immediately in George's counterargument. It is not even given the courtesy of explaining why it drops out. See George, *In Defense of Natural Law*, 206f. Finnis is more forthcoming; in *Natural Law and Natural Rights* at 217, he calls for treating women not 'as mere items in an erotically flavoured classification' but 'as full persons with personal and individual sensitivities, restraints, and life-plans.' Unfortunately, this does not go all the way to calling for treating women as having equal dignity with men. St Thomas, in denying that women have equal dignity with men, is not denying that they are full persons, though of a subordinate order. In his later book, *Aquinas*, Finnis makes substantial amends for this omission. He admits that even when read with 'great caution' St Thomas's statements about the subordination of women 'seem seriously flawed' (171); he asserts roundly that women should be regarded as fully equal in rights to men (172); he argues that a foundation for this equality (as well as for the rejection of slavery) can be found in St Thomas's basic account of freedom and equality (176).

9 Forty days after conception for males; 80, for females. *ST*, 1a, Q.118, 2. The figures are not given in the text, but in a note by the translator in the Blackfriars edition; I have not so far found the text in St Thomas. It has been argued in Catholic circles up to the present day that abortion during those periods would not be homicide; but it would still be ruled out by the prohibition of contraception. See Germain G. Grisez, *Abortion: The Myths, The Realities, and the Arguments* (New York: Corpus Books, 1970), 282.

10 I have been delighted to have this account of what is to be made in the first instance of the paramount passage in St Thomas confirmed – after writing my account out – by reading the brief but pregnant article by Columba

Ryan, OP,' The Traditional Concept of Natural Law,' in Illtud Evans, OP, ed., *Light on the Natural Law* (London: Burns and Oates, 1965), 13–37, which strives to make the traditional concept of natural law attractive to modern thinking by taking a stand on its general approach rather than on particular conclusions. It is a view very distant from particular strict regulations of sexual activity. I am much readier than Ryan, however, to go on from the paramount passage to specific prohibitions in other matters.

11 Anthony J. Lisska, *Aquinas's Theory of Natural Law: An Analytical Reconstruction* (Oxford: Clarendon Press, 1996), 119.

12 In their books, respectively, *Natural Law and Moral Philosophy: From Grotius to the Scottish Enlightenment* (Cambridge: Cambridge University Press, 1996), and *The Invention of Autonomy: A History of Modern Moral Philosophy* (Cambridge: Cambridge University Press, 1998).

13 *Thomas Hobbes and the Natural Law Tradition*, trans. D. Gobetti (Chicago: University of Chicago Press, 1993).

14 'In Defense of Natural Law,' in Sidney Hook, ed., *Law and Philosophy* (New York: New York University Press, 1964), 105–21.

15 *The Invention of Autonomy*, 145, 151, 155.

16 'Promises, Promises, Promises,' in *Postures of the Mind* (Minneapolis: University of Minnesota Press, 1985), 174–206, at 176.

17 *Natural Law and Justice* (Cambridge, Mass.: Harvard University Press, 1987), 83.

18 (New York: Oxford University Press).

19 (Oxford: Clarendon Press, 1980).

20 See Finnis's *Aquinas*, vii.

21 Russell Hittinger, *A Critique of the New Natural Law Theory* (Notre Dame, Indiana: University of Notre Dame Press, 1987), 5.

22 Finnis, *Aquinas*, vii.

23 Finnis, Grisez, Boyle, and George seem to be arrayed in current Catholic thinking against the 'proportionalists,' represented by figures like Garth Hallett, Richard McCormick, and (in a volume of essays edited in honour of Grisez by George, namely, *Natural Law and Moral Inquiry* (Washington, DC: Georgetown University Press, 1998) Edward C. Vacek, SJ. Proportionalists try to moderate the application of categorical prohibitions regarding such things as abortion and contraception. But they are almost as frightened of references to 'consequences' in moral decisions as Finnis et al. None of these writers seem to allow properly in theory for having consequences brought in only under some principled constraints, which is the utilitarian position; or for proceeding tentatively, and thus without having to know all the consequences in advance. On the first point, see my essay 'The Concept

of Needs, with a Heartwarming Offer of Help to Utilitarianism,' in Gillian Brock, ed., *Necessary Goods* (Latham, Md.: Rowman and Littlefield, 1998) and 'Utilitarianism with a Difference,' my critical notice in *Canadian Journal of Philosophy* (3 [Dec. 1973], 303–31) of Rawls's *A Theory of Justice*. On the second point, see David Braybrooke and C.E. Lindblom, *A Theory of Decision* (New York: Free Press, 1963), chaps. 9–10.

24 'Natural Law,' *International Encyclopedia of the Social Sciences* (New York: Collier-Macmillan).

25 *A History of Political Theory*, 3rd ed. (New York: Holt, Rinehart and Winston, 1961), 544; and see chap. 27 ('The Decadence of Natural Law') with the section in the chapter (29) on Hume and Burke entitled 'The Destruction of Natural Law.' Stephen Darwall, in his *The British Moralists and the Internal 'Ought': 1640–1740* (Cambridge: Cambridge University Press, 1995), 4–7, is another writer who finds 'classical natural law' opposed to 'modern natural law.' Darwall, in my view, fails to appreciate the extent to which (as one would expect of a Christian thinker) St Thomas is well aware of the sinfulness of human beings or the effect of his theoretical position that natural tendencies to heed the natural law have been offset since original sin by widespread fractiousness. This brings him into substantial convergence with Grotius's position that self-interest may lead people to flout norms 'essential to the social order.'

26 Schneewind, *Autonomy* (see 12 above).

27 Knud Haakonssen can be read in support of this point; see, e.g., Haakonssen, 6, 44, 50, 61; and support can be found also in Stephen Buckle, *Natural Law and the Theory of Property* (Oxford: Clarendon Press, 1991).

28 Buckle endorses the view that natural law theory, in the seventeenth and eighteenth centuries, was a secular theory, the possibility of which can be found maintained by Finnis and Lisska as well (see below, chap. 2, note 20). Buckle says (*Property*, 261), 'Developing a system of morals in which God plays no part need not be seen as a problem, even from a theistic point of view,' for 'God will ... be absent, but not denied, in any account of the natural moral order if the constitution of nature is indeed a fully interlocking system capable of harmonious functioning without relying on the cosmic repair man.' Given that God created the system, 'the extent to which [an account of the system] avoids a role for special divine action will be directly proportionate to its conception of the efficacy of the original divine creative act.'

29 In referring to 'a hierarchy of ends,' I do not mean to be taking a position on the contention by Finnis, Grisez et al. that basic human goods are incommensurable, doubtful as I am inclined to think the contention. 'Hierarchy' here may have just to do with levels of vital complexity.

30 Richard Tuck finds two distinctive features in natural law theory as it was worked out in the seventeenth century by Grotius, Hobbes, and others: First, that it was designed, as medieval natural law theory was not, to deal with scepticism; second, that following Grotius's lead, the design fell back on self-preservation as its ground. 'The "modern" theory of natural law,' in Anthony Pagden, ed., *The Languages of Political Theory in Early-Modern Europe* (Cambridge: Cambridge University Press, 1987), 99–119. The design may have given more prominence to self-preservation than St Thomas did, though it was prominent in his view, but self-preservation did not become (in the authors that I treat) the sole principle – what would be the sole axiom were the theory to be set forth systematically. Though Hobbes begins with avoiding self-destruction, Locke ranks the preservation of others almost as high as the preservation of oneself; Hume and Rousseau make a good deal of the emotions that impel people to mutual aid – humanity and pity, respectively. Tuck cites Grotius as asserting a principle forbidding 'wanton injury' to other human beings.

31 *On Kingship*, trans. G.B. Phelan, rev. I.T. Eschmann (Toronto: Pontifical Institute, 1949), 25–9.

32 Richard Tuck, *Natural Rights Theories*: Their origin and development (Cambridge: Cambridge University Press, 1979), chap. 1.

33 Finnis, *Natural Law and Natural Rights*, chap. 8. In his later work, *Aquinas* (1998), Finnis shifts his position somewhat and purports to find the concept of rights freely in use by St Thomas himself. However, Finnis admits that St Thomas 'never uses a term translatable as "human rights"' (136) and that 'the modern language of rights' at least as employed by Hobbes, 'is certainly different from Aquinas' [language] in very significant ways' (180). Referring back to his earlier book for an explanation of the difference and his earlier position regarding it, I think I prefer the more cautious position taken in the earlier book, that the modern concept of rights offers a congenial and useful addition to St Thomas's doctrine, whether or not it is present there.

34 A point worked out by Keith McLaughlin in a master's essay at the University of Texas in 1991.

35 It is noteworthy that Schneewind is (he says) not quite sure that Bentham fits into the perspective of autonomy. The objective of the Greatest Happiness is to be achieved by adopting rules that empirical evidence implies would be effective in this regard; hence Benthamism is a variety of naturalism. In spite, however, of the family connection with his own position, Bentham denounced natural law theory because of his opposition to the routine misuse of natural law terminology in received jurisprudence. See *Introduction to the Principles of Morals and Legislation* (New York: Hafner,

1948), chap. 2, ss. 14–18, with Bentham's footnotes. Bentham – in the footnote to the first chapter of *Morals and Legislation* that says the Greatest Happiness Principle is the only one that can be recommended by someone speaking to the community – in effect recognizes the Kantian conditions for moral legislation. Thus Benthamism is both an ethics with an empirical foundation and one that means to appeal to every rational agent ready to act only on publicly defensible reasons.

36 See, e.g., Haakonssen, 6, 46, 50–1, 71, 90, 107.

37 Ibid., 48–9, 55–8, 65, 68.

38 Sabine, 424, 598–604.

39 See Finnis, *Natural Law and Natural Rights*; Finnis and Grisez, 'The Basic Principles of Natural Law: A Reply to Ralph McInerny, *American Journal of Jurisprudence*, 26 (1981), 21–31; Grisez, Boyle, and Finnis, 'Practical Principles, Moral Truths, and Ultimate Ends,' *American Journal of Jurisprudence*, 32 (1987), 99–151.

40 A story told by St Thomas: *ST*, 1a2ae, Q.96, 6.

2 Locke's Natural Law and St Thomas's: Secular in Content, Empirical in Foundation

1 John Locke, *Questions concerning the Law of Nature*, with an introduction, [Latin] text, and translation by Robert Horwitz, Jenny Strauss Clay, and Diskin Clay (Ithaca, New York: Cornell University Press, 1990). Horwitz strongly insists upon calling the ingredients of the book *Questions*, taking them to be set up as disputations of the medieval type. The manuscript was first published in an edition and translation by W. von Leyden, who gave it the title *Essays on the Law of Nature* (Oxford: Clarendon Press, 1954). I shall refer to *Essays/Questions*, citing the translations in the Horwitz edition.

2 Princeton: Princeton University Press, 1992.

3 See above, in chap. 1.

4 Simmons does argue that Locke's doctrine of natural rights can be given a secular guise, 104. He also finds 'secular and religious conceptions of humankind and morality' so intermingled in the body of Locke's arguments as to invite 'pursuing a secular, but nonetheless Lockean project in moral and political philosophy,' 45. So, even if he does not go about pursuing it in my way, I would not expect to find him opposed to the results.

5 Richard Hooker, author of *Laws of Ecclesiastical Polity*, a work often cited by Locke in his *Second Treatise on Civil Government*.

6 *Essays/Questions*, 169.

7 Ibid., 231.

8 Ibid., 115.

9 Ibid., 125.

10 Ibid., Question V, 169.

11 Instead of 'our happiness,' a broader term might be used – 'our happiness about ourselves and about each other,' which could be taken to include sensual and spiritual happiness from moment to moment and as well contentment with our lives and life-plans (maybe very loose ones) on reviewing them.

12 *Essays/Questions*, 237.

13 Simmons, 48.

14 Simmons also cites, ibid., (among other paragraphs more suited to his reading) par. 159, but there Locke identifies the 'Fundamental Law of Nature and Government' as 'that as much as may be, *all* the Members of the Society are to be *preserved*' (Locke's italics).

15 Simmons, 48.

16 Haakonssen reports that Locke was in continual trouble with his contemporaries about a tendency to make God's activity with respect to natural law redundant. Knud Haakonssen, *Natural Law and Moral Philosophy* (Cambridge: Cambridge University Press, 1996), 55–8. Schneewind suggests that the contemporaries thought the empiricist cast of Locke's approach led either to making God redundant or to making him an arbitrary ('voluntaristic') tyrant. J.B. Schneewind, *The Invention of Autonomy* (Cambridge: Cambridge University Press, 1998), 158–9. The contemporaries were not reacting to the *Essays/Questions*, my main reliance, but to later works, published in Locke's lifetime. But just with the *Essays/Questions* in mind, and my analysis of the a posteriori argument and its relation to the official argument there, I would say, the trouble is very understandable. Schneewind (159) portrays it as the main difficulty into which Locke was led by 'empiricism.' Since my position is that the natural law is arrived at on empirical grounds, without any essential reference to God, this is no problem for me.

17 See below, chapter 5.

18 See below, the discussion in chapter 7 of Copp's *Morality, Normativity, and Society.*

19 Schneewind, in a passage of rather strained argument (149–52), makes Locke out by implication to be a voluntarist, and thus subject to additional trouble. Simmons takes him to be 'predominantly' a voluntarist (33–4), but finds a strong intellectualist strain running in Locke's thinking as well (38–9).

20 Notably, Anthony J. Lisska, who aligns St Thomas with Aristotle in his

reliance on the empirically discovered essences of things. See Lisska's *Aquinas's Theory of Natural Law: An Analytic Reconstruction* (Oxford: Clarendon Press, 1996), Chapter 4, see 137. My friend Arthur Monahan, a historian of medieval and modern political thought, takes the same view. John Finnis in *Natural Law and Natural Rights* (Oxford: Clarendon Press, 1980), 48–9, holds on different grounds that St Thomas's natural law theory can be laid out without invoking God. See also the passage cited in the previous chapter from Stephen Buckle's *Natural Law and the Theory of Property.* In all these passages, the question of content takes precedence over the question of authority.

21 In *ST,* 1a2ae, Q.91, 3, St Thomas cites Cicero for the point that the natural laws arise by custom and are approved thereby because of their utility. Nothing is said about the custom being associated with theistic belief; nor does the account of the procedures of practical reason in the same passage make any reference to theistic beliefs. In article 2 of the same Question St Thomas does invoke Divine providence and the Divine light by which – through participation in the Eternal Reason – we discover natural law; but even there St Thomas does not insist that the light is imparted only to believers.

22 *ST,* 1a2ae, Q.95, 1. The assertion at the beginning of this passage that 'man has a natural aptitude for virtue' seems to have reached some later writers, e.g., Stephen Darwall, *The British Moralists and the Internal 'Ought'* (Cambridge: Cambridge University Press, 1995, 4–5), unaccompanied by what follows about how without training man is inclined 'above all' to undue pleasures and evil-doing.

23 As explicitly maintained by Lisska, who adopts it in expounding St Thomas.

24 The mind, reeling from the impact of multiple sense-experiences, like an army in rout, rallies, takes a stand at one point, then at another, and seizes the universal, feature by feature (Aristotle, *Posterior Analytics,* II, xix).

25 This is the view of rules elaborated with my co-authors Bryson Brown and P.K. Schotch in *Logic on the Track of Social Change* (Oxford: Clarendon Press, 1995). See esp. chap. 2.

26 Finnis, *Aquinas,* 86–7.

27 Grisez, 'The First Principle of Practical Reason: A Commentary on the *Summa Theologiae, 1–2, Question 94, Article 2,'* *Natural Law Forum,* 10 (1965), 168–201.

28 Among these commentators are some very distinguished ones, including Peter Laslett, in his edition of Locke's *Two Treatises of Government* (Cambridge: Cambridge University Press, 1988, see 81–2) and C.E. Vaughan, in his *Studies in the History of Political Philosophy Before and After Rousseau* (reprinted New York: Russell and Russell, 1969, see vol. 1, 163). But I think

they take such expressions as 'knowable by the light of nature' or even 'inscribed in the heart' ('writ in the hearts of men') as too literally opposed to easily acquiring knowledge of the laws from experience in a way expectable of everybody, given human nature and circumstances. Vaughan, in particular, says things that straightjacket Locke rather than understand him: 'If there ever was an innate idea, it is the law of nature, as expounded in the *Civil Government* of Locke. It springs fully armed from the brain of man, at the very dawn of his history. It owes nothing to experience. It is the gift of intuition, pure and simple.' This is not the way that Locke treats knowledge of the natural laws in *Essays/Questions* – he treats it as something acquired from experience by the use of our natural faculties, and nothing in the *Treatises*, allowing in both works for some slippage in terminology, requires abandoning that treatment. For further discussion of this point, see the chapter to follow comparing (and combining) Locke's and Hume's doctrines of private property.

29 See Horwitz's references to James Tyrell, in his introduction to *Questions concerning the Law of Nature*, 28, 44.

30 Ibid., 28–9.

31 'Somewhat less straightforwardly' because the principle comes up in a discussion of what laws a lawgiver, human or divine, must treat as 'indispensable' and not on the face of the passage in a discussion of self-evidence, demonstrability, or universality. But the principle mentioned is given as an example of the precepts that 'contain the very preservation of the Common Good, or the very order of justice and virtue.'

32 St Thomas illustrates self-evidence of this sort with the case of angels: Someone who does not understand that circumscription in space is not a property of angels will treat seriously the question of how many angels can be in a given place (say, the head of a pin). *ST*, 1a2ae, Q.94, 2.

33 A point, with this example, made by Richard Holtzman in a seminar at The University of Texas.

34 For instance, Finnis, in *Aquinas*, 154–70, on 'exceptionless norms.' Besides not slaying the innocent, Finnis treats not telling the truth (when asked) as an example. St Thomas does hold that lying is always prohibited (*ST*, 2a2ae, Q.110, 3). He would permit you to tell the secret police 'a diversionary truth' to protect a comrade in hiding, but does not consider that you may not be able in the excitement of the moment to think of an adequately diversionary one (2a2ae, Q.110, 3). Finnis himself seems ready to allow that lying in such an instance is though wrong excusable (160–1). I prefer to make the most here and elsewhere of the side of St Thomas's doctrine that makes an impressive case for expecting every non-tautological norm specific enough for the question about exceptions to arise to have exceptions.

35 What in *Logic on the Track of Social Change* by Braybrooke, Brown, and Schotch (Oxford: Clarendon Press, 1995), are called 'technically fully expressed rules,' 23–9. I am drawing here on that passage, about the comparison of rules between cultures; and on the form used in *Track* (see 38–9) for symbolizing rules.

36 I might note as a nuance here that in principle it would make better sense to deduce rules not one by one from the pursuit of the Common Good, but from that pursuit given the other rules in place. A sort of partial equilibrium analysis would be called for, and maybe, beyond, a theory of general equilibrium for the optimization of rules as sets. But I shall give general equilibrium the go-by entirely, and not attempt to be explicit about partial equilibrium. Other rules would come into account if they conflicted with the one under consideration; and the conflict would be an argument against adopting it, at least as first framed.

37 Edited, abridged, and introduced by I.T. Ramsey (Stanford: Stanford University Press, 1958).

38 *Reasonableness*, 55.

39 Including the notions of 'our happiness about ourselves' and 'our happiness about each other.'

40 See Levi's autobiography *The Flutes of Autumn* (London: Harvill, 1983).

41 J.L. Mackie, *The Cement of the Universe* (Oxford: Clarendon Press, 1974), 62.

42 See Simmons, 55, on the difficulty of identifying either the ideal code of rule-utilitarians or 'the set of ideal rules that follow from the fundamental law of nature,' which Simmons takes to be 'the preservation of mankind as a whole' (49–50).

43 See the article in *The International Encyclopedia of Social Sciences* cited in the Introduction.

44 *Second Treatise of Civil Government*, par. 21.

45 Patrick Riley, in 'On Finding an Equilibrium between Consent and Natural Law in Locke's Political Philosophy,' *Political Studies*, 22(4) (1974), 432–52, cites with approval a dictum of Richard Aaron's on the relation for Locke between his social contract theory and the law of nature: 'In one sense the former is the corollary of the latter. In nature all men are equal, but in political society some are rulers and others ruled. This difference needs to be explained and is explained by the theory of the social contract' (Aaron, *John Locke* [Oxford: Clarendon Press, 1936], 272). The dictum expresses precisely the position adopted by Rousseau at the beginning of *Du Contrat Social*.

46 See below, chapter 8, where Locke's and Hume's teachings about private property are compared.

47 *The Invention of Autonomy*, 144, with numbers inserted by me. The phrase 'unsocially sociable psychology' may be a slip. Wouldn't it have made more sense to speak of 'unsociably social psychology?' 'Social psychology' might deal with both sociable and unsociable people.

48 *Autonomy*, 143–4.

49 On charity, vigorously asserted as a qualification to the right of private property on the part of those in a position to help those with 'pressing Wants,' see the *First Treatise of Government*, pars. 41, 42.

50 *An Essay Concerning Human Understanding*, ed. Peter H. Nidditch (Oxford: Clarendon Press, 1975), book 2, chap. 20.

51 *Human Understanding*, book 4, chaps 3, 4.

52 See Philip Hanson and Bruce Hunter's introductory essay, 'Return of the A Priori,' in the collection with the same name that they edited and published (*Canadian Journal of Philosophy Supplementary Volume 18*, 1992: Calgary: University of Calgary Press), 1–51.

3 Rousseau and St Thomas on the Common Good

1 John Finnis, *Aquinas: Moral, Political, and Legal Theory* (Oxford: Oxford University Press, 1998), 132–3; 225–6; 235–7.

2 Ibid., 132, 308.

3 Ibid., 113, 115–16.

4 Ibid., 127.

5 See, e.g., *Émile*, in Michel Launay, ed., Rousseau, *Oeuvres Complètes*, vol. 3 (Paris: Seuil, 1971), IV, 165, 175n, 202, and in *Du Contrat Social* (Launay), I, chap. 4, 520, 'Aucun homme n'a une autorité naturelle sur son semblable, et … la force ne produit aucun droit … Renoncer à sa liberté, c'est renoncer à sa qualité d'homme, aux droits de l'humanité, meme à ses devoirs.' ['No man has any natural authority over his fellow-man, and … force is not the source of any right … To give up his liberty is to give up his standing as a man, the rights of humanity, even his obligations.'] Also II, chap. 4, 527, 'La nature donne à chaque homme un pouvoir absolu sur tous ses membres … [le] droit naturel dont [les citoyens] doivent jouir en qualité d'hommes' ['Nature gives to every man an absolute power over all his body-parts … the natural right that citizens enjoy through having the status of men'], and chap. 6, 530, 'Toute justice vient de Dieu, lui seul en est la source … Sans doute il est une justice universelle emanée de la raison seule.' [All justice comes from God, He alone is its source … Without a doubt it is a universal justice emanating from reason alone.'] These statements are interwoven with a contrast between the state of nature and the moral condition of man

in civil society; and I am not bold enough to claim that Rousseau treats the contrast with unfailing consistency.

6 Jean Roy, 'Burn with a Hard Gem-Like Flame!' *Bulletin de la société d'études rousseauistes* (Sept. 1980), 3–6. (My translation from Roy's French.)

7 George H. Sabine, *A History of Political Theory*, 3rd ed. (New York: Holt, Rinehart and Winston, 1961), 585.

8 Cited by Sabine, *History*; Jean-Jacques Rousseau, 'Political Economy' (1755), Launay, vol. 2, 278.

9 Rousseau, ibid.

10 *Contrat*, I, chap. 7, 523.

11 Kenneth J. Arrow, *Social Choice and Individual Values* (New York: Wiley, 1951), 85.

12 Rousseau, *Contrat*, II, chap. 3, 527.

13 Ibid. 'May' because though the will of everyone is 'often [*sic*] very different from the General Will,' in happy circumstances the two may coincide (IV, chap. 1–2, 563–4). The coincidence, as my account of these matters will bring out, comes about through the enlargement of one's own interest to include all aspects of the common interest.

14 *Contrat*, II, chap. 3, 527.

15 John G. Head, *Public Goods and Public Welfare* (Durham, NC: Duke University Press, 1974).

16 *Contrat*, I, chap. 7, 523–4.

17 Ibid., II, chap. 1, 525–6; IV, chap. 1, 564.

18 Rousseau uses the phrase 'the common interest' more often than the phrase 'the common good,' but I take the terms to be interchangeable. Alternatively, we could regard 'the common interest' as expressing a concept that is the product of an analysis of 'the common good' in terms of the interests of members of the community.

19 Compare Zev M. Trachtenberg, *Making Citizens: Rousseau's Political Theory of Culture* (London: Routledge, 1993), 22, 27–28, 37, and 264 n22. Trachtenberg, in a stimulating treatment of the General Will given in this book, offers a different interpretation from mine. According to Trachtenberg, any set of public goods answering to the General Will consists of so many public goods in respect to which in more than 50 per cent of the comparisons of voters pair by pair on the array of voters' wants against a given set of public goods, the sizes of the differences are less than 50 per cent. (If there are 10 goods and Voter A and Voter B agree in wanting or not wanting six of them, the size of the difference between them is 40 per cent.) Trachtenberg seems to assume that the set is for any given society at any given time unique and coextensive with all the public goods then and there available.

The most important difference between our approaches, however, is that Trachtenberg, taking his stand with economists in relativizing interests to preferences (varying without any stipulated limit), makes the Common Good relative to the preferences of the voters and the distribution of the preferences. There is still (as Trachtenberg maintains) something to cognize in the Common Good: It is whether there is more than 50 per cent convergence 50 per cent of the time in the pair by pair comparison of the preferences of voters. However, though this cognized fact makes a difference to whether or not the citizens will welcome legislation bringing the goods in question into being, it is not something on which the voters express an opinion by their votes; they need just record their preferences and the Common Good can then be determined mechanically by scoring the differences in the array.

20 We must also brave Plamenatz's contention that taken literally the condition about pluses and minuses is 'sheer nonsense.' Taking it literally, for Plamenatz, meant giving it a certain algebraic interpretation: 'Let John's will be $x + a$, Richard's $x + b$, and Thomas's $x + c$; x being what is common to them all, and a, b, and c, what is peculiar to each. If the general will is what remains after the 'pluses' and 'minuses' have canceled each other out, it is x; but if it is the sum of the differences it is $a + b + c$. Whichever it is, it cannot be both; and the second alternative is too absurd to be considered.' This interpretation led Plamenatz to admonish, 'Beware of political philosophers who use mathematics, no matter how simple, to illustrate their meaning! God will forgive them, for they know [not?] what they do, but we shall not understand them.' Plamenatz, *Man and Society*, vol. 1 (London: Longmans, 1963, 393). It did not occur to Plamenatz that it might have been his algebraic interpretation rather than Rousseau's original statement that calls for the warning. Plamenatz defines a, b, and c without mentioning mutual destruction; and he dismisses their sum as an alternative answering to the General Will. Plamenatz goes on to recognize that x might answer without absurdity – thus making his consideration of $a + b + c$, or of this sum plus x as well, a wild aberrancy. However, he rules x out as unrealistic and as inconsistent with the possibility that people's opinions of what x consists of might change with the deliberation that Rousseau expects to precede the deliverances of the General Will. Plamenatz would have done better to consider what x might consist of were the deliberation to run its course.

21 Nannerl O. Keohane, *Philosophy and the State in France* (Princeton: Princeton University Press, 1980), 439–42.

22 *Émile* (Launay), IV, 157; 241; *Contrat*, III, chap. 15 (Launay, vol. 2, 558).

23 *Émile*, IV, 165; 176. I owe these quotations, in the first instance, to Joshua Cohen.

24 *Contrat*, II, chap. 3 (Launay, 527); III, chap. 12 (Launay, 555–6). I am inferring these points from these passages.

25 *Contrat*, II, chap. 1 (Launay, 525–6); III, chap. 15 (Launay, 558–9). See the discussion in Andrew Levine, *The Politics of Autonomy* (Amherst: University of Massachusetts Press, 1976).

26 William H. Riker, *Liberalism Against Populism* (San Francisco: Freeman, 1982), 241–6.

27 *Contrat*, II, chap. 2; and III, chap. 15.

28 Law, the 'organ of the will of all [*sic*] ... is the celestial voice that dictates the precepts of public reason to every citizen, and teaches him to act in conformity with the maxims of his own judgment' (article on 'Political Economy,' Launay, vol. 2, 280). The problem solved by the social contract is 'to find a form of association ... By means of which each, uniting with all, nevertheless obeys only himself and remains as free as before.' *Contrat*, I, chap. 6 (Launay, 522).

29 *Contrat*, IV, chap. 2. The double expression of opinion and commitment rests upon the social contract and the comprehensive authorizing commitment embodied therein: 'Each of us puts his person and his full power in common under the supreme direction of the General Will' (I, 6). 'Everyone submits to the conditions which he imposes on others' (II, 4). The opinions bearing on the Common Good of the whole body of citizens must take into account the opinions of the whole body of citizens, not any subgroup with a different cast of opinions.

30 Compare, in my book *Meeting Needs* (Princeton: Princeton University Press, 1987), having citizens in the policy-making population decide on more or less extensive Lists of Needs and more or less generous Minimum Standards of Provision according to the commitments that they are ready to make under the Principle of Precedence, that the needs of others as well as of themselves are to take precedence over their own mere preferences.

31 As Peter Van Dusen pointed out during a session of my graduate seminar on Rousseau at The University of Texas in the spring of 1998.

32 Could this difficulty be overcome by having the whole body of citizens ratify tentative decisions about legislation that the representatives might come to? Rousseau says, 'Any law which the People has not ratified in person is null; it is not a law' (*Contrat*, III, chap. 15, 558). This makes some allowance for ratification, and the ratification might bear on the results of one of James Fishkin's national deliberative polls as well as upon the deliverances of a legislature. James S. Fishkin, *Democracy and Deliberation: New Directions for*

Democratic Reform (New Haven: Yale University Press, 1991); also Fishkin, *The Voice of the People: Public Opinion and Democracy* (New Haven: Yale University Press, 1995). Unless the deliberations of the poll or of the legislature turn out to be redundant, which would be the case if the whole body of citizens deliberated over the same ground, a good deal of care would have to be taken to enable the whole body of citizens – the people – to assess the headway that the representatives (or the poll participants) had made with the issues when they report back. Perhaps it might suffice to give a synopsis of the arguments considered, conveniently indexed in a full record also made available, for the use of any citizen who wanted to check points in the synopsis.

33 That is to say, to the advantage of the collective body considered as affected by the laws. *Contrat*, IV, chap. 1, 564.

34 Andrew Levine, in a discussion of the General Will that is otherwise one of the most penetrating in the literature, holds that in Rousseau's view, 'The majority is certainly right if only it is properly interrogated.' Levine, *Autonomy*, 68. Neither the text of Rousseau nor Levine's own preceding discussion bears him out, unless we assume that 'properly interrogated' means the majority is to understand the question so well as to give the right answer. Rousseau himself gives some colour to this tautological interpretation by saying, 'If, when the people, sufficiently informed, deliberate, the Citizens have no private discussions among themselves, from the great number of little differences the general will always results and the deliberation will always be good' (*Contrat*, II, chap. 3, 527). But Rousseau also holds that the approach to being right varies with the size of the majority. *Contrat*, IV, chap. 2, 564. At the beginning of Book II, chap. 3, (again), he says, 'The General Will is always right and tends always towards public utility: but it does not follow that the deliberations of the people always have the same degree of correctness. One always wants one's good, but one does not always see what it is. The people are never corrupted, though they are often misled' (527).

35 A point stressed by Christopher Morris and John Ferejohn in various sessions of the summer institute on public choice theory held at Dalhousie University, August 1984. *Contrat*, II, chap. 3, 527.

36 Levine follows Brian Barry in *Political Argument* (London: Routledge and Kegan Paul, 1965) in citing the theorem. Barry in turn cites Duncan Black, *The Theory of Committees and Elections* (Cambridge: Cambridge University Press, 1958). I rely on Black's account (170–1) for the point that a larger majority is more likely to be right than a smaller one. Barry understands, as I do, Rousseau's reliance on majority voting as reliance on an empirical hypothesis about its performance.

37 *Contrat*, II, chap. 7.

38 In most other connections, too, whether these have to do with public goods or with schemes for producing and distributing private goods, citizens must now deal with questions on which they might reasonably regard expert advice as decisive – if they could identify the right experts. I would not deny that in consequence the application of the theory of the General Will is much less easy to carry through than Rousseau, with much simpler societies in mind, treats it as being. Before we consider how far the theory is relevant to our times, however, we need to see how far it is intelligible on the assumptions that Rousseau was working with.

39 In John Rawls's *A Theory of Justice* (Cambridge, Mass.: Harvard University Press, 1971), consider not only the original position argument, but also the argument invoking fraternity and other considerations (103–6) and appealing to reasons why both those better off and those worse off under a current scheme of such a kind might be content to accept it. I rely in part on such arguments in David Braybrooke, 'Making Justice Practical,' in Michael Bradie and David Braybrooke, eds. *Social Justice* (Bowling Green, Ohio, The Applied Philosophy Program: Bowling Green University, 1982) and David Braybrooke, 'Justice and Injustice in Business,' in Tom Regan, ed. *Just Business* (New York: Random House, 1984). (Both these articles have been reprinted in my *Moral Objectives, Rules, and the Forms of Social Change* (Toronto: University of Toronto Press, 1998.)

40 Very likely one could invent other allocations that would attract some people more and lead to cyclical voting; but the very prospect of confusing issues in this way stands against introducing other proposals for allocations unless they are in the circumstances cycle-proof improvements.

41 Thus, as my colleague Robert Eden, in a stimulating comment, has pointed out to me, my analysis rests rather on Books I and II of *Du Contrat Social* than on Book III.

42 Roy, 'Burn with a Hard Gem-Like Flame!'

43 In enumerating these features of the Common Good fully developed I am drawing on the article that Arthur P. Monahan and I wrote on the Common Good for the *Encyclopedia of Ethics*, L. and C. Becker, eds. as revised for the 2nd ed. of that work (forthcoming, 2001).

44 Tawney, *Equality* (London: George Allen and Unwin, 4th ed., 1964), 112–13.

45 I have benefited from comments of Joshua Cohen, Jules Coleman, and Kurt Baier at the session of the summer institute on public choice theory at which this paper was read, as well as from the comments of Robert Eden afterward. Earlier, Russell Hardin and Jane Mansbridge helped the project

forward with general encouragement. It was Jane Mansbridge who insisted that I take into account *Émile*. Later, I had useful comments from audiences at the meeting of the Atlantic Provinces Philosophical Association at Acadia University, late in October 1984, and at the University of Western Ontario, where I read the paper in early November. At Acadia, Serge Morin presented a long, acute, and learned comment, which put my argument into an historical perspective that I do not command, founded on the literature in French. It seemed to me that his comments were generally consistent with my argument. Finally, I have had some comments from Frederick Barnard, as well as the advantage of reading his recent article on Rousseau in *Political Studies* (1984), and taken some reassurance therefrom.

46 *The Third Wave: Democratization in the Late Twentieth Century* (Norman: University of Oklahoma Press, 1991).

47 John S. Dryzek, *Discursive Democracy* (Cambridge: Cambridge University Press, 1990); Robert A. Dahl, *Democracy and Its Critics* (hereafter *DIC*) (New Haven: Yale University Press, 1989).

48 Why they do not agree in reasoning that way about the distribution of automatic and semi-automatic weapons or even handguns is a puzzle arising in part from confusion about constitutional rights (confusion rooted in the ambiguous phrasing of the Second Amendment). It also arises in part from the sad fact that the rate of homicide in the United States, staggering by comparison with the rates in Japan, the United Kingdom, and even Canada, reflects the disproportionate amount of violence in central cities, suffered by black citizens rather than white ones. Most Americans – by far – like every Canadian can count on getting to the grocery store without encountering automatic rifle fire. A fallacy of composition also plays a part in American attitudes: From the fact that had someone with public spirit and a firearm been present during one of the massacres that have occurred now and then the perpetrator could have been taken out of action, it is fallaciously deduced that the whole population would be safer if everyone or almost everyone were armed. This tangled puzzle about opposition to gun control does not refute the thesis about competency, any more than the blockage that obstructs giving effect to majority opinion favouring some sort of arms control derogates from it.

49 The Common Good and other universal principles are 'too general to offer much guidance for distributing different types of goods, much less distributing goods in specific cases; or else if they are specific enough to provide guidance, they are inappropriate for some kinds of goods and all the more so for specific cases.'

4 Hobbes Allied with St Thomas: An Axiomatic System of Laws

1 See, above, Introduction.

2 Ibid.

3 Bobbio, trans. Daniela Gobetti, *Thomas Hobbes and the Natural Law Tradition* (Chicago: University of Chicago Press, 1993).

4 *In foro externo* – in actual, observable conduct. The contrast is with *in foro interno* – being disposed to obey, but maybe having no opportunity to do so safely.

5 The view that all rules can be reduced to prohibitions is an important feature of the treatment of rules in David Braybrooke, Bryson Brown, and Peter K. Schotch, *Logic on the Track of Social Change* (Oxford: Clarendon Press, 1995).

6 As A.P. Martinich recalled for my benefit. In the English version of *De Cive*, the First Law of Nature is given in the two-branch form, 'That Peace is to be sought after where it may be found; and where not, there to provide our selves for helps of War.' That both branches are prescriptions can be directly gathered from the Latin *De Cive*, without going by way of the argument that the definition of the Law of Nature (what I am calling 'the basic statement') implies that a law has two branches, both of them prohibitions: 'Quaerendam esse pacem ubi haberi potest; ubi non potest, quaerendam esse belli auxilia.' But the argument is not at all tenuous. (For bibliographical references see Appendix 4.1.)

7 As my colleague Robert Causey pointed out.

8 See Bas C. van Fraassen, *The Scientific Image* (Oxford: Clarendon Press, 1980); Ronald N. Giere, *Explaining Science: A Cognitive Approach* (Chicago: University of Chicago Press, 1988).

9 See Pars. 4 and 5 of *Leviathan*, chap. 14.

10 See David Gauthier, *Morals by Agreement* (Oxford: Clarendon Press, 1986), 174: With translucency, other persons' 'dispositions to co-operate or not may be ascertained ... not with certainty, but as more than mere guesswork.'

11 One might argue for this point simply from the very great difficulty of putting through any project of instituting a Sovereign by a social contract. Edwin Curley, in the introduction (xxxiv) to his meticulous edition of *Leviathan* (Indianapolis: Hackett, 1994), quotes from the Review and Conclusion that Hobbes appended to *Leviathan*, 'There is scarce a commonwealth in the world whose beginnings can in conscience be justified,' and Curley goes on to say, 'The implication seems to be that most governments were in fact founded by an act of conquest, and that most of these conquests resulted

from wars whose claims to justice were dubious.' The implication that most governments were not instituted by a general social contract seems even more straightforward; indeed, I think it understates the case.

12 *Leviathan*, chap. 15, at the end.

13 See my 'The Insoluble Problem of the Social Contract,' *Dialogue* 15 (March 1976), 3–37.

14 Arthur P. Monahan, in *From Personal Duties towards Personal Rights: Late Medieval and Early Modern Political Thought, 1300–1600* (Montreal and Kingston: McGill-Queen's University Press, 1994, 133, footnote 13, cites *ST*, 1a, QQ.95–9.

15 See Monahan, 134–5.

16 'Hobbes is not trying to overthrow morality nor trying to replace an old morality with a new morality ... Hobbes is trying to provide a new foundation or theory for the content of the old morality, a theory that is consistent with orthodox Christianity.' A.P. Martinich, *The Two Gods of Leviathan* (Cambridge: Cambridge University Press, 1992), 119; see also 122. Curley, in his introduction to *Leviathan* (xxix) says, 'It is helpful to see Hobbes, not as an amoralist, but as someone defending (something like) traditional morality against skeptics.' It seems appropriate enough to expect him to have some place for all the traditional virtues.

17 See, *ST*, 2a2ae, Q.108, 3, gives as a list of illustrative and evidently acceptable forms of punishment: death, stripes, retaliation, slavery, imprisonment, exile, fines, ignominy. Yet in general tenor, his treatment emphasizes like Hobbes's forward-looking considerations.

18 In quoting the laws in each case I first give, in parentheses, Hobbes's catchword or phrase (in the margin of his text) for the content; then the full statement of the law.

19 Documentation will follow, as I take up these virtues and the rules associated with them one by one.

20 *ST*, 2a2ae, Q.81, 1, 4.

21 Charity is one of the three theological virtues, along with faith and hope. *ST*, 1a2ae, Q. 62. A secular version of natural law can perhaps leave faith in religion and hope for immortality along with the redemption of sins to theology without trouble; and it must disengage 'love thy neighbour' from 'love God,' as it cannot dispense with 'love thy neighbour.' It may also in practice need to have people ready to be hopeful about the prospects of peace and of cooperation with others. Whether such hopefulness is to be counted as a secular virtue, along with faith in oneself and the goodness of other human beings, I shall not try to say.

22 *Leviathan*, chap. 15.

23 Vol. 44 of the Blackfriars translation of *ST*.

24 This is precisely the virtue that Rousseau ascribes to women, in particular to the great ladies of Paris and to his heroine Julie. See *La Nouvelle Héloïse*, part 2, letter 21; compare the role that Julie plays as the mistress of her husband's household, part 5, letter 2.

25 In *ST*, 2a2ae, Q.30, 1, St Thomas takes his cue from St Augustine: 'Mercy is heartfelt compassion for another's misery.'

26 Paul Grice, *Studies in the Way of Words* (Cambridge, Mass.: Harvard University Press, 1989), 26.

27 Even if he was influenced by the difficulty. At the beginning of the *Leviathan*, chap. 14, he had been at pains to distinguish between 'law' and 'right;' the one 'determineth and bindeth' while the other 'consisteth in liberty to do or to forbear.' How can one be commanded (even conditionally) to do rather than forbear without losing half the right? Yet the statement – the axiom – from which the First Law is deduced does forbid giving up the means of preserving one's life; and failing success in the project of obtaining peace, the right of nature and the exercise of it are the means. Perhaps we should understand the First Law to be saying that 'every man ought to endeavour peace, as the better means of preserving his life, so far as he has hope of obtaining it; but when he cannot obtain it, preserve himself by the means at his disposal in the right of nature.' The trouble comes from Hobbes's insisting without qualification on the 'liberty to do or forbear,' combined with his conception of the right of nature as having while it continues unabridged no limitation of any kind. Rights as ordinarily conceived go hand in hand with obligations: For one thing, if you are obliged to do something, you have the right to do it. Moreover, sometimes obligations are taken on or imposed precisely with the effect of prescribing that someone shall exercise a free-standing prior right in one way rather than another: People may both have a right to vote and be under an obligation to do so. It could have been in part just to avoid the present difficulty that Hobbes changed his terminology in *Leviathan*, calling the prescription to seek peace by itself 'the First Law.' But he did not carry the change all the way through; the alternative formulation figures in the same passage and has not been accommodated to the change.

5 David Hume: Natural Law Theorist and Moral Realist

1 In the Introduction to *Essays on Moral Realism*, ed. Geoffrey Sayre-McCord (Ithaca: Cornell University Press, 1988), 5.

2 See Moore's essay, 'Law as a Functional Kind,' in Robert P. George, ed.,

Natural Law Theory (Oxford: Clarendon Press, 1992), 188–242, at 189–92. See also his useful review of the present state of the discussion of moral realism, 'Moral Reality Revisited,' *Michigan Law Review,* 90 (1992), 2424–33, at 2425.

3 J.L. Mackie, *Ethics: Inventing Right and Wrong* (Harmondsworth, England: Penguin, 1977); C.L. Stevenson, *Ethics and Language* (New Haven: Yale University Press, 1944), 273–6; Simon Blackburn, 'How to Be an Ethical Antirealist,' *Midwest Studies in Philosophy,* 12 (1988), 361–75, at 362.

4 Robert P. George, *In Defense of Natural Law* (Oxford: Clarendon Press, 1999), 84.

5 Annette Baier, 'Promises, Promises, Promises,' in her *Postures of the Mind* (Minneapolis: University of Minnesota Press, 1985), 174–206, at 176.

6 There is no mention of God, except for one rhetorical flourish at the end of Appendix I to the *Inquiry,* in any of the passages in which Hume expounds his view of ethical theory.

7 Baier, 'Promises,' 176.

8 *Treatise,* 465. All references in this form are to the Selby-Bigge edition of *A Treatise of Human Nature* (Oxford: Clarendon Press, 1888).

9 Baier, *Postures,* 176–7. See also *ST,* 1a2ae, Q.97.

10 There may be such even if apart from the fundamental laws Hume would shy away from natural law theory and not in any case be comfortable with having his teachings classed with it. However, I do not agree with Annette Baier that Hume's overall inclination to stress virtues rather than rules implies so much distaste for rules as not to accept the weight that natural law theory – in particular, natural law theory in St Thomas's version – puts on rules along with virtues. See the passage below on virtues and rules.

11 Stephen Buckle, in *Natural Law and the Theory of Property* (Oxford: Clarendon Press, 1991), 234, takes Hume to be a serious contributor to natural law theory just on the point of explaining how people are motivated to practise what Hume makes out to be the artificial virtue of justice. See Buckle, 90–1.

12 Henry Sidgwick, *The Methods of Ethics,* 7th ed. (London: Macmillan, 1907).

13 *An Inquiry Concerning the Principles of Morals,* ed. C.W. Hendel (New York: Liberal Arts Press, 1957).

14 See Richmond Campbell, *Illusions of Paradox: A Feminist Epistemology Naturalized* (Lanham, MD: Rowman and Littlefield, 1998), 70–4.

15 G.H. von Wright, *Norm and Action* (London: Routledge, 1963), 103–5.

16 *Inquiry,* Conclusion, part 1, at the end.

17 But see Germain Grisez, 'The First Principle of Practical Reason,' *Natural Law Forum,* 10 (1965), 168–96, who holds that practical reason in St Thomas's doctrine does its own generalizing. We saw above one way in

which this might happen, through the emergence of a convention not explicitly reasoned out as such.

18 Peter Jones, in his *Hume's Sentiments* (Edinburgh: The University Press, 1982), cites, p. 108 from Hume's 'The Standard of Taste' (in Thomas Hill Green and Thomas Hodge Grose, eds., *Essays Moral, Political, and Literary*, [London: 1875], 268), the statement, which Hume took from Shaftesbury, 'No sentiment represents what is really in the object.' This may seem stronger. But, putting aside any fine distinctions about what 'represents' might mean, the statement is not from Hume speaking in his own person, but from Hume setting forth a position that he means to transcend, especially as regards a further feature in it, namely, the thesis that 'a thousand different sentiments, excited by the same object, [are] all right.' Furthermore, the passage continues, glossing on the statement about no sentiment representing, 'It only marks a certain conformity or relation between the object and the organs or faculties of the mind.' Thus, Hume takes the statement to imply that something like secondary qualities are at issue; and true or false apply literally to observations of secondary qualities. Even if (as Jones supposes) Hume is going to stand by the statement in his own transcending doctrine, it does not bring down either an analogy with moral realism or the fact of it.

19 The *Oxford English Dictionary* (*OED*) gives as a meaning current in both centuries: 'What one feels with regard to something; mental attitude (of approval or disapproval, etc.); an opinion or view of what is agreeable.' *OED* gives also 'a wider sense,' now rated obsolete, but with citations from 1695 and 1760 and also one from as late as 1838: 'An opinion, view (e.g., on a question of fact or scientific truth).' See Annette Baier, in *A Progress of Sentiments* (Cambridge, Mass.: Harvard University Press, 1991), chap. 6, 129–51, on the cognitive features of passions and sentiments. Baier shows how the cognitive features of the passions of love and hatred, as treated in Book II of the *Treatise*, lend strength to the cognitive features of sentiments in Book III. The case for looking upon Hume as a moral realist becomes even stronger if we take the analysis of the passions into account; but it is already very strong if we rest it on the treatment of the sentiments in Book III and in the *Inquiry*; and it is notable that Hume does not discuss the passions at any length in the *Inquiry*.

20 Richard N. Boyd, 'How to Be a Moral Realist,' in Geoffrey Sayre-McCord, ed., *Essays on Moral Realism* (Ithaca: Cornell University Press, 1988), 181–228.

21 Edward J. Bond, *Reason and Value* (Cambridge: Cambridge University Press, 1983).

22 Cited by J.L. Mackie, in his 'The Subjectivity of Values,' Sayre-McCord, 95–118, at 106.

23 *A Progress of Sentiments*, 24–5.

24 See David Braybrooke, 'How Are Moral Judgments Connected with Dis-plays of Emotion?', *Dialogue*, 4 (September 1965), 206–23.

25 See *Treatise*, III, part I, section I, toward the end: 'Vice and virtue ... may be compar'd to sounds, colours, heat and cold, which, according to modern philosophy, are not qualities in objects, but perceptions in the mind.' Hume's own full position is that they do not fail to be full-fledged qualities of objects because of their dependence, such as it may be, on perceptions in the mind.

26 As Baier points out, *A Progress of Sentiments*, 194, Hume also likens moral judgments to judgments of size and shape. The analogy with colour suf-fices to capture truth and falsity even if it is a secondary quality; but the analogy with size and shape is stronger for anyone who accepts the distinc-tion between primary and secondary qualities. Hume does not, when, as in the passage just cited, he is pressing scepticism of the senses to the limit; and he may not when he has left scepticism behind to speak as one person among others in ordinary life.

27 Challenged by J.L. Mackie and Simon Blackburn – see Blackburn, in 'How to Be an Ethical Antirealist,' 366–7; defended by John McDowell in 'Values and Secondary Qualities,' in T. Honderich, ed., *Morality and Objectivity* (London: Routledge, 1985), 110–29.

28 See Campbell, 172, on morality as composed of two systems of social con-trol, one (the product of human evolution) consisting of quick habitual responses, the other reflective and critical.

29 See David Wiggins, 'A Sensible Subjectivism,' in his *Needs, Values, Truth* (Oxford: Blackwell, 1987) for a statement of sensibility theory; and P.A. Boghossian and J.D. Velleman, 'Colour as a Secondary Quality,' *Mind*, 98 (389) (1989), 81–103, for the charge of circularity, also advanced by Stephen Darwall, Allan Gibbard, and Peter Railton in 'Toward *Fin de siècle* Ethics: Some Trends,' *Philosophical Review*, 101 (1992), 115–89.

30 Xiusheng Liu treats the charge of circularity at length in his dissertation (The University of Texas at Austin, 1998) and in a derived paper. What I say in the present paragraph has been much influenced by his treatment.

31 Blackburn holds that moral qualities are 'projections' with only 'quasi-realist' results, not realist ones, in his *Spreading the Word* (Oxford: Clarendon Press, 1984), though even so they must conform to 'the constraints upon proper projection' (186). It is not easy to discover just what constraints Blackburn has in mind; and one must wonder whether the constraints that Hume offers are not effectively the same. Why do they not suffice in both cases to ensure the correctness of the ascriptions and the reality of the qual-ities described? In 'Realism, Antirealism, Irrealism, Quasi-Realism,' *Mid-west Studies in Philosophy*, 12 (1988), 25–49, Crispin Wright points out, most

clearly 35, that Blackburn's quasi-realist program leads projectivism into 'a rather obvious dilemma. Either his program fails – in which case he does not, after all, explain how the projectivism that inspires it can satisfactorily account for the linguistic practices in question – or it succeeds, in which case it makes good all the things the projectivist started out wanting to deny: That the discourse in question is genuinely assertoric, aimed at truth, and so on.'

32 'Giving alms to common beggars is naturally praised; because it seems to carry relief to the distressed and indigent: but when we observe the encouragement thence arising to idleness and debauchery, we regard that species of charity rather as a weakness than a virtue,' *Inquiry*, part II, section 2.

33 In my 'No Rules without Virtues; No Virtues without Rules,' *Social Theory and Practice*, 17 (Summer 1991), 139–56 (reprinted in my collection *Moral Objectives, Rules, and the Forms of Social Change* [Toronto: University of Toronto Press, 1998], 233–48), I may not have made enough of this distinction between kinds of rules.

34 Of which Harvey Cormier reminded me.

35 Even the *OED* does not give a precedent for using 'kidnap' as a noun, but I am willing to set a precedent in the present phrasing. Language is evolving. Indeed, I am not alone: In an article on contemporary slavery contributed to *The Manchester Guardian Weekly*, 20 June 1999, 25, Kevin Bates speaks of 'laws against kidnap and slavery.'

36 *A Progress of Sentiments*, 235–6.

37 Compare, in the *Human Development Report 1998* of the United Nations Development Programme (New York: Oxford University Press, 1998), the entries for Norway and the Netherlands, 128, under 'Human Development Index,' with the entries for those countries under 'Aid Flows,' 196.

38 A version of this chapter, read to the weekly colloquium of the Department of Philosophy at Dalhousie, elicited a vigorous and to me very useful discussion. I have made a number of additions in response to comments made on this occasion, especially those by Richmond Campbell, Wayne Fenske, Duncan Macintosh, and Sheldon Wein. I benefited afterwards from a Canadian Philosophical Association discussion at Ottawa, especially from Annette Baier's comments on the paper before the symposium and during it.

6 From Private Property in Hume and Locke to the Universality of Natural Laws

1 Locke did not just disregard the claims of the Indians. He vigorously

argued that the claims were negligible, on the ground (among others) that the Indians were not making so productive a use of the land as the colonists would. See James Tully's incisive and unsettling article, 'Rediscovering America: The Two Treatises and Aboriginal Rights,' in G.A.J. Rogers, ed., *Locke's Philosophy: Content and Context* (Oxford: Clarendon Press, 1994), 165–96.

2 For full discussion, see David Braybrooke, 'The Social Contract and Property Rights across the Generations,' in Peter Laslett and James S. Fishkin, eds. *Justice between Age Groups and Generations* (Philosophy, Politics, and Society, Sixth Series) (New Haven: Yale University Press, 1992), 107–26.

3 See Morton J. Horwitz, *The Transformation of American Law 1780–1860* (Cambridge, MA: Harvard University Press, 1977), a work to which my colleague Gretchen Ritter called my attention.

4 See, again, my article, referred to in n2 above.

5 'There are, no doubt, motives of public interest, which determine property; but I still suspect, that these rules are principally fixed by the imagination, or the more frivolous properties of our thought and conception' (*Treatise*, III, part 2, section 3).

6 A full account of Marx's position on justice is given in chap. 7, 'Justice in the Marxist Dialectic of Rules,' of David Braybrooke, Bryson Brown, and Peter K. Schotch, *Logic on the Track of Social Change* (Oxford: Clarendon Press, 1995).

7 The favourable circumstances would not nowadays be thought to require anything like the geographical assumption about personal territories lined up along a peninsula like Digby Neck, Nova Scotia, that was invoked to put Hume's theory through with naïve literality in David Braybrooke, 'The Insoluble Problem of the Social Contract,' *Dialogue*, 15 (1976), 3–37.

8 Stephen Buckle, in his *Natural Law and the Theory of Property* (Oxford: Clarendon Press, 1991), 235, considers that taking a stand on this pleasure, from the overall operation of the rule, is Hume's most important contribution to natural law theory, since it explains how one can be morally motivated to heed justice even in cases where heeding it has no direct moral appeal. I am happy to endorse this explanation, though for me an even more important contribution is Hume's account of how natural laws (or approximations thereto) are discovered by a gradual process, consolidated only after successive experiments.

9 Or at least the institution extended to external goods might be said to arise so. Locke assumes that before we acquire any external goods we have property in our own persons, a doubtful and certainly unfamiliar notion. Buckle, 169–70, recognizing the anomaly ('an otherwise curious doctrine')

and asserting that the use of 'property' in this connection is 'a terminological variation' from received natural law theory, convincingly explains that
what Locke has in mind is the notion of 'one's own' (*suum*) as found in Grotius and Pufendorf.

10 That separating the item is assumed to occur simultaneously with the mixing forestalls Nozick's wisecrack about mixing one's property with the sea.
Anarchy, State, and Utopia (New York: Basic Books, 1974), 174–5. Buckle, 152
(including n86) discerns a deeper obstacle: Locke is steadily assuming that
the labour in question is productive labour, which improves the human
condition.

11 See Elinor Ostrom's account of how herders, farmers, and fishermen in various places learn only through a protracted period of trial and error what
rules they need to govern the joint exploitation of common pool resources:
Ostrom, 'A Behavioral Approach to the Rational Choice Theory of Collective Action,' *American Political Science Review*, 92(1) (1998), 1–22, at 8.

12 For one, David Crockett, a student one year in my seminar, notably obsti-
nate on this point; and, no doubt among other distinguished company,
Alan Ryan. Ryan, as I noted earlier, slips into the extravagance of saying
that a natural law theory without God is 'simply incoherent' (Ryan, quoted
by Lisska). How English this is, relishing trenchancy without much care for
accuracy! But it ignores the history of the secular version, which as I noted
earlier some scholars attribute to St Thomas himself, in the sense that the
arguments establishing the content of the natural laws and even sufficient
moral force to make them binding need not invoke theistic belief on the
part of people subject to them.

13 Bands that do this typically pool the catch of game, but in some cases they
let the individual gatherers appropriate the nuts and berries that they find.
But not in all cases: In some cases, men who contribute nothing to the food
supply, are fed regardless and without reproach. Moreover, it may be 'out
of the question' for someone to hoard what she has gathered while others
are hungry. See John Gowdy's wonderful collection, *Limited Wants, Unlimited Means* (Washington, DC: Island Press, 1998), esp. the article by James
Woodburn, 'Egalitarian Societies,' 87–110.

14 Notably, in the examples cited, arrangements for property or in lieu of
property come in combination with distinctive arrangements for family life,
even (e.g., in the case of the Oneida Community) for sexual relations. Richard H. Beis, in an article, based on anthropology, still valuable as a general
antidote for cultural relativism and ethical relativism, but fully alert to the
variations in particular arrangements between societies, cites the Bantu as
looking upon pre-marital sexual experiments as a helpful prelude to mar-

riage, which they regard as mainly an arrangement about property with relatively easy permission for nontraumatic divorce. Both this way and the orthodox Western way, Beis comments, 'seem to have their advantages and disadvantages.' 'Some Contributions of Anthropology to Ethics,' *The Thomist*, 28(2) (1964), 174–224, at 185.

15 Before this suggestion is dismissed as a naive pastoral myth, the comparative evidence needs to be sifted carefully. In the *Guardian Weekly*, 21 March 1999, Mari Marcel-Thekaekara, reports the reactions of six members of Adivasi tribal people who were taken from India to visit Germany: 'They did not look at the West as a kind of materialist Mecca, in complete contrast to most visitors who go there either as immigrants or tourists, but always with shopping lists. The Adivasis didn't hanker after German consumer goods. '"It's very nice to be here," Chathi, one of the six, [said]. "But I couldn't live here. It's not my place. A man needs his family, his community, his own people around him. Just money can't give you a life. You'd shrivel up and die."' The Adivasis 'were speechless when they saw an old people's home. "How can children send their old parents to live alone?" they eventually asked in wonder. And later, in a meeting, Radhakrishnan, another of the six, solemnly resolved, "We must ensure that such things never happen in our society, no matter how much we progress" ... The Adivasis were shocked at the spectre of unemployment that haunted some of our young German friends. They were particularly upset when Karl, whose home they lived in, came back preoccupied by the news that he might soon be made redundant. Bomman worried all night about him. In the morning he announced, "I have an idea. I can make bamboo flutes and Karl can sell them here till he finds a job."' (On the other hand, the Adivasis greatly valued being treated 'with respect and dignity' in Germany as they had not in India.)

16 Richard B. Lee, article cited in Gowdy, 54–6. See also John Zerzan, 'Future Primitive,' in Gowdy, 255–80, at 263 and 272. Compare Rousseau in the *Discourse on Inequality*, beginning of part 2: 'The first man who, having enclosed a piece of ground, to whom it occurred to say *this is mine*, and found people sufficiently simple to believe him, was the true founder of civil society. How many crimes, wars, murders, how many miseries and horrors Mankind would have been spared by him who, pulling up the stakes or filling in the ditch, had cried out to his kind: Beware of listening to this impostor; you are lost if you forget that the fruits are everyone's and the Earth no one's.' Victor Gourevitch, ed. and trans., *Rousseau: The Discourses and Other Early Political Writings* (Cambridge: Cambridge University Press, 1997).

17 See Hobbes, *Leviathan*, chap. 21, on how one has a right to disobey an order to abstain from food, even if it is an order from the Sovereign.

18 See Gowdy, 99.

19 These three rules are different from the three that Hume associates with property: recognition; transfer by consent; contract. See *Treatise*, III, part 2, sections 2–6. My three fall in with Hume's first. As Steven Burns reminded me in a discussion at Dalhousie, my three rules together correspond at least roughly to the principle, 'From all according to their ability to all according to their needs,' which I myself have cited in treating the Common Good.

20 Richard B. Lee, 'What Hunters Do for a Living,' in Gowdy, 43–63, at 47.

21 See Geoffrey W. Conrad and Arthur A. Demarest, *Religion and Empire* (Cambridge: Cambridge University Press, 1984), 28–9, 38, 42, 44.

22 *Communist Manifesto*, part 1, at the end.

23 See T.S. Ashton, *The Industrial Revolution* (Oxford: Oxford University Press, 1972), 108–9; Ashton, 'Economics Responsible for Living Conditions,' in T.S. Ashton and F.A. Hayek, eds., *Capitalism and the Historians* (Chicago: University of Chicago Press, 1954); compare M.C. Buer, *Health, Wealth, and Population in the Early Days of the Industrial Revolution* (New York: Howard Fertig, 1968), 55–6.

24 For Marx's continuing use of the concept of justice, in spite of his repudiation of a theory of justice like Hume's (and Locke's), see again, *Logic on the Track of Social Change*, chap. 7.

25 Locke does not have this problem because of his assumption, discussed earlier, that we have property in our selves (our bodies) in the same sense as we have property in external goods. So murder and assault attack our property. But this, as I remarked earlier, is a doubtful use of the notion of property, certainly for present day readers, and Hume is better off not indulging in it. Locke also formally provides for laws against murder and assault (as well as against kidnapping and confinement) by officially defining the property that civil society as well as the state is to respect in the case of every person as 'life, liberty, and estate.'

26 See James Buchanan and Gordon Tullock, *The Calculus of Consent* (Ann Arbor: University of Michigan Press, 1962).

27 A person who in an exchange relationship with another 'tu' does not seek the other's welfare is a 'non-tuist;' he may in other relationships with other people not be an egoist.

28 John Rawls, *A Theory of Justice* (Cambridge, MA: Harvard University Press, 1971), 60.

29 Chap. 4, section 42.

30 See above, chap. 4 in this book.

7 With Us Still: Natural Law Theory Illustrated Today in the Work of David Copp

1 Copp, 23.
2 A lucid use of the distinction between a standard or norm and a rule can be found in Michel Foucault, *Discipline and Punish*, trans. A. Sheridan (New York: Vintage Books, 1995), 184, and in the discussion just preceding.
3 As Copp himself allows in a reference to Alan Gibbard's views, Copp, 20.
4 It can be taken from David Braybrooke, Bryson Brown, and Peter K. Schotch, *Logic on the Track of Social Change* (Oxford: Clarendon Press, 1995).
5 One might say that the first part (having to do with the reference to a moral rule) fits what Stephen Darwall calls 'morality/reasons internalism,' which holds that a moral proposition entails for anyone who believes it, applied to himself, that he has a reason to act accordingly. 'Reasons, Motives, and the Demands of Morality: An Introduction,' in Stephen Darwall, Alan Gibbard, and Peter Railton, eds., *Moral Discourse and Practice* (New York: Oxford University Press, 1997), 306. The reason might not be operative with that person at that time, however. At the same time, one might say that the second part of the combination (having to do with the subscription to the rule) falls under what Darwall distinguishes under 'reasons/motives internalism' as the 'judgment' variety, which holds that if someone makes assertions of a certain sort (here, that he subscribes to the rule) then 'necessarily, she has some motivation to do A' (Darwall, 308). Judgment internalism, it is true, does not, as Darwall defines it, contemplate separating the subscription to the rule from the assertion of the connected moral proposition. Copp himself says, puzzlingly, that his theory is 'neutral between internalism and externalism about reasons and motives.' It does not entail a necessary connection between the truth of a moral judgment and the reasons or motivations of the agent who believes it (Copp, 34). But if believing that an action is prescribed by a justified moral rule does not give a reason to do it, even if it is not operative in the present case – what would? Perhaps Copp (as the alternation between 'reasons' and 'motives' suggests) is thinking of operative reasons.
6 Campbell, *Illusions of Paradox: A Feminist Epistemology Naturalized* (Lanham, Md: Rowman and Littlefield, 1998), 170. Campbell also offers an arresting explanation of how, abnormally, the two functions can pull apart in some cases: We have 'two systems of social control,' one internalized as children without any assessment of the merits of the rules so internalized, the other, a later and more sophisticated development, oriented toward evaluating the purpose or worth of moral rules and resolving conflicts between them.

What we feel to be wrong, having internalized the first system, may not be what we have in principle been convinced is wrong in the perspective of the second.

7 *Ethics: Inventing Right and Wrong* (Harmondsworth, England: Penguin, 1977).

8 G.H. von Wright, *Norm and Action* (London: Routledge, 1963), 101.

9 Copp, 37, 228–9.

10 Ibid., 227–8.

11 Ibid., 222–3, 238.

12 Or some of the same rules up to the point of allowing for different exceptions. See the discussion in *Logic on the Track of Social Change*, 23–8, of the two ways in which societies may have the same rules: Literally, the same rules with the same exceptions; or the same core rules, ignoring differences in exceptions. Canada and the United States, in respect to the law forbidding homicide, come close to illustrating the first sort of case; but Canada does not make an exception for capital punishment, while the United States does. Strictly speaking, therefore, they belong with the second sort of cases; they have the same core rule forbidding homicide, but a difference in exceptions.

13 This is not to say that the distinction, as regards personal choices, fails to make an advance on the distinction between matters of need and matters of preference only. At the social level, even so, the distinction may have to be put aside as a complication interfering with due attention to statistics about needs.

14 Copp, 155–9. For the significance of moving from needs to preferences as the basis for evaluating social policies, see David Braybrooke, *Meeting Needs* (Princeton: Princeton University Press, 1987), esp. chap. 5.

15 Copp, 191–3.

16 Ibid., 193–4.

17 Ibid., 127–8.

18 Ibid., 147.

19 I owe this radically illuminating point about how to understand the rule about good and evil to Germain Grisez, 'The First Principle of Practical Reason: A Commentary on the *Summa Theologiae*, 1–2, Question 94, Article 2,' *Natural Law Forum*, 10 (1965), 168–96. Grisez holds that every moral rule (at least every basic rule) stands on its own feet, self-evident and underived. But this is not self-evident as many would understand it; nor does it deprive the rules of an empirical footing, though the footing would rest directly on the fit between the human purposes reflected in the concept of morality and the fate of those purposes in experience.

20 See R.M. Hare on the convergence of his views in this connection with Sartre's. Hare, *Freedom and Reason* (Oxford: Clarendon Press, 1963), 38.

21 In one rather astonishing passage, 116, Copp treats 'non-epistemic reasons' as 'irrelevant to determining whether [a] code is justified.' 'Non-epistemic reasons' would include all reasons except finding a moral rule or code on the evidence one that had the status of meeting the needs of a society and hence rationally to be chosen and morally to be subscribed to (as desired to be current). The epistemic reasons would say nothing about whether anyone cared to have the needs of the society met, or was on that ground moved to subscribe morally to the rule or code. Even if we could agree that epistemic reasons alone establish whether a code is justified, what is to be done about a justified code requires bringing in non-epistemic reasons. Otherwise the connection to ethical conviction is incomplete.

22 The parenthetical qualification figures here to allow for uses of moral rules as models or metaphors applied to actions solely of personal concern, as in discussions of duties to oneself. The existence of such duties is and always has been so much a matter of doubt as to suggest that the allowance is not really called for.

23 Copp, 117. Copp cites as an example the theory put forward by Patricia S. Greenspan in *Practical Guilt* (New York: Oxford University Press, 1994). He might well have cited Hume, who is particularly explicit in justifying in this way the moral obligation to heed the rules of justice, though Hume's theory does not insist upon optimum effectiveness, which Copp implies is demanded by Greenspan's.

24 Compare Gibbard's sketch, referred to by Copp, 17, which is in effect a systematic application of the position taken by von Wright, in *Norm and Action*, about propositional schemes shadowing schemes of non-propositional moral arguments.

25 See *Illusions of Paradox*.

26 *Norm and Action*, 102.

27 Copp, 35. Campbell's hybrid theory, in *Illusions of Paradox*, is less question-begging.

28 Ibid., 37.

29 Ibid., chap. 3. Richmond Campbell sets forth this dilemma with great clarity and cogency in his critical notice of Copp's book, *Canadian Journal of Philosophy*, 27(3) (1997), 423–44. For the view that justification is feasible see Copp, 103–4, 112, 116, 190–4.

30 This is what Campbell recommends in the critical notice cited.

31 Copp, 37.

32 Ibid., 104, 162.

33 Brought up in a seminar discussion at Texas by W. Harrod.
34 See *Contrat*, IV, chap. 1. 'State' here is interchangeable with Copp's 'society.' Compare *Contrat*, I, chap. 6, at the end.
35 See, above, n21, for 'epistemically justified reasons'; for 'operative reasons,' see n5.
36 Copp, 116.
37 The distinction drawn by Copp, 84, is that to subscribe to a rule does not entail any reference to other people's conforming to it; to subscribe to a rule as a moral rule does entail desiring that others conform to it.
38 Copp, 197–8.
39 Ibid., 194.
40 Ibid., 203–4; compare 176.

8 Moral Education

1 John Knoblock, *Xun Zi* (Stanford: Stanford University Press, 1988), 85–7; A.C. Graham, *Disputers of the Tao* (LaSalle, Illinois: Open Court, 1989), 245–51.
2 See David Braybrooke, 'The Insoluble Problem of the Social Contract,' *Dialogue*, 15 (March 1976), 3–37.
3 An alternative approach to these matters lies through evolutionary psychology, which furnishes reasons for thinking that rational egoists and groups composed wholly of them do not have the best prospects of surviving. I take this to be corroborative of my approach, and a way of magnifying the force of calling motivations aligned with group-membership and the Common Good of a group 'natural.' Selfish motivations are natural, too, but there are natural advantages for groups and people as well in fostering unselfish ones and increasing their relative strength. See Elliot Sober and David Sloan Wilson, *Unto Others: The Evolution and Psychology of Unselfish Behavior* (Cambridge, MA: Harvard University Press, 1998).
4 London: Heinemann, 1987. The passage that follows comparing the achievement of personhood by animals and infants is based even on points of detail on a paper that I worked on off and on for a while with Victoria McGeer, which somehow has not yet got finished up for publication. I may not have been entirely clear when we left off work as to the division of responsibilities; and I am certainly not clear now how much she and I respectively contributed to the passage presented here; but I am very grateful for her collaboration, and the fun of working with her.
5 *The Mental and Social Life of Babies* (Chicago: University of Chicago Press, 1982).

6 Hearne, 21.

7 Ibid., 118–21; 152.

8 I am indebted to Xiusheng Liu for collecting these examples from the texts.

9 Alan Fogel would emphasize the importance of learning from peers (I am relying here on the comment, 'How Do Relationships Create Persons?,' which he contributed to a conference with Vicki Hearne, Victoria McGeer, and me in Austin in 1992). In this respect, he falls in line with Piaget, who thought peers had much more and better to contribute to children's moral development than parents (as reported by Daniel K. Lapsley, *Moral Psychology* (Boulder: Westview Press, 1996), 16–17). Lapsley also reports (24) that Piaget's thesis that peer group participation encourages moral development has been 'largely supported' by subsequent investigations. I argue that even parents can successfully serve as moral mentors; no doubt they can also do very badly, but they can succeed in a variety of ways, some more authoritarian, some very much less so. Were I to make more of peer mentoring, the implications for successful moral education in the natural laws might be even more favourable.

10 Hearne says in one passage that she would not be satisfied that Belle, her pit bull terrier, was fully trained until Hearne was 'willing to bet a month's pay that if Belle hadn't eaten for two days and the track she was on led her directly through the middle of a platter of hot prime ribs, she would regard the food as a reminder to keep working, regarding it with impatience and disgust if anything' (96); and that though Belle ordinarily loves comfort she will cheerfully sit on ice for minutes on end if she has her tracking harness on and knows that an enterprise of tracking is about to begin (158).

11 See Gauthier, in *Morals by Agreement* (Oxford: Clarendon Press, 1986), 347–8.

12 Lapsley, 5.

13 Ibid., 21.

14 Ibid., 11 (on Piaget); 66 and 70–1 (on Kohlberg).

15 Lapsley, 170, in a passage that also mentions Eisenberg, quotes Radke-Yarrow et al.: 'Children ... are not only egocentric, selfish and aggressive; they are also exquisitely perceptive, have attachments to a wide range of others, and respond prosocially across a broad perspective of interpersonal events in a wide variety of ways and with various motives.' This, I think, is just what anyone who has had to do at length with children would expect, along with findings by psychologists that young children even from babyhood are responsive to the emotional displays of others and manifest 'prosocial behaviour' (any behaviour that is intended to benefit another), for instance by sharing or giving away their toys (166–8). These expecta-

tions and findings are consistent with allowing that 'empathetic awareness and awareness of abstract, internalized moral norms increase with age, whereas hedonistic, needs-oriented, and stereotypic consideration, and the desire for interpersonal acceptance and approval, decrease with age' (162), without ever, one supposes, becoming insubstantial, as they should not.

16 Ibid., 168–9. 'To be a part of a collaborative activity with adults, especially parents, is a source of great pride to the child.'

17 See Martin Sanchez Jankowski, *Islands in the Street: Gangs and American Urban Society* (Berkeley: University of California Press, 1991) on joining gangs, though Jankowski, I think, makes too much of self-interested choice.

18 Ostrom, 'A Behavioral Approach to the Rational Choice Theory of Collective Action,' *American Political Science Review*, 92 (1) (1998), 1–22, at 11.

19 In this paragraph, I am responding to some well-taken comments by Neera Badhwar about allowing for self-striving along with cooperation. The deviation toward rational egoism can be illustrated by, among other things, the reported tendency of students who take economics at university becoming more egoistic the more economics that they study.

20 Consider Weber's reference to 'the iron cage' of modern economic organization: Max Weber, *The Protestant Ethic and the Spirit of Capitalism*, trans. T. Parsons (London: Routledge, 1992), 181.

21 Michel Foucault, *Discipline and Punish*, trans. A. Sheridan (New York: Vintage Books, 1995), in which the prison becomes the model of modern society.

22 See Gauthier, *Morals by Agreement*, e.g., 4.

23 *Leviathan*, chap. 15, par. 10.

24 *Summa Theologiae*, 1a2ae, Q.95, 1.

25 See Ronald A. Heiner, 'The Origin of Rules in Uncertainty,' in David Braybrooke, ed., *Social Rules* (Boulder, Colorado: Westview Press, 1996), 217–32.

26 See *ST*, 1a2ae, Q.87; (also 2a2ae, Q. 108, 3) and the commentaries by Thomas Gilby, 'Reward and Punishment,' at the end of his translation of 1a2ae, QQ. 18–21 (Blackfriars edition, vol. 18, London: Eyre and Spottiswoode, 1966), and 'Coercion and Law,' at the end of his translation of 1a2ae, QQ.90–97 (Blackfriars edition, also 1966).

27 On the distinction between various forms of anarchism by the strength of their opposition to rules, see the doctoral dissertation by Todd Mason-Darnell, The University of Texas at Austin, 1997.

28 *ST*, 1a2ae, Q.96, 6.

29 *ST*, 2a2ae, Q.120, 1. Xiusheng Liu has told me that Xun Zi has an equivalent term, 'Quon.'

30 David Braybrooke, Bryson Brown, and Peter K. Schotch, *Logic on the Track of Social Change* (Oxford: Clarendon Press [Clarendon Library of Logic and Philosophy], 1995).

31 See Skinner, *Science and Human Behavior* (New York: Macmillan, 1953).

32 *Leviathan*, chap. 21.

33 It does so, moreover, without preventing us from treating rules in deontic logic as functions connecting actions or sequences of actions with outcomes, which is another feature of the logic developed under Schotch's lead for *Logic on the Track of Social Change*.

34 *Logic on the Track of Social Change*, 38–9.

35 In this paragraph and the next, I am following closely the text in *Logic on the Track of Social Change*, 43–4. The distinction between 'correction' and 'punishment' is taken from Hearne, 44–5. Hearne credits the animal trainer William Koehler with the distinction.

36 Paul Ziff, in *Semantic Analysis* (Ithaca: Cornell University Press, 1960), denounces the idea that there are rules governing natural language. He is not concerned with the assumption, definitive of rules for many, that rules are accompanied by negative sanctions; but if we move away from thinking of rules as even usually being so accompanied, one ground for agreeing with his thesis disappears.

37 In this paragraph, and the one succeeding it, I follow closely the text in *Logic on the Track of Social Change*, 49–50, as I do in appending this note: Actual practice with rules lends itself to representation in a three-panel structure. In the first panel, which is the site of basic teaching, the blocking operations, physical and verbal, that come under the rule continually impinge upon the people whose conduct is to be regulated. In the centre panel, people are left to themselves with the expectation that the rule itself, now that they have learned it, will suffice to produce the desired conduct. Blocking operations occur only rarely here, and then just to remind people of the rules; sanctions do not occur at all. Sanctions appear only in the third panel. There verbal and physical sanctions (reprimands, imprisonments) back up rules that otherwise do not work often enough with enough people for the number of deviations to be tolerable. Compared to the continual blocking operations in the first panel, however, the sanctions are used rather rarely; and though they were brought in long ago for some rules, there are many rules, perhaps if we consider the rules of language, the preponderant number, that work well enough without them. Among those rules may figure the rules that can be ascribed to people who manifest one or another virtue and who thereby set examples for others, which the others follow out of admiration rather than compulsion.

38 See *Living Morally: A Psychology of Moral Character* (Philadelphia: Temple University Press, 1989). I am relying directly, however, not on the book, but on a lecture given by Thomas at the Atlantic philosophical meetings in October 1990.

39 Anne Norton has given a rich and subtle exploration of these matters in her book *Reflections on Political Identity* (Baltimore: The Johns Hopkins University Press, 1988). See esp. chap. 1.

40 A good point made by a member of the audience when I delivered an ingredient of the present chapter at a philosophical meeting in Atlantic Canada.

41 Ostrom, 'A Behavioral Approach.'

42 Ostrom, 14.

43 Ostrom, 10.

44 I am not sure that evolutionary psychology pronounces one way or another on the advantages or disadvantages of carrying attachment to a social group this far.

45 One of the people who says this is a leading writer on the Holocaust, Elie Wiesel, cited by Paul Marcus, *Autonomy in the Extreme Situation* (Westport: Praeger, 1999), 88: 'Within the system of the concentration camp ... the first to give in, the first to collaborate – to save their lives – were the intellectuals, the liberals, the humanists, the professors of sociology, and the like. Because suddenly their whole concept of the universe broke down.'

46 Marcus, 87–8, cites Bruno Bettelheim, Primo Levi, Jean Amery, and Anna Pawelczynska. Bettelheim himself, in *Surviving* (New York: Knopf, 1979), 56–8, singles out 'the *non-political middle-class prisoners*' as being 'least able to withstand the initial shock. They found themselves utterly unable to comprehend what had happened to them' and after their attempts at rationalization failed 'they seemed to disintegrate' and began cheating on other prisoners and spying on them.

47 I have no doubt that Dutch soldiers, trained and properly led, can be as steadfast as any. In Srebrnica, they seem to have been badly trained or badly led.

48 Philip J. Ivanhoe, Xiusheng Liu, and Zev Trachtenberg have done me the favour of reading this chapter in draft; and I am grateful for their remarks, both corrective and encouraging. The idea of linking 'ritual' in ancient Chinese ethical thought with the social practices in which cooperative behaviour and moral attitudes are generated came to me from a paper that Ivanhoe read when he came to Texas to join me in examining Liu on the latter's dissertation; and from the discussion at the defence of the dissertation.

9 Epilogue: The Lasting Strength of Natural Law Theory in Jurisprudence

1 See John Rawls's perception of 'the aggregative/distributive dichotomy' as one of the chief challenges to social ethics: *A Theory of Justice* (Cambridge, MA: Harvard University Press, 1971), 36–9, 44.

2 Jeffrie G. Murphy and Jules L. Coleman, *The Philosophy of Law* (Totowa, NJ: Rowman and Allanheld, 1984), 18–19. In the midst of this passage, in a part that I have suppressed above, Murphy says, 'There are many rules in any society that are surely laws but are just as surely morally neutral – e.g., some law requiring that one have one's validated registration tag on the auto license plate prior to March 1. Aquinas sensibly admits that such rules are laws, but the degree to which the admission is compatible with the literal wording of his definition is unclear.' Here Murphy has missed St Thomas's distinction between laws that can be deduced from the principles of natural law and laws that are optional constructions (determinationes) for giving the principles effect (*ST*, 1a2ae, Q.95, 2). Suppose that there is a rule of natural law according to which people are to be held responsible for actions that pose dangers of injury to others; the responsibility of drivers for the operation of their vehicles will fall under this rule by deduction. Suppose further that licence plates are an effective means of tracing drivers whose actions have been dangerous or injurious. Then the law about licence plates will come in as an optional construction, a measure for bringing home to drivers their responsibilities. Alternatively, consider a rule of natural law about raising revenue for a legitimate government, options regarding particular taxes, and options for making sure that no one is able to evade paying his share of the particular tax on motor vehicles. In both cases, fixing a date may be looked upon as a further construction for making sure of current adherence to the rules.

3 *Natural Law and Justice* (Cambridge, MA: Harvard University Press, 1987), 8. By 'deontological' Weinreb means a theory that holds, 'what is properly called (positive) law satisfies [must satisfy] moral requirements.' This description, in spite of his belief to the contrary, embraces as a special case traditional natural law theory, with its beliefs about human nature and the indispensable means of obtaining the benefits of society. (For Weinreb, 'deontological' theory came in with Kant; traditional natural law theory was, according to a distinction Weinreb leaves mysterious, 'ontological.')

4 Weinreb, 100.

5 Weinreb, 8, 116–17. Compare David A.J. Richards, *The Moral Criticism of Law* (Encino and Belmont, Calif.: Dickenson, 1977), 31–6. By 'methodological natural law theory' Richards seems to mean, chiefly, keeping in view the

moral arguments that are reflected in current laws and in judicial reasoning about them.

6 An example of the former sort of passage is *ST*, 1a2ae, Q.96, 4: 'Human positive laws are either just or unjust ... Laws are unjust in two ways.' Murphy's pieced-together quotation from St Thomas draws on both sorts of passages. See John Finnis, *Natural Law and Natural Rights* (Oxford: Clarendon Press, 1980), 364–5 (cited by Deryk Beyleveld and Roger Brownsword, *Law as Moral Judgment* [London: Sweet and Maxwell, 1986], 112). Beyleveld and Brownsword spell out (13) various ways in which they think an 'intelligible' natural law theory could avoid invoking the traditional claim or slogan which so embarrasses Finnis, though they themselves seem to stand by it (12). Weinreb points out that though Finnis asserts that he knows of 'no theory of natural law in which [the slogan], or anything like it, is more than a subordinate theorem ' (351), Finnis all but adopts it himself, in agreement with St Thomas and St Augustine (Weinreb, 99, footnote; compare Finnis, 23–4, 360–1). What is 'a subordinate theorem?' One the truth of which is so obvious, given other theorems, that it is idle to set up a demonstration for it? Subordinate or not, if it is a theorem (which, given St Thomas's remarks in defining law, above, it seems to be) it still has a firm place in natural law theory. Finnis devotes a complex and concentrated passage to showing how positive law derives from natural law (ibid., chap. 10, Section 7, 281–90).

Can any ground for jettisoning the slogan be found in the fact that (in English) the quotation from St Augustine in which it makes its appearance with St Thomas says, 'seems to be' rather than categorically 'is'? 'A law that is not just seems to be no law at all.' But in *ST*, 1a2ae, Q. 96, 4 (which Murphy draws upon) St Thomas brings in the quotation to corroborate what he says for his own part just previously in the same sentence: 'Such [unjust laws] are acts of violence rather than laws,' which is categorical, as is his statement at the end of Q.92, 1: 'A tyrannical law is not according to reason, and therefore is not straightforwardly a law, but rather a sort of crooked law (*perversitas legis*).' Equally categorical is what he says in Q. 95, 2, where he makes the same quotation from St Augustine, and goes on to say, 'Hence a command has the force of law to the extent that it is just ... If on any head [what is laid down by men] is at variance with natural law, it will not be law, but spoilt law (*legis corruptio*).' He is bound to be categorical, given his definition of law, summed up in *ST*, 1a2ae, Q.90, 4: 'Law is naught else than an ordinance of reason for the Common Good made by the authority who has care of the community and promulgated.' Returning to the passage in which St Augustine is quoted, one might wonder why after being so categorical himself, St Thomas brings in the quotation at all. Is it because, though a weaker statement, less than categorical, it shows that a great authority was at least tending in the same direction? This is a question to which a decisive answer can be given by consulting the passage in the Latin original. There the quotation from St Augustine reads, 'Lex esse non videtur quae justa non fuerit.' Videtur (videor, the passive counterpart of video, to see) has a wider range than English 'seems,' which is normally used to signify at most tentative assent, pending corroboration, or to signify a contrast with 'really is so.' Videtur may mean 'is seen'; hence esse ... videtur, 'is seen to be.' The idiomatic translation that best fits the passage and the context of St Thomas's definition of law is: 'It is evident that there has not been a law that was not just.'

7 How, one might ask, can it be said to be a slogan invented by the positivists when it can be found endorsed by St Thomas? See the first quotation from St Thomas given above, in particular the statement cited from St Augustine at the end of the quotation.

8 *A Theory of Law* (Cambridge, MA: Harvard University Press, 1984), 51.

9 Ibid.

10 Ibid.

11 Soper, 55. 'The slight modification' consists in requiring only 'that legal directives aim at serving the Common Good, however wide of the mark they may fall.' (Will the modification remain slight 'however wide of the mark' the directives may be?)

12 Not to speak of Bentham and Austin, who could find utilitarian grounds for most if not all of the content of M*, allies could include Hans Kelsen, the very prototype of a Basic Positivist. See his *General Theory of Law and State*, trans. Wedberg (Cambridge, MA: Harvard University Press, 1945), 5, 50. At the end of the first, eponymous chapter of *What Is Justice?* (Berkeley: University of California Press, 1971), Kelsen defends the moral seriousness of the 'relativism' to which he adheres (22) and then says, 'The most important thing in my life, justice, is that social order under whose protection the search for truth can prosper. 'My' justice, then, is the justice of freedom, the justice of peace, the justice of democracy – the justice of tolerance' (24). Hobbes has shown us how at least a very large part of the content of natural law can be deduced from a first principle of seeking peace (*Leviathan*, chaps. 14, 15). One might expect just from the remarkably sympathetic account of natural law theory that H.L.A. Hart sets forth (in *The Concept of Law* [Oxford: Clarendon Press, 1961]) before reaffirming the Positivist Criterion (205–6) that Hart would be an even readier ally than Kelsen.

13 Or here, for this purpose, to prescriptions that it stands by along with any other reasonable ethics.

14 For Weinreb the persistence of natural law is not only itself a puzzle; to his great credit, he senses that the persistence, puzzle and all, is 'an indication that something more lies hidden beneath the jurisprudential debate'(8). I shall solve at least in part Weinreb's puzzle about the persistence of 'natural law'; I shall not solve it, however, by bringing to light what he has in mind as the 'something more' that 'lies hidden beneath the jurisprudential debate.' What he has in mind is a supposed 'antinomy' between freedom and causation, which he believes makes the realization of any comprehensive and consistent scheme of justice impossible (Weinreb, 10–11). This is not what I have in mind; I do not even find this plausible.

15 I regard the Positivist Criterion, taking its stand on enactment as the decisive consideration for the existence of a law, as leaving open the other topics mentioned. Even on the question whether laws are commands or rules, the Criterion leaves open, as a matter for supplementary consideration, which for purposes of my argument need not be gone into, whether 'enactment' issues only in rules that fit a sophisticated account of rules (in this and other respects the Criterion may be regarded as a minimal expression of positivist views). I think that enactment does issue only in such rules; but that is not the direction in which my argument will unfold the meaning of enactment. The Criterion, as it enters into my argument, certainly leaves open the question whether good or bad fortune is deserved as a matter of natural law by the people to whom the fortune, good or bad, falls. I shall not treat this topic either. Weinreb may be correct in thinking that an affirmative answer to this question can be found in Greek tragedy and connected by argument with Greek notions of natural law. However, if such an answer is, as Weinreb holds, an essential feature of what he calls the 'ontological' view of natural law (Weinreb, 1–2, 7, 10, 41–2, 125), which he ascribes to St Thomas, among others, it is irrelevant to what I bring of traditional natural law theory into the present discussion.

16 H_a implies that agents are not merely self-interested, since M* goes beyond self-interest to require commitment to a community and readiness to make sacrifices for its Common Good; but if M* is replaced by a set of rules that do no more than maximize the rational self-interest of agents, a hypothesis parallel to H_a will emerge that will go a good part of the same distance. The two hypotheses will part company when questions arise about admitting new members to a given society who cannot pay their own way or ejecting old members who have ceased to be able to do so.

17 The 'opinion leaders' could be distributed through all social classes, and every human being might have immediate access to at least one of

them – the picture given for contemporary politics in Elihu Katz and Paul F. Lazarsfeld, *Personal Influence* (Glencoe, IL: The Free Press, 1955).

18 This is an example that Weinreb launches against the indeterminacy which he finds in Finnis's theory of natural law (Weinreb, 114).

19 In Monahan, *Consent, Coercion and Limit* (Kingston and Montreal: McGill-Queen's University Press, 1987).

20 *ST*, la2ae,Q.90, 3: 'The chief and main concern of law properly so called is the plan for the Common Good. The planning is the business of the whole people or of their vicegerent.' Blackfriars trans., vol. 28 (London: Eyre and Spottiswoode, 1966), 13.

21 Compare Juergen Habermas's notion of 'the ideal speech-situation,' with its implications for agreement in ethics and politics. See, e.g., Habermas, *Legitimation Crisis*, trans. Thomas McCarthy (Boston: Beacon Press, 1975), 105, 108.

22 Kenneth J. Arrow, *Social Choice and Individual Values*, 2nd ed. (New York: Wiley, 1963). Robert A. Dahl, *A Preface to Democratic Theory* (Chicago: University of Chicago Press, 1956), 128, demonstrates that a candidate can win by taking a minority position on all the issues of a campaign, provided that the minorities who support him on each of these issues care more about having their way on each of them than they do about having their way on other issues.

23 *ST*, 1a2ae, Q.90, 3 again. See also 2a2ae, Q.104, 5 and 6.

24 *ST*, 1a2ae, Q.96, 5, Reply to Objection 3.

25 *ST*, 1a2ae, Q.96, 4.

26 John Locke, *Second Treatise on Civil Government*, pars. 135, 210, 240.

27 See Hart, 24, with what he offers feature by feature as a theory of law that does not rest on force alone, or just with what is already present of these features in his intermediate summing up, 76.

28 Have we got any further, Hart might be asked, when he brings up oppressive ruling coalitions (Hart, 196), from a gunman than to a gang of gunmen?

29 What Hart says (196) about coalitions keeping for themselves 'the minimal protections and benefits' of law and accepted morality is not perfectly consistent with what he says earlier (167) about some rules 'obviously required for social life' conformity with which must be 'a matter of course among any group of individuals, living in close proximity to each other' if we are not to doubt 'the description of the group as a society' and be 'certain that it could not endure for long.'

30 I came upon this pithy translation from St Thomas on a church bulletin board, early one sunny morning when I was young, walking across the Green in New Haven.

31 Weinreb, 105–7. He goes on to say, (108), 'Over time, law and morality are likely to converge, by a gradual interactive process or, occasionally, by a more dramatic confrontation and elimination of dissimilarities. A person who subscribes generally to both is likely to find that his legal obligations are reinforced by their conformity to what he and others in the community regard as their moral (and social) obligations. None of that supports a distinct natural law theory or, indeed, asserts anything with which legal positivists disagree.'

32 On core rules, see David Braybrooke, Bryson Brown, and Peter K. Schotch, *Logic on the Track of Social Change* (Oxford: Clarendon Press, 1995), Introduction, 23–8. Will the shared subset be empty, or will so little be left for the basic prohibition to do even with a shared subset that is not empty, given all the occasions for action that fall under one or another head of exception not universally shared, that the core rule hardly ever operates? One will just have to look to see.

33 See above, chaps. 3, 6.

34 In outline, I gave the argument of this paper in a talk at the Faculty of Law, Queen's University, with a discussion following, from which I trust I benefited. An earlier version of the paper, once written up, elicited spirited and helpful comments from the participants in a departmental colloquium at Dalhousie; I wish to thank especially Duncan MacIntosh, for support, and Robert Martin, for stout ordinary language objections. Two anonymous referees for the *Canadian Journal of Philosophy* supplied me with a good deal of incitement, some useful comments, and even more useful bibliographical references; I thank them, too. An intermediately revised version was given to the Legal Theory Workshop of the Faculty of Law, University of Toronto; and in this connection I received helpful comments from a number of people, for which I am grateful. Above all, however, I must thank David Copp, who went far beyond the normal obligations of an editor to provide me with a critique both thorough and always to the point – as well as patient general encouragement.

Appendix Part 1 Ibn Khaldun Modernized

1 For the prototype of the theory, see David Hume's theory of justice in *A Treatise of Human Nature*, Book II, Part 2, Sections 1 and 2.

2 See Hamilton A.R. Gibb, 'Islamic Background of Ibn Khaldun's Political Theory,' in *Studies on the Civilization of Islam* (Boston: Beacon Press, 1962) on the tendency to exaggerate the independence or originality of Ibn Khaldun's thought.

3 H.E. Barnes, 'Sociology Before Comte,' *American Journal of Sociology*, 23 (1917), 197–8.

4 Nathaniel Schmidt, *Ibn Khaldun: Historian, Sociologist and Philosopher* (New York: Columbia University Press, 1930), 4.

5 Ibid., chap. 1.

6 Ibn Khaldun, *The Muqaddimah*, trans. by Franz Rosenthal, ed., N.J. Dawood (Princeton: The Bollingen Series/Princeton University Press, 1967), 45. John Locke, *The Second Treatise of Government* in *Two Treatises of Government*, ed., Peter Laslett (New York: Cambridge University Press, 1988), sect. 6.

7 *Muqaddimah*, 336 and *The Second Treatise*, sects. 6 and 25.

8 *Muqaddimah*, 45 and 152.

9 Ibid., 297, and *The Second Treatise*, sect. 25.

10 *Muqaddimah*, 46.

11 Ibid., 47.

12 Thomas Hobbes, *Human Nature* in *Elements of Law Natural and Politic*, ed., J.C.A. Gaskin (New York: Oxford University Press, 1994), 78.

13 Hobbes, *Leviathan*, ed., Edwin Curley (Indianapolis: Hackett), 74.

14 *Muqaddimah*, 238–42.

15 Ibid., 63–4.

16 For Rousseau, agriculture, along with metallurgy, are the two professions most responsible for the development and subsequent degeneration of humans. See, e.g., Jean-Jacques Rousseau, *Discourse on the Origin of Inequality* in *The Discourses and Other Early Writings*, trans., ed., Victor Gourevitch (New York: Cambridge University Press, 1997), 168.

17 Rousseau, too, argues that humans became softer as they become more civilized.

18 *Muqaddimah*, chap. 4, sections 17–18.

19 For a nice discussion of a similar argument in Machiavelli, see T.K. Seung, *Intuition and Construction* (New Haven: Yale University Press, 1993), 135–6.

20 *Muqaddimah*, 136–8.

21 Ibid., 10. See also 249.

22 Ibid., 154–60. See also Erwin I.J. Rosenthal, 'The Theory of the Power State and Ibn Khaldun's Study of Civilization,' in *Political Thought in Medieval Islam: An Introductory Outline* (Cambridge: Cambridge University Press, 1958), 100–2.

23 See Niccolo Machiavelli, *The Discourses on Livy*, Book 5, chap. 2; Jean-Jacques Rousseau, *The Social Contract*, Book II, chap. 7; and Alexis de Tocqueville, *Democracy in America*, vol. 2, Part 1, chap. 5; vol. 2, Part 2, chap. 9; vol. 2, chaps. 9 and 15.

24 I will use the term rational theology instead of Ibn Khaldun's term meta-

physics. Rational theology is faithful to Ibn Khaldun's meaning, and avoids the problems typically associated with metaphysics, i.e., that metaphysics are omnipresent and no ethical system can escape such claims. For a good version of this argument as applied to liberal theorists, see David L. Williams, 'Dialogical Theories of Justice,' *Telos* 114 (Winter 1999), 109–31.

25 Hamilton A.R. Gibb, 'The Islamic Background of Ibn Khaldun's Political Theory,' 171. See also Muhammad Mahmoud Rabi, *The Political Theory of Ibn Khaldun* (Leiden: E.J. Brill, 1967), chap. 4 and the General Conclusion.

26 *Muqaddimah*, 388–90, 398–405.

27 See Majid Fakhry, 'Theological Reaction and Reconstruction,' in *The History of Islamic Philosophy* (New York: Columbia University Press, 1970).

28 *Muqaddimah*, 398.

29 See Immanuel Kant's claim that reason must be set aside to make room for faith in *The First Critique*.

30 See Muhammad Mahmoud Rabi, *The Political Theory of Ibn Khaldun*, 43–4.

31 Benedict de Spinoza, *Ethics*, trans. R.H.M. Elwes (New York: Dover, 1955), 78.

32 David Copp, *Morality, Normativity, and Society* (New York: Oxford University Press, 1995), 218–30.

33 *Muqaddimah*, 285.

34 Copp, 127–8.

35 *Muqaddimah*, 136–8.

36 See Erwin Rosenthal, 'The Theory of the Power State and Ibn Khaldun's; Study of Civilization,' in *Political Thought in Medieval Islam*, 100.

Appendix Part 2 Natural Law in Classical Chinese Philosophy

1 It should be noted that some scholars suggest that we could, even in St Thomas, make sense out of natural law without the presupposition of a divine being.

2 Philip J. Ivanhoe has argued that the divine legislator may not be necessary for the notion of natural law. In a different context, he says that the Chinese 'had well articulated and comprehensive views comparable to "natural law" sans lawgiver.' ('China and the Scientific Revolution,' paper presented to the American Philosophical Association, Pacific Division Meeting, 1998, 8.)

3 See Fung Yu-Lan, *History of Chinese Philosophy*, in *San Song Tang Quan Ji*, vol. 2 (He Nan People's Press, 1988), 43. Zhang Dainian, *Concepts of Classical Chinese Philosophy* (Beijing: Zhong Guo She Hui Ke Xue Press, 1989), 20–2.

4 See John C.H. Wu, 'Mencius' Philosophy of Human Nature and Natural Law,' in *Chinese Culture*, (1), (1957), 13.

5 *Book of Odes*, in *Commentaries on Thirteen Classics* (*Shi San Jing Zhu Su*) (Beijing: Zhong Hua Press, 1979), part 1, 568.

6 Ibid., 522.

7 Ibid., 583.

8 See Wing-Tsit Chan, *A Source Book in Chinese Philosophy* (Princeton: Princeton University Press, 1963), 3–8. Fung Yu-Lan, *Chinese Philosophy*, 36–45.

9 *Book of Shang*, vol. 8, in *Commentaries on Thirteen Classics*, part 1, 160. See also Fung Yu-Lan, *Chinese Philosophy*, 42.

10 Cited by Fung Yu-Lan, *Chinese Philosophy*, 42–3.

11 Ibid., 46–51. See also Liang Qichao, *Chinese Political Thought before Qin*, 6th ed. (Taipei: Taiwan Zhong Hua Press, 1972), 30.

12 See Wing-Tsit Chan, *Chinese Philosophy*, 174; *Dao De Jing*, in *Zhu Zi Ji Cheng*, vol. 3 (Beijing: Zhong Hua Press, 1986), 45.

13 See Wing-Tsit Chan, *Chinese Philosophy*, 152–3; *Dao De Jing*, in *Zhu Zi Ji Cheng*, 14.

14 *Zhuang Zi*, vol. 17, *Autumn Water*, in *Zhu Zi Ji Cheng*, volume 3, 105. Also see Wing-Tsit Chan, *Chinese Philosophy*, 207.

15 Ibid.

16 *Analects*, 18: 5, 18: 6, 18: 7. See also Fung Yu-Lan, *Chinese Philosophy*, 80.

17 *The Doctrine of the Mean*. See also Zhu Xi, *Si Shu Zhang Ju Ji Zhu* (Gaoxiong: Fu Wen Press, 1985), 17; and James Legge, *Confucian Analects, The Great Learning, and The Doctrine of the Mean* (New York: Dover, 1971), 383. It is arguable as to whether Confucius himself uttered that sentence. But it is certain that the idea was already in Confucius.

18 See Wing-Tsit Chan, *Chinese Philosophy*, 78.

19 See Zhang Dainian, *Studies of Chinese Moral Thought* (Taipei: Guan Ya Wen Hua, 1991), 178–9.

20 *Xun Zi*, in *Zhu Zi Ji Cheng*, vol. 2 (Beijing: Zhong Hua Press, 1986), 205. See also John Knoblock, *Xun Zi: A Translation and Study of the Complete Works*, vol. 3, books 17–32 (Stanford: Stanford University Press, 1994), 14.

21 *Xun Zi*, 206.

22 Ibid., 211. See also Knoblock, *Xun Zi*, 20–21.

23 *Mo Zi*, in *Zhu Zi Ji Cheng*, vol. 4, 122–3.

24 Ibid., 120.

25 *Mo Zi*, 121–2. See also Zhang Dainian, *Chinese Philosophy*, 21. Universal love, in Mo Zi, can be better understood in terms of benefiting people without discrimination or preference than in terms of cultivated feelings.

26 *Mo Zi*, 163. See also Wing-Tsit Chan, *Chinese Philosophy*, 221–2. Mo Zi may

have some Confucians in mind when he uses the word 'fatalists.' If so, he misunderstands Confucianism. For Confucianism does not discourage human effort due to any pre-determined *Ming*.

27 Hu Shi, 'The Natural Law in Chinese Tradition,' in *Natural Law Institute Proceedings, No 5* (Notre Dame: University of Notre Dame Press, 1953), ed., Edward F. Barrett, 119–53. Joseph Needham, *A Shorter Science and Civilization in China*, vol. 1 (Cambridge: Cambridge University Press, 1978), 279. ('There was ... a *jus naturale* which the sage kings and the people had always accepted; this was what the Confucians called *li* [*Li*] ...') See also Hyung I. Kim, *Fundamental Legal Concepts of China and the West: A comparative Study* (London: National University Publications, Kennikat Press, 1981).

28 See Fung Yu-Lan, *Chinese Philosophy,* 75; Liang Qichao, *Chinese Political Thought,* 67.

29 See Fung Yu-Lan, *Chinese Philosophy,* 78; and Wing-Tsit Chan, 'Chinese and Western Interpretations of Jen (Humanity),' *Journal of Chinese Philosophy,* 2 (1975), 107–9.

30 For an instructive summary and an original interpretation, see Philip J. Ivanhoe, 'Reweaving the "one thread" of the *Analects,*' *Philosophy East and West,* vol. 40, no. (1), 17–34.

31 See Fung Yu-Lan, *A Short History of Chinese Philosophy* (New York: Macmillan, 1948), 43; and Zhang Dainian, *Chinese Philosophy,* 159.

32 See Zhang Dainian, *Chinese Moral Thought,* 27–30.

33 Ibid.

34 See Zhang Dainian, *Chinese Philosophy,* 144; Fung Yu-Lan, *Chinese Philosophy,* 312–16; Kwong-loi Shun, 'Jen and Li in the Analects,' *Philosophy East and West,* 43 (July 1993), 457–78; Donald Munro, *The Concept of Man in Early China* (Stanford, CA: Stanford University Press, 1969), 27–8.

35 Liang Qichao, *Chinese Political Thought,* 67–84.

36 Cited by Zhang Dainian, *Chinese Moral Thought,* 53. See also Liang Qichao, *Chinese Political Thought,* 72 (the English edition of the book: *History of Chinese Political Thought* (London: Kegan Paul, Trench, Trubener & Co, 1930), trans. L.T. Chen, 44).

37 Ma Zhenduo, for example, is one of those critics. See *Humanity, the Way of Human: Confucius' Philosophy* (Beijing: Zhong Guo She Hui Ke Xue Chu Ban She, 1993), 95.

38 Zhang Dainian, *Chinese Moral Thought,* 113–27.

39 For Mencius, human nature is '*ren zhi suo yi yi* yu *qin sho zhe*' (4B19) or '*qi suo yi yi yu shen shan zhi ye ren zhe*' (7A16). '*zhi suo yi yi yu*' or '*suo yi yi yu*' means 'that which gives rise to the differences ...' He does not say that

human nature is 'ren yi yu *qin sho zhe*' or '*ren* yi yu *ye ren zhe*.' 'yi yu' simply means 'that which is different.' See also Ma Zhenduo, *Confucius' Philosophy*, 236.

40 In a similar context, Wei-ming Tu also uses 'moral sense' to characterize Mencius' concept of human nature. 'On the Mencian Perception of Moral Self-Development,' *Monist* 61 (1), 78.

41 See Ma Zhenduo, *Confucius' Philosophy*, 234; Yang Zebo, *Study on Mencius' Theory of the Goodness of Human Nature* (Beijing: Zhong Guo She Hui Ke Xue Chu Ban She, 1995), 120–30.

42 Zhang Dainian, *An Outline of Chinese Philosophy (Zhong Guo Zhe Xue Da Gang)* (Beijing: Zhong Guo She Hui Ke Xue Chu Ban She, 1982), 250–3.

43 Roger T. Ames, '*ren xing*' in *Meng Zi*. See 'The Mencian Conception of Ren Xing: Does it Mean "Human Nature?"' in *Chinese Texts and Philosophical Contexts*, ed. Henry Rosemont, Jr (La Salle, Ill: Open Court, 1991): 143–78. For detailed discussions on that topic, see Kwong-loi Shun, 'Mencius on Jen-Hsing' and Irene Bloom, 'Human Nature and Biological Nature in Mencius,' *Philosophy East and West*, 47 (1), 1–20, and 21–32; Xiusheng Liu, *The Place of Humanity in Ethics: Combined Insights from Mencius and Hume* (PhD Dissertation, 1999, The University of Texas at Austin), chapter 3.

44 Zhang Dainian, *Outline of Philosophy*, 233.

45 *Si* means thinking, reasoning. In *Meng Zi* it characteristically means reflecting or to reflect. See also Yang Zebo, *Goodness of Human Nature*, 111.

46 See Zhang Dainian, *Outline of Philosophy*, 233; Yang Zebo, *Goodness of Human Nature*, 178.

47 Zhu Xi, *Si Shu Zhang Ju Ji Jie*, 238.

48 Ibid., 328.

49 Ibid., 372.

50 David Hume, *A Treatise of Human Nature*, 2nd ed. (Oxford: Clarendon Press, 1987), 340.

51 *Ren* has been translated as humaneness, human-heartedness, etc. Those translations are not perfect, but acceptable. Many translators also translate it as benevolence. That translation, however, may be problematic. Benevolence may have no naturalistic roots, as it is closely associated with major Western religions. Very often, it is universal love, and its practice requires God's help more than human effort. *Ren* in Confucianism is a purely naturalistic concept; it is consistent but not universal love. The best model of it is the kind of love found in a family setting. And its practice requires not God's help, just human effort.

52 Kwong-loi Shun, *Mencius and Early Chinese Thought* (Stanford: Stanford University Press, 1997), 56–63.

53 Ibid., 56.
54 Ibid., 62.
55 Ibid., 63.
56 Chen Chun, *Neo-Confucian Terms Explained*, sections 48 and 59. English Edition, translated by Wing-Tsit Chan (New York: Columbia University Press, 1986), 70, 75.
57 See Ma Zhenduo, *Confucius' Philosophy*, 87.
58 Chen Chun, *Neo-Confucian Terms Explained*, English Edition, 69–85. See also Ma Zhenduo, *Confucius' Philosophy*, 87.
59 Ma Zhenduo, *Confucius' Philosophy*, 87.
60 Chung-ying Cheng, 'On *yi* as a universal principle of specific application in Confucian morality,' *Philosophy East and west*, 32 (3), 269–80.
61 That *Yi* consists of characteristically (true) moral judgments should not affect Yi's status as a virtue. *Phronesis*, for example, is a virtue in ancient Greek philosophy and it essentially refers to sound judgments.
62 Chung-ying Cheng, 'Confucian morality,' 269–70.
63 See Legge, *Confucian Analects*, 208.
64 See Ma Zhenduo, *Confucius' Philosophy*, 91.
65 See Zhang Dainian, *Chinese Philosophy*, 214.
66 *Zhi* as wisdom sometimes refers to the exception of general rules (*epieikeia*), i.e., *Quan*. That meaning of *Zhi* is very important in classical Confucianism.
67 Chen Chun, *Terms Explained*, section 48; see English ed., Wing-Tsit Chan, 70.
68 Ibid., 59; English ed., Chan, 75.
69 Ibid., 67; English ed., Chan, 80.
70 David Hume, *Enquiries Concerning Human Understanding and Concerning the Principles of Morals* (Oxford: Clarendon Press, 1975), 214.
71 Chen Chun, *Terms Explained*, 70; English ed., Wing-Tsit Chan, 81.
72 See Wing-Tsit Chan, *Chinese Philosophy*, 61; and Legge, *The Works of Mencius* (New York: Dover, 1970), 135.
73 Zhang Dainian, *Chinese Moral Thought*, 30.
74 Legge, *Mencius*, 251–2.
75 See Legge, *Mencius*, 201; Fung Yu-Lan, *A Shorter History of Chinese Philosophy*, 75; Liang Qichao, *Chinese Political Thought*, 85.
76 See Legge, *Mencius*, 130.
77 Ibid., 147–8.
78 Ibid., 131, 245.
79 Ibid., 131, 242. Fung Yu-Lan, *Chinese Philosophy*, 118; Liang Qichao, *Chinese Political Thought*, 90.
80 See Legge, *Mencius*, 202; Fung Yu-Lan, *Chinese Philosophy*, 125.

81 See Fung Yu-Lan, *Chinese Philosophy,* 125; Liang Qichao, *Chinese Political Thought,* 86; Zhang Dainian, *Chinese Moral Thought,* 114.

82 Liang Qichao, *Chinese Political Thought,* 86. Zhang Dainian says that Mencius holds the right against only private interest. That is not correct in this context (Zhang Dainian, *Chinese Moral Thought,* 114). Critics also compare Mencius with Kant. Actually they are quite different. Kant would not allow the feeling of sympathy or indeed any feeling to serve as moral motivation.

83 Thomas Hobbes, *Leviathan* (New York: Penguin, 1985), 160.

84 Ibid., 160–1.

85 'On Human Nature as Evil,' *Xun Zi,* in *Zhu Zi Ji Cheng,* vol. 2, 289. See also Knoblock, *Xun Zi,* vol. 3, 151; Wing-Tsit Chan, *Chinese Philosophy,* 128; Homer H. Dubs, *The Works of Hsuntze* (London: Arthur Probsthain, 1928), 301.

86 Hobbes, *Leviathan,* 188.

87 'On Human Nature as Evil,' *Xun Zi,* 293. See also Knoblock, *Xun Zi,* vol. 3, 156.

88 Philip J. Ivanhoe has argued vigorously against the translation of Xun Zi's view of *xing'e* as *human nature is evil.* See his 'Human Nature and Moral Understanding in the *Xunzi,'* in *Virtue, Nature, and Moral Agency in the Xunzi* (Indianapolis/Cambridge: Hackett, 2000), eds. T.C. Kline III and P.J. Ivanhoe, 237–46, esp. 243. Ivanhoe's major argument is that the idea of human nature as evil presupposes the Augustinian notion of sin as a willful rejection of God's will. I do not want to suggest, by my translation of *xing'e* as *human nature is evil,* that Xun Zi is similar to Augustine. (No Confucians, indeed, no early Chinese thinkers, are similar to Augustine in their views of human nature.) I adopt the translation simply because of the striking similarity between Xun Zi and Hobbes – they both characterize human nature in virtue of what Hobbes calls 'the Felicity of this life.' I am grateful to Ivanhoe for comments on this point.

89 Fung Yu-lan, *A Shorter History of Chinese Philosophy,* 145.

90 'On Human Nature as Evil,' *Xun Zi,* 290. See also Knoblock, *Xun Zi,* vol. 3, 152.

91 'On Li,' *Xun Zi,* 243. See Knoblock, *Xun Zi,* vol. 3, 66.

92 'On Human Nature as Evil,' *Xun Zi,* 290. See also Knoblock, *Xun Zi.* vol. 3, 152. Scholars have different interpretations and thus different translations of the phrase '*tian zhi jiu ye.*' Ivanhoe, e.g., suggests the following translation to me: 'Human nature is our natural tendencies.'

93 See Zhang Dainian, *Outline of Philosophy,* 188–92; and Ma Zhenduo, *Confucius' Philosophy,* 243.

94 Ivanhoe has criticized the view that Mencius and Xun Zi use the term

'human nature' in different senses. His criticism is directed to scholars who, deriving no sufficient textual support, hold the view simply because they want to 'mend the rift [between Mencius and Xun Zi] in the Confucian family.' *Confucian Moral Self Cultivation* (Indianapolis/Cambridge: Hackett, 2000), 33.

95 Ivanhoe has argued that 'in terms of their ethical philosophies, Mengzi's and Xunzi's agreement went fairly deep.' See also *Confucian Moral Self Cultivation*, Chap. 3.

96 'On Human Nature as Evil,' *Xun Zi*, 290. See also Knoblock, *Xun Zi*, vol. 3, 152.

97 'On Human Nature as Evil,' *Xun Zi*, 291. See also Knoblock, *Xun Zi*, vol. 3, 153–4.

98 'On Human Nature as Evil,' *Xun Zi*, 295. See also Knoblock, *Xun Zi*, vol. 3, 157.

99 Hobbes, *Leviathan*, 215.

100 'On Human Nature as Evil,' *Xun Zi*, 296. Both *ke* and *neng* can mean either capacity or ability. In the context of human potentials for morality in Xun Zi, however, *ke* means capacity and *neng* means ability. Mencius speaks of *liang neng*. In that context, *neng* means capacity.

101 Ibid. See also Knoblock, *Xun Zi*, vol. 3, 160; Ma Zhenduo, *Confucius' Philosophy*, 241–2. See also Aristotle on first and second potentiality.

102 'On Human Nature as Evil,' *Xun Zi*, 296.

103 Ibid. See also Zhang Dainian, *Chinese Moral Thought*, 85.

104 'Kingly Government,' *Xun Zi*, 104. See also Dubs, *Hsuntze*, 136.

105 'On Rectification of Names,' *Xun Zi*, 274. For Xun Zi, emotions have a cognitive significance.

106 Ibid., 274, 284.

107 Ibid., 274; 'On Li,' ibid., 231. See also Knoblock, *Xun Zi*, vol. 3, 55. Dubs, *Hsuntze*, 301.

108 'On Human Nature as Evil,' *Xun Zi*, 289. See also Ma Zhenduo, *Confucius' Philosophy*, 243.

109 'The Great Compendium,' *Xun Zi*, 322. See also Knoblock, *Xun Zi*, vol. 3, 209.

110 'On Self-Cultivation,' *Xun Zi*, 20. See also Dubs, *Hsuntze*, 51.

111 See Liang Qichao, *Chinese Political Thought*, 96.

112 'On Li,' *Xun Zi*, 237. See also Knoblock, *Xun Zi*, vol. 3, 61; Dubs, *Hsuntze*, 225.

113 'The Great Compendium,' *Xun Zi*, 327; 'On Self-Cultivation,' ibid., 14.

114 See Liang Qichao, *Chinese Political Thought*, 94.

115 Ibid., 95.

116 'Kingly Government,' *Xun Zi*, 104–5. See also Dubs, *Hsuntze*, 137.

117 'Enriching the Country,' *Xun Zi*, 113. See also Dubs, *Hsuntze*, 151.

118 'Of Honor and Disgrace,' *Xun Zi*, 44. See also Knoblock, *Xun Zi*, vol. 1, 195.

119 'Contra Physiognomy,' *Xun Zi*, 50. See also Knoblock, *Xun Zi*, vol. 1, 206; Fung Yu-Lan, *Chinese Philosophy*, 281; Liang Qichao, *Chinese Political Thought*, 95.

120 'Contra Physiognomy,' *Xun Zi*, 50.

121 Antonio S. Cua, 'Hsun Tze and the Unity of Virtues,' *Journal of Chinese Philosophy*, 14(4), 381–400.

122 Ibid., 382.

123 'On *Tian*,' *Xun Zi*, 208.

124 'Dispelling Blindness,' *Xun Zi*, 262. See also Knoblock, *Xun Zi*, vol. 3, 102–3.

125 'Dispelling Blindness,' *Xun Zi*, 262; 'On Rectification of Names,' ibid. 286.

126 'Ru Xiao,' *Xun Zi*, 77. See also Zhang Dainian, *Chinese Philosophy*, 27.

127 'The Great Compendium,' *Xun Zi*, 325.

128 Cua, 'Virtues,' 384.

129 'The Great Compendium,' *Xun Zi*, 324–5. See also Knoblock, *Xun Zi*, vol. 3, 212; Liang Qixong, *Commentaries on Xun Zi* (Beijing: Zhong Hua Press, 1983), 368.

130 'On *Li*,' *Xun Zi*, 237.

131 'An Encouragement to Study,' *Xun Zi*, 7. See also 'Xiao Ru,' *Xun Zi*, 77.

132 'The Great Compendium,' *Xun Zi*, 330. See also Knoblock, *Xun Zi*, vol. 3, 222; and Zhang Dainian, *Chinese Moral Thought*, 114.

133 See Fung Yu-Lan, *Chinese Philosophy*, 276.

134 'Zheng Lun Pian,' *Xun Zi*, 216. See also Fung Yu-Lan, *Chinese Philosophy*, 282.

135 'Zheng Lun Pian,' *Xun Zi*, 214–8. See Fung Yu-Lan, *Chinese Philosophy*, 283–4.

136 'Universal Love,' part 1, in *Mo Zi, Zhu Zi Ji Cheng*, vol. 4 (Beijing: Zhong Hua Press, 1986), 62–3. See Liang Qichao, *Chinese Political Thought*, English ed., 93; Yi-Pao Mei, *The Ethical and Political Works of Motse* (Westport: Hyperion Press, 1973), 78–9.

137 'Universal Love,' part 3, in *Mo Zi*, 70–1. See also Burton Watson, *Basic Writings of Mo Tzu, Hsun Tzu, and Han Fei Tzu* (New York: Columbia University Press, 1967), 39.

138 'Universal Love,' part 3, in *Mo Zi*, 71. See also Burton Watson, *Basic Writings*, 40.

139 'Against Music,' part 1, in *Mo Zi*, 155. See also Watson, *Basic Writings*, 110.

140 See Fung Yu-Lan, *A Shorter History of Chinese Philosophy*, 54.
141 Ibid., 92.
142 'Against Music,' part 1, in *Mo Zi*, 156.
143 Fung Yu-Lan, *A Shorter History of Chinese Philosophy*, 94.
144 See also Liang Qichao, *Chinese Political Thought*, 122–3.
145 'Dispelling Blindness,' *Xun Zi*, 261.
146 'Shang Tong,' part 1, in *Mo Zi*, 44. There is, however, a difference between Hobbes and Mo Zi that must be noted. Unlike Hobbes, Mo Zi stresses that social disorder arises from conflicting ideologies rather than simply fighting over limited material goods. I am grateful to Philip J. Ivanhoe for his comments on this point.
147 'Shang Tong,' part 1, in *Mo Zi*, 47.
148 See Liang Qichao, *Chinese Political Thought*, 122–3.
149 'Shang Tong,' part 1, in *Mo Zi*, 44.
150 'Shang Tong,' part 3, in *Mo Zi*, 55.
151 See Liang Qichao, *Chinese Political Thought*, 127.
152 Ibid., 127.
153 'The Will of Heaven,' part 1, in *Mo Zi*, 120.
154 See also Liang Qichao, *Chinese Political Thought*, 130.
155 'The Will of Heaven,' part 1, in *Mo Zi*, 120.
156 Ibid., 119.
157 See Legge, *Confucius*, 357–9.
158 I am grateful to David Braybrooke, Philip J. Ivanhoe, and an anonymous reader for their comments on an earlier version of the essay.

Index

abortion, 5, 8, 221

a posteriori argument, without God, for natural law, 27, 29–31, 34, 36, 41, 91, 128–9

Aquinas. *See* Thomas (St Thomas Aquinas)

Aristotle, 32, 39–40, 111, 281

Arrow, Kenneth, 58, 232

autonomy, 194–5

axiomatic system of natural laws, 19–20, 26–7, 33, 38–9, 42–6, 53, 79, 91–124, 129, 136, 176; Hobbes's contribution, 26–7, 79, 91–124, 136; not inconsistent with empirical basis, 24–6, 53, 93, 96–7; not seriously pursued by Locke, 33; or by St Thomas, in spite of place reserved for deduction, 38–9, 44–6

Aztecs, 161

Baier, Annette, 10, 126, 136–7, 140–5, 194

Bedouin culture and group feeling (*asabiyah*), 248–51

Bentham, Jeremy, 48, 51, 73

Berkeley, George, 137

bindingness, implied by justification in Copp's theory, 186–7, 190–5

Blackburn, Simon, 125–6, 140

Bobbio, Norberto, 10, 91

Bolsheviks, 83–4

Boyd, Richard, 136

Boyle, Joseph M., Jr, 14–16

Buddhism, 294

Campbell, Richmond M., 181, 187

Causey, Robert L., 118, 120–4

Chinese philosophy, classical, as locus of natural law theory, 28, 243, 258–94

Cicero, 37

cognitivism, 180–1. *See also* Hume

Coleman, Jules, 223

Common Good, the, 14, 21, 23–4, 26–7, 41, 55–89, 145, 147–8, 160–1, 171, 173–5, 182, 197, 204, 208, 217–9, 228–35; anchored in meeting needs, 81, 173, 183, 194; correlated by Rousseau with the General Will and interpreted by the economic theory of public goods, 24, 57–80, 91, 192, 196, 221; including all members of a given society, 160–1;